WITHDRAWN

D1595691

African Music:
A Pan-African Annotated Bibliography

African Music:
A Pan-African Annotated Bibliography

Carol Lems-Dworkin

HANS ZELL PUBLISHERS
London • Melbourne • Munich • New York • 1991

Hans Zell Publishers
is an imprint of Bowker-Saur Ltd, a Reed International Books Company.
Borough Green, Sevenoaks, Kent, England TN15 8PH

British Library Cataloguing in Publication Data

A catalogue record for this book is available from the British Library.

Library of Congress Cataloging-in-Publication Data

Lems-Dworkin, Carol.
African music : a pan-African annotated bibliography / Carol Lems-Dworkin.
400p. 240cm.
Includes indexes.
ISBN 0-905450-91-4 (alk. paper)
1. Music -- African -- History and criticism -- Bibliography. I. Title.
ML120.A35L4 1991
018.78'098--dc20 91-33581
CIP
MN

Cover illustration: Kora players, from *Musique de l'Afrique,* by Francis Bebey. Paris: Horizons de France, 1969. (Hao-Qui)

Cover design by Robin Caira

Printed on acid-free paper.

Printed in Great Britain
by Antony Rowe Ltd, Chippenham, Wiltshire.

Dedicated to my beloved daughter,

Kristin Lems

CONTENTS

Illustrations in this book comprise: small appliquéd figures by the Fon, symbolic of former Dahomean kings, and freehand copies of Tanzanian bird combs, a Bambara antelope mask, and an anthropomorphic mask from Zimbabwe.

ACKNOWLEDGEMENTS

Had Edward Gogol, Computer Consultant and family friend, anticipated exactly what he was getting into when he kindly offered his services for this book, he undoubtedly would have run the other way. Unwittingly he had committed himself to what turned out to be two and a half years of unrelenting, frustrating, joyless work that drew upon just about every one of his extraordinary computer and teaching skills. Many a time he must have wanted to extricate himself, but, good man that he is, he stayed with the project up to the, in this case, happy end. Apparently, the only way out was through.

Edward Gogol has proven to be a "man for all seasons," with many exceptional qualities, both technical and humanistic, that work together. The services he rendered were indispensible, ranging from installation and debugging of equipment, to formatting, technical advice, and trouble shooting. Suffice it to say that were it not for Edward Gogol, this book would not be in your hands today.

There have been three other persons who have played extremely important roles in making this book a reality. I have known Hans E. Panofsky, now Curator of Africana Emeritus, Northwestern University, for many years. During a long association, he and his wife Giana have always shown themselves to be supportive friends. With reference to this book in particular, Hans has extended himself in countless enthusiastic and facilitating ways, showing sincere good will, suggesting, advising, cautioning, answering questions, and making the myriad resources of the Africana Library he was instrumental in building, available to me. I recall the night my research on this book was "launched." Hans had spread out a number of key works for examination - like a book fair - all over his dining room table! I shall be ever grateful to Hans for his abundant help and well-wishing.

The fame of Yvette Scheven, Bibliographer for African Studies at the University of Illinois (Urbana Champaign), long preceded our first meeting - fame not only for her excellence as a bibliographer, but for her outstanding personal qualities as well. These claims proved to be well-founded, apparent even during the first long distance telephone call, when I introduced myself and sought her help. I could not get used to such modesty in a person so accomplished. Through these challenging times for me, Yvette has proven herself always to be steadfast, a gracious adviser who has been available at all times, always supportive, always encouraging, knowledgeable, wise, soothing. I am one of her fans, and I thank her sincerely.

No one at Northwestern University Library was so understanding, helpful, and facilitating as Rolf H. Erickson, Circulation Services Librarian. This man of unusual empathy deals with the public in an intelligent, friendly, efficient, unruffled way, dispatching needed materials to eagerly waiting hands, saying yes more times than no. His positive cheerful attitude reminds one of earlier times when librarians really cared. Because of Rolf's help, I secured a library carrel which I sometimes filled with as many as 75 books. I also thank Sharon Smith, Circulation Assistant, for her special help. The Interlibrary Loan Department did a spectacular job in getting requested materials. I thank the Head, Kathryn Deiss, and Bradley Cornell, Carole Johnson, and Michael Nealon for their assistance. Gratitude is also expressed to Don Roberts, Head of the Music Library, and two of his excellent staff, Dean Justmann, and Deborah Campana. Appreciated is the work of the head of the African Cataloging Unit, Dawn E. Williams, who was most helpful in rushing through needed materials. Particular thanks goes to Mette Shayne, Francophone African Bibliographer for her special help, to the Africana staff, and especially to Patricia Ogedengbe for her ever-cheerful, expert assistance. Many thanks also go to Charles Fineman, Humanities Bibliographer, whose long conference helped to clarify a number of areas of my work, and to Brian Nielsen, for technical advice.

Special gratitude goes to Daniel Kodzo Avorgbedor, outstanding scholar and long-time friend, whose patience and generosity never flagged despite my countless long distance calls to him, seeking advice about Ghanaian music and other musical subjects, for which his fund of knowledge is limitless. My gratitude goes as well to Elkin M. T. Sithole, Ethnomusicologist, a man I have known for years and deeply respect, for his informed and wise counsel on South African music. I appreciate the meticulous professionalism of Sue Baugh, the Author Indexer, and Janet Russell, the Subject Indexer, who made the dense information of this bibliography accessible. Thanks go also to Vera Teixeira, who helped with the Portuguese; Muhammad Sani Umar, for help with Arabic; William O'Brien, Leni Weil, and Meta Less, for German assistance; and Rótìmí Ògúnṣuyì, for help with Yorùbá. I am grateful to Jane Cacharelis, Librarian, for her well-executed research project, and my daughter, Kristin Lems, for encouragement and editorial comments. Appreciation goes to Akbar Virmani, of the Program of African Studies, for his part in obtaining my Visiting Scholar status at Northwestern University, and to Isaac R. Amuah, Kwasi Aduonum, Marta Nicholas, and Isaac B. Laudarji. Most of all, I give thanks to my publisher, Hans Zell, for giving my dream wings.

INTRODUCTION

Purpose

Perhaps the strongest motivation for writing this book was to update prior African music bibliographies by Varley, Merriam, Thieme, and Gaskin. It seemed important to document 1960 to the present time, a period that has been particularly important in the evolution of African musicology. But there were other reasons as well.

I wanted to approach the subject of African music from a broader, and at the same time, more unified perspective than had been manifested in earlier works. The majority of these bibliographies focused on subSaharan Africa. I wanted to cover the entire continent of Africa, including its islands, as well as African-influenced music of the Western Hemisphere. I was also convinced that African music should not be treated as a thing in itself, but regarded as the integral part of culture it truly is, playing a major role in African education, history, politics, social life, and frequently associated with religion, dance, art, theater, and oral performance. I have often marveled, in fact, at the number of significant works on Africa that make no mention whatsoever of music, even though music is almost life itself to African people.

History

Before 1960, most writings on African music were in periodicals. Bibliographies often contained a long list of journal articles that was separated from a far shorter list of other kinds of publications. With expansion of the field in more recent years, however, the number of significant books, dissertations, monographs, and essays increased as well, some written by less well-known scholars, others by luminaries whose works might also be found regularly in professional journals. Not only were these later categories of publications important because of their quality and in-depth treatment of a subject, but they were apt to contain comprehensive bibliographies of their own that included the author's works and those of others, along with discographies and other aids for the researcher.

At the same time that books, monographs, and dissertations increased, so also did the number of new journals appearing on the scene. New ways had to be found to keep up with such a voluminous and continuing flow of important material. Some periodicals fortunately indexed their own articles. There was also that major professional journal,

Ethnomusicology, which, besides indexing its own articles, listed countless articles from other sources by geographic area.

The Music Index (1949-) continued to survey the periodical scene on a worldwide basis, listing a respectable number of articles on African and African-related music, and adding new periodicals regularly to its roster, including *African Music*, that pioneer journal published in South Africa from 1954 on. *RILM Abstracts of Music Literature*, begun in 1967, had the additional merit of not only listing articles and other publications on African music the world over, but abstracting them as well (the only disadvantage being a several year time lag between a current date and the appearance of a new volume).

In 1976, a unique journal appeared that served as a kind of large screening device for locating articles on African music: *Current Contents Africa*. Still published today, it features photocopies of the contents pages of countless African periodicals. Even though no more than the title of an article on music and the number of its first page can be viewed, this is often enough to decide whether or not to pursue a work to its original source.

The Bibliography

Because of my own concern with unity, I have structured this book as a totality organized alphabetically by author name. This means that one can go directly to a name, and, with few exceptions, see as one bloc the included works of that person - dissertation, articles, and books, all together. Traditionally, large bibliographies have tended to be divided into subject sections. In this case the Subject Index at the end of the bibliography performs the same function.

The present bibliography includes: books, monographs; reference works; key chapters from books; papers from collections (such as symposia, colloquia, festivals, *festschriften*, and the like); dissertations and theses; periodical and series titles - all categories of printed material that were less numerous in the past, or often overlooked because of the attention given to periodical articles.

The relatively small number of journal articles included in this book is not meant to minimize their extreme importance, but simply to emphasize other categories of works on African music that have often been neglected. Those articles that have been entered were selected mainly because of their usefulness in indicating the general kind of material covered by a given periodical whose title appears as an entry. This means that although such inclusions may be of high quality, they do not necessarily represent the most significant articles on a given subject.

There are other bibliographies that are useful for locating periodical articles besides the four mentioned in the first paragraph - particularly more recent ones by Aning (**100**), de Lerma (**446**), and Gray (**640**). These bibliographies, and a number of current abstracting and indexing periodicals, some of them online, have entries in the present bibliography.

Particular attention has been given to dissertations and theses. As many as possible have been gathered together under one umbrella, undoubtedly for the first time. These works, monuments to untold years of scholarly dedication, have often lain moldering in obscure university archives for decades, unseen and unknown. Hopefully, their inclusion will not only aid researchers working in related fields and serve as catalysts for new studies, but also inspire their own authors to take up the yoke again.

I have personally seen and examined the majority of items in this book. Annotations do vary considerably in type, style, and length - from none at all, to some that total 100 words. However, differences in lengths of annotations do not in themselves represent value judgments. Neither do the total entries for any one author imply merit, or lack thereof (the only exception being the "Titans" in the field whose names are in capitals and bold print, often with cross-references leading to their biographies or bibliographies). It should also be mentioned that if an author is not found in the bibliography, as regrettable as this might be, it is due either to the lack of accessible materials, or because those available did not fit into the scope of this bibliography. Any omissions were inadvertent.

The Subject Index of this book leads to countless headings and sub-headings that have in common only the African or African-influenced music at their core. The Index by itself, in fact, almost says more about the power and magnitude of African music than any description could.

Entry titles are in French, German, English, Spanish, Portuguese, Arabic, Yorùbá and a few other African languages, but English language titles are best represented, followed by titles in the Romance Languages. Entries for the New World start as far north as the Bronx, pass through the Caribbean, and continue down to Brazil. Almost all African countries are represented, from Algeria to South Africa, from Cape Verde to the islands of the Indian Ocean, although in this initial gathering of such widely disseminated materials, some countries and geographic areas are better represented than others.

It will be seen that only chapters or parts of composite works that actually treat the subject of this bibliography are cited, since this was not intended to be a general review of materials but a focus on African music and related topics. Hopefully, a person intrigued by the title of a compound work will return to it for further examination. On the other hand, I sometimes have given considerable attention to the photographs or art work in a book if they relate to music or dance. In this way, a book can be seen as a totality also, and any artistic augmentation to be an integral part of it.

With very few exceptions, included works were either published some time after 1960, or are reprints of earlier works. Gaskin's famous bibliography (**614**), published in 1965, is the most important source for overseeing the past history of African musicology. For good reason Gaskin claims to cover "all known works of relevance or significance."

Very few items in this book concern jazz or blues, those major African-American forms, markedly influenced by Africa, that have come virtually to identify the United States abroad. Unless there were a specific section on the African component of this music, as in Gunther Schuller's brilliant, *The history of jazz* (**1428**), these subjects were left to the thousands of treatises that already honor them. There are a few occasions, however, in which jazz and blues are mentioned in connection with their presence on *African* soil. Generally these music forms are treated only as part of the marvelous, gigantic, intercontinental call-and-response that has been going on for centuries between Africa and its people of the diaspora - now spreading out, as though from an African epicenter, to the whole world.

In light of changing times, a considerable number of entries on African urban music are listed in this book. Ronnie Graham defines contemporary African music in *The Da Capo guide to contemporary African music*, **638**, as "basically the electrified popular music which first appeared in the mid-1950s." Even though in former times distinctions did not exist in Africa between traditional and popular music, Africans have come to accept the foreign term "popular" as applied to their infectious, highly danceable, rhythmic, electrified (and electrifying) urban music. An enlightening explanation and historical overview of contemporary African music occurs in the first chapter of Graham's book. It discusses the music industry and the manifestations of its tight-fisted global control. (See also works by Kwaku Lynn, **1001**, and Wallis and Halm, **1643**, who also feel that there are genuine reasons for concern about what Graham calls, "the cultural consequences implicit in the organisation of music for profit." Atta Annan Mensah, **1072**, **1075**, however, is less pessimistic, as is also Lazarus Edward Nnanyelu Ekwueme, **504**.)

A few entries in the book fall into the Western category of "art music," used here to mean "composed" works transmitted by writing, as contrasted with the African, traditionally oral, means of transmission. Examples are by African musicians writing in a Western style, and Westerners writing in an African style. There was no hesitation in including entries of this sort in the book.

Problems

Numerous triumphs and depredations experienced by the continent of Africa are reflected in the titles and contents of works in this bibliography. During the thirty years covered, countries fought for and achieved independence, changed their names and languages, changed boundaries and governments in a ceaseless restlessness for a better life, while Africa's people experienced everything from neocolonialism to misguided socialism, despotism, droughts, famine, civil war, poverty, and now the new scourge, AIDS. All of the previously mentioned afflictions have made it extremely difficult for African musicians, and greatly limited resources available for the study of African music.

It has not always been easy to obtain the works of Africans published in Africa. Even specialist librarians are often at a loss when it comes to tracing down a particular monograph, or finding out what has happened to an African periodical not heard from for years. By using the exceptional resources of the Africana Library of Northwestern University, however, I was fortunately able to meet this challenge and to ferret out enough information so that this bibliography includes a far greater number of African authors than was formerly possible. It happily, also includes more women writers than in past times.

In the New World, terms for peoples of African descent also went through permutations (though never agreed upon by all), so that what was an acceptable designation at one time might not be so a few years later. Dealing with this sensitive issue has required careful thought. It was the decision of the subject indexer, Janet Russell, to use the term "Africa" and "Africa subSaharan" to refer to Continental Africa, and "Black culture," and "Black music" to refer to the people of African heritage in the rest of the world.

A more sticky problem concerns those obsolete, pejorative words that cannot be exorcised from titles and contents of certain works. A few such entries have urged their way into this bibliography because of their historical significance, or because they have certain merits that outweigh their obvious flaws. Fortunately, these flaws are generally recognized for what they are, and discounted by Africanists. However, I could not always resist the impulse to make an editorial comment.

Another area of concern has been the spelling of words for peoples, instruments, languages, and geographic areas that vary during different historical periods, even when the same language is used. This is further complicated by the myriad languages in Africa, both indigenous and European, that have different words for identical phenomena.

Diacritics present a special problem in that they are often inserted or omitted in texts inconsistently, probably owing as much to the inadequacies of various printing devices, as to the lack of knowledge of - or concern for - standardized language practices. Every effort was made to verify spelling with native speakers.

Conclusion

On the human level, writing this bibliography has had deep personal meaning for me that I had not anticipated. Until it was well along, I had no idea how many entries were written by people I have known personally - some of the "Greats" whose courses I have taken or whose books I have used, those whose lectures I have attended, whose recordings I own, or who were guest lecturers or participants in my own courses or workshops later on, not to mention all the friends of today, those scholars, advisers, and enthusiastic and helpful well-wishers whose names cheer me.

It is my sincere hope that this book will be of use not only to people in the fields of African Studies and Ethnomusicology, but other areas. Offhand, I should think that undergraduate or graduate students in other fields, or even the browsing lay person, might find in the bibliography useful and interesting inclusions, and perhaps become enthusiastic about African music as a result.

Just as in Shona *mbira* music there are always new patterns and textures to discover, and just as Robert Farris Thompson describes narrow-strip "rhythmized" African fabrics as meant to be "scanned metrically, in visual resonance with the famed off-beat phrasing of melodic accents in African and Afro-American music," I hope that new insights, textures, and rhythms will also resonate from this book.

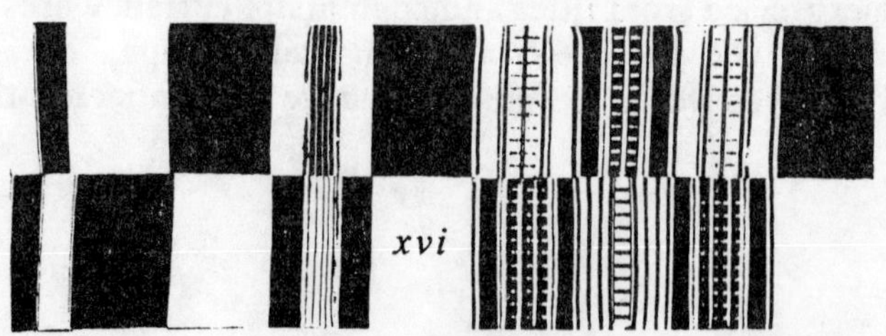

USER'S GUIDE

ABBREVIATIONS: These are used as little as possible. Occasionally there will be an: **s.l.** (no place of publication given); **s.n.** (no publisher given); **n.d.** (no date given); and **n.f.** (abbreviation in German for "new series"). Rarely, abbreviations appear as parts of entries in which they were not further explained. (Nicholas Slonimsky expresses his same dislike for abbreviations in the preface to the 6th edition of *Baker's biographical dictionary of musicians*, "No more the impenetrable jungles of Ztsch., Vsch., ves., mvt., or Kgt.")

ARTICLES FROM PERIODICALS: Titles are enclosed by quotation marks.

BOOKS AND MONOGRAPHS: Titles are italicized.

CROSS REFERENCES: Many of these are built into the bibliography itself, the purpose being to spare the reader any unnecessary ping-pong games with the indexes. Cross references also occur in the indexes.

DIACRITICS: As described in the Introduction, every possible effort was made to execute diacritics correctly, even to the point of risking inserting them when they were not found in the original source.

DISSERTATIONS AND THESES: Titles are entirely in capital letters. For the sake of simplicity of treatment, degrees are classified arbitrarily either as Master's Theses, or Dissertations.

ENTRIES FROM ESSAY COLLECTIONS, BOOK CHAPTERS, SYMPOSIA: In general, these are listed alphabetically by author under main entries, but also as separate entries enclosed by quotation marks.

FILING: Umlauts are ignored in filing. "Mc" words are not filed as Mac."

INDEXES: Content and scope are explained at the beginnings of the Author Index and the Subject Index.

PERIODICALS: Recognizable by their bold, upper case letters.

SERIES: Titles are bold in main entries, but in lower case (with the exception of proper nouns and the first letters of first words).

A

BIBLIOGRAPHY

AICP
See: **ANTHROPOLOGICAL INDEX TO CURRENT PERIODICALS IN THE LIBRARY OF THE MUSEUM OF MANKIND LIBRARY, 110.**

ASA = African Studies Association
See: **ASA NEWS, 1.**

1. **ASA NEWS.** Vol. 14- , 1981- . Atlanta, Georgia: African Studies Association.
Issued quarterly for members of ASA. (Continues **AFRICAN STUDIES NEWSLETTER**, which sometimes appeared as **AFRICAN STUDIES ASSOCIATION NEWSLETTER**, a publication that ran from 1968-1981.) Useful for musicologists to examine because of new book listings (with annotations), and an update of recent doctoral dissertations divided by subject - not to mention all the other kinds of timely information to be found in a professional newsletter of this sort).

2. **Abarry, Abu.** "A traditional poetry of the Ga of Ghana." **JOURNAL OF BLACK STUDIES** 14, no.4 (1984): 493-506.

3. **ABBIA.** 1963-1979. Yaoundé, [Cameroon].
"Revue culturelle camerounaise. Cameroon cultural review." In French and English. During its tenure, this periodical published a number of essays on African music by such scholars as Kubik, Bebey, Eno Belinga, and others. Originally issued quarterly, later issues tended to be less frequent, the last issue incorporating numbers 34-37, but nothing on music. It is worthwhile to examine the run of this journal for the occasional fine articles on music.

4. **Abdulkadir, Dandatti.** THE ROLE OF AN ORAL SINGER IN HAUSA/FULANI SOCIETY: A CASE STUDY OF MAMMAN SHATA. Dissertation, Indiana University, 1975. 338pp.
Bibliography.

Abimbola, Wande
See: **Seminar on Yorùbá Oral Tradition, 1438.**

5. **ABSTRACTS IN ANTHROPOLOGY.** 1970- . Amityville, New York: Baywood Publishing Company.
An abstracting index that covers the fields of archaeology, physical anthropology, linguistics, and cultural anthropology. Some periodicals included in this bibliography are abstracted here. Indexed in **AICP, 110.**

6. **Accam, T. N.**, comp. *Klama songs and chants.* Legon: Institute of African Studies, University of Ghana, 1967. 73pp.
Except for the title page, which is in English, the entire book consists of texts of

songs and chants in the Adangme language. *Klama* is a musical type of the Adangme of Ghana with several subcategories: *klama* for each of the principal cults, *klama* for the *tegble* heroic association, *klama* for puberty festivals, and proverbial and historical *klama* that may be sung in appropriate contexts.

7. **Achinivu, Achinivu Kanu.** *Ikoli Harcourt Whyte, the man and his music: a case of musical acculturation in Nigeria.* 2 vols. Verlag der Musikalienhandlung Wagner, 1979. (Beiträge zur Ethnomusikologie, vol. 7)
Originally presented as the author's dissertation at Freie Universität Berlin. Achinivu explains that little has been known about composer/choirmaster, Ikoli Harcourt Whyte, by the Christian and musical worlds beyond his native Nigeria. Consequently, Achinivu chronicles all aspects of the artist's life and works, and highlights his profound contribution to the development of African sacred art music. A master composer of anthems, Whyte's works have been performed widely in Nigeria, particularly in the Protestant Churches of Igboland. Those appearing in Volume 2 have Igbo and English texts. A bibliography, Nigerian maps, Igbo pronunciation guide, and German summary.

8. **Acta ethnologica et linguistica.** Vienna.
The entire series is distinguished, but the following works on African music, listed alphabetically, appear as separate entries in this bibliography. Other volumes, however, might also be worth examining for music references.
•**Kubik, Gerhard.** *The Kachamba Brothers' Band*, 1972.
•**Low, John** *Shaba diary*, 1982.
•**Ngumu, Pie-Claude.** *Les Mendzan*, 1976.
•**Òjó, Jerome.** *Yorùbá customs from Ondó*, 1976.

9. **Adams, Charles Robert.** ETHNOGRAPHY OF BASOTHO EVALUATIVE EXPRESSION IN THE COGNITIVE DOMAIN "LIPAPALI" (GAMES). Dissertation, Indiana University, 1974. 294pp.
The author himself best summarizes: "The research presented here as an ethnographic case study of the meaning of evaluative expression in the Basotho cognitive domain *lipapali* (games) has attempted to show specifically in the realm of 'values' that a fruitful integration of the orientation of ethnographic semantics to the study of axiological processes is possible." He feels that the Basotho viewpoint of *lipapali* as life-enriching and consciousness-expanding, exemplifies Levi-Strauss' belief that music provides a "middle way between aesthetic perception and the exercise of logical thought..." (Was this a precursor of left/right brain theory?)

10. **Adébọ́nọ̀jọ, Mary Bunton.** TEXT-SETTING IN YORÙBÁ SECULAR MUSIC. Master's Thesis, University of California, Berkeley, 1967. 125pp.

11. **Adédèjì, Joel Adéyínká.** THE ALÁRÈNJÓ THEATRE: THE STUDY OF A YORÙBÁ THEATRICAL ART FROM ITS EARLIEST BEGINNINGS TO

THE PRESENT TIMES. Dissertation, University of Ìbàdàn, 1969. 415pp.
This is abstracted in **Nigerian universities dissertation abstracts, 1178.** There is mention of the root elements of Yorùbá art being the mask, the chant, and the dance, but that a performance is the sub total of all of these and the unified product of gesture and costume.

12. **Adédèjì, Joel Adéyínká**. "The literature of the Yorùbá opera." In *Essays on African literature*. Edited by W. L. Ballard, 55-78. Atlanta, School of Arts and Sciences, Georgia State University, 1973. (Spectrum. Monograph series in the arts and sciences, vol. 3)

13. **Adédèjì, Joel Adéyínká**. "Theatricalism and traditional African theatre." In **The arts and civilization of Black and African peoples.** Edited by Joseph Ohiomogben Okpaku, Alfred Esimatemi Opubor, and Benjamin Ọlátúnjí Ọlọ́runtìmẹhìn, Volume 1: 102-120. Lagos: Centre for Black and African Arts and Civilization, c1986.
The essay examines select models of African theatrical traditions from the following categories: The Story Theatre, Festival Theatre, Ritual Theatre, and Masque Theatre. Those chosen are described in the order in which events occur during a given presentation. In many cases, places where music and dance occur are indicated. Few details about the actual music, however. Lengthy bibliography.

14. **Adégbìtẹ́, Adémọ́lá Moses**. ORÍKÌ: A STUDY IN YORÙBÁ MUSICAL AND SOCIAL PERCEPTION. Dissertation, University of Pittsburgh, 1978. 241pp.
Illustrations, map, music, bibliography.

15. **Adinku, William Ofotsu**. "The *kpatsa* dance of the Dangme." **JOURNAL OF THE PERFORMING ARTS** 1, no. 1 (1980): 66-82.
Brief discussion of dance itself. There are song texts, descriptions of musical instruments, information on ensembles, on occasions for performance and how performance is organized. Officer's responsibilities are mentioned.

16. **Adler, Bill**, comp. *Growing up African*. Edited by Jay David and Helise Harrington. Foreword by Edris Makward. New York: Morrow, 1971. 287.
A collection of writings by historical, political, and literary figures makes interesting reading. A remarkable excerpt from *The African Child* (or *The Dark Child*) conveys the mystery and awe surrounding the fashioning by Camara Laye's father, a well-known metalsmith, of a trinket of gold. Smithing was an art and way of life, and the smith was considered to be in close communion with the spirit of creation. This moving recollection affords a rare glimpse into a ritual in which the praise-singer plays an essential role. Elsewhere are song texts from the Sudan, Ghana, Central Africa, and Malaŵi.

17. **Aduonum, Kwasi**. A COMPILATION, ANALYSIS, AND ADAPTATION OF SELECTED GHANAIAN FOLKTALE SONGS FOR USE IN THE

ELEMENTARY GENERAL MUSIC CLASS. Dissertation, University of Michigan, 1980. 492pp.
In the framework of the compilation, analysis, and adaptation of selected Ghanaian folktale songs for use in the elementary general music class, the author discusses the importance of the use of *mmoguo* (folktale songs) as a major component in the training of children. Chapter contents are briefly described. In the sixth chapter, besides summarizing and elaborating the results of his study, Aduonum discusses the extreme importance of music to African culture, and describes the African view of music as a "referential art rather than a formalistic one." **(UMI)**.

Adzinyah, Abraham Kobena
See: **Let your voice be heard! 965.**

18. **Afre, S. A.** *Ashanti region of Ghana: an annotated bibliography, from earliest times to 1973.* Boston: G. K. Hall, [1975]. 494pp.
The music section of the subject index, pages 405-412, also includes dance. Most often entries are periodical articles or unpublished theses. In the index, one can search under: Music, Musical Instruments, Musician, Dance, and Dancing for a few other items, though most of these already occur in the pages mentioned. Under the subject heading, Vernacular Literature, are listed a number of works by Nketia, for which the annotations sometimes indicate that there is music along with the text. A list of newspapers and periodicals published in Ashanti is useful.

19. **AFRICA: JOURNAL OF THE INTERNATIONAL AFRICAN INSTITUTE.** 1928- . London.
Issued quarterly. A venerable old journal that continues to have major articles on Africa, with an emphasis on sociology and anthropology, but not exclusively. Through the years, its pages have contained countless important articles on African music. Indexed by **HISTORICAL ABSTRACTS, CURRENT CONTENTS AFRICA, AICP, PAIS**, and others. A few examples have been randomly chosen for listing:
- **Àjùwọ̀n, Bádé**. "The preservation of Yorùbá tradition through hunters' funeral dirges," vol. 50, no. 1 (1980): 66-72.
- **Alnaes, Kirsten**. "Living with the past: the songs of the Herero in Botswana," vol. 59, no. 3 (1989): 267-299.
- **Krige, Eileen Jensen**. "Girl's puberty songs and their relation to fertility, health, morality, and religion among the Zulu," vol. 38, no. 2 (1968): 173-198.

20. **Africa**. Edited by Phyllis M. Martin, and Patrick O'Meara. Bloomington: Indiana University Press, c1977. 482pp.
This first version contains a general bibliography by Jean E. Meeh Gosebrink with a Music/Dance section. Music references in the index are precisely indicated. Only two of the twenty-four essays pertain directly to music: Alan P. Merriam's, "Traditional Music of Black Africa" **(1092)**, and John E. Kaemmer's, "Changing Music in Contemporary Africa." **(803)** Each of these essays has its own bibliography.

21. **Africa**. Edited by Phyllis M. Martin, and Patrick O'Meara. 2d ed. Bloomington: Indiana University Press, c1986. 456pp.
Bibliography at end by Gosebrink again lists Music/Dance. Index well done. The two music essayists new to this edition are Ruth M. Stone, "African Music Performed" (**1504**), and Delé Jẹ́gẹ́dẹ́, "Popular Culture in Urban Africa." (**759**) Each essay has notes and suggestions for further reading.

22. **AFRICA BIBLIOGRAPHY**. 1985- . (International African Institute) Manchester, England, Manchester University Press
Issued annually. The entire continent of Africa and associated islands are included, the stated purpose being to record publications of interest to students of Africa principally in the social sciences, humanities, and arts. Periodicals surveyed are listed at the beginning, and the main body of the book is divided into subject headings that correspond to major geographic areas of Africa. Arts, one of a number of subheadings, includes music. Entries have many abbreviations. Author index.

23. **África en América Latina**. Edited by Manuel Moreno Fraginals. Mexico: Siglo Veintiuno Editores, 1977. 436pp.
This is the original version in Spanish, issued later as the English translation directly following. The same indicated noteworthy essays appear but with Spanish titles and text. Bibliography, index.

24. **Africa in Latin America: essays on history, culture, and socialization**. Manuel Moreno Fraginals, Editor. Translated by Leonor Blum. New York: Holmes and Meier, 1984. 342pp.
(This is an English translation of *África en América Latina*, published 1977 in Mexico by Siglo Veintiuno Editores.) Although this represents a most valuable collection of essays, only those listed alphabetically below pertain to music. The bibliography does not contain all sources mentioned by some of the authors, nor do the authors always give enough information about a quoted work to make tracking-down easy. Still, the bibliography has enough music entries to make it worthwhile. Book has biographical information on each essayist.
•**Aretz, Isabel**. "Music and dance in continental Latin America," 189-226.
•**Carvalho, José Jorge de**. "Music of African origin in Brazil," 227-248.
•**Feijoo, Samuel**. "African influence in Latin America: oral and written literature," 145-169.
•**Urfé, Odiolio**. "Music and dance in Cuba," 170-188.

25. **AFRICA INSIGHT**. 1971- . Pretoria, South Africa: African Institute of South Africa.
This is a continuation of **SOUTH AFRICAN JOURNAL OF AFRICAN AFFAIRS**, and not to be confused with **AFRICAN INSIGHT**, published at Indiana University and running from 1973-1978. Indexed by **CURRENT CONTENTS AFRICA**, and others. Available on microfilm from **UMI**, which also provides reprint services. This publication is a good source for articles on African music. Three samples are chosen for listing:
•**Dargie, David**. "Musical bows in southern Africa," vol. 16, no. 1 (1986): 42-52.
continued

•**Erlmann, Veit**. "Traditional African music in black education," vol. 16, no. 2 (1986): 114-119.
•**Trowbridge, Antony V**. "Hugh Travers Tracey," vol. 15, no. 1 (1985): 4-9.

26. AFRICA INTERNATIONAL. 1958- . Dakar, Senegal.
Appears monthly. Contains good features on African politics and economics. There is always a culture section that frequently has articles on African contemporary music. In French.

27. AFRICA MUSIC. 1981- . London: Tony Amadi International Ltd.
This publication calls itself "The International Entertainment Magazine." Appears irregularly. Popularly written and highly commercial, the focus is primarily on well-known African performers of contemporary music. More serious articles on music have appeared from time to time. There are countless dramatic publicity photos, many in brilliant color, and accompanying, simply written articles. Some famous black musicians beyond the continent of Africa are also featured, including Michael Jackson, and Bob Marley.

28. AFRICA REPORT. 1957- . Denville, New Jersey: African-American Institute.
Bi-monthly. Even though this journal is primarily concerned with African political and economic development, it includes articles on African music. A few have been selected randomly for listing below. Indexed in **MLA, PAIS, CURRENT CONTENTS AFRICA**, and others.
•**Kazadi, Pierre Cary**. "Congo music: Africa's favorite beat," vol. 16, no 4, 1971.
•**Lewis, Ida**. "Songs with soul: Dorothy Masuka talks about her music," vol. 15, no. 6, 1970.
•**Merriam, Alan P**. "Music." [Merriam was in charge of this special section from 1963 to 1969.]

Africa south of the Sahara: index of periodical literature
See: **Library of Congress. African Section, 974.**

29. AFRICAN ABSTRACTS: A QUARTERLY REVIEW OF ETHNOLOGICAL, SOCIAL AND LINGUISTIC STUDIES APPEARING IN CURRENT PERIODICALS. 1950-1972. London: International African Institute.
An abstracting periodical appearing quarterly during its tenure, and published with the assistance of UNESCO. (The title page was also in French: **BULLETIN ANALYTIQUE AFRICANISTE**.) Each issue had at the end a list of periodicals that had been abstracted. The last General Index, which was helpful for finding music-related items, was in 1966, the exception being the final issue. The usual author and periodical indexes were not as easy to use. Abstracts were thorough and generous in length. A concordance covers volumes 1-17 of **AFRICAN ABSTRACTS**, with the exception of the linguistic abstracts. See **Schneider, Harold K., 1424.**

African all stars
See: **Stapleton, Chris, and Chris May, 1497.**

29a. **African art: five year cumulative bibliography, mid-1983 through 1988.** Edited by Eugene C. Burt. Seattle, Washington: Data Arts [1990?]. 170pp. (EthnoArts index supplemental publication, no. 3)
There are entries for musical instruments, and indexes for locating them in either Subject, Author, or Culture indexes. Succinct annotations.

30. **AFRICAN ARTS**. 1967- . Los Angeles, California: University of California, Los Angeles.
A splendid publication with magnificent, full-color photographs. Bilingual, French and English, until 1970. Now only in English. Originally, the Music and Dance editors were Klaus P. Wachsmann and Mantle Hood, and in those earlier days there were "plums" by such scholars as Ames, Anderson (Lois), Akpabot, and many more. (See selected examples below.) Now, though most articles concern the visual arts, music articles that are not highly technical are still welcome, according to the Editor. Annual index, cumulative indexes, back issues available. Microform, reprint services available from **UMI**. Indexed in **ART INDEX, CURRENT CONTENTS AFRICA, MLA, AICP**, others.
•**Bassani, Ezio**. "A Kongo drum stand," vol. 11, no. 1 (1977): 35-37, 92.
•**Knight, Roderic**. "Mandinka drumming," vol. 7, no. 4 (1974): 24-35.
•**Òjó, Jerome O.** "*Ògbóni* drums," vol. 6, no. 3 (1973): 50-52, 84.
•**Vidal, Túnjí**. "African *orí kì* in traditional Yorùbá music," vol. 3, no. 1 (1969): 56-59.

31. **African Bibliographic Center**. *The beat goes on: a selected guide to resources on African music and dance 1965-1967.* Washington, D.C.: African Bibliographic Center, March 1968. 14pp. (Current Reading List Series 6, no. 2)
Divided into four sections: 1. A selected guide to periodicals, 2. General works, 3. Dance, 4. Music and musical instruments. An excellent survey of scholarly works for the indicated two years. Brief annotations. Emphasis on periodical articles, but there is also a selected guide to periodicals by their titles.

32. **African Bibliographic Center**. *Phase two of the beat goes on: a supplementary guide to resources for African music and dance.* Washington, D.C.: African Bibliographic Center, 1969. 7pp. (Current Reading List Series no. 7, no. 2)
This short supplement to the immediately preceding entry includes materials mostly for the years 1967-1968. Some of the items have very brief descriptive statements. The introduction to the supplement suggests that in order to keep up-to-date on "this theme on a continuing basis," [i.e., African music and dance], one should consult the Center's monthly journal, **A CURRENT BIBLIOGRAPHY ON AFRICAN AFFAIRS**. This serial ran from 1962-1967; the new series, starting with volume 1, began in 1968. Divided into General, Dance, Music.

33. **African culture: Algiers Symposium July 21st - August 1st, 1969.** *The first Pan-African cultural festival.* Alger: S.N.E.D.

(Société Nationale d'Édition et de Diffusion), 1969. 403pp.
This is an important and impressive publication. Includes texts of messages and addresses by key political figures and heads-of-state of that period - mostly, but not all, from Africa. Incorporated is a list of the "Pan-African Cultural Manifesto" that grew out of the Symposium, and a list of participants, guests and observers. The section that follows, called Communications, is really a collection of scholarly papers written on a variety of African-related subjects. Those concerned primarily with music, or that incorporate significant sections on music, are listed below. There is a two-page index.

- **Ballmoos, Agnes von.** "The collection, notation and arrangement of Liberian folk songs," 105-107.
- **Eze, Leopold Françoise.** "The *nkul*, that marvelous traditional medium of social communication," 316-320.
- **Nacib, Youssef.** "Oral tradition and the Algiers festival," 357-362.
- **Omídèyí, Ọláolú.** "The place of traditional music in African society (with particular reference to Nigeria)," 243-245.

AFRICAN ECCLESIAL REVIEW
See: **AFRICAN ECCLESIASTICAL REVIEW, 34.**

34. **AFRICAN ECCLESIASTICAL REVIEW**. 1959-1978. Kampala.
This journal was issued bimonthly, and was continued by **AFRICAN ECCLESIAL REVIEW**, 1978- , published in Eldoret, Kenya. The following articles appeared under the earlier title:

- **Carroll, Kevin**. "African music," vol. 3, no. 4 (1961): 301-307.
- **Thiel, Paul van**. "Divine worship and African church music," vol. 3, no. 1 (1961): 73-76; vol. 3, no. 2 (1961): 144-147.
- **Thiel, Paul van**. "Text, tone and tune in African sacred music," vol. 6, no. 3 (1964): 250-257; vol. 8, no. 1 (1966): 53-62.

35. **The African experience**. Edited by John N. Paden, and Edward W. Soja. 4 vols. Evanston: Northwestern University Press, 1970.
Of this 4 volume series, Volume 1, Essays, is the most valuable. (See the Wachsmann's title below.) Volume 2, Syllabus, contains two light essays: Traditional Music, and Visual Arts and Music (the latter, having to do with contemporary Africa, and followed by a brief, annotated bibliography). Volume 3a, Bibliography, includes a few new bibliographic items as compared with the Traditional Music section of Volume 2. Volume 3b, Guide to Resources, is useful for a listing of general reference sources for African studies, and for journals and newspapers. Only three periodicals are listed under Visual Arts and Music.
See: **Wachsmann, Klaus P.** "Ethnomusicology in Africa," 128-151, **1636.**

36. **African heritage: an anthology of black African personality and culture**. Edited by Jacob Drachler. London: Collier-Macmillan Ltd., 1964.
A collection of stories, poems, songs, folk tales and essays. There is a preface by Melville J. Herskovits. Part One, called African Voices, includes in its first chapter, texts to two songs from what was then Southern Rhodesia - a Sudanese mother's song to her first-born, and six songs from Dahomey. Part Two is entitled, Afro-American Responses. This is a brilliant collection by famous

African and non-African literary figures, poets, scholars, historians, political dignitaries. A few names that stand out are: Senghor, Kenyatta, Primus, Césaire, Davidson, Tutùọlá.

37. AFRICAN LANGUAGE STUDIES. 1-17; 1960-1980. London: School of Oriental and African Studies, University of London.
No more published. Any journal having to do with African languages is certain to include articles having to do with tone or intonation. This fine publication usually had one to three items yearly relating to music. Not only the tonal aspects of languages were examined, but songs too received attention, and articles could range from a study of Zulu praise songs, to a *jali*'s view of his profession. Other surprisingly relevant items are to be found for the searching. Examples follow, only from volume 13.
•**Andrejejewski, B. W.** Allusive dictation in Galla hymns in praise of Sheikh Hussein of Bale," vol. 13 (1972): 1-31.
•**Innes, Gordon**. "Mandinka circumcision songs," vol. 13 (1972): 88-112.
•**King, Anthony**. "The construction and tuning of the *kora*," vol. 13 (1972): 113-136.

38. AFRICAN MUSIC. 1954- . Grahamstown, South Africa: Rhodes University. (International Library of African Music.)
In English and French. Formerly the *Newsletter* of the African Music Society. Edited by Andrew Tracey, this is *the* African music journal. Nothing is comparable to this exceptional and pioneer publication that for decades has been faithful to its main concern - African music. Writings of some of the world's most renowned musicologists continue to appear, though there is always room for the lesser-known scholar. The journal is issued (to quote **ULRICH'S**) "approximately" annually, and has book reviews and cumulative indexes. Abstracted regularly in **RILM**, indexed in **MUSIC INDEX, CURRENT CONTENTS AFRICA** and others. Back issues are available.

39. **African music: meeting in Yaoundé (Cameroon) 23-27 February 1970, organized by** UNESCO. Paris: *La revue musicale*, 1972. 154pp.
Includes an Introduction, a Report on the Yaoundé meeting by Charles Duvelle, Recommendations, and a List of Participants. This is a translation of **La musique africaine, réunion de Yaoundé (Cameroun)** [sur les traditions musicales de l'Afrique subsaharienne], **23-27 février 1970, organisée par l'UNESCO**, 1972. The French version is also listed in this bibliography, and there are entries for essays in both their French and English forms. This is reviewed by Eileen Southern in **THE BLACK PERSPECTIVE IN MUSIC**, vol. 1, no. 2 (1973): 179-180.
•**Almeida, Renato**. "The influence of African music in Brazil," 137-141.
•**Collins, Elizabeth**. "Musical traditions in Liberia," 143-144.
•**Daniélou, Alain**. "The musical languages of Black Africa," 51-57.
•**Duvelle, Charles**. "Oriental music in Black Africa," 95-117.
•**Eno Belinga, Samuel**. "The traditional music of West Africa: types, styles and influences," 71-75.
•**Euba, Akin**. "Creative potential and propagation of African traditional music," 119-125. *continued*

•**Ismail, Mahi**. "Musical traditions in the Sudan," 89-94.
•**Kakoma, George W**. "Musical traditions of East Africa," 77-88.
•**Kebede, Ashenafi**. "African music in the Western Hemisphere," 131-135.
•**Mensah, Atta Annan**. "The modern African's contact with music: the Zambian experience," 127-129.
•**Nketia, J. H. Kwabena**. "The musical languages of Subsaharan Africa," 7-42.
•**Nketia, J. H. Kwabena**. "Sources of historical data on the musical cultures of Africa," 43-49.
•**Ṣówándé, Fẹlá**. "The role of music in traditional African society," 59-69.

African Music Society
See: **AFRICAN MUSIC, 38.**

40. AFRICAN MUSICOLOGY. 1983- . Edited by Asante Darkwa and Washington A. Omondi. Kenya: University of Nairobi, Institute of African Studies. (See also the next entry with same title, **41.**)
Only Volume 1, Number 1 could be located, though it is listed as being issued annually. (The anticipated publication date of 1979 had been delayed because of various factors explained in the introduction to this first volume, which appeared in 1983.) The journal is intended to "serve the dual purpose of a newsletter and a journal for music educators and musicologists, and others concerned with African music." Footnotes and bibliographies abound. Beautifully executed, this initial publication contains scholarly articles by highly respected musicologists. (Abstracted in **RILM**, 1985.)
•**Allen, Jim de Vere**. "A note on the nomenclature of side-blown horns on the Swahili Coast (East Africa)," 14-17.
•**Anyumba, Henry Owuor**. "Contemporary lyres in eastern Africa," 18-33.
•**Bastin, Marie-Louise**. "Instruments de musique, chants et danses des Tshokwe région de Dundo district de la Lunda Angola," 45-66.
•**Brown, Ernest**. "Drums on the water: the *kuomboka* ceremony of the Lozi of Zambia," 67-78.
•**Gansemans, Jos**. "La morphologie des chants Luba (Shaba-Zaïre)," 34-40.
•**Nzewi, Meki**. "Philological derivations of melo-rhythmic improvisation," 1-13.
•**Omondi, Washington A**. "The lyre in Luo society: an observation," 41-44.

41. **African musicology: current trends: a festschrift presented to J. H. Kwabena Nketia**. Edited by Jacqueline Cogdell DjeDje and William G. Carter. [Atlanta, Georgia: Crossroads Press, 1988]- .
Besides the excellent essays in this collection, the work is extremely valuable because of its Biobibliographic Portrait of J. H. Kwabena Nketia that includes a list of Nketia's major works from 1949 through 1987. The section entitled, "Essays in honor of J. H. Kwabena Nketia," starts with an essay, "African musicology: an assessment of the field," by DjeDje and Carter. This is followed by articles that fall into several subject categories: Theoretical Perspectives, Aspects of Performance Practice, Music and Gender, and Musical Style and Composition. The book has information on the contributors and editors. There are music notations, sketches, photographs, charts, and an index. Individual essays have bibliographies:
•**Aning, Ben A**. "Kakraba Lobi: master xylophonist of Ghana," 93-110.
•**Chernoff, John M**. "The relevance of ethnomusicology to anthropology: strategies of inquiry and interpretation," 59-92. *continued*

•**DjeDje, Jacqueline Cogdell, and William G. Carter**. "African musicology: an assessment of the field," 39-44.
•**Fiagbedzi, Nissio**. "Toward a philosophy of theory in ethnomusicological research," 45-57.
•"**J. H. Kwabena Nketia: a biobibliographical portrait**," 3-29.
•**Kimberlin, Cynthia Tse**. "Ornaments and their classification as a determinant of technical ability and musical style," 265-305.
•**Kubik, Gerhard**. "Àlọ́ - Yorùbá chantefables: an integrated approach towards West African music and oral literature," 129-182.
•**Monts, Lester P.** "Vai women's roles in music, masking and ritual performance," 219-235.
•**Robinson, Gertrude Rivers**. "Moods for Flute and Piano, I and II," 321-331.
•**Schmidt, Cynthia E.** "Womanhood, work and song among the Kpelle of Liberia," 237-263.
•**Simon, Artur**. "Trumpet and flute ensembles of the Berta people in the Sudan," 183-217.
•**Slawson, Wayne**. "Features, musical operations, and composition: a derivation from Ewe drum music," 307-319.
•**Vidal, Túnjí**. "The role and function of music at Yorùbá festivals," 111-127.

African rock
See: **Stapleton, Chris, and Chris May**. *African all stars*, **1497**.

42. AFRICAN NOTES. 1963- . Ìbàdàn, Nigeria: Institute of African Studies, University of Ìbàdàn.

None were published 1973-1979. Issued semiannually. Indexed in **MLA, HISTORICAL ABSTRACTS**, and others. A few selections follow:
•**Armstrong, Robert G.**, *et al.* "*Èkìtì* traditional dirge of Lt. Colonel Adénkúnlé Fájùyì's funeral," vol. 5, no. 2 (1969): 63-94.
•**Ògúnbà, Oyinadé**. "The poetic content and form of Yorùbá occasional festival songs," vol. 6, no. 2 (1971): 10-30.
•**Ọláyẹmí, Val**. "Forms of the song in Yorùbá folktales," vol. 5, no 1 (1968): 179-207.

43. **African songs and rhythms for children**: a selection from Ghana by W. K. Amoaku. Mainz: Schott, c1971. 32pp. (Orff-Schulwerk in the African tradition)

In the preface, Nketia mentions that the traditional African approach to musicianship, through speech, rhythms and movement, is very close to that of Orff-Schulwerk. Working under the guidance of Dr. Carl Orff, Amoaku, a Ghanaian musician, launched the first volume of this series based entirely on African materials. Twelve notated works are included, largely songs in Ga and Ewe, but also some simplified rhythmic patterns of traditional Ghanaian dance forms. Black and white photographs of an *adowa* drum ensemble, one of several idiophones. Songs texts in English. Twi and Ewe names for instruments are given.

44. **African studies: papers presented at a colloquium at the British Library, 7-9 January 1985.** Edited by Ilse Sternberg, and

Patricia M. Larby. London: British Library in association with SCOLMA, 1986.
The following two essays are included:
- **Duran, Lucy**. "British Library African resources: (2) archival; The National Sound Archive: traditional African music," 238-245.
- **Vickers, Jonathan**, "British Library African resources: (2)archival; The National Sound Archive: spoken recordings," 231-237.

African Studies Association
See: **ASA NEWS, 1.**

African Studies Association of the United Kingdom
See: **Symposium on African Art, Music and Literature, 1522.**

African studies information resources directory.
See: **Gosebrink, Jean E. Mech, 633.**

AFRICAN STUDIES NEWSLETTER
See: **ASA NEWS, 1.**

AFRICAN URBAN NOTES
See: **AFRICAN URBAN STUDIES, 45.**

45. **AFRICAN URBAN STUDIES.** no. 1, 1978- . East Lansing, Michigan: African Studies Center, Michigan State University.
Appears three times a year, and supersedes **AFRICAN URBAN NOTES.** Starting with Number 1, published in the spring of 1978, issues are called the "New Series." Articles on African music between 1960-1977 appear under the older title. Indexed in **HISTORICAL ABSTRACTS, AMERICAN HISTORY AND LIFE, CURRENT CONTENTS AFRIKA**, and other indexing journals listed in **ULRICH'S**. Following are four items selected from both old and new series, with the reminder that in 1970, a number of other articles appeared on African music.
- **Euba, Akin**. "Traditional elements as the basis of new African art music," vol. 5, no. 4 (1970): 52-62.
- **Hooker, Naomi W.** "Popular musicians in Freetown," vol. 5. no. 4 (1970): 11-18.
- **Kazadi wa Mukuna**. "The origins of Zaïrean modern music: a socio-economic aspect," vol. 6 (1979-1980): 31-39.
- **Mbabi-Katana, Solomon**. "Similarities of musical phenomenon over a large part of the African continent as evidenced by the *irambo* and *empango* side-blown trumpet styles and drum rhythms," vol. 5, no. 4 (1970): 25-41.

46. **African-American baseline essays**. Rev. ed. Portland, Oregon: Multicultural/Multiethnic Education Office, Portland Public Schools, 1990.
Included because of the essay on "African and African-American contributions to world music." See **Lawrence-McIntyre, Charshee, 958.**

African-American Institute's African Performing Artist Program.
See: **Music of Africa, 1132.**

The Africana conference paper index
See: **Melville J. Herskovits Library of African Studies, 1063.**

47. AFRICANA MARBURGENSIA. 1968- . Marburg: Germany. Universität Marburg.

The text is in English, French, and German. Issued semiannually. Occasional papers on African music. Available on "exchange basis." Concerned with religious, social, economic and legal aspects of African studies. Indexed in **MLA, CERDIC, CURRENT CONTENTS AFRICA**. A few examples follow:

- **Erlmann, Veit**. "Musik und Trance: Symbolische Aspekte des Bori Bessessenheits Kultes der Hausa in Maradi (Niger)," vol. 15, no. 1 (1982): 3-24.
- **Johnston, Thomas F.** "Aspects of Tsonga history through song," vol. 6, no. 1 (1973): 17-36.
- **Johnston, Thomas F.** "Humanized animal and bird figures in Tsonga songtexts." vol. 11 (1978): 15-16.

48. **Africana Museum (Johannesburg, South Africa).** *Catalogue of the musical instruments in the collection of Percival R. Kirby*. Compiled by Margaret M. De Lange. Johannesburg, 1967. 155pp.

Kirby's unique collection of musical instruments is now preserved in the Africana Museum in the Johannesburg Public Library. There are some 400 instruments. See also: **Kirby, Percival Robson, 865-869.**

49. **Africanisms in American culture.** Edited by Joseph E. Holloway. Bloomington: Indiana University Press, c1990. 249pp. (Blacks in the diaspora)

- **Maultsby, Portia K.** "Africanisms in African-American music," 185-210.

50. AFRIKA HEUTE. 1957- . Bonn: Progress Dritte Welt. Bimonthly. Title varies: AFRIKA-INFORMATIONS-DIENST, 1962. Continued by 3. WELT MAGAZIN, 1975- .

This journal changed names a number of times, but it appears that no more were published after the May, 1979 issue. When it was called **AFRIKA HEUTE**, a number of papers on African music were published: an earlier one by A. M. Dauer, in 1961; in 1966, one by Nketia, and another by Kubik; in 1968, a paper by Maurice Djenda; and in 1969, a paper by G. T. Nurse. There may have been others. The following essays have been selected at random for listing:

- **Dauer, A. M.** "Musik - Landschaften in Afrika," no. 23 (1966): 1-7.
- **Kubik, Gerhard**. "Musikaufnahme in Malaŵi: Probleme der Durchführung," no. 4, 1968.
- **Kubik, Gerhard**. "Neue Musikformen in Schwarzafrika. Psychologische und musikethnologische Grundlagend," no. 4, 1965.
- **Kubik, Gerhard**. "Probleme der Tonaufnahme afrikanischer Musiker," no. 15-16, 1966.

AFRIKA INFORMATIONS DIENST
See: **AFRIKA HEUTE, 50.**

A

51. **AFRIKA UND ÜBERSEE: SPRACHEN, KULTUREN**. 1910- . Berlin: D. Reimer.

A large number of articles on African music have appeared in this durable journal. It appears semiannually (though irregularly). Indexed by **MLA** and **AICP**. Examples follow:

- **Biebuyck, Daniel, and Kahombo Matene**. "Chante Hunde," vol. 48, no. 1 (1966): 157-169.
- **Johnston, Thomas F**. "Hand pianos, xylophones and flutes of the Shangana-Tsonga," vol. 57, no. 3 (1974): 186-192.
- **Knappert, Jan**. "Swahili songs with double entendre," vol. 66, no. 1 (1983): 67-76.

52. **AFRIKA-TERVUREN**. 1955- . Tervuren, Publiée sous les auspices des Amis du Musée royal de l'Afrique Centrale.

(A title variant is **CONGO-TERVUREN**.) The text is in French or Flemish. The last issue seems to have been in 1986, with volume 32. During this journal's tenure, a number of articles on African music were published. A few are listed below:

- **Dechamps, R**. "Note préliminaire concernant l'identification anatomique des espèces de bois utilisée dans la fabrication des tambours à fente de l'Afrique Centrale," vol. 18, no. 1 (1972): 15-18.
- **Gansemans, Jos**. "De Jachtliederin der Luba-Shankadi. [Hunting songs of the Luba-Shankadi]," vol. 14, no. 2 (1972): 2-5.
- **Lestrade, A**. "La flute traditionnelle au Rwanda," vol. 16, no. 1(1970): 30.

53. **L'Afrique noire en marionettes**. Compiled and edited by Olenka Darkowska-Nidzgorska. English translation by Prudence Borgniet, iconography by Denis Nidzgorski, editorial assistance by Sylvie Jupinet. [Charleville-Mézières, France: Unione internationale de la marionette, 1988]. 80pp.

An informative book about African puppets, with parallel text in English and French. There are two pages of information on the giant wooden trumpet "puppets" of the Bembe. (See **Lehuard, Raoul** for an earlier paper, **960**.) Darkowska-Nidzgorski and students tried in vain to find any signs remaining of these puppets in Mouyondzi, Congo, where they "could be seen 30 years ago." A photo of the puppets being carried is the same one pictured in Lehuard's paper, and in Nketia's book, *The music of Africa*, **1205**.

54. **AFRO MUSIC**. 1976-1978. Paris: Media International.

In French, appeared monthly. Starting with Number 14 (April, 1977) issued in magazine format similar to a Sunday newspaper supplement. The main concern was personalities associated with popular music - stars more than music. Large, full-color sensational photographs fill the pages, accompanied by short, popularly written articles. African musicians were featured, but with no neglect of stars from the United States and Jamaica. Although the emphasis was primarily on celebrities of African heritage, there were occasional exceptions. Included were editorials, a correspondence section, and other regular features such as are found in similar publications designed for popular consumption. Sexist.

55. **Afro-America sings.** [Detroit, Board of Education of the City of Detroit, 1971]. 182pp.
A handsomely-designed collection of approximately 85 songs, scored principally for solo voice or chorus, with piano accompaniment. Though most of the songs are African-American, there are 8 from the Caribbean, and 13 from Africa that have been adapted and arranged. Explanatory notes precede the songs, and there are attractive illustrations and abundant photographs. Some American work songs are included, though any possible Africanisms are not detectable. Interesting is an excerpt from Samuel Coleridge-Taylor's, *The Bamboula* (a strongly African dance performed by slaves). The book was prepared by a Detroit Public School workshop directed by Ollie McFarland.

56. **AFROPOP WORLDWIDE. LISTENER'S GUIDE.** 1989- . Washington D.C.: National Public Radio.
This colorful, envelope-sized treasure is published annually. To date issues have contained: a program roster; a Glossary of African Music Terms; dramatic maps of Africa or other areas, showing countries or islands associated with particular Afropop personalities or groups; a world-wide discography; suggested reading (quality books and periodicals); **AFROPOP WORLDWIDE** radio stations; festivals; record stores; and information on the nightclub circuit. Guest essays, listed below, appear in each issue. Many bright photos. (The publishers regret that they can only provide copies of the current guide by subscription from "libraries or institutions.")
•**Palmer, Robert**. "Introduction," [on African popular music] 1990: 4-7.
•**Pareles, Jon**. "Introduction," [on African popular music] 1989: 2-5.
•**Thompson, Robert Farris**. "Afro-Atlantic music in the nineties: making space for African futures," 1991: 2-6.

57. **Agbenyega, Stephen Tete.** LIBATION: MUSIC WRITTEN FOR TWO PIANOS AND ELECTRONIC TAPE WITH ESSAY ON SPACE-TIME AND IMPLICATIONS FOR AFRICAN MUSIC. Dissertation, Columbia University, 1983. 292pp.
Libation is a twelve-tone composition. In his essay the author says, that an objective notion of space-time is possible, and that space-time is inseparable and interlocked. He sees the earth's "time-line" relative to time-lines described by other planets, each having its "own internal tempo." [Any connection to Music of the Spheres?] He concludes that "the possibility of multi-linear temporal relations escaping the domination of strict one-dimensional causation for the entire universe, in the Newtonian sense, appears to be real," and uses pre-Renaissance Western music, and particularly African music, to substantiate this idea. Agbenyega anticipates the "ontological" study of African arts. **(UMI)**

58. **Agu, D. C. C.** INDIGENOUS CHORAL MUSIC IN AFRICAN CHRISTIAN WORSHIP: AN ANALYTICAL STUDY OF THE YOUTH SONGS IN THE NIGER DIOCESE OF NIGERIA. Dissertation, Queen's University of Belfast (Northern Ireland), 1984. 824pp.

59. **Agyemang, Fred M.** *Amu, the African: a study in vision and courage*. Accra: Asempa Publishers, Christian Council of Ghana,

1988. 208pp.
Biography of Ephraim Amu, renowned and distinguished Ghanaian. A prolific composer, and also a devout Christian who taught religion, agriculture, music, drumming, and African musical instruments, Amu distinguished himself early in his career by advocating a return to African ways. He promoted the use of African music and instruments, African attire, languages, food, utensils. He also had much to do with integrating African culture into the Christian liturgy. (This was at a time when Ghana was still emulating the West, so that Amu's unwavering insistence on affirming traditional African mores made him a controversial figure.) Index, photographs.

Ajíbọ̀lá, J. O.
See: **Orin Yorùbá, 1295.**

60. **Àjùwọ̀n, Bádé**. *Funeral dirges of Yorùbá hunters.* New York: NOK Publishers International, c1982. 134pp.
In English and Yorùbá. Bibliography.

61. **Àjùwọ̀n, Bádé**. "The metaphorical language of *ìrèmọ̀jé* chants." **ODÙ** New Series no. 18 (1978): 106-116.
Texts of Yorùbá hunters' funeral dirges. The dirges are performed by trained and respected artists who have excellent improvisational skills. Notes.

62. **Àjùwọ̀n, Bádé**. "The preservation of Yorùbá tradition through hunters' funeral dirges." **AFRICA** 50, no. 1 (1980): 66-72.

63. **Àjùwọ̀n, Bádé**. THE YORÙBÁ HUNTER'S FUNERAL DIRGES. Dissertation, Indiana University, 1977. 346pp.

64. **Akpabot, Samuel Ekpe**. "The conflict between foreign and traditional culture in Nigeria." In **Reflections on Afro-American music**. Edited by Dominique-René de Lerma, 124-130. [Kent, Ohio] Kent State University Press [1973].
Akpabot exhorts Nigerians not to get caught up in the "passing fancy" of American dance, but to reaffirm their own traditional dances, and return to other traditional Nigerian creative arts, as well. (The soul music of the day - obviously not his favorite - he describes as "100-decibel twanging guitars, the roar of electric organs, and the fanfare of blazing trumpets.")

65. **Akpabot, Samuel Ekpe**. *Foundation of Nigerian traditional music.* Ìbàdàn: Spectrum Books; Channel Islands, United Kingdom: Compendium House, 1986. 113pp.
Bibliography.

66. **Akpabot, Samuel Ekpe**. "Fugitive notes on notation and terminology in African music." **THE BLACK PERSPECTIVE IN MUSIC**
continued

4, no. 1 (1976): 39-45.
Includes music.

67. **Akpabot, Samuel Ekpe.** FUNCTIONAL MUSIC OF THE IBIBIO PEOPLE OF NIGERIA. Dissertation, Michigan State University, 1975. 156pp.

68. **Akpabot, Samuel Ekpe.** *Ibibio music in Nigerian culture.* [East Lansing]: Michigan State University Press, 1975. 102pp.
Bibliography, illustrations.

69. **Akpabot, Samuel Ekpe.** INSTRUMENTATION IN AFRICAN MUSIC: THE EVIDENCE OF NIGERIA. Master's Thesis, Trinity College of Music, 1967.

70. **Akrofi, Eric Ayisi.** THE STATUS OF MUSIC EDUCATION PROGRAMS IN GHANAIAN PUBLIC SCHOOLS. Dissertation, University of Illinois at Urbana-Champaign, 1982. 224pp.
As a result of his study, Akrofi was able to indicate the prevalence in Ghana of Western-based notions of music education. Tangible suggestions for correcting this inappropriate situation resulted from a questionnaire sent to 10 selected Ghanaian music educators. It was felt that the objectives of the music education program should [in compressed form]: be geared to Ghana, use African music as the focus, expose students to world musics, give opportunities for all to participate in musical performances. It was further recommended that regional and district organizers supervise the music program, and that specialists meet regularly to discuss problems and share ideas. **(UMI)**

71. **Alagoa, Ebiegberi Joe.** *War canoe drums and topical songs from Nembe, Rivers State.* Rivers State, Nigeria: University of Ìbàdàn, Institute of African Studies, 1974. 13pp.
The war canoe was an instrument of battle, and a political and social instrument of several kingdoms of the Eastern Nigerian Delta. This pamphlet describes the symbolism of the boat, and the roles of various drums as they praise the chief (seated on a center platform), communicate to other war canoes, or "talk" to warriors on the same vessel. Paddle rhythms and words of topical songs in Nembe are given with English translation, two pertaining to the Biafran war. A demonstration record is (was?) available from the University of Ìbàdàn.

72. **Alájá-Browne, Afọlábí.** AYỌ̀ BÁNKỌLÉ: HIS LIFE AND WORK. Master's Thesis, University of Pittsburgh, 1981.

73. **Alájá-Browne, Afọlábí.** JÙJÚ MUSIC: A STUDY OF ITS SOCIAL HISTORY AND STYLE. Dissertation, University of Pittsburgh, 1985. 187pp.
Jùjú music originated in Lagos in the third decade of this century. Chapters cover its development: from 1929-1939, from the early 40s to late 60s, and in more recent times. Alájá-Browne indicates the relationship between jùjú and the "oil-

decade of Nigeria's petroleum-dependent economy." The fourth chapter studies the nature and elements of jùjú style exemplified by Abdulrafiu Babátúndé King. Chapter five is a summary, with suggestions for future research. Alaja-Browne states that jùjú "emerged and subsequently developed out of a set of structural relations between musicians and the total context in which they performed." (UMI)

Algiers Symposium July 21st - August 1st, 1969.
See: **African culture: Algiers Symposium, 33.**

74. **Allen, Jim de Vere.** "A note on the nomenclature of side-blown horns on the Swahili Coast (East Africa)." **AFRICAN MUSICOLOGY** 1, no.1 (1983): 4-17.
Bibliography.

75. **Almeida, Renato.** "L'influence de la musique africaine au Brésil." In **La musique africaine, réunion de Yaoundé (Cameroun)** [sur les traditions musicales de l'Afrique subsaharienne], **23-27 février 1970, organisée par l'UNESCO**, 135-140. Paris: *La revue musicale*, Richard-Masse, 1972.
Original French version of entry that follows.

76. **Almeida, Renato.** "The influence of African music in Brazil." In **African music: meeting in Yaoundé (Cameroon) 23-27 February 1970, organized by UNESCO**, 137-141. Paris: *La revue musicale*, 1972.
Translation from French of the preceding entry.

77. **Alnaes, Kirsten.** "Living with the past: the songs of the Herero in Botswana." **AFRICA** 59, no. 3 (1989): 299.
This is about a people who were originally refugees from the Herero war against the German colonial power in 1904. Defeated and annihilated in large numbers, some managed to survive in the agonizing retreat across the Kalahari desert. (Today the Herero regard themselves as citizens of Botswana.) Abundant notes, long bibliography, song texts. Brief French summary at end.

78. **Alvarenga, Oneyda.** *Música popular brasileira.* 2d ed. São Paulo: Livraria Duas Cidades, 1982. 374pp. (*Coleção O Baile das quatro artes*)
An important book, written in Portuguese, with many references to the African presence in music, dance and ritual. There are detailed notes on instruments. Fascinating photographs include people playing instruments, as well as still shots of a musical bow, and drums and rattles straight out of West Africa! No index, but watch for key words such as Xangô, Bahia, Candomblé, Afro-brasileiro, and others. An eight-page bibliography, of predominantly Portuguese entries, is included. Some music, principally unaccompanied melodies.

79. **Alvarez Nazario, Manuel.** *El elemento afronegroide en el español de Puerto Rico: contribución al estudio del negro en America.* 2d ed., revised and augmented. San Juan: Instituto de Cultura Puertorriqueña, 1974. 489pp.
Includes a bibliography and index. Contains information on the *bomba*, a name signifying drum-dances in Puerto Rico of African and Afro-Antillean origin. (The dances are accompanied by drums of the same name.)

80. **Alves, Henrique L.** *Bibliografia afro-brasileira: estudos sobre o negro.* Apresentação de José Honório Rodrigues; [capa, Studio Cátedra]. 2d ed., revised and amplified. Rio de Janeiro: Livraria Editora Cátedra, 1979. 181pp. "Em convênio com o Instituto Nacional do Livro."
In Portuguese. The bibliography is entirely alphabetical by last names of authors, and one misses a subject index. With careful probing, however, certain key words can be found within a title: i.e., música, Xangô, Candomblé, and Portuguese words for certain dances, etc. All in all, though the book does not seem to have an overwhelming number of music references, it does provide the names of significant Brazilian periodicals that might regularly feature articles on African-related music and dance.

81. **Amankulor, Jas. N.** "Ekpe festival as religious ritual and dance drama." IKENGA 1, No.2 (1972): 37-47.
Describes the role of drumming and song in the Ekpe festival. Amankulor says that in response to the question "Who am I?" (the same one asked by Oedipus), Africa's answer lies in a "return to the roots of culture and back to the realm of traditional ritual and religion." He believes that Epke "provides a possibility for this return, and that "through its media of song and dance great drama could be forged."

82. **Amegatcher, Adelaide.** THE CONCERT PARTIES: A MANIFESTATION OF POPULAR DRAMA IN GHANA. Master's Thesis, University of North Carolina, 1968.

83. **América Latina en su música.** Edited by Isabel Aretz. Paris: UNESCO, 1977. 344pp. (Serie América Latina en su cultura)
(Note: This entry also appears under the editor's name, with a slightly longer annotation, **121**.) A collection of essays by different authors, written in Spanish. With patience, one might ferret out a few references to Africa. There is a 20 page bibliography, an index by authors, and a subject index by country, instruments, serials, and music education. Chapter 3 appears to be the most useful; subheading 4, entitled "Aporte Africano," is pertinent:
•**Locatelli de Pérgamo, Ana María.** "Raíces musicales," 35-52.

American and Canadian doctoral dissertations and master's theses on Africa, 1886-1974
See: **Sims, Michael,** *et al.*, **1460.**

American and Canadian doctoral dissertations and master's theses on Africa, 1974-1987
See: **Lauer, Joseph J.** *et al.*, **951.**

84. **Ames, David W.** "Hausa drums of Zaria." **ÌBÀDÀN** vol. 21 (1965): 62-79.

85. **Ames, David W.** "A sociocultural view of Hausa musical activity."In *The traditional artist in African societies.* Edited by Warren L. d'Azevedo, 128-161. Bloomington: Indiana University Press, -[1973].

86. **Ames, David W., and Anthony V. King.** *Glossary of Hausa music and its social contexts.* Evanston: Northwestern University Press, 1971. 184pp.
Divided into sections for: Instruments and Their Parts, Professional Performers, Patrons, Occasions, and Music Performance. Hausa and English-Hausa indexes are followed by several pages of well-defined black and white photos of performing musicians. Two administrative and cultural areas of Hausaland, Katsina and Zaria, are the primary focus. A most thorough collaborative work by a musicologist and an anthropologist.

87. **Amoaku, William Komla.** *African and African-American music traditions.* Portland, Oregon: Portland Public Schools, [198-?]. 115pp.
This Ghanaian ethnomusicologist overviews a vast subject. Of particular value is his lucid presentation of the traditional African world view and how this is expressed in rituals involving music, dance and visual art, also in the New World. He discusses Africanisms in United States religious music, worksongs and blues, and in music and dance of other New World areas. From the section on Classic Blues to Jazz Today, standard information on African-American music and musicians is given. There are 24 chapters and a bibliography. Spiral-bound.

88. **Amoaku, William Komla.** SOME ASPECTS OF CHANGE IN TRADITIONAL INSTITUTIONS AND MUSIC IN GHANA. Master's Thesis, University of Illinois, Urbana-Champaign, 1971.

89. **Amoaku, William Komla.** SYMBOLISM IN TRADITIONAL INSTITUTIONS AND MUSIC OF THE EWE OF GHANA. Dissertation, University of Pittsburgh, 1975. 328pp.
Illustrations, maps, music, bibliography.

90. **Amoaku, William Komla.** "Toward a definition of traditional African music: a look at the Ewe of Ghana." In **More than drumming: essays on African and Afro-Latin music and musicians**. Edited by Irene V. Jackson, 31-40. Westport,

Connecticut: Greenwood Press, c1985.
Bibliography. Abstracted in **RILM**, 1985.

Amoaku, William Komla
See also: **African songs and rhythms for children, 43.**

91. **Amrouche, Jean.** *Chants berbères de Kabyile.* Preface by Mouloud Mammeri. Transcribed and edited by Tassadit Yacine. Bilingual edition. Paris: Édition L'Harmattan, 1988. 264pp.
Kabyle song texts and poetry. In French and Kabyle. Bibliographical references.

92. **Anderson, Ian.** "Roots at risk: the music of Madagascar is at a dangerous crossroads says Ian Anderson." **FOLK ROOTS** no. 95 (1991): 20-22.

93. **Anderson, Lois Ann.** "The *entenga* tuned-drum ensemble." [Buganda] In **Essays for a humanist: an offering to Klaus Wachsmann**, 1-57. Spring Valley, New York: Town House Press, 1977.
The author studied with Buganda musicians, members of the *entenga* tuned-drum ensemble from 1964 to 1966, until national poltical events forced the emsemble out of existence. There are figures, charts, notations, a bibliography, and photographs.

94. **Anderson, Lois Ann.** "The interrelation of African and Arab musics: some preliminary considerations." In *Essays on music and history in Africa.* Edited by Klaus P. Wachsmann, 143-169. Evanston: Northwestern University Press, 1971.
Includes 92 footnotes, and a chart with brief information about the seven men chosen by Abu Bakr, b. Mujahid (d. A.H. 324/A.D. 936) [Abū Bakr Mujāhid] to be authoritative Koran readers.

95. **Anderson, Lois Ann.** THE 'MIKO' MODAL SYSTEM OF KIGANDA XYLOPHONE MUSIC (WITH) VOLUME II: TRANSCRIPTIONS OF THE AMADINDA REPERTOIRE. [Buganda] 2 vols. Dissertation, University of California, Los Angeles, 1968. 370pp.
Anderson undertook extensive studies of the *amadinda* xylophone after playing xylophone in a Balinese *gamelan*, reading an article on the Kiganda instrument by G. Kubik, and being "struck" by possible similarities in playing techniques. She learned all aspects of the 12-tone *amadinda*, worked with the Kabaka's Royal Musicians of 1964-1966, and far more. Ninety-two *amadinda* transcriptions are included. Her stunning dissertation offers a basis for comparative studies in music even beyond Africa. She is unprepared, however, pending further investigations of actual xylophone traditions, to draw any conclusions regarding the mere *presence* of the xylophone in Africa, Indonesia, and Southeast Asia.

96. **Anderson, Lois Ann**. "Multipart relationships in xylophone and tuned drum traditions in Buganda." In **Studies in African music**. Co-editors, J. H. Kwabena Nketia, and Jacqueline Cogdell DjeDje, 121-144. [Los Angeles]: Program in Ethnomusicology, Department of Music, University of California, Los Angeles, 1984.
Map, notations, charts, notes, diagrams, bibliography, photographs.

97. **Andersson, Muff**. *Music in the mix: the story of South African popular music.* Johannesburg: Ravan Press, c1981. 189pp.
The subjects are: 1. The Background of the South African Music Scene, 2. Music as Propaganda: an Instrument of Apartheid, 3. Repercussions - the Damage Done, Trends of the Future. Lighter commercial music and popular resistance forms are the main concentration. The book is bold and dramatic, with many photographs of musicians, variations in print size and style, and quotations in the margins. The author says that the book "attempts to be not only a comment on the plight of an art form/expression of life, but also a comment on a very peculiar society: the two ideas cannot be separated." Index, bibliography.

98. **Andrejejewski, B. W**. "Allusive dictation in Galla hymns in praise of Sheikh Hussein of Bale [al-Shaykh Ḥusayn]." AFRICAN LANGUAGE STUDIES 13, (1972): 1-31.

99. **Aning, Ben A.** *Adenkum, a study of the music of Akan female bands.* Post-Graduate Diploma, University of Ghana, Institute of African Studies, 1964. 296pp.
Concerns the Ghananian recreational music known as *adenkum*, named for a gourd stamping tube that is a fundamental component. The author carefully analyzes *adenkum* musically, and goes on to more recent changes in its function, instrumentation, and the newer role of women in its performance. Three female bands from different regions are studied and compared. Includes a bibliography, transcriptions of 43 songs, their texts in Twi and English, and a few photos. A tape of the music accompanies the work.

100. **Aning, Ben A.** *An annotated bibliography of music and dance in English-speaking Africa.* Legon: Institute of African Studies, University of Ghana, 1967. 47pp.
A small book, about ¼" thick, organized by region. There are 132 entries, comprising books and periodicals, and they are annotated. The author mentions in the preface that he makes no claims to have covered the subject completely, adding that the bibliography was undertaken to indicate what still needs to be done with regard to existing literature in the field. He mentions prior bibliographies of Merriam, Varley, Thieme, and Gaskin. By including music and dance, Aning shows his appreciation of the close unity of these arts in Africa. This is another important reference book in the field of African music.

101. **Aning, Ben A.** "*Atumpan* drums: an object of historical and anthropological study." In **Essays for a humanist: an offering to Klaus Wachsmann**, 58-72. Spring Valley, New York: Town House Press, 1977.

Discusses the construction, symbolic significance, and musical roles of the Akan talking drum, *atumpan*. Photographs, bibliography.

102. **Aning, Ben A.** "Kakraba Lobi: master xylophonist of Ghana." In **African musicology: current trends: a festschrift presented to J. H. Kwabena Nketia**. Edited by Jacqueline Cogdell DjeDje, and William G. Carter, 93-110. [Atlanta, Georgia: Crossroads Press, 1988]- .

An informative human interest biography, with notes, bibliography, brief song texts, two photographs. (One recalls the virtuosity displayed by Kakraba Lobi during a lecture performance years ago at Northwestern University, the flying sticks as he gave his mischievous version of American jazz. Remembered too is his demonstration of *gyil* funeral music for a dead wife, the overlapping dialogue between hands, one lamenting, the other answering with words of comfort.) See also the entry under Grace Moore, a short study written during Kakraba Lobi's Evanston stay, **1107**.

103. **Aning, Ben A.** "Melodic analysis of Adenkum." In **Papers in African studies**, 64-80. Legon: University of Ghana, Institute of African Studies, 1968.

Adenkum is the name of a gourd stamping tube played by Akan women of Ghana. It is also the name of a type of recreational music accompanied by this instrument. Notated music examples, five tables, illustrations. See also Aning's other works on *adenkum*, **99, 101**.

104. **Aning, Ben A.** "The music and musical instruments of West Africa." In **Brief sketches in Akan (Ghana) art symbols, literature, music, and African theater**, 9-14. Washington, D.C.: Association for the Study of Negro Life and History, c1972.

105. **Aning, Ben A.** *NWƆNKORƆ*: A STUDY OF STABILITY AND CHANGE IN TRADITIONAL MUSIC. Master's Thesis. University of Ghana, 1969. 239pp.

Nwɔnkorɔ is a women's recreational music. The study considers several extra-musical factors, such as social behavior, social organization, and social institutions as they relate to the music.

106. **Aning, Ben A.** "Tuning the *kora*: a case study of the norms of a Gambian musician." JOURNAL OF AFRICAN STUDIES 9, no. 3 (1982): 164-175.

Includes 17 figures, notes.

107. **Aning, Ben A.** "Wangara xylophone and its music." In **Papers in African studies.** 57-63. Legon: University of Ghana, Institute of African Studies, 1968.

This is based on Aning's interview with musician-informant, Musa Wangara. There are photographs and a staff notation of pitches used on the *cholhu* (the Buamu name for the xylophone; the Bobo call it *balam*). Aning lists the names of six pieces recorded during his interview with Wangara on April 4, 1967 at the Institute of African Studies, University of Ghana. It is not indicated whether the University became a repository for this recording.

108. **Ankermann, Bernhard.** *Die afrikanischen Musikinstrumente.* Leipzig: Zentralantiquariat der Dt. Demokrat. Republic, 1976. 134pp.

This is a reprint of the 1901 edition published by Haack, Berlin, which was issued as Volume 3, Book 1 of Ethnologisches Notizblatt. On African musical instruments. Includes bibliographical references.

109. **Anku, William Oscar.** PROCEDURES IN AFRICAN DRUMMING: A STUDY OF AKAN/EWE TRADITIONS AND AFRICAN DRUMMING IN PITTSBURGH. Dissertation, University of Pittsburgh, 1988. 406pp.

The purpose of the study was: (1) to identify the distinguishing features of African drumming; (2) to devise a theoretical framework for its analysis; and (3) to establish the procedures and processes that guide the interplay of composite rhythmic elements in drumming. Anku believes in the value of performance as a tool for musicological research, and consequently learned to play in the traditions being investigated, i.e., Akan and Ewe. Ultimately, his attention was focused on African drumming observed in Pittsburgh that had a "peculiar African character." He describes the laboratory techniques used for transcribing music played by these local experts. **(UMI)**

110. **ANTHROPOLOGICAL INDEX TO CURRENT PERIODICALS IN THE LIBRARY OF THE MUSEUM OF MANKIND LIBRARY.** 1963- London, England: Royal Anthropological Institute of Great Britain and Ireland.

This publication, issued quarterly, contains about 2,000 titles of articles published in current journals worldwide that cover all aspects of anthropology, archaeology, ethnography, and linguistics. Periodicals so indexed in this bibliography are indicated by the acronym, **AICP**. This was formerly known as, **ROYAL ANTHROPOLOGICAL INSTITUTE OF GREAT BRITAIN AND IRELAND. LIBRARY. ANTHROPOLOGICAL INDEX.** Back issues are available.

111. **ANTHROPOLOGICAL LITERATURE: AN INDEX TO PERIODICAL ARTICLES AND ESSAYS.** 1979- . Harvard University: Tozzer Library, Cambridge, Massachusetts.

Issued quarterly starting 1988. Provides an author and subject index to 10,000 articles in approximately 1,000 serials and edited works. Articles are primarily focused on the fields of archaeology, biological and physical anthropology, cultural and social anthropology, and linguistics. Volume 6 (1984) to volume 10, number 4 (fall, 1988) were published in microfiche format.

112. **The anthropology of the body**. Edited by John Blacking. New York: Academic Press, 1977. 426pp. (A.A.A. monograph, 15)
Of these papers presented at a conference sponsored by the African Studies Association, one relates in particular to African music:
- **Kubik, Gerhard**. "Patterns of body movement in the music of boy's initiation in South-east Angola," 253-274.

113. **ANTHROPOS: REVUE INTERNATIONALE D'ETHNOLOGIE ET DE LINGUISTIQUE**. 1906- . Fribourg, Switzerland: Editions Saint-Paul (Anthropos Institute)
Obviously a durable journal. Published twice a year, with text in English, French, and German. Discusses ethnological issues. Articles on African music have appeared throughout the years. Indexed in **MLA, AICP, SOCIAL SCIENCE INDEX**, others. Following are a few randomly selected items:
- **Hartwig, Charlotte Mae**. "Music in Kerebe culture," vol. 68, no. 3/4 (1972): 449-464.
- **Johnston, Thomas F**. "Tsonga musical performance in cultural perspective," vol. 70, no. 5/6 (1975): 761-799.
- **Merriam, Alan P**. "Music change in a Basongye village," vol. 72, no. 5/6 (1977): 806-846.

114. **Anya-Noa, Lucien, and Basile Juléat Fouda**. *Berçeuse Beti*. [s.l.: s.n., 1982]. (Yaoundé: Impr. Saint-Paul), 31pp.
Eleven Beti lullabies of southern Cameroon are translated into French, following an introductory section in which the lullaby is treated as a literary genre and explored in an objective manner suggestive of a philosophical treatise. A poignant Bambara funeral chant is translated into French, the theme being that the Child is the only medicine - the only remedy - for the irrevocability of Death. Texts only.

115. **Anyidoho, Kofi**. "The Haikotu song and dance club of Wheta: a communal celebration of individual poetic talent." **Cross rhythms** 1 (1983): 173-192.
This is within the musical and poetic traditions of the Anlo-Ewe of south-eastern Ghana.

116. **Anyidoho, Kofi**. ORAL POETICS AND TRADITIONS OF VERBAL ART IN AFRICA. Dissertation, University of Texas at Austin, 1983. 514pp.
The study is partly a survey, and partly an in-depth examination of selected traditions of verbal art in Africa. The Ewe tradition is given central consideration. Though the emphasis is on verbal art, there is some discussion of the interplay of poetry and music. In Part Three, attention is given to the relationship between verbal structures and musical patterns in Ewe song texture. A song of the Haikotu Dance Club of Wheta receives what Anyidoho calls, "multifocal analysis." **(UMI)**

117. Anyumba, Henry Owuor. "Contemporary lyres in eastern Africa." **AFRICAN MUSICOLOGY** 1, no.1 (1983): 18-33.
Bibliography, charts, tables. Abstracted in **RILM**, 1985.

118. Anyumba, Henry Owuor. *A musical profile of some Kalenjin songs.* [Nairobi, Kenya]: University of Nairobi, Department of History [1973]. 26pp. (Staff seminar, University of Nairobi, Department of History)
Anyumba originally intended to cover the music of all Kalenjin peoples, but ended up describing only Sabaot and Pokot music. Aside from the concerns of his specific research, the writer raises a number of questions pertinent to the field of ethnomusicology. Following an historical overview of the music area concept, he mentions his own traditional, comparative methodology, but adds that his ultimate intention is to test the validity of cantometric methods over the whole Kalenjin area. Song types are stressed, but instruments, musical style, and elements of music are also not neglected. Texts and English translation of 19 songs. Bibliography.

119. Appleby, David P. *The music of Brazil.* Austin: University of Texas Press, 1983. 209pp.
Primarily on Western art music and its composers. In Chapter 4, entitled Folk, Popular and Art Music, one can find brief mention of music, dance and religious practices of African-derivation. Key words are Eshu, umbigada, coco, call-and-response, samba, batuque, terreiros, congada, lundu, batuque, Candomblé, Macumba, Xangô, Escolas de Samba. A few observations by well-known Brazilian and United States ethnomusicologists are given. There is very little about the many Africa-related musical instruments of Brazil. Notes, Index, Glossary, Bibliography.

120. Aretz, Isabel. "African characteristics in the folkloric music of Venezuela: Afro-Venezuelan instruments and acculturation and change." In **INTERNATIONAL MUSICOLOGICAL SOCIETY. Congress. Report**, 53-54, 1977. Berkeley, California.

121. Aretz, Isabel. *América Latina en su Música.* 2d ed. Paris: [UNESCO], 1977. 344pp.
A collection of essays in Spanish by scholars representing a number of different disciplines. Mention of Africa is surprisingly rare considering the magnitude of the African influence in Latin America. Chapter 2, "Expressiones musicales: sus relaciones y alcance en las clases sociales," has a brief subsection - really a paragraph - called, "El elemento Africano." Chapter 3, by Ana María Locatelli de Pérgamo, "Raíces musicales," includes a 2 page subsection, "Análisis de los elementos musicales de procedencia africano," that is more substantial. The book itself has an impressive and useful general bibliography, which could lead to more useful items concerning the African connection. (See also the slightly different annotation for this, entered under its title, **83.**)

122. **Aretz, Isabel.** "Music and dance in continental Latin America, with the exception of Brazil." In *Africa in Latin America: essays on history, culture, and socialization.* Edited by Manuel Moreno Fraginals, 189-226. New York: Holmes and Meier, 1984.
A dizzying, dazzling compilation with much about the African connection. The earlier section on instruments is excellent, and the several excerpts from historical records as far back as the 16th century, fascinating. Admittedly the topic is a tall one, but starting about the half-way point, the essay does not seem to evolve logically, but flits almost randomly from subject to subject. Also, there are no footnotes. This meritorious essay deserves to be expanded into a carefully structured book. Some rather long transcriptions, and a brief discography.

Aretz, Isabel
See also: •**América Latina en su música.**
•**Aretz de Ramón y Rivera, Isabel** (alternate version of name), **123, 124.**

123. **Aretz de Ramón y Rivera, Isabel.** *Instrumentos musicales de Venezuela.* Cumaná, UDO, 1967. 317pp
A complete inventory of Venezuelan instruments, organized according to the Sachs-Hornbostel system. Brief notations, charts, bibliography. Includes a number of instruments that can be recognized to be of African derivation.

124. **Aretz de Ramón y Rivera, Isabel, and Luis Felipe Ramón y Rivera.** *Resumen de un estudio sobre las expresiones negras en el folklore musical y coreográfico de Venzuela.* [Caracas] Institutos de Antropologia y Historia y de Filologia "Andres Bello," Facultad de Humanidades y Educación, Universidad Central de Venezuela [19??). 11pp.
One need not find the actual word "Africa" in a paper on "Negro" expressions in music and dance of Venezuela to be able to recognize African continuities when they are encountered. Drums and rhythm get brief mention in this brief paper.

Aretz de Ramón y Rivera, Isabel
See also: **Aretz, Isabel** (alternate, shortened version of the name), **120-122.**

125. **Armstrong, Robert G.,** *et al.* "*Èkìtì* traditional dirge of Lt. Colonel Adénkúnlé Fájùyì's funeral." AFRICAN NOTES 5, no. 2 (1969): 63-94.

Armstrong, Robert G.
See also: ***Ìyèrè Ifá*: the deep chants of Ifá, 744.**

126. **Arneson, Arne Jon.** *The music educators journal: cumulative index 1914-1987: including the Music supervisors' bulletin and the Music supervisors' journal.* Stevens Point, Wisconsin:

Index House, 19867. 380pp.
Since a number of articles on African and African-American music have appeared in the **MUSIC EDUCATORS JOURNAL**, this is a useful tool.

127. **Arnoldi, Mary Jo**. PUPPET THEATRE IN THE SEGU REGION IN MALI. Dissertation, Indiana University, 1983. 275pp.
Chapter 5 has information on song, dance, mime, and drums used in conjunction with the puppet theater of Mali. An interesting statement is that the puppets are generally voiceless, and that song is the only means of verbal communication between a puppet and its audience. Puppet song texts [!] are included, along with a glossary, and bibliography.

128. **Arom, Simha**. *Conte and chantefables ngbaka-ma'bo (Rêpublique centrafricaine)*. Jacqueline M. C. Thomas, collaborator. [Paris]: Société pour l'étude des langues africaines, 1970. 237pp. (Bibliothèque de la SELAF, 21-22)
Issued in portfolio. Includes summary in English, French, German, Spanish and Russian. Bibliography.

129. **Arom, Simha**. "La 'mémoire collective' dans les musiques traditionelles d'Afrique Centrale." **REVUE DE MUSICOLOGIE** vol. 76, no. 2 (1990): 149-162.
Music notations, English summary.

130. **Arom, Simha**. "The music of the Banda-Linda horn ensembles: form and structure." In **Studies in African music**. Co-editors, J. H. Kwabena Nketia, and Jacqueline Cogdell DjeDje, 173-193. [Los Angeles]: Program in Ethnomusicology, Department of Music, University of California, Los Angeles, 1984.
Many transcriptions, some lengthy. Map, notes, bibliography, photographs.

131. **Arom, Simha**. *Polyphonies et polyrythmies instrumentales d'Afrique centrale: structure et méthodologie*. 2 vols. Paris: SELAF, c1985. 905pp. (Ethnomusicologie, 1)
The book is concerned with polyphony and polyrhythms in Central Africa, and contains brief summaries in English, German, and Spanish. Six self-contained parts make up the two volumes and can be read separately. The Introduction has to do with social and typological aspects of Central African music; Part 2 discusses the execution of polyphonic music; Part 3 is on technological tools; Part 4 discusses conceptual tools; Part 5 deals with temporal structuring; and in Part 6, the focus is on diverse polyphonic and polyrhythmic techniques. Bibliography, discography, illustrations, music.

132. **Arom, Simha**. "Time structure in the music of Central Africa: periodicity, meter, rhythm and polyrhythmics." **LEONARDO** 22, no. 1 (1989): 91-99.
Bibliography, illustrations.

133. **Arom, Simha.** "The traditional music in the Central African Republic." In **Creating a wider interest in traditional music: proceedings of a conference held in Berlin in cooperation with the International Music Council, 12th to the 17th June, 1967.** [Edited by Alain Daniélou and others], 135-140. Berlin: International Institute for Comparative Music Studies and Documentation, [1967?].

134. THE ART INDEX. 1929- . Bronx, New York: H. W. Wilson Company.
Appears quarterly. This is an author and subject index to domestic and foreign art periodicals and museum bulletins, covering archaeology, art history, arts and crafts, city planning, fine arts, industrial design, etc. There are not apt to be an overwhelming number of articles on African music, but occasionally one is listed, found in a journal whose prime concern is usually visual art, rather than music. Covers at least two journals whose subject is specifically African art. A list of periodicals indexed appears at the beginning. Items might be found under: "Music, African," or under "African" and subheadings.

135. **Arthur, Appianda.** ABISA FESTIVAL: A GHANAIAN (NZEMA) MUSIC INSTITUTION. Dissertation, Wesleyan University, 1977. 263pp.

136. **Arthur, George E.** A DESCRIPTIVE ANALYSIS OF GHANAIAN FOLK TUNES RECOMMENDED FOR THE AMERICAN GENERAL MUSIC PROGRAM. Master's Thesis. State University of New York, Fredonia, 1974. 100pp.

137. **The arts and civilization of Black and African peoples.** 10 vols. Edited by Joseph Ohiomogben Okpaku, Alfred Esimatemi Opubor, and Benjamin Ọlátúnjí Ọlọ́runtìmẹhìn. Assisted by Jacob Olúgbénga Adéṣidà, and Thomas Okpaku. Lagos: Centre for Black and African Arts and Civilization, c1986.
We are considering here only Volume One, "Black civilization and the arts." The Appendix lists contents of the other volumes, but these are not on music or related arts. The colloquium, of which this is a part, was organized by the planners of FESTAC '77, held in Nigeria, who were "concerned with projecting a true understanding of African States and societies, and the inter-relationships between various parts of the continent." The first essays are concerned with the arts of continental Africa, the later ones, with the arts of black people of the New World. The following essays treat African music:
- **Adédèjì, Joel Adéyínká.** "Theatricalism and traditional African theatre," 102-120.
- **Bokelenge, Lonah M.** "Modern Zaïrian music: yesterday, today and tomorrow," 132-151.
- **Ekwueme, Lazarus Edward Nnanyelu.** "Contemporary African music: functions and influences," 121-131.
- **Kavyu, Paul N.** "The role of traditional instruments in music," 152-165.
- **Mensah, Atta A.** "African civilization and the performing arts," 64-82.
- **Quarcoo, A. K.** "Black civilization and the arts," 35-53.

138. **ARTS AND HUMANITIES CITATION INDEX**. 1976- . Philadelphia, Pennsylvania: Institute for Scientific Information.
Indexes a number of periodicals listed in this bibliography. Includes a Source Index, Citation Index, Corporate Index, and Permuterm Subject Index. It is multidisciplinary, indexes all fields of arts and humanities. In **ULRICH'S (1601)**, this is abbreviated as **A&HCI**.

139. **ARTS D'AFRIQUE NOIRE**. 1972- . Villiers-le-Bel, France.
Published quarterly. (Number 1 has the title, **ARTS D'AFRIQUE**.) Articles are almost exclusively in French, some having been translated from English into French. Works of art are magnificently photographed, and without doubt, are the main concern of the periodical. Special art collections are frequently featured. Sometimes, however, African music gets slipped in sideways. A separately issued index, covering numbers 1-57 (to 1986), helps in locating these articles. Following is a list of those that mention African music - even though the mention be secondary (or even tertiary):

- **Laffont, Elisabeth**. "Les cordophones congolaise: survie des harpes de l'antique Egypte dans les cordophones Zande et Mangbetu," 6 (1973): 16-23.
- **Lehuard, Raoul**. "Trompes anthropomorphes du Bas-Congo," 4 (1973: 4-15.
- **Söderberg, Bertil**. "Les instruments de musique africains et leurs décoration," 24 (1977): 18-33.
- **Söderberg, Bertil**. "Les sifflets sculpté du Bas-Congo," 9 (1974): 25-44.
- **Valbert, Christian**. "L'avenir des danses traditionnelles en Côte d'Ivoire," 29 (1979): 7-23.
- **Volavka, Zdenka**. "Le *Ndunga*: un masque, une danse, une institution social au *Ngoyo*," 17 (1976): 28-43.
- **Widman, Ragnar**. "Le culte du *Niombo* des *Bwendé*," 2 1972): 13-41.

140. **Arvey, Verna**. "Negro dance and its influence on Negro music." In **Black music in our culture: curricular ideas on the subjects, materials, and problems.** Edited by Dominique-René de Lerma. Kent State University Press [1970].
The theme is the close association of music and dance in Africa, and extensions of this phenomenon to the New World. Arvey starts with the Dan (Côte d'Ivoire) who have only one word for song, dance and instrumental music, continues with other African examples, followed by references to black music and dance forms of the Caribbean, Mexico, Brazil, and the United States. Mentioned also are African-influenced compositions by Western composers, including those by her own husband, William Grant Still. The contributions of innumerable famous and lesser known black dancers are chronicled. An incredible amount of valuable information is synthesized - comfortably.

141. **Aryee, Enoch A.** ADAAWE: A STUDY OF GAME SONGS OF THE GA WOMEN FOLK. Master's Thesis, University of California, Los Angeles, 1973. 193pp.

142. **Asempa hymns: with orders for Holy Communion and Mass.** Drawings and cover design by Abraham Yeboah. Accra, Ghana:
continued

Asɛmpa Publishers, 1978. 190pp.
This book is designed for African schools and colleges, and is another edition of **Good news hymns** (which differs in not including communion services). There are 200 familiar hymns that are common to usual hymn books but modernized to remove "thee," "thou," and other archaic expressions. Includes 92 items from Ghana, 22 hymns and songs from other African countries, and 20 hymns from China, India and other parts of Africa. See also: **Ghana praise, 621.**

Ashenafi Kebede
See: **Kebede, Ashenafi, 841-848.**

143. **Asiama, Simeon D.** ABƆFOƆ: A STUDY OF AKAN HUNTERS' MUSIC. Dissertation, Wesleyan University, 1977. 304pp.
The music of Akan hunters of Ghana. Abɔfoɔ means hunters, the name of hunters' music and dance, and one of the pieces played by the *kete* drum ensemble. Illustrations, maps, music, bibliography.

144. **Asiama, Simeon D.** "African musical instruments." In **Curriculum materials for teachers**. 2d ed., 178-184. Urbana, Illinois: University of Illinois at Urbana-Champaign, [1985].
Illustrations, bibliography, discography, films and slides.

145. **Asiama, Simeon D.** "An African musician's thoughts on teaching in American schools." In **Curriculum materials for teachers**. 2d ed., 185-187. Urbana, Illinois: University of Illinois at Urbana-Champaign, [1985].
Includes the names of five University of Illinois resources on African music, but gives no further information about them.

146. **Asiama, Simeon D.** *Music and dancing in a Ghanaian community (Pokuase)*. University of Ghana, 1965.

147. **Asiama, Simeon D.** "Singing games from Ghana." In **Curriculum materials for teachers**. 2d ed., 270-278. Urbana, Illinois: University of Illinois at Urbana-Champaign, [1985].
Includes music, words, pronunciation and meaning of 7 Ghanaian songs.

148. **Asiama, Simeon D. and Louise Crane**. "Listening to African music: some resources." In **Curriculum materials for teachers**. 2d ed., 328-333. Urbana, Illinois: University of Illinois at Urbana-Champaign, [1985].
Discography divided into: Instrumental Music, Traditional Music (Instrumental and vocal), Political/Patriotic Music, Religious Music (Christian), Popular Music, Music of Contemporary Composers, and Children's Music. Also includes a list of producers/distributors of Africa records.

Association for the study of Negro Life and History
See: **Brief sketches in Akan (Ghana) art symbol, literature, music and African theater, 285.**

149. **Atakora, Theophilus Apea.** "Mmoguo: song interludes in Akan folk tales." Diploma in African Music, University of Ghana, 1964. 357pp.
Following a brief survey of song interludes in Akan folktales, there is a chapter on story-telling techniques of the Akan people of Ghana. Song texts have been collected from Ashanti, Akuapim, Kwaku, and the Fanti areas of Ghana. These are placed into three categories according to the role they play in Akan folklore, and thereafter arranged by length and simplicity.

150. **Atakpu, Benedict Ozengbe.** A GUIDE TO SELECTED TRADITIONAL DANCES OF THE BENDEL STATE OF NIGERIA. Dissertation, Middle Texas State University, 1988. 170pp.
Indicates the musical instruments associated with various dances.

151. **Atigbi, I. A.**, ed. *Nigeria: traditional festivals: a guide to Nigeria's cultural safari.* Lagos: Nigerian Tourist Association, [197-?]. 60pp.
Primarily a tourist guide (with advertising), but it does contain a summary of all leading Nigerian festivals throughout the year with descriptive information as to their significance and essential characteristics. One can see at a glance which ones involve song, drumming, dancing. For an additional tourist guide, also edited by Atigbi, but with less information, see also **Nigeria tourist guide, 1175.**

152. **Augier, Pierre.** "La musicologie africaine à l'Institut National des Arts d'Abidjan." **RECHERCHE, PÉDAGOGIE ET CULTURE** no. 65-66 (1984): 55-63.

153. **Avorgbedor, Daniel Kodzo.** "Double bell techniques among the Anlo-Ewe of Ghana." **PERCUSSIVE NOTES** 20, no. 2 (1981): 77-80.
The *gankogui* is a double-bell idiophone that performs important musical and nonmusical functions among the Anlo-Ewe of Ghana. There are four basic techniques of playing the instrument that combine mutes and open sounds. Body parts, such as the thigh and the chest, are employed in effecting mutes, and a metal wristlet helps the performer to diversify tone and rhythm.

154. **Avorgbedor, Daniel Kodzo.** "The interaction of music and spoken texts in the context of Anlo-Ewe music." **BLACK ORPHEUS** 6, no. 1(1986): 17-25.
In some musical genres, the Anlo-Ewe emphasize the integration of spoken text, drummed phrases, dramaturgy, and the regular song mode to effectively communicate meaning and affect. Musical examples, notes, bibliography.

155. **Avorgbedor, Daniel Kodzo.** MODES OF MUSICAL CONTINUITY AMONG THE ANLO EWE OF ACCRA: A STUDY IN URBAN

ETHNOMUSICOLOGY. Dissertation, Indiana University, 1986. 340pp.
Music of Anlo Ewe immigrants in Accra is analyzed, hoping to broaden and refine the theories, methods, and materials of ethnomusicology. The study centers on "a 'symbiotic' relationship between music and society as reflected in the urban Anlo voluntary associations; the impact of urban temporal orientation on modes of musical performance and organization; and parameters that define musical innovation in the urban Anlo context." The effects of demographics, socioeconomics, and spatio-temporal features of Accra on urban Anlo music are studied. Questioned is the concept of Western influence as a major element in explaining "all West African urban musical phenomena." **(UMI)**

156. **Avorgbedor, Daniel Kodzo.** THE MUSICAL VALUES OF INDIGENOUS GHANAIAN SOUND INSTRUMENTS IN WORSHIP WITHIN THE FRAMEWORK OF CONTEMPORARY GHANAIAN SOCIETY. Master's Thesis, Northeast Missouri State University, 1978. 94pp.
The subject is primarily instrumental music in Ghanaian traditional worship. Avorgbedor, Ghanaian by birth and a rigorously trained ethnomusicologist, has himself participated in the music events he describes, which gives additional meaning to his meticulous scholarship. The five chapters, each with subdivisions, are: The Introduction, Synopsis of Musical Types in Ghana, Organology, Musical Values, and the final Summary. An illustrative music cassette accompanied the original version. Included are many plates, figures, and a definition of several important terms used in the thesis. Bibliography.

157. **Avorgbedor, Daniel Kodzo.** "The transmission, preservation and realisation of song texts: a psycho-musical approach." **Cross rhythms** 2 (1985): 67-92. Bloomington, Indiana: Trickster Press.
(Dictated by the author) "In order to achieve an affective musical communication, the Anlo-Ewe employ music, dance, iconic images, gesticulation, and mime. The concept of repetition as associated with 'redundancy' is not supported by the Ewe example. The performers employ shifting spacial and temporal orientation in order to imbue song texts with fresh meaning." Musical example, chart, bibliography, notes. (Avorgbedor was coeditor of **Cross rhythms** 1983, 1985, (399).

158. **Axelsson, Olof.** "African music and its relation to education." In **Symposium on Ethnomusicology.** (3rd: 1982: University of Natal) [4th: 1983: Rhodes University] *Papers presented at the Third and Fourth Symposia on Ethnomusicology,* Music Department, University of Natal, Durban, 16th to 19th September 1982; Music Department, Rhodes University, 7th to 8th October 1983, 61-63. Grahamstown, South Africa: International Library of African Music, 1984.
Note that this paper is in the 4th Symposium. (The 3rd and 4th Symposia are in one volume.)

159. **Axelsson, Olof.** "The development of African church music in Zimbabwe." In **Symposium on Ethnomusicology.** (2nd: 1981:

Rhodes University) *Papers presented at the Second Symposium on Ethnomusicology, Music Department, Rhodes University, 24th to 26th September, 1981.* Edited by Andrew Tracey, 2-73. Grahamstown: International Library of African Music, Institute of Social and Economic Research, Rhodes University, 1982.

159a. **Ayestarán, Lauro.** "El tamboril Afro-Uruguayo," In **Music in the Americas**. Edited by George List and Juan Orrego-Salas, 23-27. [Bloomington]: Indiana University Research Center in Anthropology, Folklore and Linguistics, 1967.
On an African-derived Uruguayan drum that comes in four sizes. Notes, photographs, illustrations.

160. **Ayu, Iyorchia D.** *Creativity and protest in popular culture: the political music of Fẹlá Aníkúlápó-Kútì.* [Nigeria]: Positive Review in association with Nigerian Democratic Review, [1985]. 40pp. (Revolutionary monographs on culture and society in Africa. Series 1, no. 1, 1985)
This is the same essay appearing as part of Ayu's book, listed directly below. (161)

161. **Ayu, Iyorchia D.** *Essays on popular struggle.* Oguta, Nigeria: Zim Pan African Publishers, 1986. 203pp.
The first essay is entitled: "Creativity and protest in political culture: the political protest in popular music of Fẹlá Aníkúlápó-Kútì." This is followed by two other essays by Ayu - a sociologist - that are essentially political in nature and unrelated to music. Fẹlá Aníkúlápó-Kútì's music is compared to revolutionary music of Chile and the Caribbean, to show the connection. Lyrics are given detailed analysis. This is not a "romantic celebration" of Fẹlá, though he is basically treated as a hero. A number of criticisms are also unabashedly levied against him. Includes bibliographical references and an index.

Azevedo, Warren L.
See: **d'Azevedo, Warren L., 441-442.**

162. **Azuonye, C.** THE NARRATIVE WAR SONGS OF THE OHAFIA IGBO: A CRITICAL ANALYSIS OF THEIR CHARACTERISTIC FEATURES IN RELATION TO THEIR SOCIAL FUNCTION. Dissertation, London University, 1979. 546pp.

163. **BĀ SHIRU**. 1970-1987. Madison, Wisconsin: University of Wisconsin at Madison, Department of African Languages and Literature, Madison, Wisconsin.

During its tenure, this fine journal was concerned primarily with African literature. It was issued twice a year. The following articles - and several more - were on music:

- **Bẹ́kọ̀ní, Olúrọ́pọ̀**. "Mechanism and meaning in Yorùbá *ìjálá*," vol. 8, no. 1 (1977): 31-36.
- **Davis, Charles N.** "Melodic and harmonic movement in indigenous Ghanaian music," no. 4 (1972): 1-10.
- **Ojaide, Tanure**. "The poetry of the *udje* songs," vol. 12, no. 1 (1981): 31-38.

164. **Babalọlá, S. A.** "The characteristic features of outer form of Yorùbá *ìjálá* chants." ODÙ 1, no. 1 (1964):33-34; Part 2, vol. 1, no. 2 (1965): 47-77.

Ìjálá is the oral poetry of Yorùbá hunters. The author includes three of the rules governing the position of minimal stress, with examples and detailed explanations. Chant texts and footnotes.

165. **Babalọlá, S. A.** *The content and form of Yorùbá ìjálá.* Oxford: Clarendon Press, 1966. 395pp. (Oxford library of African literature)

Songs in English and Yorùbá. Bibliography.

166. **Babalọlá, S. A.** trans. "An *ìjálá* chant." BLACK ORPHEUS vol. 3, no. 4 (1976): 11-13.

This chant is part of a larger section that runs from pages 4-13 and is entitled, Five Chants. Translated by others are: An Alekwu Chant; an Ìsọ̀ko Heroic Chant, an Ọfọ̀ Chant, and a Mmonwu Chant. Texts, no music.

167. **Babalọlá, S. A.** *The poetic characteristics of Yorùbá ìjálá chants.* [Ìbàdàn: 1964]. 69pp.

At head of title: Institute of African Studies, University of Ifẹ̀, Ìbàdàn Branch, Ìbàdàn. Seminar 1963/64/7.

168. **Backus, Le Roy M.** STYLISTIC DEVELOPMENT OF REGGAE MUSIC IN JAMAICA, WEST INDIES. Master's Thesis, University of Washington, 1978. 118pp.

169. **Baines, Anthony**, ed. *Musical instruments through the ages.* Baltimore: Penguin Books, [1961]. 383pp.

The book begins with a section on percussion instruments that includes frequent mention of Africa. Body percussion as a musical component is also considered. Wachsmann's essay, "Primitive Musical Instruments," though it scans the world, seems to have a larger number of illustrations of African instruments. In this case, at least, that antediluvian word, "primitive," is defined as meaning instruments fashioned from natural products, instruments that are not mass produced, or instruments without complicated parts. Bravo to all such resourceful instrument-makers and those who play their instruments! Interesting photographs are located in the center of the book. Bibliography.

170. **Bakan, M.** "West African drum languages." **PERCUSSIONIST** 24, no. 2 (1986): 29-30.

171. **Baker, David N.** "A periodization of black music history." In **Reflections on Afro-American music**. Edited by Dominique-René de Lerma, 143-160. [Kent, Ohio] Kent State University Press [1973].
A good deal about African music is contained in this essay, before Baker, a university professor and acclaimed jazz musician, leads into African-American music and a succinct history of jazz.

172. **Baker, Philip**, comp. *International guide to African studies research = Études africaines, guide international de recherches*. Edited by the International African Institute. Second fully revised and expanded edition. London: Published for the International African Institute (by) Hans Zell, 1987. 264pp.
An exceptional reference tool for all Africanists. Areas and countries are listed in the thematic index, and music appears as a subheading frequently. The main body has a bold heading by country on each page, with noticeable entry numbers. Data on music courses, degrees offered, library holdings, and a personnel index are included. This is a dense, tidy little masterpiece, attractively designed, with space-saving symbols explained on a novel, inward-folding strip inside the back cover that might be overlooked. Key explanations in French as well as in English. Good to take abroad!

173. **BALAFON: POUR LA CONAISSANCE DE L'AFRIQUE NOIRE**. 1965-1988. (Air Afrique). Éditions Voyages. Paris, France.
Some choice gems follow, and there are still more by Bebey in other issues.
- **Bebey, Francis**. "Le monde ambigu des griots; troubadours, historiens, conteurs et même magiciens, les griots assument des fonctions importantes dans la société africaine. Pourtant ils sont souvent méprises. Pourquoi?" no. 58 (1983): 54- .
- **Bebey, Francis**. "La musique traditionelle au Senegal," no. 48 (1980): 36-40.
- **Bebey, Francis**. "La sanza, le petit piano portatif africain," no. 53, (1981): 54-60.

174. **Ballantine, Chris.** "'Africans in America.'" "'Harlem in Johannesburg:'" the ideology of Afro-America in the formation of black jazz and vaudeville in South Africa before the mid-1940s." In **Symposium on Ethnomusicology**. (7th: 1988: Venda, South Africa). *Papers presented at the 7th Symposium on Ethnomusicology: Department of Anthropology and Ethnomusicology, University of Venda, 3rd to 5th September 1988*. Edited by Andrew Tracey, 5-10. Grahamstown, South Africa: Rhodes University, 1989.

175. **Ballantine, Chris.** "Taking sides - or music, music departments and the deepening crisis in South Africa." In **Symposium on Ethnomusicology**. (3rd: 1982: University of Natal) [4th: 1983: Rhodes University] *Papers presented at the Third and Fourth Symposia on Ethnomusicology*, Music Department, University of Natal, Durban, 16th to 19th September 1982; Music Department, Rhodes University, 7th to 8th October 1983, 52-55. Grahamstown, South Africa: International Library of African Music, 1984.
Note that this paper is in the 4th Symposium. (The 3rd and 4th Symposia are in one volume.)

176. **Ballard, W. L.**, ed. *Essays on African literature.* Atlanta, School of Arts and Sciences, Georgia State University, 1973. 195pp. (Spectrum. Monograph series in the arts and sciences, vol. 3)
•**Adédèjì, Joel Adéyínká.** "The literature of the Yorùbá opera," 55-78.

177. **Ballmoos, Agnes Nebo von.** "The collection, notation and arrangement of Liberian folk songs." In **African culture: Algiers Symposium July 21st - August 1st, 1969.** *The first Pan-African cultural festival*, 105-107. Alger: S.N.E.D. (Société Nationale d'Édition et de Diffusion), 1969.
Ballmoos describes what is involved in collecting, notating and arranging Liberian songs. A list is given of Kra instruments with their description, and similar lists for the Bassa and Gola. She speaks of the difficulties of being solely dependent upon the oral tradition as the source for her studies.

178. **Ballmoos, Agnes Nebo von.** THE ROLE OF FOLKSONGS IN THE LIBERIAN SOCIETY. Master's Thesis, Indiana University, 1973.

179. **Bamboté, Makombo.** *Chant funèbre pour un héros d'Afrique. Précédé d'un chant populaire adapté par Sembène Ousmane.* Tunis: [Société nationale d'édition et de diffusion], 1962]. 73pp. (J'exige la parole, 11)

179a. **Bame, Kwabena N.** *Come to laugh: a study of African traditional theatre in Ghana.* With an introduction by John Povey. Accra New-Town (P.O. Box K. 189, Accra New-Town): Baafour Educational Enterprises, Publishing Division, c1981. 102pp.
Bame is concerned with comic plays as staged by concert parties, the latter described as "itinerant theatre groups in Ghana." The history of the plays is given, along with chapters on: the actors, humor, presentation, thematic sources, comedians and their audience, audience response, and the social function of the play. In Chapter 4, on music and dancing, the musical instruments are listed that comprise the equipment of a typical concert party. Song texts, generally sentimental or philosophical, are given, along with music transcriptions. An appendix gives brief synopses of 12 plays. Bibliography.

B

179b. **Bame, Kwabena N.** THE CONCERT PARTIES: A MANIFESTATION OF POPULAR DRAMA IN GHANA. Master's Thesis, University of North Carolina, 1968.
Includes the role of music in the concert party.

180. **Banfield, Beryle.** *Africa in the curriculum: a resource bulletin and guide for teachers.* New York: Edward B. Blyden Press, Inc., 1968.
This modest-appearing paperback has surprising contents. An amazing amount of factual material is included - even recipes! Particulars of the historical, political and sociological contents are too numerous to be elaborated here, but two chapters are of special interest: Traditional Literature, and Traditional Music, Dance, Art. The final chapter, called Teaching About Africa, is an excellent guide for teachers. Banfield, a professional dancer, born in Panama where Garvey and Du Bois were household words, travelled extensively throughout the Caribbean collecting folkloric materials. Photographs, illustrations, charts, resource materials for both teachers and children.

Bangura, Ibrahim
See: **Temne stories and songs, 1538.**

181. **Bantje, Han.** *Kaonde song and ritual*, by Hans Bantje. *La musique et son rôle dans la vie sociale et rituelle Luba*, by Jos Gansemans. Tervuren: Musée royale de l"afrique centrale, 1978. 121pp. (Annales - Musée royal de l'Afrique centrale: Series in-8°. Sciences humaines, no. 95)
Bantje examines the role of music in ritual and social life of the Kaonde people. Gansemans does the same for the Luba. In English or French. Includes bibliographies.

182. **Bantu music, with special reference to South Africa = Bantoe-musiek, met klem op Suid-Afrika.** Pretoria, Republic of South Africa: State Library, [1971]. 20pp. (Bibliographic Department, list no. 71/13 = Bibligrafiese Afdeling, lys no. 71/13)
The bibliography incorporates 32 books and 174 periodical articles on the subject, many rather old, but others more recent. A good number of entries are by Hugh Tracey, incorporating many of his articles and those of other musicologists that have appeared in the journal, *African Music.* Articles by Percival Robson Kirby also appear frequently. A good resource, despite the title.

183. **Barber, Karin.** "Popular theatre and music: a new field." In *New directions in African bibliography.* Edited by Patricia M. Larby, 51-68. London: Standing Conference on Library Materials on Africa, 1988.
A most thoughtful, provocative essay. Just about every question of methodology and aesthetics is raised regarding the study of pop art, not the least of which has to do with the difficulty inherent in trying to convert an essentially oral,

improvisatory and interactive genre, such as the Ghanaian concert party play, to writing. (The author describes a "research pack" as one possible third-dimensional approach to the problem.) This brilliant essay can generate new thinking and respect for arts that have mass appeal. A short bibliography incorporates a few play texts. A brief discussion by attendants at the conference follows.

184. **Barony, Laurence.** "Introduction à la musique africaines." In *Musiques africaines.* Edited by Nanie Bridgman. [Paris]: Musique de tous les temps, [1967]. 1 vol. (unpaged, but approximately pages 21-44, including plates). (Musique de tous les temps, 44/45)

185. **Bascom, William.** "Folklore and literature." In *The African world: a survey of social research.* Edited by Robert A. Lystad for the African Studies Association, 469-490. New York: Praeger, (1965).
There are enough scattered though brief references to song texts and their uses to warrant this article's inclusion. The unofficial national anthem of Central and South Africa, "God Bless Africa" (*Nkosi Sikelel' iAfrika*) is mentioned, along with other songs used for political purposes. Praise poems receive some attention. Bibliography and cited literature appear at end of book.

186. **Bascom, William, and Melville J. Herskovits**, eds. *Continuity and change in African cultures.* [Chicago]: University of Chicago Press [1962]. 309pp.
(Originally published in 1959.) A major work, consisting of 15 important essays on a variety of subjects, written by eminent Africanists. Chapter 4, which appears as a separate entry in this bibliography, is the only one concerned with music: **Merriam, Alan P.** "African Music," 49-86.

187. **Bassani, Ezio.** "A Kongo drum stand." **AFRICAN ARTS** vol. 11, no. 1 (1977): 35-37, 92.

188. **Bastide, Roger.** *African civilizations in the New World.* Translated from the French by Peter Green, with a foreword by Geoffrey Parrinder. New York: Harper and Row [1971]. 232pp. (A Torchbook library edition).
Many of Bastide's works were originally written in French. This is a translation of *Les civilisations africaines dans le Nouveau Monde.* Since many of his writings are concerned with African or African-derived religions in the New World, concomitant music references are also likely to be found. Comments on music are scattered throughout this book, reachable via the index, or hopefully come upon as one reads the book in entirety. Examination of other of Bastide's myriad and frequently-quoted publications is recommended.

189. **Bastin, Marie-Louise.** "Instruments de musique, chants et danses des Tshokwe région de Dundo district de la Lunda Angola." **AFRICAN MUSICOLOGY** 1, no.1 (1983): 45-66.
Bibliography. In French.

190. **THE BEAT: REGGAE•AFRICAN•CARIBBEAN•WORLD MUSIC.** 1988- Los Angeles, California: Bongo Productions.
Published bi-monthly. **AFROPOP WORLDWIDE Listener's Guide** calls this "the best journal available in U.S. that covers African and Caribbean music." In 1982, the publication was merely a newsletter; from 1983-1988, it was called **THE REGGAE AND AFRICAN BEAT**. In 1988 it assumed its present title. The journal provides information, news, interviews, discographies, and cultural features. It features the works of top writers, artists and photographers. Following are two randomly selected examples:
•**Scaramuzzo, Gene.** "*Zouk*: magic music of the French Antilles," vol. 5, no. 4 (1986): 27-33.
•**Smith, C. C. and Gerard Tacite Lamothe.** "Legends of Haitian music," vol. 6, no. 2 (1987): 14-18.

191. **Bebey, Francis.** *African music: a people's art.* Translated from the French by Josephine Bennett. New York: Lawrence Hill, 1975. 184pp.
This is a translation of *Musique de l'Afrique* (1969) written by renowned Cameroonian musician, poet, and film-maker, Francis Bebey. Popular in style, loose in structure. Profusely illustrated. Emphasis on wide range of instruments and their performance, including earth bow and friction drum. Selective discography, updated by Richard Hill, is in four sections: basic elements, and classification by country, theme, and instrument. Tacked on is a brief list of "Recent Recordings," and a half page of U.S.A. distributors. There are several pages of notes relating to the chapters. Lack of an index makes use of book frustrating.

192. **Bebey, Francis.** "Le monde ambigu des griots; troubadours, historiens, conteurs et même magiciens, les griots assument des fonctions importantes dans la société africaine. Pourtant ils sont souvent méprises. Pourquoi?" **BALAFON** no. 58 (1983): 54- .

193. **Bebey, Francis.** "La musique africaine moderne." In **Colloque sur l'art nègre**. Rapports. Vol. 1 (1967): 499-516. [Paris: Présence africaine, 1968]

194. **Bebey, Francis.** *Musique de l'Afrique.* [Paris]: Horizons de France, [1969]. 207pp.
See also the preceding English translation, **191.** If a person has a reading knowledge of French, it's worth trying to obtain this original version primarily because the photographs of performing musicians are so exceptional. The paperback, annotated above, despite its other merits is photographically drab by

comparison. It lacks that awesome, magnificent, full-color portrait on the cover of the hardback of an intense *alghaïta* player with cheeks puffed to huge apples. Discography and 33 1/3 disc in book pocket. Illustrations.

195. **Bebey, Francis.** "La musique traditionelle au Senegal." **BALAFON** no. 48 (1980): 36-40.

196. **Bebey, Francis.** "La sanza, le petit piano portatif africain." **BALAFON** no. 53, (1981): 54-60.

197. **Bebey, Francis.** "Vivante et ancestrale musique de l'Afrique." **COURIER** 25, no. 10 (1972): 14-19.

198. **Begho, Felix O.** BLACK DANCE CONTINUUM: REFLECTIONS ON THE HERITAGE CONNECTION BETWEEN AFRICAN DANCE AND AFRO-AMERICAN JAZZ DANCE. 2 vols. Dissertation, New York University, 1984. 710pp.

An unprepossessing title but a powerhouse work for those involved in African or African-related arts. By now the close bonding of music and dance in Africa is so well established that it is reasonable to say that one can learn almost as much about the one from studying the other. Begho, a chief's son, thoroughly explores the commonalities/differences of African dance and African-American jazz dance, treats their associated musics similarly, and makes informed and pertinent sociocultural observations that bring new insights to a complex field. Countless photographs, resource lists, a vast and eclectic bibliography.

Behaghel, Anne
See: **Chansons et proverbes lingala, 334.**

199. **Béhague, Gerard.** "Notes on regional and national trends in Afro-Brazilian cult music." In **Tradition and renewal: essays on twentieth-century Latin American literature and culture.** Edited by Merlin H. Forster, 68-80. Urbana: University of Illinois Press, [1975].

200. **Béhague, Gerard.** "Patterns of Candomblé music performance: an Afro-Brazilian religious setting." In **Performance practice: ethnomusicological perspectives.** Edited by Gerard Béhague, 222-254. Westport, Connecticut: Greenwood Press, c1984.

A deep study, with notes, bibliography, and a much-appreciated glossary of main terms used in Bahian Candomblé.

201. **Béhague, Gerard.** POPULAR MUSICAL CURRENTS IN THE ART MUSIC OF THE EARLY NATIONALISTIC PERIOD IN BRAZIL, CIRCA 1870-1920. Dissertation, Tulane University, 1966. 283pp.

Examines music and society of the second half of the nineteenth century, considers folk songs and dances and their transformation into urban popular forms. Popular and art music composers are discussed. Three Brazilian popular music composers are credited with nationalizing European dances, popularizing the *modhina* and *lundu*, and introducing the "new popular aspects of the *tango*, *maxixe*, and the early urban *samba*, from which the vernacular music emerged." He finds the systematized syncopation of "all Afro-American music" to be common to *all* popular, and *most* art music of that time. Transcriptions, bibliography.

202. **Béhague, Gerard**. Reflections on the ideological history of Latin American ethnomusicology." In **Comparative musicology and anthropology of music: essays on the history of ethnomusicology**. Edited by Bruno Nettl and V. Bohlman, 56-68. Chicago: University of Chicago Press, 1991.

Béhague, Gerard
See also: **Performance practice: ethnomusicological perspectives, 1324.**

203. **Beiträge zur Ethnomusikologie**. Hamburg, Germany.
The following volumes of the series appear as separate entries (alphabetical by last name):
- **Achinivu, Achinivu Kanu**. *Ikoli Harcourt Whyte, the man and his music: a case of musical acculturation in Nigeria*, vol. 7, 1979.
- **Branda-Lacerda, Marcos**. *Kultische Trommelmusik der Yorùbá in der Volksrepublik Benin: Bàtá-Sàngó und Bàtá-Egúngún in der Städten Pobè und Sakété*, vol. 19, 1988.
- **Simon, Artur**. *Studien zur ägyptischen Volksmusik*, vol. 1, 1972.
- **Touma, Habib**. *Der Maq̄am Bayati im arabischen Taqsīm*, vol. 3, 1976.
- **Vogels, Raimund**. *Tanzlieder und liturgische Gesänge bei den Dagaaba in Nordwestghana: zur Verwendung einheimischer Musik im katholischen Gottesdienste*, vol. 18, 1988.

204. **Bẹ́kọ̀ní, Olúrọ́pọ̀**. "Mechanism and meaning in Yorùbá *ìjálá*." **BĀ SHIRU** vol. 8, no. 1 (1977): 31-36.

Belinga Eno
See: **Eno Belinga, Samuel-Martin, 523-531.**

205. **Bemba, Sylvain**. *Cinquante ans de musique du Congo-Zaïre, 1920-1970: de Paul Kamba à Tabu-Ley*. Paris: Présence africaine, c1984. 188pp.
Popular music and musicians of Congo and Zaïre. Dedicated to Joseph Kabasele Tshamala (1930-1983), "le père de la musique Congolaise moderne." Photographs range from Tabu-Ley, to an either rejoicing - or frantic? - Louis Armstrong carried aloft on a *tipoye!* An eight-page chart, has a column for dates (1808 to 1978), ones for "Zaïre" and "Congo," and a remaining column headed, "Monde et Afrique." The latter has unexpectedly juxtaposed items, such as the invention of tango music in Africa, the birth of Langston Hughes, presentation of the rumba in Chicago, and the invention of hi-fi in London. Bibliography.

206. **Bemba, Sylvain**. "En direct du Congo: musique traditionelle: realités Congolaises d'aujourd'hui." **RECHERCHE, PEDAGOGIE ET CULTURE** no. 29-30 (1977): 49-52.

207. **Bemba, Sylvain**. "La naissance du discours amoureux dans la vie quotidienne chantée au Congo-Zaïre." In **Chansons d'Afrique et des Antilles**, 39-53. Paris: Harmattan, c1988.

208. **Bender, Wolfgang**. "Ebenezer Calender: an appraisal." In *Perspectives on African music.* Edited by Wolfgang Bender, 43-68. Bayreuth, Germany: Bayreuth University, c1989.

209. **Bender, Wolfgang**. *Moderne afrikanische Musik auf Schallplatten: ein kommentierter Katalog für die Schallplattenbar der Ausstellung, Neue Kunst in Afrika: Mainz, Mittelrheinisches Landesmuseum, Bayreuth, Universität Bayreuth und Hypo-Bank, Wörgl/Österreich, Galerie Perlinger.* Edited by Institut für Ethnologie und Afrika-Studien, Johannes Gutenberg-Universität, Mainz: Das Institut, 1980. 67pp. ("Neue Kunst in Afrika")
A catalog with commentary on African urban music groups and their recordings. The groups are categorized according to regions. Photocopies of a number of album covers done in pop art style are of interest. Discography of popular music. Discography of jazz.

210. **Bender, Wolfgang**. *Sweet mother: modern African music.* Translated by Wolfgang Freis. Chicago: University of Chicago Press, 1991. 248pp. (Chicago studies in ethnomusicology)
This is a comprehensive cultural history of modern African music. Bender discloses how changes that occur in the music tie into the cultural complexities of modern Africa. Profusely illustrated, bibliographical references, discography. (The next entry is the original edition, written in German.)

211. **Bender, Wolfgang**. *Sweet mother: moderne afrikanische Musik.* Münich: Trickster Verlag, c1985. 241pp.
"Popular" African music. Bibliography, discography.

Bender, Wolfgang
See also: •**Perspectives on African music, 1326.**
•**Ìwàlewà-Haus Bayreuth** (two entries are listed under this heading, **742, 743**)

212. **Benjei**. *The origin of the white race: stories.* Freetown: People's Educational Association of Sierra Leone, 1987. 47pp. (Stories and songs from Sierra Leone, 34)
Songs, tales. Page 2 indicates that the stories by Benjei were collected at

Towaama Village, Bo District, Southern Province, on the 1st of May, 1986. Includes songs of Sierra Leone in addition to tales.

213. **Bennett, Carolyn La Delle.** AFRICAN SURVIVALS IN THE RELIGIOUS MUSIC TRADITION OF THE UNITED STATES NEGRO: AN ETHNOMUSICOLOGICAL STUDY WITH SPECIAL EMPHASIS ON THE CONGREGATIONAL SPIRITUAL. Master's Thesis, Greencastle, Indiana: Depauw University, 1969. 143pp.

214. **Bensignor, François.** *Sons d'Afrique.* [Alleur, Belgium]. Marabout, [1988]. 124pp. (Compact book)
This is a square, hand-sized popularly written book about the contemporary music scene in Africa. It starts with a map of Africa that has shaded geographic areas by music type, and the names of a few associated musicians. Some basic information about the music by region follows, with biographical facts and photos of a number of key musicians of the day. Each section ends with a listing entitled, References and Notes, but which is primarily a discography. The photographs are interesting but they often lack identifying labels.

215. **Benson, Mary, and Liz Nickson.** *Free Nelson Mandela: a festival concert book.* Foreword by Winnie Mandela. New York: Penguin, 1988. 16opp.
This is a large picture book of events and musicians featured at a concert held at London's Wembley Stadium, June 11, 1988, in honor of Mandela's 70th birthday. White and black artists from all over the world were part of the 72,000 people in attendance at the spectacular concert. Some of the African musicians or groups present were: *Amamponda* (of South Africa), Salif Keita, Youssou N'Dour, Miriam Makeba, and Hugh Masekela. Light background information accompanies candid or posed portraits of performers. Earlier, Mandela's life and political activities are documented, and there is an equivalent biography of Winnie Mandela.

216. **Berceuses du Zaïre.** Compiled by Mbuyamba Lupwishi and Ngoma Nlolo, with collaboration of Mondo M., Pwono M., and Tshiamala M. Kinshasa: Presses universitaires du Zaïre, 1983.
Notated, unaccompanied melodies. Words to the lullabies are in various African languages, and are also translated into French. The accompanying text is in French.

217. **Bergman, Billy**. *African pop: goodtime kings.* Poole, Dorset, United Kingdom: Blandford; New York, N.Y.: Prepared and produced by Quarto Marketing, 1985. 143pp.
Includes a bibliography and index.

218. **Bergman, Billy**, *et al. Reggae and Latin pop.* Blandford, Poole, 1985.
This work is reviewed by Paul Oliver in **KESKIDEE** no. 1, 1986. No further information is presently available. Oliver is even uncertain about the title, since

it appears in three different forms on the cover. The work contains a small number of essays on Afro-Latin music. Bergman writes on *reggae*, soul calypso (known as *soca*), and Haitian *rara*. Isabelle Leymarie has two chapters on *salsa*, and Tony Sabournin talks of the spread of *salsa* to Central and South America. Rob Baker has a brief outline of Brazilian popular forms. Andy Schwartz writes on Reggae after Marley.

219. Berliner, Paul. THE MEANING OF THE MBIRA, NYUNGA-NYUNGA. Master's Thesis, Wesleyan University, 1970. 114pp.
Bibliography, illustrations, tape.

220. Berliner, Paul. THE SOUL OF MBIRA: AN ETHNOGRAPHY OF THE MBIRA AMONG THE SHONA PEOPLE OF RHODESIA. Dissertation, Wesleyan University, 1974. 439pp.
Illustrations, music, bibliography.

221. Berliner, Paul. *The soul of mbira: music and traditions of the Shona people of Zimbabwe.* With an appendix: Building and playing a Shona Karimba. [Updated Edition.] Berkeley: University of California Press, 1981. 312pp.
A *magnum opus.* This book is without doubt the definitive work on the *mbira*, highly esteemed and oft-quoted by scholars. Originally it was an unpublished dissertation completed at Wesleyan University, 1974. (See preceding entry, **220.**) Later, in 1978, it was published by the University of California Press. The present updated edition includes the appendix on building and playing a Karimba, and is meant to be accompanied by two Nonesuch recordings. Includes illustrations, music, bibliography, discography.

222. Berque, Jacques. *Arabies: entretiens avec Mirèse Akar.* Paris: Stock, c1978. 307pp.
This biographical interview is included because of two paragraphs (pages 156-158) in which Akar gives his sensitive recollections of music and instruments heard as a child in Algeria. In French.

223. Berry, Jack. "Is Caribbean English a tone language?" In **Essays for a humanist: an offering to Klaus Wachsmann**, 95-104. Spring Valley, New York: Town House Press, 1977.
An interesting exploration, and probably the only entry in this bibliography concerned with tone language beyond the continent of Africa. Bibliography.

224. Bertonoff, Deborah. *Dance towards the earth: on a* UNESCO *grant in Ghana.* Translated from the Hebrew by I. M. Lask. Tel-Aviv, Alityros, 1963. 233pp.
On Ghanaian dance, and percussion instruments.

225. **Berzez Sesel = Berceuses des Seychelles.** Victoria, Seychelles: Seksyon resers, Divizyon Kiltir, Minister Ledikasyon ek Lenformasyon, [1981?]. 34pp.
Contains 36 lullabies in French and French Creole of the Seychelles. Words only are presented, no music. At the beginning, there is a general essay in both languages on popular oral traditions of Seychelles, followed by two and one-half pages concerned only with the lullabies. Words and certain expressions used in a few lullabies are explained at the end of the book.

226. **Besmer, Fremont E.** HAUSA COURT MUSIC IN KANO, NIGERIA. Dissertation, Columbia University, 1971. 344pp.
Music, bibliography.

227. **Besmer, Fremont E.** *Horses, musicians, and gods: the Hausa cult of possession-trance.* South Hadley, Massachusetts: Bergin and Garvey, 1983. 290pp.
Bori is defined in the book's glossary as "Hausa cult of possession-trance; a supernatural spirit." Chapter 3 contains some 30 pages under the heading, Musicians: Their Society, Instruments and Music. Chapter 6, the Summary and Conclusion, includes 2 pages on music. This is an example of high-level scholarship. Appendices include 27 musical transcriptions, a Hausa glossary and index, the Houses of Jangare, and an abundance of photographs, primarily of people in various states of possession. Bibliography.

228. **Besmer, Fremont E.** *Kídàn dárán sállà: music for the eve of the Muslim festivals of 'Id al-Fiṭr and 'Id al-Kabīr in Kano, Nigeria.* Bloomington, African Studies Program, Indiana University, 1974. 84pp.
Every imaginable aspect of the festivals is examined and explained with meticulous attention to detail. Dárán Sállà marks the end of the difficult fast-month for Moslems known as Ràmàdân. Besmer says in his conclusion that the purpose of the paper has been to demonstrate an approach to the structural analysis of a significant musical event in the annual cycle of activities of the court musicians of the Emir of Kano. No bibliography, but copious notes.

229. **Bethel, Edward Clement.** MUSIC IN THE BAHAMAS: ITS ROOTS, DEVELOPMENT AND PERSONALITY. Master's Thesis, University of California, Los Angeles, 1978.

230. **Bibliographie des arts zaïrois.** Kinshasa/Gombe: Bibliothèque nationale, 1974. 13pp.
Includes music and literature.

231. **Bichi, Abdu Yahya.** WEDDING SONGS AS REGULATORS OF SOCIAL CONTROL AMONG THE HAUSA OF NIGERIA. Dissertation, University of Pennsylvania, 1985. 201pp.
Bichi believes that the field of wedding songs has not been fully investigated, and

that more research is needed to understand its significance in African folklore scholarship. Hausa wedding songs are the prime concern. They are generally believed among the Hausa to establish approved ways of behavior regarding married life. Moreover, they are directed not only to the bride and bridegroom, but also to adolescent youth. Examples are given of songs used for didactic purposes. Bibliography, index. **(UMI)**

232. **Biebuyck, Daniel, and Kahombo Matene.** "Chante Hunde." **AFRIKA UND ÜBERSEE** 48, no. 1 (1966): 157-169.

233. **Bigalke, Erich Heinrich.** AN ETHNOMUSICOLOGICAL STUDY OF THE NDLAMBE OF SOUTHEASTERN AFRICA. Dissertation, Queen's University of Belfast (Northern Ireland), 1982. 302pp.
The author studied the musical life of "almost a thousand" members of the Ndlambe in a village in the eastern Cape Province of South Africa. He sought the answers to two questions: "Why, in a male-dominated society with a patrilineal descent system and a strong lineage organization, music seems to be mainly the preserve of women?" - and - "In view of the strength of the lineage principle, why is music-making a communal activity rather than restricted to descent groups alone?" Notes were kept regarding interviews and communal events. Music recorded on a cassette tape recorder was later transcribed. **(UMI)**

234. **Bigalke, Erich Heinrich.** "An historic overview of southern Nguni musical behaviour." In **Symposium on Ethnomusicology.** (3rd: 1982: University of Natal) [4th: 1983: Rhodes University] *Papers presented at the Third and Fourth Symposia on Ethnomusicology,* Music Department, University of Natal, Durban, 16th to 19th September 1982; Music Department, Rhodes University, 7th to 8th October 1983, 38-47. Grahamstown, South Africa: International Library of African Music, 1984.
Note that this paper is in the 4th Symposium. (The 3rd and 4th Symposia are in one volume.)

235. **Bilby, Kenneth.** "Caribbean crucible." In **Repercussions: a celebration of African-American music.** Edited by Geoffrey Haydon and Dennis Marks, 128-151. London: Century Publications, 1985.
Masterfully done. Contains song texts, an extensive bibliography, discography, and many black and white photographs. Bilby, who learned Caribbean music first-hand while living with African communities in Guyana and Jamaica, is known particularly for his work in recording and annotating Caribbean music for the American Folkways record series. The essay is abstracted in **RILM** 1985, reviewed in **KESKIDEE** 1, 1986.

236. **Binkley, David Aaron.** A VIEW FROM THE FOREST: THE POWER OF SOUTHERN KUBA INITIATION MASKS. Dissertation, Indiana University, 1987. 245pp.

237. **Binon, Gisèle**. "Musique dans le Candomblé." In **La musique dans la vie, étude realisée sous les auspices l'Ocora et sous la direction de Tolia Nikiprowetzky**, 159-207. Vol. 1. Paris, Office de coopération radiophonique, 1976 - .
Illustrations, photographs, brief excerpts of chanted or sung texts. Twenty-five, easily-read transcriptions of Brazilian Candomblé music - very African - make up the larger portion of the essay, which is in French. In some cases, Yorùbá words accompany the transcriptions.

Biobaku, Saburi O.
See: **The living culture of Nigeria, 980.**

238. **Bisilliat, Jeanne, and D. Laya**, eds. and trans. *Les zamu: ou, Poèmes sur les noms: la tradition orale dans la société Songhay-Zarma*. Niamey: CNRSH [i.e., Centre nigerien de recherches en sciences humaines, 1972]. 160pp. (Tradition orales et culture, 1)
On Zarma songs, poetry based on personal names, and representing the oral tradition of Niger. Some of the *zamu* (i.e., poems on names) are meant to be sung, some meant to be recited. Words to 19 sung pieces are included, in French and/or Songhai, but no music notations. Poems and accompanying photographs are beautiful.

239. **Bispo, Antonio**. "Zur Kirchenmusik in Zaïre nach den Darstellungen in der missions- und musikwissenschaftlichen Literatur." In **Symposium musico-ethnologicum**. Edited by Johannes Overath, 364-382. **MUSICES APTATIO** 1980 (Roma: CIMS, 1980).
In German. Bibliography. Abstracted in **RILM**, 1985.

240. **Black music in Britain: essays on the Afro-Asian contribution to popular music**. Edited by Paul Oliver. Milton Keynes [England]; Philadelphia: Open University Press, 1990. 198pp. (Popular music in Britain)
Misleading title, since chapters on *Bhangra* and *Qawwali* are concerned with musics neither black nor Afro-Asian. (Surely the social sciences or humanities might have yielded more precise terms than those Oliver ultimately chose.) Part one covers black music from 1800-1950. Part two covers 1950 on. Oliver writes introductions to each section of essays, and also the conclusion. The index has some references to African-related subjects, including, African elements in concert music. Chris Stapleton's chapter, "African connections: London's hidden music scene," is the most relevant. Three chapters concern Caribbean music in Britain. Bibliography, notes, illustrations, discographies.

241. **Black music in our culture: curricular ideas on the subjects, materials and problems**. Edited by Dominique-René de Lerma. With contributions by Thomas Jefferson Anderson, Jr. [and others.

Kent, Ohio] Kent State University Press [1970]. 263pp.
Much of the information included in this book was presented as a seminar, Black Music in College and University Curricula, held at Indiana University from June 18 to 21, 1969. One of the Appendices, entitled Sample Curricular Syllabi, gives outlines of courses that include in some way the study of African music. The one essay that refers to African music and dance is by Verna Arvey, music historian, dance authority, and librettist to her composer-husband, William Grant Still.
•**Arvey, Verna**. "Negro dance and its influence on Negro music," 79-92.

242. **BLACK MUSIC RESEARCH BULLETIN**. 1978- . Center for Black Music Research, Columbia College Chicago, Chicago, Illinois.
This was formerly the **BLACK MUSIC RESEARCH NEWSLETTER**. It is published semi-annually, and covers a broad range of research in black music.

243. **BLACK MUSIC RESEARCH JOURNAL**. 1980- . Center for Black Music Research, Columbia College Chicago, Chicago, Illinois.
Semi-annual. Covers a broad range of research in black music. Indexed in **RILM**, **MUSIC INDEX, ARTS AND HUMANITIES CITATION INDEX**.

244. **BLACK ORPHEUS: JOURNAL OF AFRICAN AND AFRICAN-AMERICAN LITERATURE**. 1957- . University of Lagos, Lagos University Press, Lagos, Nigeria.
An excellent source. Described as covering African literature, music, sculpture, and other art forms. Indexed in **CURRENT CONTENTS, MLA**. A few articles have been selected at random for listing:
•**Avorgbedor, Daniel**. "The interaction of music and spoken texts in the context of Anlo-Ewe music," vol. 6, no. 1 (1986): 17-25.
•**Babalọlá, S. A.** "An *ìjálá* chant," vol. 3, no. 4 (1976): 11-13.
•**Euba, Akin**. "The potential of traditional music as a contemplative art," vol. 3, no. 1 (1974): 54-60.
•**Gbàdàmọ́sí, Bákàrè, and Ulli Beier**. "Yorùbá funeral songs," no. 22 (1967): 5-6.
•**Peek, Phil, and R. Dogbu**. "*Isoko* and *ijaw* songs," no. 22 (1967): 4-5.

245. **THE BLACK PERSPECTIVE IN MUSIC**. 1973-1990. Cambria Heights, New York.
Regrettably, this excellent journal ceased publication with the November/December issue, 1990. Published semiannually, the journal contained scholarly articles, interviews, historical reports, biographical sketches, and reviews of books and records pertaining to African-American and African music. Dr. Eileen J. Southern was the editor. Fortunately, the journal is indexed in: **MUSIC INDEX, RILM, CURRENT CONTENTS, CURRENT CONTENTS AFRICA**, and in a number of other indexes listed in **ULRICH'S**. **THE BLACK PERSPECTIVE IN MUSIC** is also available in microform through **UMI**. Reprints available. Following are randomly selected examples:
•**Akpabot, Samuel**. "Fugitive notes on notation and terminology in African music," vol. 4, no. 1 (1976): 39-45.
•**DjeDje, Jacqueline Cogdell**. "Song type and performance style in Hausa and Dagomba possession (Bori) music," vol. 9, no. 3 (1982): 166-182.
continued

•**Ekwueme, Lazarus**. "African music retentions in the New World," vol. 2, no. 2 (1974): 128-144.

•**Hampton, Barbara L**. "The contiguity factor in Ga music," vol. 6, no. 1 (1978): 32-48.

246. BLACKING, JOHN.
The loss of this outstanding musicologist and exceptional human being is still keenly felt. "John Blacking (1928-1990): a personal obituary" appears in **ETHNOMUSICOLOGY** (Volume 34, no. 2, 1990: 263-270), written by Jim Kippen, of the University of Toronto. The memorial essay is followed by a bibliography of Blacking's works. Publications run from 1954 to 1988. **POPULAR MUSIC** (New York: Cambridge University Press) calls its 10th volume, no. 1, 1991, the "John Blacking Issue." Two of the eight essays are on reminiscences of John Blacking. Three concern South African music.

247. Blacking, John. "Field work in African music." In **Reflections on Afro-American music**. Edited by Dominique-René de Lerma, 207-221. [Kent, Ohio] Kent State University Press [1973].
Blacking discusses the techniques he used in studying music in Africa between 1954 and 1969. As a guide to others, he is even candid as to some of the (forgivable) blunders he made. Further along in the essay, he answers questions put to him about the strength of the relationship between African music and African-American music, and on unity in African music.

248. Blacking, John. "Field work in African music." **REVIEW OF ETHNOLOGY** 3, no. 3, 1973.
Not seen, but this paper has the same title as the immediately preceding entry. They each appeared in 1973.

249. Blacking, John. *How musical is man?* Seattle: University of Washington Press, [1973]. 116pp. (The John Danz lectures)
"The Venda taught me that music can never be a thing in itself, and that *all* music is folk music, in the sense that music cannot be transmitted or have meaning without associations between people." Blacking explores the role of music in society, and of society and culture in music, drawing from music of the Transvaal Venda, with whom he lived and whose culture he studied in-depth, and from his own deep knowledge of Western music. Contains numerous transcriptions, diagrams, photographs. A brief biography chronicles Blacking's distinguished career. Venda music on tape is (was?) available from the publisher.

250. Blacking, John. "Introduction: Indigenous musics of South Africa." In *South African music encyclopedia*. Vol. 2. Edited by Jacques P. Malan, 265-267. Cape Town: Oxford University Press, 1979-1986.

251. Blacking, John. "Music and the historical process in Vendaland." In *Essays on music and history in Africa*. Edited by Klaus P.

Wachsmann, 185-212. Evanston: Northwestern University Press, 1971.
Notations, footnotes, map.

252. **Blacking John**. "Music of the Venda-speaking people." In *South African music encyclopedia*. Vol. 2. Edited by Jacques P. Malan, 418-508. Cape Town: Oxford University Press, 1979-1986.

253. **Blacking, John**. PROCESS AND PRODUCT IN THE MUSIC OF CENTRAL AND SOUTHERN AFRICA. Dissertation, University of the Witwatersrand 1972.

254. **Blacking, John**. "Some principles of composition in the indigenous music of South Africa." In *South African music encyclopedia*. Vol. 2. Edited by Jacques P. Malan, 294-301. Cape Town: Oxford University Press, 1979-1986.

255. **Blacking, John**. "Trends in the black music of South Africa." In **Music of many cultures: an introduction**. Edited by Elizabeth May, 172-194. Berkeley: University of California Press, c1980.
Discography, filmography, bibliography, glossary, photographs, notations, diagrams.

256. **Blacking, John**. VENDA CHILDREN'S SONGS: A STUDY IN ETHNOMUSICOLOGICAL ANALYSIS. "Part of Thesis." University of the Witwatersrand, 1967. 210pp.
A much-quoted study. The music is principally melodies with words. Illustrations, tables (some folding), diagrams. Bibliography.

Blacking. John
See also: •**The anthropology of the body, 112.**
•**The performing arts: music and dance, 1325.**

257. **Bloch, Peter**. *La-le-lo-lai: Puerto Rican music and its performers*. [New York] Plus Ultra Educational Publishers [1973]. 197pp.
An overview of Puerto Rican music of all kinds, and Puerto Rican composers and performers. References to Africa are in two chapters, The Roots, and The Afro Influence - Bomba and Plena. There is an index, bibliography, and a brief biography of the author (who identifies strongly with Puerto Ricans, their culture, their struggles). The musical exclamation "la-le-lo-lai," characteristic of Puerto Rican farmers and farm workers, is also said to exist among farm workers in Spain. Bloch conjectures that this may have been brought from the Moors, and be a case of indirect African influence on Puerto Rican folk music.

258. **Blum, Odette.** *Dance in Ghana.* Introduction by Ko̲bla Ladzekpo. New York: Dance Perspectives Foundation, 1973. 57pp. (Dance perspectives, 56)
There is a good deal in this book about the role music plays in dance and ritual in Ghana, if not much focus on the music itself. Various kinds of Ghanaian instruments are mentioned, and there are some interesting insights into the social and behavioral aspects of music/dance events - the relationship of lead drummer to dancers, for instance.

259. **Blum, Stephen.** "European musical terminology and the music of Africa." In **Comparative musicology and anthropology of music: essays on the history of ethnomusicology**. Edited by Bruno Nettl and V. Bohlman, 3-36. Chicago: University of Chicago Press, 1991.
Bibliography, notes, charts.

260. **Boateng, Atto Ampofo.** AN INSIGHT INTO THE MUSICAL CULTURE OF AFRICA THROUGH GHANA GATES. Dissertation, [Halle?], 1967. 116pp.

Bockarie, Samura
See: **Limba stories and songs, 976.**

261. **Bogniaho, Ascension.** "A la découverte de la chanson populaire au Bénin." In **Chansons d'Afrique et des Antilles**, 81-88. Paris: Harmattan, c1988.

Bohlman, Philip V.
See: **Chicago studies in ethnomusicology, 35.**

262. **Bokelenge, Lonah H.** "Modern Zaïrian music: yesterday, today and tomorrow." In **The arts and civilization of Black and African peoples**. Edited by Joseph Ohiomogben Okpaku, Alfred Esimatemi Opubor, and Benjamin Ọlátúnjí Ọlọ́runtìmẹhìn, Volume 1: 132-151. Lagos: Centre for Black and African Arts and Civilization, c1986.
A methodical and thorough survey. Contains an interesting summary, resulting from a colloquium on Zaïrian music in Kinshasa in 1968, that defines the constituent elements of Zaïrian music. No bibliography.

263. **Bonanni, Filippo.** *Antique musical instruments and their players: 152 plates from Bonanni's 18th century "Gabinetto Armonico."* With a new introduction and captions by Frank Ll. Harrison and Joan Rimmer. New York: Dover, 1964.
This is the first reprinting of Filippo Bonanni's masterpiece, *Gabinetto Armonico*, published in final form in 1723. The 152 reproductions of magnificent engravings are of ancient and contemporary musical instruments of the world.

Instruments are meticulously executed, and always shown being played. Many are almost too fantastic to be believed. Included are an African tubular drum, double bell, single bell, xylophones, rattles, sanza, a spike-fiddle, and a dancing Brazilian woman with arm bells. Drawings are interestingly naïve, captions sometimes pejorative, but any musicologist, or Africanist interested in organology should explore this exceptional book. Engravings by Arnold van Westerhout.

264. **Boncoungou, Gomzoudou, Jean-Marie.** *Ethno musicologie moderne.* [s.l.: s.n., 1978?]. 159pp.
Music of Burkina Faso, texts of 321 songs in French. Bibliography.

265. **Boot, Adrian.** *Bob Marley.* London: Hutchinson, 1981.

Borel, François
See: **Musée d'ethnographie (Neuchâtel, Switzerland), 1124.**

266. **Boulton, Laura.** *The music-hunter: the autobiography of a career.* Garden City, New York: Doubleday, 1969. 513pp.
Concerns Boulton's wanderings in 5 continents to collect music little known up until then. The African section covers 100 pages. Chapter 32 has considerable information on Ethiopian instruments. Several pages entitled, Survivals in the New World, are primarily concerned with African retentions in Haiti. Sixty-six varied photographs are historically priceless, comprising African musicians, not to mention Schweitzer, Kodàly, and other such unexpected world renowned figures. Some photos show Boulton in the field, the determined musicologist, struggling with pathetic old equipment that she somehow made work. The informative story of an inspiring, indefatigable human being. Index.

267. **Bouws, Jan.** *Solank daar musiek is...: musiek en musiekmakers in Suid-Africa (1952-1982).* Kaapstad: Tafelberg, 1982. 202pp.
In Afrikaans. Nothing about the black South African contribution. This book is included because of a few historical plates of black street musicians and a man dancing with a child near a covered wagon. Other more distasteful examples can be found. The Traceys and Kirby get brief mention. We learn something of the blackface white Minstrel Shows, but nothing of Orpheus M. McAdoo and the Virginia Jubilee Singers, which company even caused Paul Kruger to shed some tears in public. Effects of these musicians on black South African music today can be demonstrated. (See Erlmann's listed works touching on McAdoo, **537, 540, 545.**)

268. **Bowdich, T. Edward.** *Mission from Cape Coast Castle to Ashantee.* 3d ed., edited with notes and an introduction by W. E. F. Ward. [London]: F. Cass, 1966. 512pp.
Fortunately, this remarkable old work, first published in London by John Murray (1819), is available in our time. Bowdich's account of his exploratory mission from Cape Coast to Kumasi, where he was sent by the Government of the Gold Coast Colony on behalf of the British Government, still makes fascinating reading. The book contains a wealth of information on many subjects, including detailed

accounts of musical instruments and music practices. There are even transcriptions of songs. The great importance of this book lies in the fact that it was the first published authentic account of the Ashanti kingdom. Maps, tables.

269. **Bowra, Cecil Maurice.** *Primitive song.* London: Weidenfeld and Nicolson, [1962].
If one can get past the first word of the title, there might be value in some of the translations of African song texts - assuming that they are reliably done. The index has a number of references to "Bushmen" and "Pygmy" songs, apparently the only African ones selected. Notes, but no bibliography.

270. **Boyce, Carole Elizabeth.** THE TRINIDAD CALYPSO: AN ANALYSIS OF THE FUNCTIONS OF AN AFRICAN ORAL TRADITION IN THE CARIBBEAN. Master's Thesis, Howard University, 1974. 193pp.

271. **Boyd, Alan.** TO PRAISE THE PROPHET: A PROCESSUAL SYMBOLIC ANALYSIS OF "MAULIDI," [al-Mawlūd] A MUSLIM RITUAL IN LAMU, KENYA. Dissertation, Indiana University, 1981, 192pp.
To quote from the author's UMI abstract, "By concentrating attention upon the interactions within and surrounding a musical event, and relating these to the cultural definition of the situation of *maulidi* and the values that underlie that definition, it is shown that music is culturally derived, just as other behavior systems arise from the cultural base of a given society. By closely observing how *maulidi* is used to express social dynamics both of dissension and unity, it is shown that a musical event can be a valuable source of data for the understanding of the larger community."

272. **Boyd, Alan.** *The zumari: a musical instrument in the Lamu area.* [Nairobi]: University of Nairobi, Institute of African Studies, 1977. 9pp. (Seminar paper - University of Nairobi, Institute of African Studies, no. 72)

273. **Boyd, James T.** "Music in Islam: Lamu, Kenya, a case study." In **A tribute to Alan P. Merriam.** Edited by Caroline Card, *et al.*, 83-98. Bloomington, Indiana: Indiana University. (Archives of Traditional Music), c1981.
Bibliography.

274. **Branda-Lacerda, Marcos.** *Kultische Trommelmusik der Yorùbá in der Volksrepublik Benin: Bàtá-Ṣàngó und Bàtá-*Egúngún in der Städten Pobè und Sakété. 2 vols. Hamburg: Karl Dieter Wagner, 1988. v.1, 215pp; v.2, 113pp. (Beiträge zur Ethnomusikologie, vol. 19)
A highly technical study of Yorùbá music of Benin, with an emphasis on bàtá drum ensembles used for religious purposes. Bibliography and discography. Volume 1 is primarily text, with a few folded pages of music. Volume 2 is music only. Included are two rather dark photos of drum ensembles and performers.

275. Brandel, Rose. *The music of Central Africa: an ethnomusicological study.* The Hague: Martinus Nijhoff, 1973. 272pp.
This was based on - or is the same as - Brandel's doctoral dissertation, completed at New York University in 1959. Nijhoff first published the book in 1961, and this is a republication of what has become a classic in the field. Sometimes the book is listed under the name **Natanson, Rose Brandel.** Bibliography, charts, music.

276. Brandes, Edda. *Die Imzad-Musik der Kel-Ahaggar-Frauen in Süd-Algerien.* Göttingen [Germany]: Edition Re, c1989. 239pp. (Orbis musicarum, Volume 4)
On Algerian music of the Ahaggar Mountains, women musicians of that area, and bowed stringed instrument. Bibliographic references. One sound cassette.

277. Brandily, Monique. *Un chant du Tibesti (Tchad).* [Paris: s.n., 1976?] pp.[127]-192. ("Extrait du Journal des africanistes, t. 46, 1-2, 1976.")
The song that is the subject of this study is a male solo composed by a young man during a fifteen-day trip by camel that took him to the Tibesti in the Chad to Fezzan in the Murzuk region of Libya. The poem is strophic in structure, and the song, dithyrambic. It is dedicated to a woman - a "song of the saddle," as the Teda call it. Only the melody is studied here; Brandily postpones rhythm studies. She is concerned about the complex relations that exist between the music and the words. Bibliography, accompanying disc.

278. Brandily, Monique. "Un exorcisme musical chez les Kotoko." In **La musique dans la vie, étude realisée sous les auspices l'Ocora et sous la direction de Tolia Nikiprowetzky,** 30-75. Vol. 1. Paris, Office de coopération radiophonique, 1976 - .
In French, and about the Kotoko of Chad. A thorough and beautifully-done monograph divided into [translated]: Introduction, The Ceremony, The Participants, Interpretive Essay, Conclusion. The work is augmented by phótographs, music notations, footnotes, and a bibliography.

279. Brandily, Monique. *Instruments de musique et musiciens instrumentistes chez les Teda du Tibesti.* Tervuren: Musée royal de l'Afrique centrale, 1974. 260pp. (Musée royal de l'Afrique centrale, Tervuren, Belgium. Annales: Série in-8°. Sciences humaines, no. 82)
Music and musical instruments of the Tibbu of Tibesti [Chad]. Bibliography, indexes.

280. Brandl, Rudolf Maria. MÄRCHENLIEDER AUS DEM ITURI-WALD: DIE LIEDER AUS DEN ERZÄHLUNGEN DER WALDNEGER UND PYGMÄEN VON DER KONGO-EXPEDITION, 1958-59. Dissertation, Vienna, 1969. 211pp.

281. **Brandt, H. M.** AN ETHNOMUSICALOGICAL [*sic*] STUDY OF THREE AFRO-VENEZUALAN [*sic*] DRUM ENSEMBLES OF BAROVENTO. Dissertation, Queen's University of Belfast (Northern Ireland), 1978. 353pp.
Source is **The BRITS index.**

282. **Brandt, Hans.** FORTY TRADITIONAL AFRICAN CHILDREN'S SONGS: SELECTIONS FROM THE ACHOLI, HAUSA, SHONA AND YORÙBÁ. Master's Thesis, University of California, Los Angeles, 1970. 212pp.

283. **Brempong, Owusu.** AKAN HIGHLIFE IN GHANA: SONGS OF CULTURAL TRANSITION. 2 vols. Dissertation, Indiana University, 1986. 712pp.
The author studied highlife songs in order to identify, analyze, and interpret their form, style, and content. He also wanted to determine the patterns of interaction between their traditional and non-traditional components. In studying the functions of highlife songs in urban as well as rural Akan communities, Brempong found that although the songs are largely intended for entertainment, they also serve as powerful socializing elements with "didactic" messages. Illustrations, maps, music, bibliography. **(UMI)**

284. **Bridgman, Nanie,** ed. *Musiques africaines*. [Paris]: Musique de tous les temps, [1967]. 1 vol. (unpaginated). (Musique de tous les temps, 44/45)
Almost like a museum catalog, since there are photographic studies of African sculpture on each right hand page. Starts with a poem by Senghor, followed by an essay on African culture. Pertinent for our purposes are Laurence Barony's "Introduction à la musique africaines," and Marius Schneider's, "Le langage tambouriné des Doula." The latter has a number of music transcriptions. A sound disc in pocket has music from the Central African Republic described by Simha Arom. Bibliographical references.

285. **Brief sketches in Akan (Ghana) art symbol, literature, music, and African theater.** Washington, D.C.: Association for the Study of Negro Life and History, c1972. [19]pp.
One essay is concerned with music:
Aning, Ben A. "The music and musical instruments of West Africa," 9-14.

Brincard, Marie-Thérèse
See: **Sounding forms, 1484.**

286. **Brissonnet, Lydie Carmen.** THE STRUCTURATION OF COMMUNITAS IN THE CARNAVAL OF SALVADOR, BAHIA (NORTHEASTERN BRAZIL). Dissertation, Indiana University, 1988.
The author says that themes and songs of Afro-Bahian clubs have always revealed a concern with African roots. Music, musician status and behavior, song texts, dance, and religious affiliations associated with these clubs are discussed, primarily in Chapter 7 of this probing socio-political study of Bahian Carnaval

behind-the-scenes. Brissonnet dispels what she calls "the myth of racial democracy," contrasting elite carnaval clubs featured during prime hours, with Afro-Bahian clubs relegated to the night. She further describes this "white/black, upper class/lower class polarization" that directly contradicts official propaganda. Bibliography.

British Library African Resources: National Sound Archive.
See: •**Duran, Lucy, 489.**
•**Vickers, Jonathan, 1621.**

287. **The BRITS index: an index to the British theses collections, 1971-1987 held at the British Document Supply Centre and London University.** 3 vols. Godstone, Surrey, England: British Theses Service, c1989.
The first volume is an author index, the second is a subject index, and the third is a title index. Dissertations on African music were easily located.

288. **Brodber, Erna, and J. Edward Greene.** *Reggae and cultural identity.* St. Augustine, Trinidad and Tobago: Department of Sociology, University of the West Indies, 1981. 30pp. (Working papers on Caribbean society. Series C, Contemporary issues, no. 7)
On reggae music and social conditions in Jamaica. Bibliography

289. **Brooks, Christopher Antonio.** DÚRÓ LÁDIPỌ̀ AND THE MOREMI LEGEND: THE SOCIO-HISTORICAL DEVELOPMENT OF THE YORÙBÁ MUSIC DRAMA AND ITS POLITICAL RAMIFICATIONS. Dissertation, University of Texas, 1989. 287pp.
The Moremi legend is a traditional Yorùbá myth that was converted to a music drama by the late Nigerian composer, Dúró Ládipọ̀, and presented at the annual Edi festival in Ilé-Ifẹ̀. He had been inspired by the Festival to incorporate the legend into his musical stage work in the 1960s. This was during a time that Nigeria was experiencing its greatest internal political turmoil since independence. The author wonders how drawing from the myth and festival might invigorate musical and dramatic works, and also inspire an audience to develop a national identity and sense of shared destiny. **(UMI)**

290. **Broster, Joan A.** *The Tembu: their beadwork, songs, and dances.* Introduction by Kaiser Mantanzima. Cape Town; New York: Purnell, c1976. 118pp.

291. **Broszinsky-Schwabe, Edith.** *Kultur in Schwarzafrika: Geschichte, Tradition, Umbruch, Identität.* Leipzig: Urania-Verl., 1988. 355pp.
On subSaharan African arts, and written entirely in German. There are writings on African music in the Song and Dance section, pages 240-247, that incorporate line drawings and reproductions of old illustrations of African musicians from as far back as 1869. Included are other varied, historical photographs and

illustrations. The book ends with dazzling examples of contemporary African art. Bibliography and index.

292. **Brown, Ernest.** DRUMS OF LIFE: ROYAL MUSIC AND SOCIAL LIFE IN WESTERN ZAMBIA. Dissertation, University of Washington, 1984. 800pp.
The music of the royal xylophone and drum ensembles of the Nkoya and Lozi of western Zambia are studied. The dissertation attempts to analyze the relationship between royal music and changing social structures by comparing Nkoya and Lozi royal music. Illustrations, maps, music, bibliography. **(UMI)**

293. **Brown, Ernest.** "Drums on the water: the *kuomboka* ceremony of the Lozi of Zambia." **AFRICAN MUSICOLOGY** 1, no.1 (1983): 67-78. Bibliography. Abstracted in **RILM**, 1985.
Kuomboka and *nalikwanda* are ceremonies that accompany the exodus and return of the Lozi due to floods. On these occasions, there are performances of royal music. Some instruments, including *maoni* drums, are symbols of power.

294. **Brown, Ernest.** *Songs of the spirits: the royal music of the Nkoya of Zambia.* [Lusaka, Zambia]: University of Zambia, Institute for African Studies, 1976. 34pp. (University of Zambia Seminar, Institute for African Studies)
There is an informative general essay, followed by notes. Appendix 1 lists Senior Nkoya Chiefs; Appendix 2 is a transcription of one song, "Mushilunga, The Grave," from the Kuandamisa repertoire; Appendix 3 consists of song texts. Several instruments are illustrated.

Brown, Lalage
See: **International Congress of Africanists, 1st, Accra, 1962.**

295. **Bryer, Valerie.** *Professor Percival Robson Kirby: a bibliography of his works.* Johannesburg: Johannesburg Public Library, 1965.

296. **Buchner, Alexandr.** *Folk music instruments.* Translated by Alžběta Nováková [of *Hudební nástroje národů*]. New York: Crown, 1972. 292pp.
The section on Africa contains a general essay on African musical instruments, with a one-page focus only on Ethiopia. This is a large book with dazzling black/white and color photographs of instruments and people playing them. The Arabic Countries section has only scattered, scanty information about North African instruments. The bibliography is old, but good. Buchner spends some time on modern Arabic music theory. In speaking of West Africa, the book says at one point, "Every orchestra must without fail contain one drum called the 'Owner' or 'Landlord.'" Can something have been lost in the translation?

297. Buchner, Alexandr. *Handbuch der Musikinstrumente.* Translated by Anna Urbanová. Hanau (Germany): Dausien, 1981.) 352pp.
The book consists chiefly of illustrations of musical instruments the world over. There is a separate section on "Schwarzafrika" (pages 257-264), in which a variety of African instruments in performance are pictured, and a section, "Arabische Völker" (pages 265-274) that includes a few instruments from northern Africa. The bibliography incorporates primary names in the Africana field such as Brandel, Carrington, Farmer, Günther, and Laurenty.

298. Burnim, Mellonee V. SONGS IN MENDE FOLKTALES. Master's Thesis, University of Wisconsin-Madison, 1976. 170pp.

298a. Burt, Eugene C. *An annotated bibliography of the visual arts of East Africa.* Bloomington: Indiana University Press, 1980. 371pp. (Traditional arts of Africa)
There are entries for musical instruments, and indexes for locating them in either Subject, Author, or Culture indexes. Succinct annotations.

Burt, Eugene
See also: **African art - 5 year cumulative bibliography, 29a.**

299. Butcher, Vada E. *et al. Development of materials for a one year course in African music for the general undergraduate student (project in African music).* [Washington]: Office of Education, 1970. 281pp.
The study, sponsored by the U.S. Government and undertaken by Howard University, is a treasure chest. Two separate outlines are presented for the year length course, one on African music, the other on African-American music. For each outline, with its various subdivisions, there is a detailed summary section entitled, Bibliographies, Discographies, Lists of Audio-Visual Materials. A number of pertinent essays, and scripts associated with slides and demo tapes prepared just for this book, are included. Listed below are those essays specifically on African music. There are similar ones specifically on African-American music:

- **Butcher, Vada E.** "The impact of the African idiom upon American music: an introductory lecture," 223-229.
- **Euba, Akin**. "In search of a common musical language in Africa," 85-87.
- **Euba, Akin**. "The music of Nigeria," 93-98.
- **Thieme, Darius**. "Music history in Africa," 101-104.
- **Thieme, Darius**. "Music in Yorùbá society," 107-111.
- **Thieme, Darius**. "Social organization of Yorùbá musicians," 115-117.
- **Thieme, Darius**. "Training and musicianship among the Yorùbá," 121-122.

300. Butcher, Vada E. "The impact of the African idiom upon American music: an introductory lecture." In *Development of* *materials for a one year course in African music for the general undergraduate student (project in African music).* Edited by Vada E. Butcher, *et al.*, 223-229. [Washington]: Office of Education, 1970.

301. **Butumweni, Nlandu Yambula.** "Perspectives d'avenir des musiques africaines." **INTERNATIONAL COMMITTEE ON URGENT ANTHROPOLOGICAL AND ETHNOLOGICAL RESEARCH. BULLETIN** 24, (1982): 83-88.
In French. Butumweni begins by discussing how the African music of today is not that of yesterday, and how African music is not fixed but metamorphoses with the times - and generally. He spends the rest of the essay on the problems of notating African music, saying that to date the majority of works published on this subject have focused on instruments, and the role music plays in African society. He feels that it is now necessary to focus on the notation of that music. The essay is a little over 3 pages long. The bibliography is almost that long.

302. CBMR MONOGRAPHS. 1989 - . Center for Black Music Research, Columbia College Chicago, Chicago, Illinois.
Issued annually. Covers a broad range of research in black music.

Ceeba
See: **Publications Ceeba, 1347.**

303. CERDIC. BULLETIN DU CERDIC ABSTRACTS. (CENTRE DES RECHERCHE ET DE DOCUMENTATION DES INSTITUTIONS CHRÉTIENNES)
This was an abstracting and indexing publication, mentioned a few times in this bibliography in connection with a few periodicals it formerly serviced. In the 1990-1991 edition of **ULRICH'S**, it is listed as "ceased."

304. **Cable, George W.** *The dance in Place Congo.* New Orleans, Louisiana: Faruk von Turk, c1974. 39pp. Reprinted from THE CENTURY MAGAZINE 31 (1886): 522-559.
Cable, in his disdainful manner, manages to document sights and sounds he experienced in Place Congo long ago. (On Sundays, New Orleans slaves were permitted to dance in this famous square.) Eight directly African, or African-derived, dances are described, along with descriptions of instruments, also African or African-derived in their construction or playing techniques. There are music transcriptions, song texts, and sympathetic illustrations by Edward Windsor Kemble, an artist not normally known for his kindly depictions of people of African heritage. Included with this reprint is a brief article, "The Congo dance," that also mentions dancing and instruments.

305. **Cáceres, Abraham.** "Preliminary comments on the marimba in the Americas." In *Discourse in ethnomusicology: essays in honor of George List.* Edited by Caroline Card, *et al.*, 225-250. Bloomington: Ethnomusicology Publications Group, Indiana University, c1978.

306. CAHIERS D'ÉTUDES AFRICAINES. 1960- . Paris: Mouton.
Appears quarterly. Indexed in **CURRENT CONTENTS, CURRENT CONTENTS AFRICA, MLA,** and others publications listed in **ULRICH'S.** Texts are in English and French. Music articles were more apt to appear in earlier issues. Three have been selected for listing below:
- **Makarius, Laura.** "Observations sur la legende des griots Malinke," vol. 9, no. 4 (1969): 626-640.
- **Monts, Lester Parker.** "Conflict, accommodation and transformation: the effect of Islam on music of the Vai secret societies," vol. 24, no. 3 (1984): 321-342.
- **Zemp, Hugo.** "La legende des griots Malinke," vol. 6, no. 24 (1966): 611-642.

307. **Calender, Ebenezer.** *Songs by Ebenezer Calender in Krio and English from Freetown, Sierra Leone.* [In some sources his name is spelled *Ebenezar Calendar.*] Edited by Wolfgang Bender. Transcribed and translated by Alex Johnson. [Bayreuth,

Germany]: Ìwàlewà, University of Bayreuth, 1984. 69pp. (Song texts of African popular music, no. 2)

Because composer, singer, guitarist, Ebenezer Calender was particularly well-known in the 50s and earlier 60s, these 13 song transcriptions were made from 78 rpm shellac discs. (More recently in Freetown, however, Calender was still famous, and townspeople could quote from his various songs, as Bender puts it, "on the spot.") The songs relate to daily life in Freetown, to special events, and, in general "to questions of social behavior." Texts are in English and Krio. A carpenter by trade, Calender appeared for more than twenty years on Sierra Leone radio, occasionally on TV. Known for his Maringa Band. Discography.

Camara, Seydou
See: **Kamara, Seyidu, 809-811.**

308. **Camara, Sory.** *Gens de la parole: essai sur la condition et le role des griots dans la société malinke.* Paris: La Haye: Mouton, c1976. 358pp.

In French. Concerns the griot's role in Mandingo society. Bibliography, illustrations.

309. **Campbell, Carol A.** *An introduction to the music of Swahili women.* [Nairobi]: University of Nairobi, Institute of African Studies, [1976]. 18pp. (Seminar paper - University of Nairobi, Institute of African Studies, no. 68)

Kenyan music.

310. **Campbell, Carol A.** NYIMBO ZA KISWAHILI: A SOCIO-ETHNOMUSICOLOGICAL STUDY OF A SWAHILI POETIC FORM. Dissertation, University of Washington, 1983. 298pp.

***Nyimbo*, one form of Swahili sung poetry performed by both children and adults, is the subject of this dissertation. The context in which *nyimbo* is performed, called *ngoma*, is a musical event that includes song, dance and the playing of musical instruments. The many *ngoma* styles are described in Chapter 3, and the musical structure of *nyimbo za ngoma*, in Chapter 4. The author believes that the method she has used, i.e., examining sung poetry in context of the total event, could be similarly applied to other musical events and to sung poetry of other cultures. Maps, music, bibliography. (UMI)**

311. **Campbell, Carol A.** SAUTI ZA LAMU: AN EXPLORATORY STUDY OF SWAHILI MUSIC. Master's Thesis, University of Washington, 1974. 135pp.

Includes phototapes.

312. **Campbell, Horace.** *Bob Marley lives: reggae, rasta, and resistance.* Dar es Salaam, Tanzania: Tackey BCI, [198-]. 21pp.

Primarily a biography of Bob Marley from a political and sociological perspective. History of reggae music. Includes texts for the songs: *Survival*, *Zimbabwe*, *War*, *Africans United*, and *Redemption Song*, and a few photos. The book

concludes with: "Bob Marley's music will be sung wherever men and women come together and demand justice and freedom. Bob Marley has left a legacy of hard work, a spirit of freedom and love for Black people which will prove an inspiration to many as the crisis of the Babylonian system deepens." Bibliography.

313. Campbell, James Tierney. OUR FATHERS, OUR CHILDREN: THE AFRICAN METHODIST EPISCOPAL CHURCH IN THE UNITED STATES AND SOUTH AFRICA. Dissertation, Stanford University, 1989. 419pp.
Although the AME Church is the main focus, this study also "seeks to illuminate the broader process of intellectual and cultural interchange between black Americans and black South Africa" between 1890 and 1930. Pages 119 to 130 pertain to musical contact across the ocean. The author draws on works of Coplan and Erlmann, but includes additional enlightening material of his own. We hear more about Orpheus McAdoo's Jubilee Singers, and prominent South African composers, performers, singers-become-missionaries. A comprehensive bibliography. Written in an engaging style rare in dissertations. Masterfully done.

314. CANADIAN JOURNAL OF AFRICAN STUDIES/REVUE DES ÉTUDES AFRICAINES. 1967- . Association of African Studies, Ottawa, Ontario, Canada.
Published three times a year. Text is in English and French. It contains articles on African music rarely. Indexed in **CURRENT CONTENTS, HISTORICAL ABSTRACTS, MLA, AICP,** and more. Supersedes **BULLETIN OF AFRICAN STUDIES IN CANADA.**

- **Nketia, J. H. Kwabena.** "African music and Western praxis: a review of Western perspectives on African musicology," vol. 20, no. 1 (1986): 36-56.
- **Olema, Debhonvapi.** "Société Zaïroise dans le miroir de la chanson populaire," vol. 18, no. 1, (1984): 122-130.

315. Card, Caroline. THE MUSIC OF THE TUAREG TRIBES OF THE CENTRAL AND SOUTHERN SAHARA. Master's Thesis, Hunter College, 1972. 102pp.
This study addresses the problem of how identity concepts affect musical creation and behavior, and how changing concepts of identity affect musical change. The musical traditions and social behavior of the Tuareg people of Algeria and Niger are examined, both the role of music in the Tuareg identity system and the effects of that role upon the music. Attention is given to how music is used to express social attitudes and affiliations, and how individuals interact by means of musical symbols. Illustrations, map, music, bibliography. **(UMI)**

316. Card, Caroline. "Some problems of field recording for research purposes." In *Discourse in ethnomusicology: essays in honor of George List.* Edited by Caroline Card [et al.], 53-64. Bloomington: Ethnomusicology Publications Group, Indiana University, c1978.
This paper is the result of Card's research in Algeria and Nigeria in 1976-1977.

C

317. Card, Caroline. "*Tende* music among the Tuareg." **Cross rhythms** 1 (1983): 155-171.

318. Card, Caroline. TUAREG MUSIC AND SOCIAL IDENTITY. Dissertation, Indiana University, 1982. 239pp.
Illustrations, map, music, bibliography.

Card, Caroline
See also: •**Discourse in ethnomusicology: essays in honor of George List, 468.**
•**A tribute to Alan P. Merriam, 1586.**

319. Carpenter, Lynn Ellen. UKOKPAN, A RECREATIONAL MUSIC OF THE ANANG IBIBIO OF SOUTH-EASTERN NIGERIA. Master's Thesis, University of California, 1974. 170pp.

320. **CARIBBEAN QUARTERLY** 1949- . Kingston, Jamaica: University of the West Indies.
Appears quarterly. Available on microform from **UMI**. Information on back issues supplied on request. Indexed by **HISTORICAL ABSTRACTS** and others listed in **ULRICH'S**, and on the inside pages of the journal itself. One relevant article is listed below. This publication is a likely source for others.
•**Elder, Jacob D.** "The male/female conflict in calypso," vol. 14, no. 3 (1968): 23-41.

321. Carr, Andrew, J. D. Elder, and W. Austin Simmons. *Independence exhibition: history of carnival, calypso, and steelband.* Port-of-Spain: Trinidad Government Printery, 1962.

322. Carrington, John F. *Talking drums of Africa.* New York: Negro Universities Press, 1969. 96pp.
(This is a reprint of the 1949 version, published by Negro Universities Press, and also by Carey Kingsgate Press, London, the same year.) Carrington is an important name in musicological circles, though regrettably, most of his works were published before the scope of this bibliography. Others of his writings may be found in earlier volumes of the periodical, **AFRICAN MUSIC** (Grahamstown, South Africa), and in other journals listed in Gaskin's and Thieme's bibliographies. Perhaps this is Carrington's best-known publication, since it is cited frequently by other scholars, and listed in many bibliographies. Illustrations.

323. Carroll, Kevin. "African music." **AFRICAN ECCLESIASTICAL REVIEW** 3, no. 4 (1961): 301-307.
Footnotes, recordings, analysis.

324. Carter, Madison H. *An annotated catalog of composers of African ancestry.* New York: Vantage Press, c1986. 134pp.
Well-intentioned, but the end result is extremely uneven and sketchy. No biographical data is given, nor are the listings of compositions at all comprehensive. Composers of the United States represent the largest number of entries, though names of a few Africans are included: Ṣówándé, Turkson, Bánkọ́lé, Akpabot, Amu, Euba, and Nketia (the latter having only one item after his name). The subject section happily includes a heading for Women Composers, Arrangers and Editors. Realistically, however, it is always possible that the few specific facts for which one was searching just might be found here.

325. Carter, William Grandvil. ASANTE MUSIC IN OLD AND NEW JUABEN: A COMPARATIVE STUDY. Dissertation, University of California, Los Angeles, 1984. 612pp.
The impact of rapid social change on the music of the Akan of Ghana is described and analyzed within the framework of musical acculturation. Studied are: the means for regulating music in a traditional Asante state, the factors and processes that motivate and shape responses to musical change, and the mechanisms by which musical continuity is maintained. Illustrations, music, bibliography. **(UMI)**

326. Carter, William Grandvil. THE NTAHERA HORN ENSEMBLE OF THE DWABEN COURT: AN ASHANTI SURROGATING MEDIUM. Master's Thesis, University of California, Los Angeles, 1971.

327. Carvalho, José Jorge de. "Music of African origin in Brazil." In *Africa in Latin America: essays on history, culture, and socialization.* Edited by Manuel Moreno Fraginals, 227-248. New York: Holmes and Meier, 1984.
An admirable, well-researched and well-footnoted compendium. There is careful data on original slave influx, religious music, instruments, dance, religious plays, and ceremonies. This essay demonstrates just how much valuable information can be successfully compressed into a small space when there has been careful planning. Bravo!

328. Carvalho, José Jorge de. RITUAL AND MUSIC OF THE ṢÀNGÓ CULTS OF RECIFE, BRAZIL. Dissertation, Queen's University of Belfast (Northern Ireland), 1984. 628pp.

329. Cashion, Gerald Anthony. HUNTERS OF THE MANDE: A BEHAVIORAL CODE AND WORLD VIEW DERIVED FROM THE STUDY OF THEIR FOLKLORE. Dissertation, Indiana University, 1984. 899pp.
Research for this study, which analyzed selected aspects of hunters' folklore, included oral epics performed by hunters' praise singers. **(UMI)**

330. Catálogo de instrumentos musicais de Moçambique. [Edited by Gabinete Central de Organização do Festival de Canção e Música

Tradicional]. [Mozambique]: Ministério da Educação e Cultura, [1980]. 31pp.
In Portuguese. Concerned with musical instruments of Mozambique, catalogs and collections.

CENTER FOR BLACK MUSIC RESEARCH
See: •**BLACK MUSIC RESEARCH BULLETIN, 242.**
•**BLACK MUSIC RESEARCH JOURNAL, 243.**
•**CBMR Monographs, 302.**

331. **Chabot, Irenaeus Raymond.** AN ADMINISTRATIVE GUIDELINE AND RESOURCE FOR THE INSTRUMENTAL PROGRAM OF THE ZAMBIAN CURRICULUM OF MUSIC EDUCATION. Master's Thesis, University of Lowell, 1983. 304pp.
The stated goal is "to reinforce the Zambian musical culture and not to supplant it." For the sensitivity and respect he shows, for his scholarly and humane approach to cross-cultural music education, Brother Chabot deserves an honorary Ph.D. There is information specifically directed to primary and secondary schools, and a thorough description of Zambian musical instruments and their uses. Zambian dance forms are covered. An historical account of the evolution of musical instruments through the ages emphasizes band instruments, since Zambian people apparently continue to be enthusiastic about bands.

Chaker, Salem
See: **Étude touarègues, 552.**

332. **La chanson populaire en Côte d'Ivoire: essai sur l'art de Gabriel Srolou.** (Published under the direction of Christopher Wondji.) Dakar: Présence Africaine, 1986. 342pp.
Touhourou is an unwritten musical composition without composer whose origin in time cannot be determined, and which does not follow known rules nor use conventional instruments or scales. In Côte d'Ivoire, where this music has traditional roots but updated appeal, it is a national tragedy and a time for taking stock when a master exponent of *touhourou*, and cherished oral historian, Gabriel Sroulou, dies at age 38. Scholarly essays honor Sroulou, and examine the future of *touhourou*, the capacity of popular music to express the "soul" of a people, plus other sociocultural phenomena. Select bibliography, several photos.

333. **Chansons d'Afrique et des Antilles.** Preface by Bernard Magnier. Paris: Harmattan, c1988. 134pp. (Itinéraires et contacts de cultures, v. 8)
This is a collection of essays by various writers on music of Africa and the French West Indies. Writers come from Mali, Congo-Zaïre, Cameroon, Benin, Côte d'Ivoire, Madagascar, Guadeloupe-Martinique. Includes bibliographical references. The essays are listed alphabetically below:
•**Bemba, Sylvain.** "La naissance du discours amoureux dans la vie quotidienne chantée au Congo-Zaïre," 39-53.
•**Bogniaho, Ascension.** "A la découverte de la chanson populaire au Bénin," 81-88. *continued*

- **Derive, Jean**. "La chanson dans une société de tradition orale de Côte d'Ivoire: (Les Dioula de Kong)," 89-98.
- **Diabaté, Masan Makan**. "L'épopée mandingue et le titre d'honneur de Sunjata Keita," 11-19.
- **Diakhité, Drissa**. "Des hymnes à la maternité," 21-28.
- **Kayo, Patrice**. "La chanson dans la société traditionelle bamiléké," 77-80.
- **Mazauric, Catherine**. "Salif Keita, un héritier singulier," 29-37.
- **Obenga, Théophile**. "La chanson mbochi," 55-62.
- **Pius Ngandu Nkashama**. "La chanson de la rupture dans la musique du Zaïre," 63-75.
- **Rakotoson, Michéle**. Dix ans de chanson à Madagascar," 99-106.
- **Schmidt, Nelly**. "Chanson des 'nouveaux libres' de Guadeloupe et de Martinique," 107-135.

334. **Chansons et proverbes lingala**. Compiled and translated by A. Dzokanga with the collaboration of Anne Behaghel. Illustrations by Charles Popineau. Paris: Conseil international de la langue française: Edicef, c1978. 162pp. (Fleuve et flamme)
Texts in Lingala with French translation. Includes index.

335. **Chants de chasseurs du Mali**. By Mamadu Jara. 3 vols. [s.l.: s.n.], c1978- ([s.l.]: Uni edit).
On hunting songs of the Bambara people of Mali. Written in Bambara and French. The first two volumes, by Mamadu Jara, are presented by Annik Thoyer-Rozat, and transcribed by Lasana Dukure. The third volume is by Ndugace Samake, also presented by Annik Thoyer-Rozat. The bibliography is in the first volume.

336. **Chants d'enfants: en duálá et basaá**. Edited by Collège Libermann. Douala: Collège Libermann, 1982. 52pp. (Langues et littératures nationales, 9)
Children's songs from the Cameroon, 11 in duálá, 10 in basaá (including many diacritics, and at least three letters not easily reproducible using standard equipment). The French translations appear side-by-side on the right. No music transcriptions are present. The small book is stapled and appears to have been mimeographed. The editor anticipates that the included songs, part of the oral tradition, will unify younger Cameroonians, and generate pride in their past. One hopes someday to hear the languages spoken, the songs sung.

337. **Chants de vie et de beauté: recueillis chez des Peuls nomades du Nord-Cameroun**. Translated and edited by Roger Labatut. Paris: Publications orientalistes de France, c1974. 155pp. POF-études)
French and Fullah.

338. **Chants et danses sahraouis: une culture de résistance**. Groupe el-Ouali. [s.l.]: Ministère de l'information de la République arabe

sahraouie démocratique, c1983. 39pp.
Consists primarily of lyrics of songs and poems of the Western Sahara. Illustrated.

339. **Chants mongo (Rép. du Zaïre).** Edited by G. Hulstaert. Bandundu: République du Zaïre: Ceeba, 1982. 175pp. (Publications Ceeba, Serié 2, vol. 76)
Text of songs in Mongo. Translation and critical material in French. Bibliography.

340. **Chants musulmans en peul: textes de l'héritage religieux de la communauté musulmane de Maroua, Cameroun.** Introduction and translation by J. Haafkens. Leiden: E. J. Brill, 1983. 422pp.
Texts of the songs in Fulah with French translation on opposite pages. English summary of introduction. Bibliography. Includes index.

341. **Charters, Samuel Barclay.** *The roots of the blues: an African search*. Boston: M. Boyars, 1981. 151pp.
Information on West African music, and especially on the traditions of the *jali* (i.e., "griot"). Plates, illustrations.

341a. **Chase, Gilbert.** *A guide to Latin American music*. 2d ed., revised and enlarged. Washington D.C.: Pan American Union, 1962. [First edition, 1945] 411pp. (A joint publication of the Pan American Union and the Library of Congress)
George List mentions this in **Music in the Americas (1129a)** as an important reference book. The present update adds 1,100 additional entries, primarily "important monographs," though it is limited in periodical coverage for reasons the author explains. Includes South and Central America, Mexico, the West Indies, parts of the United States, in which the Hispanic influence was once predominant, and the Bahamas. Classified by country, with an introductory section for each one, followed by a general bibliography, and sometimes other subdivisions. Often includes national anthems. Annotated, but entries are of older vintage. Some might lead, by indirect route, to Africa.

342. **Chelbi, Mustapha.** *Musique et société en Tunisie*. Tunis: Editions Salammbo, c1985. 21p.
This is a kind of historical overview. The essay covers Tunisian song types, musical instruments, traditional modes, musical styles during the Golden Age of Islam, prominent musicians with their biographies (including contemporary artists who use electric equipment). Chelbi speaks often of the importance of the oral heritage and shows much concern for what he regards as the deleterious effects of mass media and foreign influence on Tunisian music. He wishes to safeguard cultural identity and calls for "pioneers" to give Tunisian music new vigor. A brief bibliography. Appendix has cited song texts in Arabic. No transcriptions of music.

343. Chenoweth, Vida. *The marimba of Guatemala*. 1964. 108pp.
Only Chapter 5, History and Development of the Marimba, mentions African instruments. The Chopi *timbila* and two other varieties of African xylophone are briefly examined. Chenoweth claims that a Portuguese missionary named Father André Fernandez, in a letter dated December 5, 1562, provided the earliest account of the marimba in Africa. The bibliography has only one item as recent as 1955; the rest are considerably older. A. M. Jones' well-known work on the xylophone (and a possible African-Indonesian connection in the past), published the same year as this book, naturally did not get included.

344. Chernoff, John Miller. "Africa come back: the popular music of West Africa." In **Repercussions: a celebration of African-American music**. Edited by Geoffrey Haydon and Dennis Marks, 152-178. London: Century Publications, 1985.
Bibliography, discography by country, photographs. The essay is abstracted in **RILM** 1985, reviewed in **KESKIDEE** 1, 1986.

345. Chernoff, John Miller. *African rhythm and African sensibility: aesthetics and social action in African musical idioms*. Chicago: University of Chicago Press, 1979. 261pp.
An important and widely acclaimed book. *Repercussions* (Haydon and Marks, **1336**) says that many believe *African rhythms and African sensibility* is "the best book on the subject ever published - certainly the best book by a non-African." An excellent 90 minute cassette correlates with the book. Notes, a bibliography, index, transcriptions of music, photographs. Chernoff is an anthropologist and drummer who has studied and participated in music intensively in Ghana. The book, which is richly informative, uses a sociological approach. Included is an Appendix (courtesy of Charles Keil) with the responses of Nigerian students to the question, "Who is your favorite musician - and why?"

346. Chernoff, John Miller. AFRICAN RHYTHM AND AFRICAN SENSIBILITY: AESTHETICS AND SOCIAL ACTION IN AFRICAN MUSIC. Dissertation, Hartford Seminary Foundation, 1974. 330pp.
This forms the basis for the book of the same title, published 1979.

347. Chernoff, John Miller. "The drums of Dagbon." In **Repercussions: a celebration of African-American music**. Edited by Geoffrey Haydon and Dennis Marks, 101-127. London: Century Publications, 1985.
Dagomba is the English term for a Ghanaian people who call *themselves* "Dagbamba," speak a language called Dagbani, and live in a traditional state called Dagbon. Various musical types and dances are discussed in their historical and cultural contexts. (The drums of Dagomba are shaped like hourglasses.) Black and white photographs; two recordings listed. The essay is abstracted in **RILM** 1985, reviewed in **KESKIDEE** 1, 1986.

348. Chernoff, John Miller. "The relevance of ethnomusicology to anthropology: strategies of inquiry and interpretation." In **African**

musicology: current trends: a festschrift presented to J. H. Kwabena Nketia. Edited by Jacqueline Cogdell DjeDje, and William G. Carter, 59-92. [Atlanta, Georgia: Crossroads Press, 1988]- .
A theoretical essay which later uses the Dagomba to illustrate certain points. Music and dance are mentioned within cultural context. Notes, extensive bibliography.

349. **Chester, Galina, and Tunde Jegede**. *The silenced voice: hidden music of the kora*. London: Diabaté Kora Arts, c1987. 48pp.
The book is divided into two sections: The Griot Tradition; and, In Exile: a Discussion with Ahmed Sheikh of the African Dawn. The African Dawn is a group living in the black community of London, its purpose being to protect African heritage and create access to *kora* music in Britain. Ahmed Sheikh, Senegalese poet, musician, and writer, is a founder of African Dawn. Included is a list of source material on *kora* music in the National Sound Archive in South Kensington, London. Excellent black and white photographs.

349a. **The Chicago manual of style: for authors, editors, and copywriters**. 13th ed., revised and expanded. Chicago: University of Chicago Press, 1982. 737pp.
A primary - almost mandatory - reference tool, packed with information of vital importance to anyone involved with writing or with books. It is rare not to find an answer to even the most complex of questions pertaining to accepted practice for abbreviations, treatment of foreign languages, names and titles, punctuation, scholarly notes, bibliographies, and much more. Almost all terms pertaining to writing, books, and book production may be found in this book. Even the long-forgotten rules for generating roman numerals are included. Meticulously organized. Bibliography and an index.

350. **Chicago studies in ethnomusicology**. Chicago, Illinois.
This series, begun in 1990, is published by the University of Chicago Press. Editors are Philip V. Bohlman and Bruno Nettl. The publisher's catalogue says that the series will represent a wide range of aesthetic and social scientific approaches. The following books appear as separate entries in this bibliography:
- **Bender, Wolfgang**. *Sweet mother*, 1991.
- **Comparative musicology and anthropology of music**. Bruno Nettl and Philip V. Bohlman, eds., 1991.
- **Erlmann, Veit**. *African stars: studies in black South African performance*, 1991.
- **Kartomi, Margaret J**. *On concepts and classification of musical instruments*, 1990.
- **Waterman, Christopher Alan Waterman**. *Jùjú: a social history and ethnography of an African popular music*, 1990.

351. **Chima, Alex B**. "The suitability of instruments in the liturgy." In **Symposium musico-ethnologicum**. Edited by Johannes Overath,

84-114. **MUSICES APTATIO** 1980 (Roma: CIMS, 1980).
The work is trilingual, in English, French, and German. Bibliography. Abstracted in **RILM**, 1985.

352. **Christopherson, Larry Lee.** TEACHING AFRICAN MUSIC WITH THE AID OF VIDEOTAPED PERFORMANCES AND DEMONSTRATIONS BY AFRICAN MUSICIANS. Dissertation, Northwestern University, 1973. 252pp.

353. **Ciparisse, Gérard.** *Le chant traditionnel: une source de documentation orale. Chants des Bampangu, Zaïre.* Brussels, CEDAF, 1972. 31pp. (Les Cahiers du CEDAF, 1972, 1. Série 1: Anthropologie)
Issued in portfolio. French or Ki-kongo. Includes phonodisc in slipcase, also issued separately as no. 5 of Opnamen van Afrikaanse muziek.

354. **Clark, Èbùn.** THE HUBERT ÒGŨNDÉ THEATRE COMPANY. Master's Thesis, University of Leeds, 1974.

355. **Clayton, Anthony.** *Communication for new loyalties: African soldiers' songs.* Athens, Ohio: Ohio University Center for International Studies, Africa Program, 1978. 56pp. (Papers in international studies. Africa series, no. 34)
Music, illustrations. War-songs.

356. **Cleaned the crocodile's teeth: Nuer song.** Translated by Terese Svoboda. Greenfield Center, N.Y.: Greenfield Review Press, c1985. 104pp.
The poet/translator learned the Nuer language, then took on the challenge of living with the Nuer, recording and transcribing their songs. The result is a work of art containing the most sensitive translations and beautiful photographs imaginable. From the treeless flat land of the Sudan emerges a lyrical poetry that conforms to the highest standards of poetry anywhere in the world. The chapters are divided into seven song categories. Preface, by Francis Mading Deng, points out "what the recording, translating, and publishing of oral literature can mean for the dignity and survival of cultures otherwise threatened with extinction."

357. **Clegg, Johnny.** "An examination of the *umzansi* dance style." In **Symposium on Ethnomusicology.** (3rd: 1982: University of Natal) [4th: 1983: Rhodes University] *Papers presented at the Third and Fourth Symposia on Ethnomusicology,* Music Department, University of Natal, Durban, 16th to 19th September 1982, 64-70; Music Department, Rhodes University, 7th to 8th October 1983. Grahamstown, South Africa: International Library of African Music, 1984.
The *umzansi* dance originated in Durban and its outlying areas. The place of

song is interwoven in this paper, with some mention also of the use of drums. The dance itself is the focus, however, and there are diagrams that demonstrate how it is performed. Note that this paper is *listed* under *4th* Symposium, but is preceded by the statement: "3rd Symposium - Durban."

358. **Clegg, Johnny**. "The music of Zulu immigrant workers in Johannesburg - a focus on concertina and guitar." In **Symposium on Ethnomusicology**. [1st: 1980: Rhodes University] *Papers presented at the Symposium on Ethnomusicology, Music Department, Rhodes University, on 10th and 11th October, 1980*, 2-9. Grahamstown: International Library of African Music, Institute of Social and Economic Research, Rhodes University, 1981.

359. **Clegg, Johnny**. "Towards an understanding of African dance: the Zulu *Isishameni* style." In **Symposium on Ethnomusicology**. (2nd: 1981: Rhodes University) *Papers presented at the Second Symposium on Ethnomusicology, Music Department, Rhodes University, 24th to 26th September, 1981*, 8-14. Edited by Andrew Tracey. Grahamstown: International Library of African Music, Institute of Social and Economic Research, Rhodes University, 1982.
Not much on music except for mention of rhythm and beat.

360. **Cole, Ann**, *et al. Children are children are children: an activity approach to exploring Brazil, France, Iran, Japan, Nigeria and the U.S.S.R.* Illustrations by Lois Axeman. Boston: Little, Brown and Company, 1978. 212pp.
A joyous book, with fanciful illustrations and countless creative activities for children as they learn about other cultures. There is background information on each country - its history, geography, languages, customs, foods. Every imaginable kind of fascinating art or craft is possible with this book's guidance. The Nigerian section encourages children to compose praise songs, make African-type instruments from local substances, perform rhythmic exercises, sing in call-response, dance in highlife style, tell stories with rhythmic accompaniment. The Brazilian section has activities relating to carnival, samba schools, song-writing, constructing Brazilian-type musical instruments. Bibliography.

361. **Collaer, Paul, and Jürgen Elsner**. *Nordafrika*. With collaboration of Brahim Bahloul...[et al.]. Leipzig: VEB Deutscher Verlag für Musik, c1983. 205pp. (Musikgeschichte in Bildern 1: Musikethnologie, Part 8)
Includes pictorial works of art pertaining to music of North Africa. Bibliography, index, illustrations, portraits.

Collège Libermann
See: **Chants d'enfants: en duálá et basaá, 336.**

362. **Collins, Elizabeth**. "Musical traditions in Liberia." In **African music: meeting in Yaoundé (Cameroon) 23-27 February 1970, organized by UNESCO**, 143-144. Paris: *La revue musicale*, 1972.
English translation of the following entry.

363. **Collins, Elizabeth**. "Les traditions musicales au Liberia." In **La musique africaine, réunion de Yaoundé (Cameroun)** [sur les traditions musicales de l'Afrique subsaharienne], **23-27 février 1970, organisée par l'UNESCO**, 141-142. Paris: *La revue musicale*," Richard-Masse, 1972.
See previous entry (362) for English translation.

364. **Collins, John**. *African pop roots: the inside rhythms of Africa.* Edited by Sylvia Moore. London; New York: W. Foulsham & Company, c1985. 120pp.
Includes index.

365. **Collins, John**. *E. T. Mensah, the king of highlife.* London: Off the Record Press, [1986?]. 51pp.
Mensah - trumpet and saxophone player, and bandleader - is known throughout West Africa as the King of Highlife, and is generally regarded as the single most influential musician in highlife's history. It was he who disseminated highlife throughout West Africa, even touring with Nkrumah as a kind of musical ambassador. Born in Ghana in 1917, Mensah's formal photo at age 18, saxophone in hand, appears at the front of the book. Mensah's famous Tempo Band performed in many styles, and delivered its songs in a variety of languages. Twelve chapters comprise this biography, six pages of plates, and a "Provisional discography."

366. **Collins, John**. *Hidden roots of African rhythm.* London: Zwan, 1988.

367. **Collins, John**. *Musicmakers of West Africa.* Washington, D.C.: Three Continents Press, c1985. 177pp.
For the most part, this book consist of interviews with West African urban musicians. Index and bibliography.

368. **Colloque sur l'art nègre**. Rapports. 1.-; 1966- . [Paris, Présence africaine].
In French. Volumes 1 (1967) and 2 (1971) of this series contain many significant writings on the arts. The Festival mondial des arts nègre, that occurred in Dakar, April 1-24, 1966, was organized by the SAC. (Societé africaine de Culture) in conjunction with UNESCO. The essays that focus primarily on African music are listed alphabetically below, though all are well worth examining. (See also the

next entry (369) for the English translation of the Colloquium.)
- **Bebey, Francis**. "La musique africaine moderne," Vol. 1, 499-516.
- **Copans, Simon**. "L'héritage africain dans la musique des Américains," Vol. 1, 231-241.
- **Eno Belinga, Samuel-Martin**. "La musique traditionelle d'Afrique Noire," Vol. 2, 189-198.
- **Lapassade, Georges**. "Un art marginal (Essai sociologique sur le dépérissement de l'art musical nègre dans le Maghreb) [al-Maghrib]," Vol. 2, 199-210.
- **Nketia, J. H. Kwabena**. "La musique dans la culture africaine," Vol. 1. 147-191.
- **Obama, Jean-Baptiste**. "La musique africaine traditionelle, ses fonctions sociales et sa signification philosophique," 193-230, Vol. 1, 193-230.
- **Pepper, Herbert**. "La notion d'unité, notion clé de l'expression nègre-africaine," Vol. 1, 231-241.

369. **Colloquium on Negro Art, Dakar, 1966: Function and significance of African Negro art in the life of the people, March 30-April 8, 1966**. Organized by the Society of African Culture (S.A.C.) [Paris, Présence africaine, 1968]. 600pp.

This publication represents the English translation of most of the essays in Volume 1 of the immediately preceding entry. Only four of those on music, listed above, are included:
- **Copans, Simon**. "The African heritage in the music of the American Negro," 369-395.
- **Nketia, J. H. Kwabena**. "Music in African culture," 143-186.
- **Obama, Jean-Baptiste**. "Traditional African music," 187-222.
- **Pepper, Herbert**. "The notion of unity: the key to Negro-African expression," 223-232.

370. **Comitas, Lambros**. *The complete Caribbeana, 1900-1975: a bibliographic guide to the scholarly literature*. Under the auspices of the Research Institute for the Study of Man. 4 vols. Millwood, New York: KTO Press, c1977. 2139pp.

The volumes treat different subjects: People, Institutions, Resources, and Indexes. In Volume 2 on Institutions, there is a subdivision, Cultural Continuities, within which are chapters on Values and Norms; Ethnic and National Identity; Religion; Folklore; Language and Linguistics; Cultural Change, and Chapter 22, on Creative Arts and Recreation. The latter chapter is a rich resource for African-related materials, some of which tie into music. Herskovits' name is well-represented, as are a number of other renowned scholars. No annotations. Entries could be more detailed. Caribbean map on lining paper.

371. **Companhia de Diamantes de Angola**. *Folclore musical de Angola: colecção de fitas magnéticas e discos. Angola folk-music: collection of magnetic tapes and discs.* Lisbon, 1961.

Angolan music - songs, instruments. Text in English and Portuguese. Maps, plates.

372. **Comparative musicology and anthropology of music: essays on the history of ethnomusicology**. Edited by Bruno Nettl and

Phillip V. Bohlman. Chicago: University of Chicago Press, 1971. 378pp. (Chicago studies in ethnomusicology)

The advance flier accurately described the book: "Essays by nineteen scholars from five countries explore significant issues in the history of ethnomusicology, its methodology and theoretical foundations, and provide a critique of the discipline." Included are illustrations, tables, bibliographical references, an index. Of the selected essays that follow, the one by Shelemay, though not specifically on African music, is considered significant to the subject of this book in light of the extraordinary and ongoing proliferation of recorded African or African-derived urban music today.

- **Béhague, Gerard**. "Reflections on the ideological history of Latin American ethnomusicology," 56-68.
- **Blum, Stephen**. "European musical terminology and the music of Africa," 3-36.
- **Shelemay, Kay Kaufman**. "Recording technology, the record industry, and ethnomusicological scholarship," 277-292.
- **Waterman, Christopher A.** "The uneven development of Africanist ethnomusicology: three issues and a critique."

The complete Caribbeana, 1900-1975.
See: **Comitas, Lambros, 370.**

373. Compositores e interpretes baianos: 50 anos de musica popular. Prepared by Bibliotecários do Estado da Bahia. [Salvador: Associção Professional dos Bibliotecários do Estado da Bahia, 1982]. 60pp.

In Portuguese. This is a catalogue with biographical information. Bibliography, index.

374. THE CONCH. 1969- . Buffalo, New York., S. O. Anozie.

This was published semiannually, but discontinued, apparently with Volume 13 in 1981. The Periodical was entitled: "A Biafran journal of literary and cultural analysis." In 1971 a special issue appeared on Igbo traditional life, culture and literature. Two of the papers on music are cited below:

- **Egudu, Romanus N.** "Igbo and Ozo festival songs and poems," Vol. 3, No.2 (1971): 76-88.
- **Nzewi, Meki**. "The rhythm of dance in Igbo music," Vol. 3, No.2 (1971): 104-108.

375. CONGO DISQUE: **revue de la musique congolaise moderne**. B.P. 6112 Kinshasa 6, Zaïre.

Information was obtained from **ULRICH'S**. Volume 5, 1967 is mentioned, but not the date the first volume appeared. It seems to be an ongoing publication.

CONGO-TERVUREN
See: AFRIKA-TERVUREN, 52.

376. Conrath, Philippe. *Johnny Clegg: la passion zoulou.* Paris: Seghers, 1988. 263pp.

C

377. **Contes et chants du Tchad (région d'Abéché)**. Edited and transcribed by Patrice Jullien de Pommerol. Directed by Gérard Troupeau. Paris: École pratique des hautes études, 4th section: Diffusion, Librairie de l'Harmattan, 1977, cover 1978. 447pp.
Chad tales, songs, folklore. Introductory comments in French. The tales themselves are in French and Arabic dialect. Maps (one folded) and notated music. Bibliography.

378. **Conway, Eugenia Cecelia**. THE AFRO-AMERICAN TRADITIONS OF THE FOLK BANJO. Dissertation, University of North Carolina at Chapel Hill, 1980. 259pp.
The author says that written records, before the exchange of folk banjo traditions by Afro-Americans and Anglo-Americans, show that slaves brought the banjo with them from Africa. Even though banjo styles and techniques have evolved and now show many influences, Afro-American traditions are given the most emphasis in this study, irrespective of whether they are any longer traceable directly to Africa. (Dena Epstein has done exhaustive research on this same subject, **533, 534**.)

379. **Cooke, Peter R.** THE GANDA NDERE: AN EXAMINATION OF THE NOTCHED FLUTE OF THE GANDA PEOPLE OF UGANDA, ITS USAGES, MANUFACTURE AND REPERTOIRE, WITH SPECIAL MENTION OF THE ROYAL FLUTE BANDS OF THE FORMER KINGS OF BUGANDA, THE SOUND TEXT COLLATED FROM TAPE NOS. 5, 16 and 35 RECORDED DURING 1965-1968. Master's Thesis, University of Wales, 1970. 96pp. and phonotape.

Cooke, Peter R.
See also: **Twenty-four songs of Uganda, 1597.**

380. **Coolen, Michael Theodore**. TO PRAISE THE PROPHET: THE XALAM TRADITION OF THE SENEGAMBIA. Dissertation, University of Washington, 1981. 192pp.
The *xalam*, found in the Senegambia region, plays an important role in the history of plucked lutes in western Africa.

381. **Copans, Simon**. "The African heritage in the music of the American Negro." In **Colloquium on Negro Art, Dakar, 1966**, 369-395. Organized by the Society of African Culture (S.A.C.) [Paris, Présence africaine, 1968]
Note that the original version that follows speaks of the African heritage on music of the "Américains," not the "American Negro."

382. **Copans, Simon**. "L'héritage africain dans la musique des Américains." In **Colloque sur l'art nègre**. Rapports. Vol. 1(1967): 231-241. [Paris: Présence africaine]
This is the original French version (translated in the preceding entry).

383. **Coplan, David B.** *Eloquent knowledge: Lesotho migrants' songs and the anthropology of experience.* [Chicago]: University of Chicago, African Studies Workshop, 1987. 25pp.
Coplan is concerned with the need for an "internal, culturally reflexive account of the experience of labor migration" from a conscious *Sotho* viewpoint. Believing that oral-literature has the most potential to reveal this, he documents the "eloquent knowledge" (an aesthetic and spiritual concept) revealed in the beautiful and heroic texts of *lifela* songs - songs that are related to, and have evolved from, praise songs of the past. Sensitively done. Bibliography.

384. **Coplan, David B.** "Go to my town, Cape Coast! The social history of Ghanaian highlife." In **Eight Urban Cultures: tradition and change.** Edited by Bruno Nettl, 96-114. Urbana: University of Illinois Press, 1978.
Bibliography. Abstracted in **RILM**, 1985.

385. **Coplan, David B.** *In the time of cannibals: Besotho working-class aurature and the meaning of Sesotho.* [Cape Town]: Centre for African Studies, University of Cape Town, 1989. 37pp. (Africa seminar)
The author uses the word "aurature" as an extension of the term "orature," popularized by Ngugi wa Thiong'o, and says that he "wants to bring the methods of cultural anthropology to bear upon indigenous genres created outside formal organizational structures in autonomous response to the social transformations wrought by colonialism, and the migrant labour system." The music of migrants, particularly the song form deriving from praise-poetry known as *lifela*, is a major interest. The broader meaning of the term "Sesotho" is explored. Song texts, no transcriptions.

386. **Coplan, David B.** *In township tonight!: South Africa's black city music and theatre.* Johannesburg, Ravan Press, 1985. 278pp.
This is based on Coplan's doctoral dissertation, "The Urbanization of African performing arts in South Africa." Christopher Waterman describes it as a "richly detailed and lucid account of the development of black popular performing arts in South Africa, making use of historical, ethnological, and musicological data." Includes a bibliography and index. This receives a lengthy review by Chris Smith in **Keskidee** no. 1, 1990.

387. **Coplan, David B.** A STUDY OF THE CULTURAL DETERMINANTS OF MUSICAL FORM AND THE ROLE OF MUSIC IN THE TRANSMISSION OF ORAL TRADITION IN A TRADITIONAL WEST AFRICAN SOCIETY. Master's Thesis, University of Ghana, 1972. 207pp.

388. **Coplan, David B.** THE URBANIZATION OF AFRICAN PERFORMING ARTS IN SOUTH AFRICA. Dissertation, Indiana University, 1980. 482pp.
continued

A superior anthropological analysis of performing arts in South Africa, primarily black music and dance from the 19th century to 1960. Coplan believes that the results of his study "advance the comparative study of processes of urbanization, especially in colonial situations," and that they "support the argument that history and social science are indispensable to an understanding of performance culture." There are 3 maps, a bibliography, examples of 9 songs. Included is a most useful glossary. (Dedicated to the memory of Alan P. Merriam.) Much of the material has been incorporated into Coplan's, *In township tonight*. Illustrations, maps, music, bibliography.

389. **Coplan, David B., and David Rycroft**. "*Marabi*: the emergence of African working-class music in Johannesburg." In **A tribute to Alan P. Merriam**. Edited by Caroline Card, [*et al.*], 43-65. Bloomington, Indiana: Indiana University. (Archives of Traditional Music), c1981.
Music, bibliography, charts, tables.

390. **Corbitt, John Nathan.** THE HISTORY AND DEVELOPMENT OF MUSIC USED IN THE BAPTIST CHURCHES ON THE COAST OF KENYA: THE DEVELOPMENT OF INDIGENOUS CHURCH MUSIC, 1953-1984. Dissertation, Southwestern Baptist Theological Seminary, 1985.
The purpose of this dissertation was to define the primary influences on the body of music used in the Baptist churches on the Coast of Kenya. Traced are the historical and musical developments of four musical styles that have become indigenous to the church. **(UMI)**

391. **Cornelius, Steven Harry**. THE CONVERGENCE OF POWER: AN INVESTIGATION INTO THE MUSIC LITURGY OF SANTERÍA IN NEW YORK CITY. Dissertation, University of California, 1989. 358pp.
Ritual music expression, as found in song, drumming and dance, is central to Santería, a Yorùbá and Catholic-influenced Afro-Cuban religion, and helps to bridge the gap between the physical and spiritual worlds. This study of Santería in New York City is concerned with how "communicative power" is generated, maintained, and manipulated, and includes a taxonomic study of musical instruments, formal analysis of musical structure, and analysis of the musician's role in religious ritual.

392. **Cornelius, Steven Harry**. "Encapsulating power: meaning and taxonomy of the musical instruments of Santería in New York City." **SELECTED REPORTS IN ETHNOMUSICOLOGY** 8 (1990): 125-141.
In the introduction Cornelius says, "Santería is a syncretic mix of Yorùbá belief with those of Catholicism." Some of the instruments examined are The Bell (i.e., *Guataca*, a metal hoe blade); *Acheré*, a small rattle; *Guiry*, a scraper; *Shekere* [Yorùbá = Ṣẹ̀kẹ̀rẹ̀], a hollowed-out gourd with beads on the outside; Conga Drum, and *Batá* [Yorùbá = Bàtá]. The Appendix has a terse chart called, "Musical Instruments and their *Orisha*" [Yorùbá = Òrìṣà]. Footnotes, bibliography, one photograph.

392a. **Corrêa de Azevedo, Luiz H.** "*Vissungos* - Negro work songs of the diamond district in Minas Gerais, Brazil." In **Music in the Americas**. Edited by George List and Juan Orrego-Salas, 64-67. [Bloomington]: Indiana University Research Center in Anthropology, Folklore and Linguistics, 1967.

This is a short paper with only a few notes, but the author says that it was not intended to be more than an objective report concerning one of the most singular examples of African culture to be found in Brazil. He claims that the work songs, called *Vissungos*, are unlike any other in Brazil, and that many are antiphonal.

Coughlan, Alice Diane
See: **Stefaniszyn, Bronislaw**. *African lyric poetry*, **1500**.

393. **COURIER**. 1948- . Paris, France: Public Information Office of UNESCO.

Issued monthly. For many years this was known as the **UNESCO COURIER**. Available in many languages, and can be obtained on microfilm and microfiche from **UMI**. Indexed in **CURRENT CONTENTS, ARTS AND HUMANITIES CITATION INDEX**, and others. Pertinent examples follows.

- **Bebey, Francis**. "Vivante et ancestrale musique de l'Afrique," vol. 25, no. 10 (1972): 14-19.
- **Euba, Akin**. "The dichotomy of African music," vol. 26, no. 6 (1973): 65-68.
- **Mbabi-Katana, Solomon**. "A song for every season: music in African life from the cradle to the grave," vol. 30, no. 5 (1977): 26-32.

394. **Courlander, Harold**. *The Drum and the hoe: life and lore of the Haitian people*. Berkeley: University of California Press, 1960. 371pp.

"A definitive masterpiece," says the *New York Times*. Abundant references to Africa. Describes many Haitian rites, and other aspects of culture having strong African roots. Information is also given on African-derived songs (in Creole), dances, various drums, and other instruments. Mieczyslaw Kolinski, who transcribed 180 songs, found that musical phrasing does not necessarily start at the same point as the word phrasing [a common Africanism]. Song texts in English are in the Appendix. Ninety remarkable photographs of Haitian music-related activities enhance the book. Bibliography, discography. Be not dissuaded by the fact that the index lists very little under Africa or Music.

395. **Courlander, Harold**. *Haiti singing*. New York: Cooper Square Publishers, 1973. 273pp. (Library of Latin-American history and culture)

This is a reprint of the 1939 edition published by the University of North Carolina Press, Chapel Hill. On Haitian Creole songs, dance music, dancing, and more. The island of Haiti is particularly rich in African retentions. Bibliography.

396. **Courlander, Harold**. *Negro folk music, U.S.A.* New York: Columbia University Press, 1963. 324pp.

continued

The title is somewhat misleading. Actually, there are numerous references throughout this book to African culture, and African music retentions in the United States, the Caribbean, and even Brazil, since Courlander's perspective is broad. Almost every chapter contains something significant about Africa, no matter whether that subject be instruments, dance, various kinds of songs, blues, ring games. Though this is an older book, its value remains. There are notes, a fine index, and an excellent bibliography that contains some references to works on African music. The discography includes African and Caribbean music, along with that of the United States.

397. Courlander, Harold. *A treasury of African folklore: the oral literature, traditions, myths, legends, epics, tales, recollections, wisdom, sayings, and humor of Africa.* New York: Crown Publishers, [1975]. 617pp.

The title mentions everything *but* music, even though the book contains such gems as: several pages of Akan drum poetry; translation of a song of the Twa of Rwanda; "Music among the Bongo," Courlander's qualifying introduction to an excerpt from Georg Schweinfurth's, *The heart of Africa*...(observations during the explorer's travels in Central Africa from 1868-1871); a fragment of a Tutsi song-poem from 1880; a brief transcription in dialogue form, by Rose Brandel, in which a *mwami* is asked for assistance, and perhaps another worthwhile item or two. Bibliography.

398. Creating a wider interest in traditional music: proceedings of a conference held in Berlin in cooperation with the International Music Council, 12th to the 17th June, 1967. [Edited by Alain Daniélou and others]. Berlin: International Institute for Comparative Music Studies and Documentation, [1967?]. 240pp.

A number of papers on various subjects were presented at this conference. The following are selected for listing:

- **Arom, Simha**. "The traditional music in the Central African Republic," 135-140.
- **Ismail, Mahi**. "Traditional music in the Sudan," 104-111.
- **El-Mahdi, Salah** [Al-Mahdī Ṣalāḥ]. "The problems of traditional music in Tunisia," 154-156.
- **Nikiprowetzky, Tolia**. "Means of preservation and diffusion of traditional music in French-speaking Africa," 132-134.
- **Nketia, J. H. Kwabena**. "Traditional music in Ghana," 120-127.
- **Santoro, Claudio**. "Means of preservation and diffusion of traditional music in Latin America," 199-203.
- **Wachsmann, Klaus**. "Traditional music in Uganda," 128-131.

399. Cross rhythms. 1983- . Bloomington, Indiana: Trickster Press, c1983- . (1983: Occasional papers in African folklore; 1985- : Occasional papers in African folklore/music)

At the time of writing, three volumes had appeared in years 1983, 1985, and 1989. Those articles specifically concerned with African music are:

•**Anyidoho, Kofi**. "The Haikotu song and dance club of Wheta: a communal celebration of individual poetic talent,"vol. 2: 173-192.
•**Avorgbedor, Daniel K.** "The transmission, preservation and realisation of song texts: a psycho-musical approach," vol. 2: 67-92.
•**Card, Caroline**. "*Tende* music among the Tuareg: the history of a tradition," vol. 1: 155-171.
•**Darkwa, Asante**. "Traditional music and dance practices of the Wataito of Kenya: a current survey," vol. 3: 155-169.
•**Kubik, Gerhard**. "The emics of African musical rhythm," vol. 2: 6-66.
•**Kubik, Gerhard**. "Subjective patterns in African music," vol. 3: 129-154.
•**Timpunza, Mvula Enoch S.** "Mngeniso ritual and Ngomi ethnic identity," vol. 3: 109-128.
•**Timpunza, Mvula Enoch S.** "Tumbuka pounding songs in the management of familial conflicts," vol. 2: 93-113.
•**Yankah, Kwesi**. "Beyond the spoken word: *aural* literature in Africa," vol. 2: 114-146.

400. **La Crotte tenace et autres contes ngbaka-ma'bo de République centrafricaine**. Compiled by Marie-José Derive, Jean Derive, and M. C. Thomas. Marcel Mavode, Collaborator. Paris: Société d'études linguistiques et anthropologiques de France: Avec le concours du Centre National de la recherche scientifique et de l'Office de la recherche scientifique et technique outre-mer, 1975. 228pp. (Langues et civilisations à tradition orale, 13)

Songs and tales of the Ngbaka-Ma'bo people of the Central African Republic. Each of 13 Ngbaka-ma'bo texts is translated into three French versions - one, word-for-word, another, into "intelligent French," and a final "literary" translation that attempts to capture the more subtle aspects of the oral tradition, incorporating speech effects, and sometimes the expression of gesture. Summaries in English, French, German, Russian, and Spanish. Bibliography, indexes, 2 sound discs.

401. **Cultural atlas of Africa**. Edited by Jocelyn Murray. N.Y. Facts on File; Oxford: Phaidon, c1981. 240pp.

The editor created this stunning book because no prior works, in her opinion, provided an introduction to Africa as a whole. Divided into: The Physical Background, The Cultural Background, The Nations of Africa. Pages 90-95, under Music and Dance, provide an informed general orientation to African music and musical instruments, drawing from writings of Nketia, Kubik, Blacking, A. M. Jones, Lomax, and Oliver. Rhythm gets particular attention. New World cultures are mentioned, and there are brilliant and unusual color photos everywhere. There is a Gazeteer, bibliography, and index that leads to passing mention of music and dance elsewhere in the book.

402. **Cuney-Hare, Maud**. *Negro musicians and their music*. New York: DeCapo Press, 1974.

This is a reprint of an old classic first published in 1936 by Associated Publishers, Washington. There is a bibliography, illustrations, and an appendix featuring African instruments (pages 286-412). Many of the perceptive insights and analyses of this musicologist, pianist, lecturer were way before her time. She wrote, for example, that black music "ignores any division of time that follows the natural pulse of a regular metrical beat," and also referred to accents being anticipated or held over beyond their expected time - subjects treated years later by Richard Waterman and A. M. Jones.

A CURRENT BIBLIOGRAPHY ON AFRICAN AFFAIRS
See: **African Bibliographic Center, 31, 32.**

403. **CURRENT CONTENTS** (Arts and Humanities). 1979- . Institute for Scientific Information. 3501 Market Street, Philadelphia, Pennsylvania 1904.
Issued bi-monthly, and described as having: "Tables of contents of the world's leading publications covering art and architecture, performing arts, language and linguistics, history, philosophy, religion, and theology." It is also available online. There is a certain ambiguity in that the term Current Contents can also apply to subjects or disciplines other than those indicated above. It is assumed that when **ULRICH'S** indicates that a journal (listed in the present bibliography) is indexed in **CURRENT CONTENTS**, the Arts and Humanities subsection is meant. **CURRENT CONTENTS AFRICA** is a separate publication.

404. **CURRENT CONTENTS AFRICA**. 1976- . Münich, Germany: K. G. Saur. (Published on behalf of the Frankfurt Stadt- und Universitätsbibliothek)
Issued quarterly. A unique and most useful periodical that gives facsimile reproductions of the contents pages of Africanist serials. Though it is somewhat frustrating not to be able to examine likely articles, or to know their inclusive pages merely from a contents page, **CCA** still represents a marvelous and even exciting screening device from which one can go an original source. At the beginning of each bound volume is a list of periodicals covered. Contents pages are arranged alphabetically, and periodicals are included from all over the world. See next entry (**405**) for the earlier version from which this continued.

405. **CURRENT CONTENTS AFRIKA**. 1975-1978. Frankfurt am Main: Stadt- und Universitätsbibliothek Frankfurt am Main.
Listed in one reference as being "completely irregular," this was the progenitor of the very useful **CURRENT CONTENTS AFRICA**, listed above **(404)** and had the same format.

406. **Curriculum materials for teachers**. 2d ed. Urbana, Illinois: University of Illinois at Urbana-Champaign, [1985]. 353pp. (African studies)
Packed with reliable information on Africa, and extremely comprehensive. The compendium, which is spiral-bound, consists of many short papers well-organized by subject. There are maps, charts, illustrations, music notations, and 13 (!) bibliographies over and beyond those in individual papers. These bibliographies sometimes also contain items on music, with indications of how they might be obtained. Pages 189-191 contain the music and the words (in a number of African

languages) to *Nkosi Sikelel' iAfrika*. The book is a "must" for teachers involved in any way with African studies, or African-American studies. Selected papers follow:

- **Asiama, Simeon**. "African musical instruments," 178-184.
- **Asiama, Simeon**. "An African musician's thoughts on teaching in American schools," 185-187.
- **Asiama, Simeon, and Louise Crane**. "Listening to African music: some resources," 328-333.
- **Asiama, Simeon**. "Singing games from Ghana," 270-278.
- **Yanco, Jennifer**. "Lingala: 'La langue la plus chantée d'Afrique,'" 233-234.

407. Curry, Beulah Agnes Bonner. AN EVALUATION OF AFRICAN AND AFRO-AMERICAN MUSIC IN SELECTED ELEMENTARY MUSIC TEXTBOOK SERIES AND RECOMMENDATIONS FOR SUPPLEMENTAL SONG MATERIALS. Dissertation, University of Houston, 1982. [208]pp.

The author studied the quantity, and quality of presentation, of African and African-American music in five major publishers' elementary music textbook series, the particular area of focus being songs in Grades 2 and 5. These songs were also compared with music of other cultures. As might have been expected, there were serious sins of omission, which Curry describes and documents. She gives specific suggestions for curricula enrichment - traditional materials in the form of singing games, recreational songs, parables, and lullabies. Considerably less African source materials than African-American.

D

408. **Dagogo-Jack, Charles E.** KALABARI CHILDREN'S PLAYGROUND SONGS. Master's Thesis, University of Jos, Nigeria, 1985.

409. **Damas, Léon-Gontran.** *African songs of love, war, grief and abuse.* Designed and illustrated by Georgina Betts. [Translated by Miriam Koshland and Ulli Beier]. Ìbàdàn: Mbari, 1961. 40pp. Translation of: *Poèmes nègres sur des airs africains*, published in Paris: GLM, 1948. (Poésie commune, 6)
Song texts, illustrations.

410. **Daniel, Francisco, Salvador.** *The music and musical instruments of the Arab: with introduction on how to appreciate Arab music.* Edited with notes, memoir, bibliography and thirty examples and illustrations by Henry George Farmer. Portland, Maine: Longwood Press, 1976. 272pp.
This is a reprint of the 1915 edition published by Scribner's, New York. The index, in German, has references to Tunisia, Egypt, Morocco, Algeria, Algiers, Cairo, Morocco, and other African cities and countries.

411. **Daniel, Yvonne Laverne Payne.** ETHNOGRAPHY OF RUMBA: DANCE AND SOCIAL CHANGE IN CONTEMPORARY CUBA. University of California, Berkeley, 1989. 461.
Since the music of rumba music is African-derived, and music is inextricably bound with the dance known as *rumba*, this dissertation is considered appropriate for inclusion here. In the author's words, "As an example of dance anthropology within the Caribbean, this study illuminates values and attitudes which are embodied in dance. Meaning in dance is revealed at the world-view, ritual and performance, symbolic, group, individual and movement levels and the multivocalic nature of dance is demonstrated. The cultural contexts of Rumba facilitate an understanding of the profound complexities surrounding change in contemporary Cuba." **(UMI)**

412. **Daniélou, Alain.** "Les langages musicaux de l'Afrique noire." In **La musique africaine, réunion de Yaoundé (Cameroun)** [sur les traditions musicales de l'Afrique subsaharienne], **23-27 février 1970, organisée par l'UNESCO**, 49-55. Paris: *La revue musicale*, Richard-Masse, 1972.
Following is the English translation.

413. **Daniélou, Alain.** "The musical languages of Black Africa." In **African music: meeting in Yaoundé (Cameroon) 23-27 February 1970, organized by UNESCO**, 5-57. Paris: *La revue musicale*, 1972.
Translation of preceding entry.

414. **Les danses du Cameroun - Cameroonian dances.** 2d ed. Yaoundé: Direction des affaires culturelles du Ministère de l'éducation, de la culture et de la formation professionelle, 1971. 127pp. (Culture camerounaise, Cameroonian culture)
Photocopied, with no great loss. One would like, however, to see the originals of photographs that can still look so good in this reproduced form. The work is comprehensive, with much to be found on music in conjunction with particular dances. Musical instruments are named, along with the texts of songs used, the general role music plays in the dance, and even the tie-in of music to entrances and exits of dancers. Most essays are by experts on a particular dance, the majority written in French, but some in English. A map indicates the dances associated with Cameroon areas.

415. **Daraca, Jerry.** *How to play congo rhythms for rock and soul.* Ontario, California: Congeros Publications, c1974. 31pp.
Perhaps a far-fetched entry, but this simple book has sketches of an African drum (probably from Uganda), and African-derived drums from Haiti, Cuba (plus similarly constructed drums from Tahiti, Panama and Asia), and instructions on how to produce open tones, tap tones and accent tones. Drawings and instructions are uncomplicated and clear. Exercises. It would be interesting to compare Daraca's methods of sound production and concepts of desirable tone with those of Africans or African-Americans, especially when the drums used are similar and played with two hands. Do any commonalities exist that extend beyond culture or style?

416. **Darah, G. G.** "Aesthetic socialization of youth through dance and music in Urhobo society." **ODÙ** New Series no. 28 (1985): 46-56.
Notes.

417. **Dargie, David.** "Group composition and church music workshops." In **Symposium on Ethnomusicology.** [1st: 1980: Rhodes University] *Papers presented at the Symposium on Ethnomusicology, Music Department, Rhodes University, on 10th and 11th October, 1980,* 10-13. Grahamstown: International Library of African Music, Institute of Social and Economic Research, Rhodes University, 1981.

418. **Dargie, David.** "Music and liberation." In **Symposium on Ethnomusicology.** (3rd: 1982: University of Natal) [4th: 1983: Rhodes University] *Papers presented at the Third and Fourth Symposia on Ethnomusicology,* Music Department, University of Natal, Durban, 16th to 19th September 1982, 9-14; Music Department, Rhodes University, 7th to 8th October 1983. Grahamstown, South Africa: International Library of African Music, 1984.
Note that this paper is in the 3rd Symposium. (The 3rd and 4th Symposia are bound in one volume.)

D

419. **Dargie, David**. "Musical bows in southern Africa." **AFRICA INSIGHT** 16, no. 1 (1986): 42-52.

420. **Dargie, David**. "Some recent discoveries and recordings in Xhosa music." In **Symposium on Ethnomusicology**. (5th: 1984: University of Cape Town). *Papers presented at the fifth Symposium on Ethnomusicology: Faculty of Music, University of Cape Town, August 30th-September 1st, 1984*, 29-35. Grahamstown: International Library of African Music, 1985.

421. **Dargie, David**. "A theoretical approach to composition in Xhosa style." In **Symposium on Ethnomusicology**. (2nd: 1981: Rhodes University) *Papers presented at the Second Symposium on Ethnomusicology, Music Department, Rhodes University, 24th to 26th September, 1981*. Edited by Andrew Tracey, 15-22. Grahamstown: International Library of African Music, Institute of Social and Economic Research, Rhodes University, 1982.

422. **Dargie, David**. *Xhosa music: its techniques and instruments, with a collection of songs*. Cape Town: D. Philip, 1988. 235pp.
Based on the author's doctoral dissertation. A probing study that includes a history of music and musicians of the Lumko District, a great deal of information on the Xhosa people and their culture, and an informed and comprehensive investigation of Xhosa music itself. Includes Xhosa lyrics with English translations. Even though transcriptions were designed "to make both pitch and rhythm immediately visible through lines and spaces," they hardly end up to be graspable at first sight. Certainly they would be difficult to reproduce from the printed page. Bibliography, recording list, 43 songs, photos, and a sound cassette.

423. **Dargie, David**. *Xhosa Zionist church music: a report for the Research Unit for the Study of New Religious Movements and Indigenous Churches in Southern Africa (NERMIC), University of Zululand*. Introduction by Andrew Tracey. [KwaDlangezwa?, Zululand]: University of Zululand; Bergvlei [South Africa]: Hodder and Stoughton Educational Southern Africa, [1987?]. 26pp.
Dargie's appointment in 1979 to the Catholic Church charged him with "doing something about African church music." This resultant publication, 8 years later, includes analyses of eight cassettes (available through NERMIC), transcriptions of 5 songs, six plates in full color, and a short bibliography. Described is the work done in collecting Zionist music material, and how the music gives an insight into Zionist thought and practice. The place of Zionists in Xhosa society is described. Characteristics of Zionist music are seen to be typically African, and as pointing an "African way ahead for all Christians in Africa."

424. **Dark, Philip J. C., and Matthew Hill.** "Musical instruments on Benin plaques." In *Essays on music and history in Africa.* Edited by Klaus P. Wachsmann, 65-78. Evanston: Northwestern University Press, 1971.
There are 25 stunning photographs, primarily of the rectangular bronze Benin plaques. In an examination of 895 of them, 295 contained representations of musical instruments. These are classified according to the Hornbostel-Sachs system. It is believed that almost all of the plaques were cast from ca. 1550 to ca. 1650. The paper is heavily footnoted.

425. **Darkowska-Nidzgorska, Olenka.** *Théâtre populaire de marionnettes bronze en Afrique sud-saharienne.* Bandundu, République du Zaïre: Centre d'études ethnologiques; St. Augustin, Rep.fed. d'Allemagne: Diffusion hors-Zaïre, Steyler Verlag, c1980. 259pp. (Publications Ceeba, Série 2, vol. 60)
This was originally presented as the author's doctoral thesis at the Université de Paris, VIII, 1976. On popular puppet theater in sub-Saharan Africa, with examples from many countries and cultures. The book mentions that marionette repertoire is composed of songs, dances, living tableaus, and that pieces are often accompanied by music. A little on dance, less on music. Bibliography. Many photographs

Darkowska-Nidzgorska, Olenka
See also: **L'Afrique noire en marionettes, 53.**

426. **Darkwa, Asante.** THE NEW MUSIC TRADITIONS IN GHANA. Dissertation, Wesleyan University, 1974. 269pp.
Music, illustrations, music.

427. **Darkwa, Asante.** *Some aspects of the preservation and promotion of traditional music and dance in University cultures.* [Nairobi]: University of Nairobi, Institute of African Studies, [1980]. 10pp. (Paper - University of Nairobi, Institute of African Studies, no. 135)

428. **Darkwa, Asante.** "Traditional music and dance practices of the Wataito of Kenya: a current survey." **Cross rhythms** 3 (1989): 155-169.

429. **Dauer, A. M.** "Musik - Landschaften in Afrika." **AFRIKA HEUTE** no. 23 (1966): 1-7.
Bibliography, one small notation.

430. **Dauer, A. M.** *Tradition afrikanischer Blasorchester und Entstehung des Jazz.* Graz, Austria: Akademische Druck- u.
continued

Verlagsanstalt, 1985. 2 vols. (Beiträge zur Jazzforschung = Studies in jazz research, 7)
Volume 1 is text, Volume 2, transcriptions. The author examines African instrumental ensembles from different parts of the Continent and traces their influence on New World jazz ensembles. The bulk of the work focuses on Africa, starting with traditional music, and proceeding to neo-traditional music by region, with mention of specific groups. The African influence on jazz bands of the New World is studied in Haiti, Mississippi, Alabama, and New Orleans. Bunk Johnson and Kid Ory are included. There are 46 glossy, black and white photos, 68 transcriptions, an index, discography, and an impressive bibliography.

Dauer, A. M.
See also: **Musik in Afrika, 1135.**

David, Jay
See: **Adler, Bill**. *Growing up African*, **16.**

431. **Davies, H. Olúfẹlá**. *The Victor Ọláìyá story*. [Maryland Ìkejà: Sankey Print. Works, between 1964 and 1967]. 52pp.
Ọláìyá is a leading Nigerian singer-composer and trumpet player, known for his unwavering dedication to highlife music for more than three decades.

432. **Davis, Charles N.** "Melodic and harmonic movement in indigenous Ghanaian music." BĀ SHIRU no. 4 (1972): 1-10.
Notes, bibliography, several notations of scales.

433. **Davis, Hartley Ermina Graham**. IN HONOR OF THE ANCESTORS: THE SOCIAL CONTEXT OF IWÌ EGÚNGÚN CHANTING IN A YORÙBÁ COMMUNITY. Dissertation, Brandeis University, 1977. 452pp.

434. **Davis, Martha Ellen**. AFRO-DOMINICAN RELIGIOUS BROTHERHOODS: STRUCTURE, RITUAL, AND MUSIC. Dissertation, University of Illinois at Urbana-Champaign, 1976. 453pp.

435. **Davis, Martha Ellen**. *Music and dance in Latin American urban contexts: a selective bibliography*. [Brockport? New York, 1973]. 20pp. (Urban anthropology bibliographies, no. 1)
An admirable small bibliography with informative annotations. Publications encompass Spanish and Portuguese-speaking countries, and the hispanic United States Southwest. The 42 entries were chosen from what was at the time of writing, "the last decade." Music and dance that are traditional (i.e., orally transmitted), and popular (i.e., commercial), are included. She defines urban music and dance, to use her own terms, "pragmatically and loosely." Art music and dance are not considered.

436. **Davis, Ruth Francis.** MODERN TRENDS IN THE MA'LŪF OF TUNISIA, 1934-1984. Dissertation, Princeton University, 1986. 296pp.
The term *ma'lūf* is used to designate the traditional Arab art music repertory of Tunisia, and this paper studies modern trends affecting the music. The Rashidiya Institute was founded in Tunis in 1934, two years after the First International Congress for Arab Music, in Cairo, in order to preserve and promote Tunisian music. According to Davis, it is ironic that "the methods the Rashidiya [Rashīdiyyah] adopted to achieve its objectives, including the expansion of the traditional ensemble format and the use of western musical notation in performance, contributed to the modernization of the very tradition they were designed to conserve." **(UMI)**

437. **Davis, Stephen.** *Bob Marley: the biography.* London: A. Barker, c1983. 248pp. [Now published by Schenkman Books, Rochester, Vermont.]
Illustrations, plates, index, bibliography. On Bob Marley, other Jamaican singers, reggae music, and the reggae group, the Wailers. John Storm Roberts says that the writer has a "talent for intermingling personal experience with more objective material."

438. **Davis, Stephen.** *Reggae bloodlines: in search of the music and culture of Jamaica.* Photographs by Peter Simon. [Garden City, New York]: Anchor Press, c1977. 2165pp.
On Jamaican music and social conditions in Jamaica. Bibliography, and "Jamaica discography, pages 211-216.

439. **Davis, Stephen, and Peter Simon.** *Reggae international.* New York: R & B [Rogner and Bernhard], c1982. 191pp.
An extraordinarily complete book on reggae. Besides the scholarship displayed in 16 essays on every imaginable reggae-related subject, the book has enough photographic razzle-dazzle to grace any coffee table. Jamaican, American and British scholars write on their particular areas of expertise, classified under: Tracein' de Riddim; The Rastafarians; Rebel Music, and Reggae International. Particularly valuable are articles covering Jamaican and reggae history, a Rasta Glossary, an article on Haile Selassie, one on dub poetry, on Ska and Rock Steady, on Women in Reggae, and much about Marley and other stars. The following essays deserve particular notice:
- **Silver, David.** "Reggae epiphanies: Freetown, Sierra Leone," 184.
- **White, Timothy.** "Rebel music: a history of Bob Marley and the Wailers," 75- 86.
- **White, Garth.** "Voices crying in the wilderness," 25-32.

440. **Davoine, Françoise.** ANALYSES ET TRANSCRIPTIONS D'UN CORPUS MUSICAL DE RÉPUBLIQUE CENTRAFRICAINE EN VUE D'UN TERRAIN. Master's Thesis, University of Montreal, 1982.

441. **D'Azevedo, Warren L.** *The artist archetype in Gola culture.* [Reno] Desert Research Institute: University of Nevada, 1966,

second printing, 1970. 80pp.

The Gola of Liberia have no general term for Music or for Musicians. Professional musicians are men, who are expected to perform well on all instruments. They are regarded as "the epitome of the irresponsible wanderer." Most professional singers are women, and they are in great demand. Pertinent to our subject area, several paragraphs are to be found in each of sections headed: Singing; Musicianship; Dancing; Storytelling and Oratory, but one must read the entire monograph to have any real understanding. Interesting is the discussion of the Gola concept of talent, virtuosity and genius. Bibliography.

442. **D'Azevedo, Warren L.** "Sources of Gola artistry." In *The traditional artist in African societies.* Edited by Warren L. d'Azevedo, 282-340. Bloomington: Indiana University Press, [1973].

443. **Debhonvapi, Olema.** "Société Zaïroise dans le miroir de la chanson populaire." **CANADIAN JOURNAL OF AFRICAN STUDIES** 8, No. 1 (1984): 122-130.

de Carvalho, José Jorge
See: **Carvalo, José Jorge de, 327, 328.**

444. **Dechamps, R.** "Note préliminaire concernant l'identification anatomique des espèces de bois utilisée dans la fabrication des tambours à fente de l'Afrique Centrale." **AFRIKA-TERVUREN** 18, no. 1 (1972): 15-18.

445. **Dehoux, Vincent.** *Chants à penser gbaya (Centrafrique).* Paris: SELAF, 1986. 219pp. (Ethnomusicologie, 2)

Summary in English, French, and Gbaya (Central African Republic). Bibliography, discography.

De Lange, Margaret M.
See: **Africana Museum (Johannesburg, South Africa), 48.**

446. **de Lerma, Dominique-René.** *Bibliography of Black music.* 4 vols. Foreword by Jessie Carney Smith. Westport, Connecticut: Greenwood Press, 1981- . (The Greenwood encyclopedia of Black music)

Nothing can compare to the comprehensiveness of this four volume compendium on black music of the world. Librarian/bibliographer de Lerma, who has demonstrated in countless ways his life-long commitment to the documentation and promulgation of black music, has ferreted-out, packed-in an almost overwhelming amount of information, much of it of vital interest to the Africanist and ethnomusicologist. Volumes are entitled, 1. Reference materials, 2. Afro-American idioms, 3. Geographical studies, and 4. Theory, education, and related studies. With the exception of Volume 2, abundant African references appear throughout., but particularly in volume 3. In-depth examination is recommended.

447. de Lerma, Dominique-René. *Reflections on Afro-American music.* [With contributions from Richard L. Abrams and others. Kent, Ohio] Kent State University Press [1973]. 271pp.
The preface, by Dominique-René de Lerma, gives the interesting background to his founding of the Black Music Center at Indiana University, which he subsequently directed for two years. Though all essays in the book make worthwhile reading, only those concerning African music have been selected for listing below:
- **Akpabot, Samuel.** "The conflict between foreign and traditional culture in Nigeria," 124-130.
- **Baker, David N.** "A periodization of black music history," 143-160.
- **Blacking, John.** "Field work in African music," 207-221.

de Lerma, Dominique-René
See also: **Black music in our culture, 241.**

448. Deluz, Ariane. *Histoire inattendue: insultes et récit épique.* Chicago, University of Chicago, African Studies Workshop, 1986. 29pp.
Songs texts of the Guro of Côte d'Ivoire, including songs of invective. Oral tradition. Bibliography.

449. Deng, Francis Mading. *The Dinka and their songs.* Oxford: Clarendon Press, 1973. 301pp.
Part I is an in-depth study of the Dinka themselves and their country, the last section dealing with the role of song in Dinka society. Part II has words in Dinka and English of songs that fit into 10 categories. The last section includes 133 selected texts, all in Dinka, but no music transcriptions. Before almost every song, there is explanatory information. Strategically-placed footnotes are also a consideration to the reader. No index or bibliography. Much careful work has obviously gone into this book.

450. Deng, Francis Mading. *The Dinka songs.* Washington, D.C.: Embassy of the Democratic Republic of the Sudan, [1976?]. [24pp.]. (Selections from Sudanese literature, no. 3)
Texts in English and Arabic.

451. Denyer, Frank. *The lyre in the northern Kerio Valley.* [Nairobi]: University of Nairobi, Institute of African Studies, [1980]. 21pp. (Paper - University of Nairobi, Institute of African Studies, no. 137)

452. Denyer, Frank. *Some preliminary thoughts concerning curricula for music education in Kenya.* [Nairobi]: University of Nairobi, Institute of African Studies, [1979]. 16pp. (Paper - University of Nairobi, Institute of African Studies, no. 120)
Concerned with music instruction and study in Kenya.

453. **Deren, Maya**. *Divine horsemen: voodoo gods of Haiti.* Foreword by Joseph Campbell. New York: Dell Publishing Company, 1970.
A profound exploration of the Voudoun religion. Deren went to Haiti on a Guggenheim Fellowship in 1947 to film dance, but become so totally involved in Voudoun that she never finished the film. She herself has experienced deep possession. The chapter entitled, Drums and Dance (pages 225-246) has the most important information on music. The book contains a Glossary of Creole Terms Referring to Voudoun, many of which pertain to music, and an important chart that classifies Voudoun Loa. There are 23 monochrome plates, 17 line drawings, copious chapter notes, a bibliography, and index. A classic.

454. **Derive, Jean**. "La chanson dans une société de tradition orale de Côte d'Ivoire: (Les Dioula de Kong)." In **Chansons d'Afrique et des Antilles** 89-98. Paris: Harmattan, c1988.

455. **Derive, M. J.** *Bamori et kowulen: chant de chasseurs de la région d'Odienné.* [Abidjan]: Ministère de la recherche scientifique, Université d'Abidjan, Institut de linguistique appliquée, 1978. 56pp. (Tradition orale, 68)
Texts of hunting songs from the Côte d'Ivoire. In French and Mandingo. Includes bibliographical references.

Derive, M. J.
See also: **La Crotte tenace et autres contes ngbaka-ma'bo de République centrafricaine, 400.**

456. **Deroff, Doug**. "The Zulu choirs: a brief introduction." **KESKIDEE: A JOURNAL OF BLACK MUSIC TRADITIONS** 1 (1986): 20-21.

457. **Desai, Desmond**. "'Cape Malay' music." In **Symposium on Ethnomusicology**. (5th: 1984: University of Cape Town). *Papers presented at the fifth Symposium on Ethnomusicology: Faculty of Music, University of Cape Town, August 30th-September 1st, 1984*, 39-44. Grahamstown: International Library of African Music, 1985.
This concerns the secular music of the Cape Muslims, referred to here as "Cape Malay" music. Lyrics are traceable to the Netherlands.

458. **De Vale, Sue Carole**. "Prolegomena to a study of harp and voice sounds in Uganda: a graphic system for the notation of texture." In **Studies in African music**. Co-editors, J. H. Kwabena Nketia, and Jacqueline Cogdell DjeDje, 285-315. [Los Angeles]: Program in Ethnomusicology, Department of Music, University of California, Los Angeles, 1984.
continued

Notes, bibliography, map. Textures of harp and voice recordings are analyzed using a two-part graphic system.

459. **De Vale, Sue Carole.** A SUDANESE GAMELAN: A GESTALT APPROACH TO ORGANOLOGY. Dissertation, Northwestern University, 1977. 302pp.

460. **Devlin, Eileen Bonnie.** "VWA GUINE": AN ORIGINAL PERFORMANCE PIECE DERIVED FROM THE HAITIAN "VODU COUCHER TAMBOUR" CEREMONY: THE SACRED AND THE AESTHETIC IN RITUAL PERFORMANCE. Dissertation, New York University, 1986. 530pp.
The purpose of this study was to create and document an original performance piece derived from the Haitian Vodu Coucher Tambour ("to sleep the drum") ceremony, and to examine the sacred and the aesthetic in associated ritual, arts and performance. From the abstract, it was not possible to determine if any associated music was analyzed, though it seems likely in light of the author's saying, "The researcher, by employing an interdisciplinary approach, was able to...delineate the Haitian Vodu Coucher Tambour ceremony, along with Vodu drumming, related arts and creative manifestations as a living tradition..." **(UMI)**

461. **Diabaté, Masan Makan.** "L'épopée mandingue et le titre d'honneur de Sunjata Keita." In **Chansons d'Afrique et des Antilles**, 11-19. Paris: Harmattan, c1988.

462. **Diabaté, Masan Makan.** *Janjon et autres chants populaires du Mali.* Preface by Djikbril T. Niane. Paris: Présence Africaine [1070] 110pp.
In French. Oral poetry and popular songs of the Bambara people, including the *Janjon*, a praise-poem in honor of Sunjata (regarded by historians to be the founder of the Mali empire). This was told to Diabaté by his uncle, *Jali* Kele-Monson Diabaté.

463. **Diakhité, Drissa.** "Des hymnes à la maternité." In **Chansons d'Afrique et des Antilles**, 21-28. Paris: Harmattan, c1988.

464. **Diégues Júnior, Manuel.** *Africa in the life and culture of Brazil: a contribution for the study of African influences and the presence of these influences in the formation of Brazilian life and culture.* Translated by Derek Wheatley. [s.l.: s.n., 1977?]. 174pp. (Cover says: 2nd World Black and African Festival of Arts and Culture, Nigeria Lagos - Kaduna, 15th January -12th February 1977. Parallel titles on cover: L'Afrique dans la vie et la culture du Brésil; A África na vida e na cultura do Brasil)
The bound volume, which includes three 54 page treatises in English, French and Portuguese, is informative regarding the African-Brazilian connection, particularly

of the past. There are records of musical activities of the slaves, accomplishments of popular and classical composers of African ancestry, mention of songs, dances and musical instruments. There is information on folklore, religion, family life and work, theater, cinema, language, "miscegenation and transculturation," and related areas of interest. Politics and heavier sociological concerns are noticeably omitted. Valuable data here, but the writer patronizes, sentimentalizes, or glosses-over subjects getting too close for comfort. No bibliography, index, photographs.

465. **Diégues Júnior, Manuel.** *A África na vida e na cultura do Brasil: contribuição para o estudo das influências africanas e sua presença na formação brasileira.* Rio de Janeiro: Artes Gráficas Schultze, [1977?]. 65pp.

This is the exclusively Portuguese version of the directly preceding entry.

466. **Dieterlen, Germaine.** "Notes sur les tambours de calebasse." **SOCIÉTÉ DES AFRICANISTES. BULLETIN** 33, Fascicle 2, 1963.

Not seen nor are pages known, but there is indication that the article includes some mention of a calabash water drum used by different populations along the river in Niger.

467. **Dietz, Betty Warner, and Michael Babátúndé Ọlátúnjí.** *Musical instruments of Africa: their nature, use, and place in the life of a deeply musical people.* Illustrated by Richard M. Powers. New York: John Day Company, [1965]. 115pp.

A handsome, well-planned, informative book that was probably designed for classroom use. Instruments are classified according to the general concepts of the Sachs-Hornbostel system, with lavish accompanying photographs from all over Africa. Some portraits show performing musicians. Other photographs are of instruments in museum cases. The introduction is by Colin M. Turnbull, whose phonodisc of field recordings is contained in the book pocket. Includes illustrations, a pronunciation guide, record notes, brief bibliography, brief discography, map, and chart showing years certain African countries achieved independence and later became U.N. members.

Discourse in ethnomusicology (no. 2)
See : **A tribute to Alan P. Merriam, 1586.**

468. **Discourse in ethnomusicology: essays in honor of George List.** Edited by Caroline Card [et. al.]. Bloomington: Ethnomusicology Publications Group, Indiana University, c1978. 298pp.

The following essays, arranged here alphabetically by last name, have been chosen because they pertain in some way to African music:

- **Cáceres, Abraham.** "Preliminary comments on the marimba in the Americas," 225-250.
- **Card, Caroline.** "Some problems of field recording for research purposes," 53-64.
- **Stone, Ruth M.** "Motion film as an aid in transcription and analysis of music," 65-68.

DISSERTATION ABSTRACTS ON DISC
See: **UMI, 1598.**

469. **Dixon, David M.** "A note on Kushite contact with the South." In *Essays on music and history in Africa*. Edited by Klaus P. Wachsmann, 135-139. Evanston: Northwestern University Press, 1971.
Dixon focuses on the Nile Valley as a possible internal source of musical culture in tropical Africa, an idea that had formerly been neglected in the field of music. This is a short paper, but very detailed and with footnotes and a map.

470. **DjeDje, Jacqueline Cogdell.** "The concept of patronage: an examination of Hausa and Dagomba one-string fiddle traditions." In **JOURNAL OF AFRICAN STUDIES** 9, no. 3 (1982): 116-127.

471. **DjeDje, Jacqueline Cogdell.** *Distribution of the one string fiddle in West Africa.* Los Angeles: Program in Ethnomusicology, Department of Music, University of California Los Angeles, 1980. 43pp. (Monograph series in ethnomusicology, no. 2)
Bibliography and discography.

472. **DjeDje, Jacqueline Cogdell.** "The interplay of melodic phrases: an analysis of Dagomba and Hausa one string fiddle music." In **Studies in African music**. Co-editors, J. H. Kwabena Nketia, and Jacqueline Cogdell DjeDje, 81-118. [Los Angeles]: Program in Ethnomusicology, Department of Music, University of California, Los Angeles, 1984.
In a scholarly study, DjeDje compares the one-string fiddle traditions of the Dagomba of Northern Ghana, and the Hausa of Northern Nigeria. Although a number of commonalities exist between one-string fiddle playing techniques and functions throughout Sudanic Africa, it is in the organization of melody - particularly the interplay of melodic phrases - that one society is distinct from another. DjeDje examines the organization of musical performance, the organization of melodic parts, the interrelationship of these melodic parts, and reaches certain conclusions. There are music notations, a long transcription, notes, photographs, a bibliography, and short discography.

473. **DjeDje, Jaqueline Cogdell.** THE ONE STRING FIDDLE IN WEST AFRICA: A COMPARISON OF HAUSA AND DAGOMBA TRADITIONS. Dissertation, University of California, Los Angeles, 1978. 1489pp.

474. **DjeDje, Jacqueline Cogdell.** "Song type and performance style in Hausa and Dagomba possession (Bori) music." **THE BLACK PERSPECTIVE IN MUSIC** 9, no. 3 (1982): 166-182.

D

475. **DjeDje, Jaqueline Cogdell.** "Women and music in Sudanic Africa." In **More than drumming: essays on African and Afro-Latin music and musicians.** Edited by Irene V. Jackson, 67-89. Westport, Connecticut: Greenwood Press, c1985.
Notes, bibliography. Abstracted in **RILM**, 1985.

476. **DjeDje, Jacqueline Cogdell, and William G. Carter.** "African musicology: an assessment of the field." In **African musicology: current trends: a festschrift presented to J. H. Kwabena Nketia.** Edited by Jacqueline Cogdell DjeDje, and William G. Carter, 39-44. [Atlanta, Georgia: Crossroads Press, 1988]- .
Bibliography.

DjeDje, Jaqueline Cogdell
See also: **•African musicology: current trends, 41.**
•Studies in African music, 1514.

Dos Santos Barbosa, Guilherme
See: **Santos Barbosa, Guilherme dos, 1410a.**

Drachler, Jacob
See: **African heritage: an anthology of black American personality and culture, 36.**

478. **Drewal, Henry John.** ÈFÈ/GÈLÈDÉ: THE EDUCATIVE ROLE OF THE ARTS IN TRADITIONAL YORÙBÁ CULTURE. Dissertation, Columbia University, 1973.
Of course the educative role of music gets its deserved attention in this study. The verbal art of Èfè songs is covered on pages 82-114. They are analyzed on the basis of style (accompaniment, presentation, structure); content, and meaning. Four major categories are delineated, according to subject matter, and one song from each category (and sub-division within a category) is examined from a number of perspectives. The author stresses that the totality of the arts is far more than the analysis of any one "art" for study purposes. Glossary. Bibliography.

479. **Drewal, Henry John, and Margaret Thompson Drewal.** *Gẹ̀lẹ̀dẹ́ art and female power among the Yorùbá.* Bloomington: Indiana University Press, c1983. 306pp. (Traditional arts of Africa)
At once, scholarly and spectacular. To quote from the book, "The Gẹ̀lẹ̀dẹ́ spectacle honors and serves spiritually powerful woman - elders, ancestors and deities." The masquerades, found originally among western Yorùbá peoples in Nigeria and Benin, are lavish affairs involving wooden headpieces, cloth costumes, dances, songs and drumming. One cannot even find Music and Dance in the index, so ubiquitous are references to these arts throughout the book. However, chapters 1, 3, and 5 probably contain the most important music references. This book got rave reviews, understandably. Bibliography, memorable photographs in brilliant colors of masked people.

480. **Drewal, Margaret Thompson, and Glorianne Jackson**, comps. *Sources on African and African-related dance.* New York: American Dance Guild, [1974], 38pp.
The bibliography, supposedly on dance, demonstrates graphically how welded dance is with music in Africa, since so many entries also pertain to music. There are separate sections for books, articles, journals, films, and other subjects, plus a good index. This bibliography is particularly valuable because the scope is so broad. There are any number of entries that pertain to music and dance in the New World as well as in Africa.

481. **Duckles, Vincent H.** *Music reference and research materials: an annotated bibliography.* 4th ed. New York: Schirmer Books; London: Collier Macmillan, c1988. 714pp.
This reference work, now in its fourth edition, has been a mainstay for musicologists since 1964. Not only does it cover Western art music, but there are also materials included on African music and Ethnomusicology, though not in great abundance. The three indexes are by subject, title, and names of author, editor or reviewer. Annotations vary in length, but are well done. This particular edition is unfavorably reviewed by D. W. Krummel, in **NOTES: QUARTERLY REVIEW OF THE MUSIC LIBRARY ASSOCIATION** vol. 46, nos. 1/2, 1989, but he eventually softens: "For all its increasingly conspicuous limitations, *Duckles 4* is no misfortune to have around."

482. **Dufrasne-Gonzalez, J. Emanuel.** LA HOMOGENEIDAD DE LA MUSICA CARIBENA: SOBRE LA MUSICA COMERCIAL Y POPULAR DE PUERTO RICO. Dissertation, University of California, Los Angeles, 1985. 478pp.
In Spanish. Africanists will have a heyday, since the researcher has a broad view of African survivals in the New World, and uses for documentation, Puerto Rican oral traditions, as compared with information on musical cultures of Mexico, Cuba, Dominican Republic, Haiti, Venezuela, Central America, the Lesser Antilles, Brazil, United States, Peru and West Africa. Historical data from Spain and Portugal is also included. Musical instruments are studied in depth - even interesting details regarding non-documented chordophones. Dance forms get their share. This is augmented by drawings, photographs, musical transcriptions. **(UMI)**

483. **Duignan, Peter.** *Handbook of American resources for African studies.* The Hoover Institution on War, Revolution, and Peace. Hoover Institution bibliographical series XXIX. (Stanford, California): Stanford University, 1967. 218p.
The purpose of this book is to document the resources of American institutions and museums and to encourage their use. Fifteen are listed under one index heading, Music and Musical Instruments. Collections described include books; traditional and popular sound recordings - discs, tapes, cylinders (some commercial, some made during major expeditions); manuscripts pertaining to recordings; instrument collections; photographs of people playing instruments and dancing, etc. Information on organizations, provided by questionnaire, varies in

length, and, since not all organizations responded, there are omissions. Major Africana libraries are described by their curators or bibliographers.

484. **Dunaway, David King.** *Field recording oral history, folklore and ethnomusicology.* Nairobi: University of Nairobi, Institute of African Studies, 1984. 28pp. (Seminar paper - University of Nairobi, Institute of African Studies, no. 161)

Makes a good case for the importance of the researcher's being well-informed about all aspects of recording before going into the field. Detailed information is given, from designing a project to carrying it through to completion. There is concern with evaluating the sound environment, what is involved in the directed interview, how to record the music proper, the equipment to use, and its maintenance, and much more. Despite our fact-paced technological world in which older equipment is constantly being supplanted, this guide can still be valuable. Bibliography.

485. **Dunaway, David King.** *Processing oral texts.* [s.l.: s.n., 1984]. 17pp. (Seminar paper. University of Nairobi, Institute of African Studies, no. 162)

By "processing," Dunway means all the stages necessary to make a collected text public. By "text," he means "a single telling of a tale, recitation of a proverb, a singing of a folk song." [Alan Dunde's definition.] Subjects covered are: Auditing, Indexing, Narrator Review and Compensation, Interview History, Depositing and Publishing Oral Texts, Cataloguing, and Theoretical Questions. The aim of the paper is to present guidelines for preparing oral texts so that they can be analyzed and used by scholars, and by the communities that preserve them. Bibliography.

486. **Dundes, Alan**, ed. *Mother wit from the laughing barrel: readings in the interpretation of Afro-American folklore.* New printing, with addendum. New York: Garland, 1981, c1973. 674pp. (Critical studies on Black life and culture, vol. 7)

Includes two essays of particular interest. Waterman's was originally included in selected papers of the **International Congress of Americanists, 29th, New York, 1949**, first published in 1952, reprinted in 1967. See entry in this bibliography, **733.**

•**Janheinz, Jahn**. "Residual African elements in the blues," 95-103.
•**Waterman, Richard Alan**. "African influence on music of the Americas," 81-94.

487. **Dunstan, Raymond David.** ST. LUCIAN CARNIVAL: A CARIBBEAN ART FORM. Dissertation, State University of New York, Stoney Brook, 1978. 374pp.

488. **Duodu, Emmanuel Ampofo.** DRUMMING AND DANCING IN AKAN SOCIETY - A STUDY OF COURT MUSICAL AND DANCING TRADITIONS. Master's Thesis, Wesleyan University, 1972. 154pp.

489. **Duran, Lucy**. "British Library African resources: (2) archival; The National Sound Archive: traditional African music." In *African studies: papers presented at a colloquium at the British Library, 7-9 January 1985*. Edited by Ilse Sternberg and Patricia M. Larby, 238-245. London, British Library in association with SCOLMA, 1986.

The article begins with quotations by J. H. Kwabena Nketia and *Jali* Nyama Suso from their recordings at the Archive that reiterate the extreme importance of music to African society, and (as extended by Duran), the need for it to be documented and preserved through recordings. To this purpose, and to provide representative coverage of all African countries, the Archive is dedicated. As ethnomusicologist of the National Sound Archive, Duran is well qualified to recount the scope of the Archive, the fascinating ups and downs of its history. Holdings, functions, and services of the Archive are thoroughly and impressively presented.

490. **Duvelle, Charles**. "La musique orientale en Afrique noire." In **La musique africaine, réunion de Yaoundé (Cameroun)** [sur les traditions musicales de l'Afrique subsaharienne], **23-27 février 1970, organisée par l'UNESCO**, 95-116. Paris: *La revue musicale*, Richard-Masse, 1972.

Original version of the entry that follows.

491. **Duvelle, Charles**. "Oriental music in Black Africa." In **African music: meeting in Yaoundé (Cameroon) 23-27 February 1970, organized by UNESCO**, 95-117. Paris: *La revue musicale*, 1972.

English translation of the preceding entry.

492. **Dwaben Ntahera**. Compiled by K. Ampom-Darkwa and K. Asante Darkwa. [Legon?]: Institute of African Studies, University of Ghana, 1973. 47pp. (I.A.S. court literature series, no. 5)

This is about a horn ensemble associated with a Ghanaian chief's court. Songs are in Twi, introduction in English. Includes music. See also the Master's Thesis of William Grandvil Carter on this same subject, **326**.

Dzokanga, A.
See: **Chansons et proverbes lingala, 334.**

E

493. **Echezona, W. Wilberforce C.** IBO MUSICAL INSTRUMENTS IN IBO CULTURE. Dissertation, Michigan State University, 1963. 200pp.
Illustrations, maps, music, bibliography.

494. **Echezona, W. Wilberforce C.** *Nigerian musical instruments: a definitive catalogue.* East Lansing, Michigan: Apollo Publishers, c1981. 236pp.
Musical instruments of Nigeria, catalogs and collections. Illustrations.

495. **Echezona, W. Wilberforce C.** UBO-AKA AND NGEDEGWU: MUSICAL INSTRUMENTS OF THE IBOS. Master's Thesis, Michigan State University, 1962.

Edet, Edna Smith
See: •**Griot sings, 642.**
•**Smith, Edna Marilyn, 1471.**

496. **Edwards, Walford I.** "Some characteristics of African music." **PAN-AFRICAN JOURNAL** 3, no. 2 (1970): 42-49.
Edwards prepares the reader by saying, "The following notes should be limited to those general aspects that would be applicable to most African musical practices." After a brief introduction, rhythm is treated in two paragraphs of two sentences each, followed by two more paragraphs on melody, and similar kernels about vocal music, scales, harmony, and a slightly elaborated section on instruments. The author concludes with suggestions for incorporating the study of African music into the classroom. Some of the generalities are valid; others are not, but one senses the author's good intentions, and nothing is disturbingly awry.

497. **Egblewogbe, E. Y.** GAMES AND SONGS AS AN ASPECT OF SOCIALIZING IN EWELAND. Master's Thesis. University of Ghana, 1967.
Following a brief outline of the ways in which Ewe society has been shaped by historical, geographical and economic factors, description is given of the social organization of Ewe society. The ways in which socialization is aided by games and songs is the concern of this thesis.

498. **Egblewogbe, E. Y.** *Games and songs as educational media: a case study among the Ewes of Ghana.* Tema, Ghana: Ghana Publishing Corporation, c1975. 111pp.
Text of songs in Ewe and English. Bibliography.

499. **Egudu, Romanus N.** "Igbo and Ozo festival songs and poems." **THE CONCH** 3, No.2 (1971): 76-88.

Ehlers, Jackie
See: **Songs of Zambia, 1483.**

500. Eight urban musical cultures: tradition and change. Edited by Bruno Nettl. Urbana: University of Illinois Press, 1978. 320pp.
This is a collection of essays, abstracted in the 1985 **RILM**. There are charts, music, bibliographies, and tables. Two essays pertain to African music:
- **Coplan, David B.** "Go to my town, Cape Coast! The social history of Ghanaian highlife," 96-114.
- **Ware, Naomi.** "Popular music and African identity in Freetown, Sierra Leone," 296-320.

501. Ekwueme, Lazarus Edward Nnanyelu. African music retentions in the New World." THE BLACK PERSPECTIVE IN MUSIC 2, no. 2 (1974): 128-144.
Music, bibliography.

502. Ekwueme, Lazarus Edward Nnanyelu. "Blackie Na Joseph: the sociological implications of a contemporary Igbo popular song." NIGERIAN MUSIC REVIEW 1, no.1 (1977): 39-65.

503. Ekwueme, Lazarus Edward Nnanyelu. "Concepts of African musical theory." JOURNAL OF BLACK STUDIES. 5, no.1 (1974): 43.

504. Ekwueme, Lazarus Edward Nnanyelu. "Contemporary African music: functions and influences." In **The arts and civilization of Black and African peoples.** Edited by Joseph Ohiomogben Okpaku, Alfred Esimatemi Opubor, and Benjamin Ọlátúnjí Ọlọ́runtìmẹhìn, Volume 1: 121-131. Lagos: Centre for Black and African Arts and Civilization, c1986.
Ekwueme concludes his paper with the following remarks: "Contemporary African music is an interesting phenomenon of continuity and change. Various elements - unity and diversity, antique and modern, elitist and popular, professional and amateur - combine to give the art a new strength and dynamism." (These are optimistic words for those who - and not without justification - fear the disappearance of traditional culture and values. Bibliography.)

505. Ekwueme, Lazarus Edward Nnanyelu. IBO CHORAL MUSIC: ITS THEORY AND PRACTICE. Dissertation, Yale University, 1972. 464pp.

506. Ekwueme, Lazarus Edward Nnanyelu. "Linguistic determinants of some Igbo musical properties." JOURNAL OF AFRICAN STUDIES vol. 1, no. 3 (1974): 335-53.

507. Ekwueme, Lucy Uzoma. NIGERIAN INDIGENOUS MUSIC AS A BASIS FOR DEVELOPING CREATIVE MUSIC INSTRUCTION FOR NIGERIAN PRIMARY SCHOOLS AND SUGGESTED GUIDELINES FOR IMPLEMENTATION. Dissertation, Columbia University Teachers College, 1988. 305pp. *continued*

Ekwueme mentions that studies of music education in Nigeria reveal the absence of a meaningful music curriculum in Nigerian primary schools. He also mentions the lack of indigenous music as a basis for music instruction, and the absence of meaningful music curriculum and materials to guide teachers in classroom instruction. In the final chapter, a basis for teacher training is provided, along with "a curriculum to be taught in a way consistent with Nigerian cultural values." **(UMI)**

508. Elder, Jacob D. *The calypso and its morphology.* Trinidad and Tobago: National Cultural Council, 1973. 32pp.
This paper analyzes changes in structure, style and content of the Trinidadian calypso over a period of more than 100 years. The calypso is regarded as an important indicator of the past history and present condition of the society from which it evolves. The approach to the study is described as "holistic, systematic and statistical." In this context, however, the components do not conflict but are complementary. The work is divided into two chapters with subdivisions, one on background and theory, the other on research design. Alan Lomax's cantometric system was part of the overall research plan. Chapter notes.

509. Elder, Jacob D. "Color, music, and conflict: a study of aggression in Trinidad with reference to the role of traditional music." In **Black society in the new world**. Edited by Richard Frucht, 315-323. New York: Random House, [1971].

510. Elder, Jacob D. EVOLUTION OF THE TRADITIONAL CALYPSO OF TRINIDAD AND TOBAGO: A SOCIO-HISTORICAL ANALYSIS OF SONG-CHANGE. Dissertation, University of Pennsylvania, 1966. 376pp.

511. Elder, Jacob D. *Folk song and folk life in Charlotteville: aspects of village life and dynamics of acculturation in a Tobago folk song tradition.* [This represents the expansion of a paper prepared for the Twenty-First Conference of the International Folk Music Council, Kingston, Jamaica, West Indies, August 27-September 3, 1971.] 61pp. It was printed in Port-of-Spain, Trinidad, by Universal Printing Products.]
A treasure-trove of information, often African-related. Melodies of 25 Tobago songs are notated. The following subject headings convey something of the breadth and depth of this treatise: The Beginnings, Migrant Musicians, Culture Clash, Singers from the Grenadines, Demographic Mix-Up, Acculturation, Song Categories and Local Spirituals, Drum Dance Music, Work Songs, Stylistic Mixture, Rites of Passage Music, Congo Music, Types of Music Makers, Conflict Over Church Music, Children's Music, Women's Banter Songs, Music for Magic, Music in Life and Death, Music and Social Conflicts, Cultural Continuities and Cultural Changes, Major Genres of Charlotteville Traditional Music. Delightful writing style.

512. **Elder, Jacob D.** *From Congo drum to steelband: a socio-historical account of the emergence and the evolution of the Trinidad steel orchestra.* St. Augustine, Trinidad: University of the West Indies, 1969. 21pp.
There is far more here than the evolvement of the steelband. Dense with vital information, this monograph, by Trinidad and Tobago's leading social scientist, starts with pre-Columbian times, continues the history of the area, its many ethnic groups, and brings us to the flowering of calypso and steelband. The term "sociohistorical" truly describes this in-depth, comprehensive study. Most valuable is the list of 23 Folk-Music Types - many having strong African ties. Associated instruments, culture groups, and supporting institutions are given for each example. (It is doubtful that such an informed and comprehensive summary exists any other place.) Imposing bibliography.

513. **Elder, Jacob D.** "*Kalinda* - song of the battling troubadours of Trinidad." **JOURNAL OF THE FOLKLORE INSTITUTE.** 3, no.2 (1966): 192-203.
This paper gives the history of a kind of stick-fight, known as *Kalinda*, that continues as a social institution in Trinidad. *Kalinda* songs are important because they are the prototype of the Calypso, and leave their melodic and poetic stamp on contemporary songs. Song texts and notated examples of *Kalinda* forms are included. (Note: this article can also be found in Vol. 1, no.2 of **ART AND CULTURE: THE QUARTERLY JOURNAL OF THE NATIONAL CULTURAL COUNCIL OF TRINIDAD AND TOBAGO**).

514. **Elder, Jacob D.** "The male/female conflict in calypso." **CARIBBEAN QUARTERLY** 14, no. 3 (1968): 23-41.

515. **Elder, Jacob D.** *Song games from Trinidad and Tobago.* Revised Edition. Port-of-Spain, Trinidad: National Cultural Council Publications, 1973. 128pp.
Convinced that song-games have been a neglected folklore genre, the author analyzes 37 examples gleaned from Trinidad and Tobago. Background information, derivation, method of performance, and sociological implications are given. All songs are notated. Africa asserts itself through the prevalence of call-response form, use of handclapping and rattles, and the syncopation added to British game-tunes. Examination of other kinds of song-game variations might yield further Africanisms to the dedicated researcher. Interesting is mention of the *banja*, an African *sanza* recreated by children, that evolved into the *basse-en-botte.* Bibliography.

515a. **Ellison, Mary.** *Lyrical protest: Black music's struggle against discrimination.* New York: Praeger, 1989. 169pp. (Media and society series)
The book is about black protest music sung in English that has either African or African-American roots. Though African references occur intermittently throughout the book, a chapter of focused attention is called, Liberation songs for South Africa. It gives a brief history of South African colonialism, the emergence of South African protest music, and surveys the strong, supportive response by

black musicians from other parts of Africa, the Caribbean, Canada, Britain, and the United States. Notes. No song texts or music.

516. **Elschekovà, Alica**. "Traditionelle afrikanische Mehrstimmigkeit: Za ihrer Typologie, Stratigraphie und historischen Erforschung." In *Musikkulturen in Afrika*. Edited by Erich Stockmann, 62-81. Berlin: Verlag Neue Musik, 1987.

In German. An analysis of polyphony in traditional African music follows a presentation of conclusions reached by earlier researchers. A chart of types and techniques of polyphony is included plus many notes and several music transcriptions.

517. **Elsner, Jürgen**. DER BEGRIFF DES MAQĀM IN ÄGYPTEN IN NEUERER ZEIT. Dissertation, Humboldt University, 1970. 155pp.

518. **Emery, Lynn Fauley**. *Black dance: from 1619 to today*. 2d rev. ed. New chapter by Brenda Dixon-Stowell. Foreword by Katherine Dunham. Salem, New Hampshire: Ayer Company, c1988. 397pp.

Emery, a social scientist and historian with a thorough knowledge of dance, also has a deep interest in Africa. In her broadly informative book, Africa weaves in and out the chapters. Early accounts of dance in Africa, and particularly those of dance in the New World, are often written in the first-person. Documentation is scholarly and thorough, and there are fascinating photographs and stories of famous dancers of the past and present. Noteworthy are chapters on plantation dances and Caribbean dances. Music references are ubiquitous. Countless African-related subject headings occur in the index. Magnificent, subdivided bibliography.

518a. **The encyclopaedia of Islam**. New ed., prepared by a number of leading orientalists. Edited by an editorial committee consisting of H. A. R. Gibb [and others]. Leiden: Brill, 1960-[1991].

At the time of writing, volume 7, through parts 115-116, had been issued and the letter "M" was almost completed. This work is a useful source for information on Islam and Islamic peoples and institutions (beliefs, practices, customs and traditions). The transliteration of Arabic words used in this book is based on the transliteration system of the **Encyclopaedia of Islam**. Volumes include illustrations, plates, folding maps, diagrams, bibliographies. Index volumes are cumulative.

519. **Engel, Hans**. *Die Stellung des Musikers im arabisch-islamischen Raum*. Bonn: Verlag für Systematische Musikwissenschaft, 1987. 350pp. (Volume 49 der Orpheus-Schriftenreihe zu Grundfragen der Musik)

This represents a complete coverage of music and musicians in Arab countries, from past to present times. The approach is historical and sociological. The index includes occasional references to a number of specific northern African countries, their peoples, musical instruments, dance. Also included in the index is the collective term, "Nordafrika." A most scholarly, broad-based, and well-documented work. Bibliography and a 5 page summary in English (though the latter does not seem to have many - if any - references to Africa).

520. **ENGLAND, NICHOLAS M.**
Some of the additional writings of this outstanding musicologist were not within the time scope of this bibliography. Upon consultation with Dr. England, however, he has agreed to forward a bibliography of his publications upon written request to: Dr. Nicholas M. England, Director of Intercultural Arts Project, California Institute of the Arts, 24700 McBean Parkway, Valencia, California, 91355.

521. **England, Nicholas M.** "Bushman counterpoint." INTERNATIONAL FOLK MUSIC COUNCIL. Yearbook 19 (1967): 58-66.

522. **England, Nicholas M.** MUSIC AMONG THE ZŨ'/'WÃ-SI OF SOUTH WEST AFRICA AND BOTSWANA. 2 vols. Dissertation, Harvard University, 1968. 775pp.
A *magnum opus* that describes the musical repertoires of the mid-twentieth century Zũ'/'wã-si (and related or more distant groups), in, to use England's own terminology, "words, music, notes, sound and sight." England studies the technical aspects of the music, the uses of music in cultural context, and gives as much historical background as was possible at the time of writing. He covers vocal and instrumental music, and instrument construction and playing techniques. Dance is not neglected. There are transcriptions, maps, diagrams, graphs, tables, a guide to orthography, photographs, an index, lengthy bibliography. (A tape accompanies the original dissertation.)

523. **Eno Belinga, Samuel-Martin.** *Découverte des chantefables beti-bulu-fang du Cameroun.* Preface by Pierre Alexandre. Paris: Klincksieck, 1970. 192pp. (Langues et littératures de l'Afrique noire, 7)
Cameroon songs. Bibliography.

524. **Eno Belinga, Samuel-Martin.** *L'Epopée Camerounaise, Mvet: Moneblum ou l'Homme Bleu.* Édit. CEPER, Yaoundé (Cameroun), 1978. 288pp.

525. **Eno Belinga, Samuel-Martin.** *Littérature et musique populaire en Afrique noire.* [Paris, Éditions Cujas, 1965]. 258pp. (Culture et cooperation, no. 1)
Popular African music and literature. Includes bibliography, music, illustrations.

526. **Eno Belinga, Samuel-Martin.** *Livret du Mvet: pour une lecture théâtrale d'un Mvet Bulu de D. Osomo Mva'a: moneblum ou l'homme bleu.* [Cameroon?]: Université de Yaoundé, [1979]. 35pp.
continued

A *mvet*, identified by some as a "harp-zither," appears on the cover, showing which hand plays which strings. Mvet is also an oral epic in which the instrument has a primary role. The epic of the Bulu of Cameroon, *Mvet Moneblum* or *L'Homme Bleu* has a complex structure, much action, and can include as many as 300 actors only portraying prisoners! Except for introductory remarks, this book is essentially a director's guide as to who sings, dances, speaks or acts for 60 listed songs. See also: **Eno Belinga (524)**, and **Mvet Moneblum (1145)** for the complete text.

527. **Eno Belinga, Samuel-Martin**. "La musique traditionelle d'Afrique Noire." In **Colloque sur l'art nègre**. Rapports. Vol. 2 (1971): 189-198. [Paris: Présence africaine]

528. **Eno Belinga, Samuel-Martin**. "La musique traditionelle de l'Afrique occidentale: genres, styles et influences." In **La musique africaine, réunion de Yaoundé (Cameroun)** [sur les traditions musicales de l'Afrique subsaharienne], **23-27 février 1970, organisée par l'UNESCO**, 69-74. Paris: *La revue musicale*, Richard-Masse, 1972.
This is the original French version. The English translation is listed under **Eno Belinga, Samuel-Martin**, "The traditional music of West Africa: types, styles and influences." (531)

529. **Eno Belinga, Samuel-Martin**. "Musique traditionelle et musique moderne au Cameroon." **INTERNATIONAL COMMITTEE ON URGENT ANTHROPOLOGICAL AND ETHNOLOGICAL RESEARCH. BULLETIN** 11 (1969): 83-90.
Sections on traditional music and religious music are followed by a discussion of varieties of dance music and modern music. Imported instruments are mentioned, such as the accordian, saxophone, and bass, as well as several Cameroonian groups and individual popular musicians. Included is a long extract of a Bulu Mvet from the Village of Nkolafendek ("selon Daniel Ossomo") 1963.

530. **Eno Belinga, Samuel-Martin**. "*Ôka'angana*: un genre musical et littéraire pratique par les femmes Bulu du Sud-Cameroun." In **La musique dans la vie, étude realisée sous les auspices l'Ocora et sous la direction de Tolia Nikiprowetzky**, 105-132. Vol. 1. Paris, Office de coopération radiophonique, 1967- .
In French. A short but detailed analysis of the genre, *ô ka'angana*, which is described as a little narration whose beauty lies in the choice of subjects, the musicality of the sung strophes, and the depth of an "ethic carefully enveloped by a sexual enigma." Examples of text, footnotes, brief bibliography.

531. **Eno Belinga, Samuel-Martin**. "The traditional music of West Africa: types, styles and influences." In **African music: meeting in Yaoundé (Cameroon) 23-27 February 1970, organized by**

UNESCO, 71-75. Paris: *La revue musicale*, 1972.
This is a translation of Eno Belinga's paper, "La musique traditionelle de l'Afrique occidentale: genres, styles et influences." (528)

532. **Enquête sur la vie musicale au Congo belge, 1934-1935.** 3 vols. Questionnaire Knosp. Tervuren: Musée royal de l'Afrique centrale, 1968. 3 vols. (Musée royal de l'Afrique centrale, Tervuren, Belgium, Archives d'ethnographie, no. 11-13)
On Zaïrian music. Illustrations, map, tables, music.

533. **Epstein, Dena J.** "The folk banjo: a documentary history." ETHNOMUSICOLOGY 19, no. 3 (1975): 347-371.
This paper, selected for listing from the "U.S. Black Music Issue" of ETHNOMUSICOLOGY, contains impressive documentation of the banjo's probable origins in Africa. There are many interesting quotations from the past, along with notes, a long bibliography, and several remarkable illustrations of life on the planation. Slaves are shown playing the banjo while others dance. Another old drawing, from 1823, shows a banjo hanging on the wall of the living quarters of a Jamaican of African descent. The paper includes a detailed table of references to the banjo, arranged in chronological order from 1621 to 1851.

534. **Epstein, Dena J.** *Sinful tunes and spirituals: Black folk music to the Civil War.* Urbana: University of Illinois Press, c1977. 433pp. (Music in American Life)
An amazing amount of dedication and high-level scholarship has gone into the creation of this superlative work. Unfortunately, the title gives no indication of the importance Epstein has given to the African component, the many references to African music and musical instruments, the myriad retentions indicated in her story of the early experiences of people of African descent in the New World. Since the author is at once a librarian and a musicologist, this work represents perfection in both disciplines. A 41 page bibliography, and an exemplary index. Epstein presents impressive evidence for the African origins of the banjo.

535. **Erian, Nabila Meleka.** COPTIC MUSIC, AN EGYPTIAN TRADITION. Dissertation, University of Maryland Baltimore County, 1986. 469pp.
The author summarizes the three aims accomplished by the dissertation: (1) It has provided comprehensive information about Coptic music in its totality and context, basic for further research. (2) It has established the uniqueness of the Coptic chant tradition by defining its possible modality, formulae and genera. (3) It has provided the historical missing link in the understanding of the Egyptian character in music, persisting from Ancient Egyptian times to the present. **(UMI)**

536. **Erigène, Valentin.** *Mystère and pouvoir des sons au temps des pharaons: à la recherche d'une science perdue.* Paris: G. Trédaniel, c1987. 170pp.
In French. Examines Egyptian music to 500, including its religious aspects. Music was regarded as sacred by the Egyptians. Sound was understood as a force able

to generate life. Even though ancient Egyptian civilization disappeared, the author believes that vestiges of Egyptian mythological and cosmological beliefs about music are to be found in other cultures, and in other areas of the world. The book includes a list of musicians of ancient Egypt, and a list of museums and archaeological documents. There is a brief section on Egyptian instruments of the past. Bibliography. Eight plates of ancient paintings and stone carvings. One pendant shows animal "music-makers!"

537. **Erlmann, Veit.** *African stars: studies in black South African performance.* Chicago: University of Chicago Press, 1991. 280pp. (Chicago studies in ethnomusicology)
A history of South African performance arts, now widely celebrated in the West. The early days of *isicathamiya* (the vocal style made famous by Ladysmith Black Mambazo) are presented. Two chapters focus on Durban between the two World Wars, the evolution of Zulu music and dance, and the transformation of *ingoma* (migrant worker's music emerging in the 1930s). The life and important work of South Africa's first black ragtime composer, Reuben T. Caluza, is given, along with a reconstruction of the concert tours in the 1890s of the African-American, Orpheus M. McAdoo, and the Virginia Jubilee Singers.

538. **Erlmann, Veit.** *Booku, eine literarisch-musikalische Gattung der Fulbe des Diamaré (Nordkamerun).* Berlin: Reimer, 1979. 294pp. (Marburger Studien zur Afrika- und Asienkunde. Serie A, Afrika, vol. 20)
Annex includes texts in Fulfulde with German translation. Bibliography.

539. **Erlmann, Veit.** "A conversation with Joseph Shabala of Ladysmith Black Mambazo: aspects of African performers' life stories." **THE WORLD OF MUSIC** 31, no. 1 (1989): 31-58.
Photographs, long bibliography.

540. **Erlmann, Veit.** *A feeling of prejudice: Orpheus M. McAdoo and the Virginia Jubilee Singers in South Africa, 1890-1898.* [s.l.: s.n., 1986]. 35pp. (African Studies seminar paper. University of the Witwatersrand, African Studies Institute, no. 196)
An illuminating work concerning a little known aspect of South African history - the effects of visiting American minstrel shows. Orpheus M. McAdoo is the focus, an American black born to slave parents in 1873 and educated at Hampton University. He and his Virginia Jubilee Singers, (not to be confused with the earlier Fisk group), made special kinds of waves during their South African residency, 1890 - 1898. The period covered is politically and sociologically complex. (Alas, the typing job is unfortunate. Large, intrusively inserted arabic numbers, correlated to copious notes at the end, interfere with the flow of text.)

541. **Erlmann, Veit.** *Die Macht des Wortes: Preisgesang und Berufsmusiker bei den Fulbe des Diamaré (Nordkamerun).* Hohenschäftlarn: K. Renner, 1980. 2 vols. (Studien zur Musik
continued

Afrikas, vol. 1)
Another brilliant and authoritative work by Erlmann. On praise songs and professional music of the Fulbe of Diamaré, northern Cameroon. The text is in German. Words to songs are in Fulah and German, and the summary is in English and French. Bibliography.

542. **Erlmann, Veit.** "Music and body control in the Hausa *bori* spirit possession cult." In **Symposium on Ethnomusicology.** (2nd: 1981: Rhodes University) *Papers presented at the Second Symposium on Ethnomusicology, Music Department, Rhodes University, 24th to 26th September, 1981.* Edited by Andrew Tracey, 23-27. Grahamstown: International Library of African Music, Institute of Social and Economic Research, Rhodes University, 1982.

543. **Erlmann, Veit.** *Music and the Islamic reform in the early Sokoto empire: sources, ideology, effects.* [Marburg]: Deutsche Morgenländische Gesellschaft; Wiesbaden: Kommissionsverlag Steiner, 1986. 68pp. (Abhandlungen für die Kunde des Morgenlandes, 48, 1)
A "holy war" (*jihad*) in the early 19th century led to the establishment of the Sokoto Caliphate, which included Northern Nigeria, parts of Niger, and North Cameroon. This detailed, highly scholarly work gives insights into early African views on African music, and also the influence of Islamic dogma on African writing about African music. There is a map, a comprehensive bibliography, 22 photographs of important documents written in Arabic, and an appendix of musical terms in Hausa and Arabic.

544. **Erlmann, Veit.** "Musik und trance: Symbolische Aspekte des Bori Bessessenheits der Hausa in Maradi (Niger)," **AFRICANA MARBURGENSIA** 15, no. 1 (1982): 3-24.

545. **Erlmann, Veit.** *"Singing brings joy to the distressed:" the social history of Zulu migrant workers' choral music.* [s.l.: s.n., 1988]. 22pp. (Africa seminar)
Title from a song recorded by the choir, Cup and Saucer, in 1984 in Durban. The author refers to a paucity of studies on migrant workers' consciousness, and examines the social history of a genre of Zulu all-male choral music, called *isicathamiya*, popularized more recently by the Durban-based group, Black Mambo, and U.S. star, Paul Simon. Erlmann traces the style to the 1930s, and its pre-history to the 19th century, when American minstrel shows visited major cities of South Africa. Orpheus McAdoo's black company had considerable influence. Many song and dance styles are mentioned. Bibliography.

546. **Erlmann, Veit.** "Traditional African music in black education." **AFRICA INSIGHT** 16, no. 2 (1986): 114-119.

Eshete, Aleme
See: **Songs of the Ethiopian revolution, 1482.**

547. **Espi-Sanchis, Pedro**. "African stories in education." In **Symposium on Ethnomusicology**. (7th: 1988: Venda, South Africa). *Papers presented at the 7th Symposium on Ethnomusicology: Department of Anthropology and Ethnomusicology, University of Venda, 3rd to 5th September 1988.* Edited by Andrew Tracey, 11-13. Grahamstown, South Africa: Rhodes University, 1989.
Not only the stories, but the accompanying music is also mentioned.

548. **Essayad, A.** "La musique berbère au Maroc." In **La musique dans la vie, étude realisée sous les auspices l'Ocora et sous la direction de Tolia Nikiprowetzky**, 241-260. Vol. 1. Paris, Office de coopération radiophonique, 1967- .
A tidy, informative analysis, with footnotes and a number of music notations.

549. **Essays for a humanist: an offering to Klaus Wachsmann.** Spring Valley, New York: Town House Press, 1977. 393pp.
This volume was presented to the eminent musicologist, Klaus Wachsmann, to honor his 70th birthday. Fifteen essays were gathered and seen through publication by his many friends, appearing exactly as they were prepared by their individual authors. The foreword, by Mantle Hood, is followed by a two-page biography of Wachsmann. A complete bibliography of his works appears on pages 390-393. The book contains illustrations, transcriptions, charts, diagrams, photographs, and a list of references. A dazzling list of well-wishers is included. Those essays that relate to African music are as follows:
•**Anderson, Lois Ann**. "The *entenga* tuned-drum ensemble," 1-57.
•**Aning, Ben A.** "*Atumpan* drums: an object of historical and anthropological study," 58-72.
•**Berry, Jack**. "Is Caribbean English a tone language?" 95-104.
•**Euba, Akin**. "Ìlù Èṣù (drumming for Èṣù): analysis of a *dùndún* performance," 121-145.
•**McLeod, Norma**. "Musical instruments and history in Madagascar," 189-215.
•**Rycroft, David K**. "Evidence of stylistic continuity in Zulu 'town' music," 216-260.
•**Welch, David**. "West African cult music retentions in Haitian urban *vaudou*: a preliminary report," 337-349.
•**Willet, Frank**. "A contribution to the history of musical instruments among the Yorùbá," 350-386.

Essays on music and history in Africa
See: **Wachsmann, Klaus P., 1635.**

550. **ESSAYS ON MUSIC IN AFRICA.** 1988 - . [Bayreuth, Germany]: ÌWÀLEWÀ Haus, Universität Bayreuth.

Volume 1

This initial volume, published in 1988, is a stellar work, meticulously executed, and containing essays only by Akin Euba. It should be a primary reference source for researchers concerned with Yorùbá music and culture, and/or African art as total art. Following are merely the titles of the five essays (in chapter order) each one of which is singularly meritorious. Bibliographies follow each essay. There are many authoritative transcriptions of music with Yorùbá texts and English translations. 139pp.

- "The music of Yorùbá gods."
- "Music fit for kings: the traditional concept of kingship music in Africa."
- "Music and masks: the use of music in the African masquerade theatre."
- "Ayọ̀ Bánkọ́lé: a view of modern African art music through the works of a Nigerian composer."
- "Jùjú, highlife and Afro-beat: an introduction to popular music in Nigeria."

Volume 2

The second volume, also by Euba, was published in 1989 and is entitled, "Intercultural Perspectives." It consists of four essays by Euba that cover the topics of popular music, music theater, and neo-African art music. Included are 44 musical examples, a selected discography, and a selected list of composers and their works. 178pp.

- "*Jùjú*, *fújì* and the intercultural aspects of modern Yorùbá popular music."
- "Concepts of neo-African music as manifested in the Yorùbá folk opera."
- "My approach to neo-African music theatre."
- "Intercultural expressions in neo-African art music: methods, models and means."

551. **ETHNOMUSICOLOGY. JOURNAL OF THE SOCIETY FOR ETHNOMUSICOLOGY.** 1953- . Bloomington, Indiana.

Published three times a year, and a primary African music source. For decades some of the most distinguished musicologists of the world have published here. Besides scholarly articles, the journal contains announcements of theses and dissertations, reviews of books, films, recordings, a current bibliography (by geographic location), lists of republications, including recordings, and other timely information. Indexed annually, sometimes cumulatively for a decade, and available on microfilm and microfiche. Articles are indexed and annotated by **RILM**. **ULRICH'S** lists as **JOURNAL FOR ETHNOMUSICOLOGY**. Recent issues of the journal, however, do not indicate a title alteration.

ETHNOMUSICOLOGY NEWSLETTER

See: **Society for Ethnomusicology**. *S.E.M. Newsletter*, **1475**.

552. **Études touarègues: bilan des recherches en sciences sociales: institutions, chercheurs, bibliographie.** Under the direction of Salem Chaker, with contributions of Mohamed Aghali-Zakara...*et al.* Aix-en-Provence: ÉDISUD, c1988. 192pp.

A compendium of information on social science research pertaining to the Tuareg

people. Included are the names and addresses of major institutions throughout the world where research is being done, and similar information regarding individual researchers studying the Tuaregs. A fine bibliography, covering Tuareg language, culture and society from 1977-1987, is accessed by three indexes (by country, discipline, and miscellaneous). "Disciplines et Domaines" incorporates music-related terms. The following two brief essays contain factual information on resources for studying Tuareg music:
•**Mecheri-Saada, Nadia**. "Ethnomusicologie," 68-72.
•**Mecheri-Saada, Nadia**. "Audiographie Touarègue," 73-77.

553. **Euba, Akin**. "Creative potential and propagation of African traditional music." In **African music: meeting in Yaoundé (Cameroon) 23-27 February 1970, organized by UNESCO**, 119-125. Paris: *La Revue musicale*, 1972.
Translation of entry **557**, below.

554. **Euba, Akin**. "The dichotomy of African music." **COURIER** 26, no. 6 (1973): 65-68.

555. **Euba, Akin**. DÙNDÚN MUSIC OF THE YORÙBÁ. Dissertation, University of Ghana, 1974.

556. **Euba, Akin**. "European influences in Nigerian musical life." **NIGERIA MAGAZINE** no. 101 (1969): 477-478.
It was learned too late for altering that the title above is only a section of an entire essay by Euba entitled, "Music in traditional society." The later comprises pages 475 to 480.

557. **Euba, Akin**. "Évolution et diffusion de la musique africaine traditionelle." In **La musique africaine, réunion de Yaoundé (Cameroun)** [sur les traditions musicales de l'Afrique subsaharienne], **23-27 février 1970, organisée par l'UNESCO**, 117-124. Paris: *La revue musicale,* Richard-Masse, 1972.
This is the original French version translated into English. (See **553**, above.)

558. **Euba, Akin**. "Ìlù Ẹ̀ṣù (drumming for Ẹ̀ṣù): analysis of a *dùndún* performance." In **Essays for a humanist: an offering to Klaus Wachsmann**, 121-145. Spring Valley, New York: Town House Press, 1977.
Photographs, bibliography.

558a. **Euba, Akin**. "The potential of traditional music as a contemplative art." **BLACK ORPHEUS** 3, no. 1 (1974): 54-60.

558b. **Euba, Akin**. *Yorùbá drumming: the dùndún tradition*. Anne McLellan, 16 Mabel Thornton House, Burma Road, London N16

9BG, England, 1991. 545pp.
Everything one would want to know about dùndún is contained in this authoritative and comprehensive work by Nigeria's foremost musicologist. The dùndún, an hourglass tension drum used extensively by the Yorùbá for music-making, also serves as an important speech surrogate instrument. An overview of the theory and practice associated with dùndún also affords a significant insight into Yorùbá drumming in general. Fourteen chapters are divided into: The Social Background; The Ensemble; The Poetry and the Music; Related Musical Types and other Art Forms. Many illustrations, music and text examples, tables, figures, graphs, tuning chart, maps, photos, appendices, bibliography.

559. **Euba, Akin**. "In search of a common musical language in Africa." INTERLINK. **The Nigerian-American Quarterly** 3, no. 3 (1967).
There may be other articles on music in this publication, begun in Lagos, NUSA Publishers, 1963. It appears to have run only through April of 1972.
Note that the next entry has the same title.

560. **Euba, Akin**. "In search of a common musical language in Africa." In *Development of materials for a one year course in African music for the general undergraduate student (project in African music)*. Edited by Vada E. Butcher, *et al.*, 85-87. [Washington]: Office of Education, 1970.
Note that this bears the same title as the preceding entry.

561. **Euba, Akin**. "An introduction to music in Nigeria." NIGERIAN MUSIC REVIEW 1, no.1 (1977): 1-38.

562. **Euba, Akin**. "Islamic music culture among the Yorùbá: a preliminary survey." In *Essays on music and history in Africa*. Edited by Klaus P. Wachsmann, 171-181. Evanston: Northwestern University Press, 1971.
Well-footnoted.

Euba, Akin. "Music in traditional society."
See: **556**.

563. **Euba, Akin**. "The music of Nigeria." In *Development of materials for a one year course in African music for the general undergraduate student (project in African music)*. Edited by Vada E. Butcher, *et al.*, 93-98. [Washington]: Office of Education, 1970.

563a. **Euba, Akin**. "Musicology in the context of African culture." ODÙ New Series no. 2 (1969): 3-18.
Bibliography.

Euba, Akin. "The poetential of traditional music as a contemplative art."
See: **558a.**

564. **Euba, Akin**. "Preface to a study of Nigerian music; in the light of references which made it what it is." **ÌBÀDÀN** 21 (1965): 53-62.

565. **Euba, Akin**. "Six Yorùbá songs." **ODÙ** [Initial Series] no. 9 (1963): 5-12.
The transcribed songs are presented, with nothing else.

566. **Euba, Akin**. "Traditional elements as the basis of new African art music." **AFRICAN URBAN STUDIES** 5, no. 4 (1970): 52-62.

Euba, Akin. "Yorùbá drumming."
See: **558b.**

Euba, Akin
See also: •ESSAYS ON MUSIC IN AFRICA, 550.
•NIGERIAN MUSIC REVIEW, 1177.

567. **Evans, David**. "Africa and the blues." **LIVING BLUES** no. 10, (1972):27-29.

568. **Evans, David**. "African elements in twentieth-century United States black folk music." In **INTERNATIONAL MUSICOLOGICAL SOCIETY. Congress. Report**, 54-66, 1977. Berkeley, California.
Source is **RILM**, 1981.

569. **Ewens, Graeme**. *Luambo Franco and 30 years of OK jazz, 1956-1986*. Discography by Ronnie Graham. London: Off the Record Press, c1986. 64pp.
This is a biography that traces three decades of the career of famed Luambo Franco, of Zaïre, and his OK Jazz group. A singer, guitarist, saxophonist, band leader, composer, arranger, and stylist, Franco held a distinguished place in the history of African urban music. In 1988, Ronnie Graham (**638**) referred to him as "beyond doubt Africa's most popular and influential musician." This book contains a short bibliography (called Sources) and a complete discography starting with Franco's early recordings in the 1950s on 78s. Not many photos, but those included are worthwhile.

569a. **Expanding horizons in African studies. Program of African Studies, Northwestern University; proceedings of the twentieth anniversary conference, 1968**. Edited by Gwendolen M. Carter and Ann Paden. Evanston, llinois, Northwestern University Press, 1969. 364pp.
continued

The following essay by Klaus P. Wachsmann is responded to directly afterward by J. H. Kwabena Nketia:

•**Wachsmann, Klaus P.** "Ethnomusicology in African studies: the next twenty years," 131-142.

570. **Explorations in ethnomusicology: essays in honor of David P. McAllester.** Edited by Charlotte J. Frisbie. Detroit: Information Coordinators, 1986. 280pp. (Detroit monographs in musicology, 9)

Contains a number of essays, a bibliography, index, and an autobiographical sketch of David P. McAllester.

•**Kebede, Ashenafi.** "Musical innovation and acculturation in African music," 59-67.

•**Stone, Ruth M.** "Unity of the arts in the aesthetics of *Kpelle* performance," 179-185.

571. **Expressively black: the cultural basis of ethnic identity.** Edited by Geneva Gay and Willie L. Baber. New York: Praeger, 1987. 372pp.

Of particular interest because of the following essay:

•**Maultsby, Portia K.** "From backwoods to city streets: the Afro-American musical journey," 109-136.

572. **Eze, Leopold Françoise.** "The *nkul*, that marvelous traditional medium of social communication." In **African culture: Algiers Symposium July 21st - August 1st, 1969.** *The first Pan-African cultural festival*, 316-320. Alger: S.N.E.D. (Société Nationale d'Édition et de Diffusion), 1969.

Reading this enthralling paper about the making of the Cameroonian talking drum, *nkul*, and about its legendary origin, its language, its uses, one *also* realizes how "marvelous" it is, and fears, along with Eze, its possible disappearance from Africa. Eze recommends that an adaptation and systematic study of the instrument and its use be undertaken on a very large scale throughout Africa. He believes that such an effort would bring African cultures and peoples closer together. Drum texts are included, and very brief staff notations of pitches.

573. **Ezegbe, Clement Chukuemeka.** THE DEVELOPMENT OF A SOCIOCULTURAL CURRICULUM IN NIGERIAN STUDIES: AN INTEGRATION OF ETHNOMUSICOLOGY AND SOCIAL STUDIES. Dissertation, University of British Columbia, 1981. 314pp.

The purpose of this study was to develop a curriculum for ethnomusicological education in Nigerian elementary schools based on the integration of ethnomusicology with social studies. Three curricula were developed, consistent with the aims of the Nigerian educational system - particularly the social studies curriculum - and field-tested in upper elementary classes in two Nigerian elementary schools. Emphasis was on increasing inter-ethnic and cross-ethnic understanding and respect in a country with more than 250 ethnic groups. Salutary results are described in the dissertation. **(UMI)**

E

574. **Ezegbe, Clement Chukuemeka.** THE IGBO UBO-AKA: ITS ROLE AND MUSIC AMONG THE NRI PEOPLE OF NIGERIA. **Master's Thesis, University of British Columbia, 1978. 307pp.**

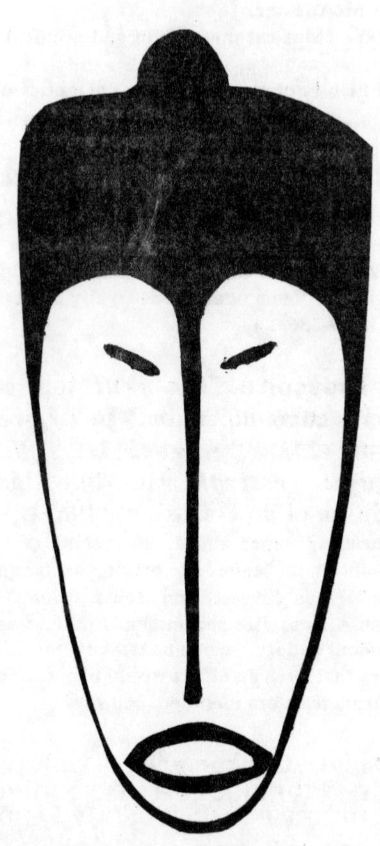

575. **Fage, John D.** "Music and history: a historian's view of the African picture." In *Essays on music and history in Africa.* Edited by Klaus P. Wachsmann, 257-266. Evanston: Northwestern University Press, 1971.
Based on his own knowledge of African history, Fage examines critically some of the strengths and weaknesses of historical approaches used by musicologists whose essays appear in the book. He indicates that the musicologist's research often serves merely to substantiate what is already known historically about an area, rather than to contribute something new. He is cautionary about the oral tradition, and about song texts as sources of reliable historical information unless carefully checked and cross-checked. But he also indicates that the historian and musicologist-historian can enlighten each other through research in their respective disciplines. Footnotes.

576. **Fallers, Margaret Chave.** *The eastern lacustrine Bantu (Ganda and Soga).* London: International African Institute, 1960. 86pp. (Ethnographic survey of Africa: East central Africa, pt. 11)
Somehow, listed under the heading, Economy, there are two pages of information on musical instruments of the area. Instruments are classified by their scientific designations: idiophones, aerophones, membranophones, and chordophones, with a brief paragraph about each category. Folding map, bibliography.

577. **Fampou, François.** *Ku sá: introduction à la percussion africaine.* Paris: L'Harmattan, c1986. 159pp.
African music, emphasis on percussion instruments. Bibliography and discography.

578. **Fanjul, Serafín.** *El Mawwāl egipcio: expresión literaria popular.* Preface by Pedro Martínez Montávez. Madrid: Instituto Hispano-Arabe de Cultura, 1976. 165pp.
On Arabic songs of Egypt. Text in Arabic and Spanish. Bibliography, discography.

579. **Fanshawe, David.** *African Sanctus: a story of travel and music.* London: Collins and Harvill Press, 1975. 208pp. [This is listed elsewhere as published by Knell in 1986].
Translations of several Masai cattle songs, and a Sudanese love song may be worthwhile. Other passing music references might also be examined by a discerning scholar, since British composer Fanshawe is not an ethnologist, but an ardent hitch-hiker who underwent years of privation and joy photographing and recording the Africa he loves. But *African Sanctus* "converts" excerpts of African music, much of it Islamic, and that of other traditional religions and cultures of East Africa, to a Christian Mass incorporating rock drums. All is subsumed - even lamentations for a dead fisherman, and certain other items recorded without approval of the people involved. Photographs. Illustrations.

580. **Farmer, Henry George.** *Islam.* Leipzig: Deutscher für Musik [1966]. 205pp. (Musikgeschichte in Bildern 3: Musik des Mittelalters

und der Renaissance, Part 2)

Primarily pictorial, but augmented by impressive scholarly writing. The focus is Islamic works of art having to do with music - particularly musical instruments - that originated in earlier phases of Islamic history. Egypt is the country most represented. There is an impressive 60 page chart that summarizes what was happening historically and culturally in Islamic countries over many centuries. A separate column is devoted to music. Though Egypt receives considerable coverage in this chart, there is even a much larger section on North Africa treated as a separate entity. Bibliography. Index is by instrumental classification.

Farmer, Henry George
See also: **Daniel, Francisco Salvador.** *The music and musical instruments of the Arab*, **410.**

581. **Farrell, Eileen Ruth.** NGOMA YA USHINDANI: COMPETITIVE SONG EXCHANGE AND THE SUBVERSION OF HIERARCHY IN A SWAHILI MUSLIM TOWN ON THE KENYA COAST. Dissertation, Harvard University, 1980.

582. **Al-Faruqi** [Al-Fārūqī], **Lois Ibsen**, comp. *An annotated glossary of Arabic musical terms.* Forewords by Ali Jihad Racy and Don Michael Randel. Westport, Connecticut: Greenwood Press, c1981. 511pp.

An extremely important reference tool if one wishes to study Arabic music in Africa or elsewhere. As is said in the Introduction, "This is the first Arabic-English glossary of musical terms to be published for the Western student or investigator of Arabian music." Five appendixes include an index of English musical terms, an index of Arabic roots, a guide to pronunciation and transliteration, a list of abbreviations, and an authors and references cited index. Phenomenal scholarship!

583. **Al-Fasi, Muhammad.** *Chants anciens des femmes de Fès.* [Cover illustration by the author]. [Paris]. Seghers, [1967]. 119pp.

Fezzan songs. Songs and music of women of Morocco. Love poetry.

584. **Feijoo, Samuel.** "African influence in Latin America: oral and written literature." In *Africa in Latin America: essays on history, culture, and socialization.* Edited by Manuel Moreno Fraginals, 145-169. New York: Holmes and Meier, 1984.

Feijoo says, "The influence of the words, euphonics, proverbs, rhythms, dances and songs of the tense personality of the Black African, inherited and transformed by the descendants of those who had been slaves, is a creative force in present-day Latin America." He dwells on this force, gives examples of sayings, stories, song texts and poetry from Brazil and Columbia, and concludes with a discussion of the influence of the *son* (a strong Cuban music and dance form) on black poetry throughout Latin America. Unfortunately, not all resource materials are clearly identified in this book's bibliography.

585. **Festac '77**. London: Africa Journal Ltd., c1977. 152pp.
This is a Souvenir book of the second World Black and African Festival of Arts and Culture, Lagos, Nigeria, 15 January-12 February, 1977. A brief essay by Senghor, entitled "Black Culture," and a four page one by Nketia, called "Music in African Culture," redeem this popularly written souvenir book packed with generalities, but enriched by some vibrant photos of musicians and dancers. An appendix with basic facts about Festac is included.

586. **Festschrift to Ernst Emsheimer on the occasion of his 70th birthday, January 15th 1974**. Edited by Gustaf Hilleström. Stockholm: Nordiska Musikförlaget, 1974. 310pp.
- **Söderberg, Bertil**. "Afrikanische Musikinstrumente und bildende Kunst," 214-223.
- **Widstrand, Carl Gösta**. "A Masai musical instrument," 252.

587. **Fiagbedzi, Nissio**. THE MUSIC OF THE ANLO-EWE OF GHANA: AN ETHNOMUSICOLOGICAL ENQUIRY INTO ITS HISTORY, CULTURAL MATRIX AND STYLE. Dissertation, University of California, Los Angeles, 1977. 491pp.

588. **Fiagbedzi, Nissio**. "Notes on membranophones of the Anlo-Ewe." **RESEARCH REVIEW** 8, no. 1 (1971): 90-97.

589. **Fiagbedzi, Nissio**. "On signing and symbolism in music: the evidence from among an African people." **JOURNAL OF THE PERFORMING ARTS** 1, no. 1 (1980): 54-65.
This essay is also found in **More than drumming** (Irene V. Jackson, Editor, c1985), pages 41-48. **(1110)** Notes, bibliography.

590. **Fiagbedzi, Nissio**. "A preliminary inquiry into inherent rhythms in Anlo dance drumming." **JOURNAL OF THE PERFORMING ARTS** 1, no. 1 (1980): 83-92.

591. **Fiagbedzi, Nissio**. *Religious music traditions in Africa: a critical evaluation of contemporary problems and challenges: an inter-faculty lecture delivered on Thursday, 17th August, 1978*. Accra: Ghana Universities Press, 1979. 30pp.
Includes bibliographical references, illustrations.

592. **Fiagbedzi, Nissio**. "Sogbadzi songs: a study of Yeve music." Diploma in Music, University of Ghana, 1966.

593. **Fiagbedzi, Nissio**. "Toward a philosophy of theory in ethnomusicological research." In **African musicology: current trends: a festschrift presented to J. H. Kwabena Nketia**. Edited

by Jacqueline Cogdell DjeDje, and William G. Carter, 45-57. [Atlanta, Georgia: Crossroads Press, 1988]- .
Although the topic is broad in scope, there are implications for African musicology, including mention of prior studies in this field. Bibliography includes references on musicology in general, African music in particular.

594. **Fiberesima, Adam Dagogo.** A FIELD STUDY OF THE KIRIOWU CULT AND AN ORIGINAL MUSICAL COMPOSITION BASED ON THE MUSIC OF THE CULT AS A CULTURAL AND EDUCATIONAL SYSTEM: THE CASE OF THE OKRIKA PEOPLE OF THE RIVERS STATE OF NIGERIA. Dissertation, Rutgers University, 1982. 177pp.
The part music plays in *Kiriowu*, a religious cult of the *Okrika* people, is analyzed. The author also includes an original composition, *Drum Symphony*, based on this music. At the time Fiberesima did his research, the average music student in Nigeria was unacquainted with *Kiriowu* music because of taboos surrounding its performance, but Fiberesima anticipates a time when the music will no longer be confined to religion. He believes that religious music can inspire and guide new art, and cherishes the artistic and spiritual values of traditional music and dance. Enlightened educational suggestions follow. Bibliography, 20 figures.

595. **Fishing in rivers of Sierra Leone: oral literature.** Edited by Heribert Hinzen,...*et al*. Photographs by Inga and Udo Quedenfeldt. Freetown: People's Educational Association of Sierra Leone, 1987. 342pp. (Stories and songs from Sierra Leone, 25)
A strange title but a handsome work dedicated to the story-tellers, singers and musicians of Sierra Leone. Though the larger part contains transcribed gems from the oral tradition - tales, riddles, proverbs, and songs from all over the country - spectacular glossy colored photos crystallize praise-singers, musicians, dancers, singers, and story-tellers in glorious moments of time. Herbert Hinzen, consummate interviewer, draws out his artist subjects with a skill issuing from sincerity and respect. Photos and life stories of Ebenezer Calender and Salia Koroma, prominent musicians, are especially appreciated. Index, map.

596. **Fitzmaurice, Robert M.** MUSIC EDUCATION IN PUERTO RICO: A HISTORICAL SURVEY WITH GUIDELINES FOR AN EXEMPLARY CURRICULUM. Dissertation, Florida State University, 1970.
The section of particular interest is under the heading, Education and Music to 1800, subheading Slave Music and Instruments (pages 19 to 24). In this section, Fitzmaurice points out the strong African influences on Puerto Rican music, naming a number of African-derived instruments and the way they are used, as well as dance forms. Lengthy bibliography.

597. **Fléouter, Claude.** *La mémoire du peuple noir*. [published by] F.R. [France-Regions] 3. Paris: A. Michel, 1979. 137pp.
Intense. Contains impressive portraits in writing and photograph of black musicians of the New World and Lagos. Besides focusing on American musicians and their music forms, the book examines reggae, the samba, and jùjú from a sociological perspective. Included are Joseph Hill (Jamaica), Fẹlá Aníkúlápó-Kútì

(Nigeria), three significant Brazilians - Milton Nascimento, Clementina de Jesus (a major figure in Candomblé), "Valdemar" (player and teacher of the *berimbau*) - not to mention countless distinguished American musicians and the music forms with which they are associated. Photographs are superb and capture the essence of each individual. African cultural connections come through strong.

598. **FOLK ROOTS.** 1979- . London, England: Southern Rag Ltd.
Appears monthly. This publication, formerly known as **SOUTHERN RAG**, contains all sorts of information on people, festivals and events, clubs and gigs, tours, reviews of cassettes, albums, videos. In one issue (no. 95, 1991) there were two articles on African music, an ad for an African group called, "Jali Role" (!), and an imposing picture of Senegal's popular, Baaba Maal on the cover. The publication is broad in coverage, and has had many other articles on African music, or music of the diaspora.

- **Anderson, Ian.** "Roots at risk: the music of Madagascar is at a dangerous crossroads says Ian Anderson," no. 95 (1991): 20-22.
- **Prince, Rob.** "Baaba Mall talks to Rob Prince about the importance of traditional music," no. 95 (1991) 34-37.
- **Stapleton, Chris.** "Golden Guinea," no. 61 (1988): 27, 29.

Forster, Merlin H.
See: **Traditional and renewal: essays on twentieth-century Latin American literature and culture, 1583.**

Fortune, G.
See: **Shona praise poetry, 1450.**

599. **Freedom is coming: songs of protest and praise from South Africa.** Songs collected and edited by Anders Nyberg. Translations by Jonas Jonson...*et al.* Uppsala, Sweden: Utryck, 1984. 36pp.
This is a beautifully executed song book with an heroic format. The songs, of a religious or otherwise spiritual nature, have been passed on orally and have never appeared in print before. Words are in Sotho, Xhosa, and Zulu, with accompanying text in English. Large bold music transcriptions are on the right side. On the left, huge black and white photographs, with succinct and dramatic captions, fill the page. Some quotations by Bishop Desmond Tutu are incorporated. Musical instructions precede songs. Performers are asked to "move" to the songs in African style. Cassette tape available (hopefully, still) from the publisher.

600. **Friedman, Robert.** MAKING AN ABSTRACT WORLD CONCRETE: KNOWLEDGE AND STRUCTURAL DIMENSIONS OF PERFORMANCE AMONG BATÁ DRUMMERS SANTERÍA. Dissertation, Indiana University, 1982.
The study examines the music of batá [Yorùbá = *bàtá*] drummers in performance events of the African-Cuban religion Santería, derived and practiced primarily by Cubans and Puerto Ricans living in the Caribbean and major urban areas of the United States. (Those who practice Santería trace it to Yorùbá belief systems of slaves brought to Cuba between the 18th and 19th centuries.) The fieldwork, done

in New York City, was centered on how batá drummers' concepts of organized sound exist within a matrix of conceptual schemes for action. **UMI.**

Frisbie, Charlotte J.
See: **Explorations in ethnomusiolcogy: essays in honor of David P. McAllester, 570.**

601. **Frontera, Nélida Muñoz de.** A STUDY OF SELECTED NINETEENTH CENTURY PUERTO RICAN COMPOSERS AND THEIR MUSICAL OUTPUT. 4 vols. Dissertation, New York University, 1988. 810pp.
For sheer bulk (4 volumes, countless photos and documents) this dissertation takes all prizes! The four composers, Felipe Gutiérrez y Espinosa, Manuel Gregorio Tavarez Ropero, Juan Morel Campos, and José Ignacio Quinton Rosario, are only part of a vast exploration of many other subjects - probably too ambitious for one dissertation. Frontera says that the four musicians had "some African blood," were largely self-taught, yet she apparently finds no African traces in their music, except for Campos (based primarily on his titles). The bibliography indicates a deficiency in primary materials on African music and African music retentions, which may explain things.

602. **Frucht, Richard,** ed. *Black society in the New World.* New York: Random House, [1971]. 403pp.
See the following essay:
•**Elder, Jacob D.** "Color, music, and conflict: a study of aggression in Trinidad with reference to the role of traditional music," 315-323.

603. **Fyle, C. Magbaily.** *Tradition, song and chant of the Yalunka.* Freetown: People's Educational Association of Sierra Leone, 1986. 32pp. (Stories and songs from Sierra Leone, 22)
This work derives from research undertaken by the author at an earlier time. Three sections are included, each with an introduction and text in English. The first, an epic recorded in Sierra Leone in 1973, is entitled "Yeli Foday and Long Ago." *Yeli* Foday Samura, one of the most popular *Yeliba* [i.e., *jali*] of the Koinaduga District, is characterized as usually playing "an instrument closely resembling a xylophone." [If it isn't a xylophone, what *is* it?I The second section is entitled, The Power of Hunters. Two Female Initiation Songs comprise the third section. No music transcriptions are included.

604. Galand-Pernet, Paulette. *Recueil de poèmes chleuhs.* Paris: Klincksieck, 1972- (Études linguistiques, 16)
Berber songs. Text in Berber and French but without the music. Commentary in French.

605. Galeota, Joseph. DRUM MAKING AMONG THE SOUTHERN EWE PEOPLE OF GHANA AND TOGO. Master's Thesis, Wesleyan University, 1985.

606. Gansemans, Jos. *Les instruments de musique du Rwanda: étude ethnomusicologique.* Tervuren, Belgium: Koninklijk Museum voor Midden-Afrika, 1988. 361pp. (Menswetenschappen = Sciences humaines. Annales, vol. 127)
Begins with information about the country, its history, population, and music life. Rwandan instruments are classified and described, and 93 beautiful photographs show every category of Rwandan instrument (even dog bells) and close-ups of musicians enjoying their favorite sport. Several variations of a given instrumental type are pictured. The stages of fashioning a drum are shown from beginning to end. An 18 page bibliography and short discography augment this fine work.

607. Gansemans, Jos. *Les instruments de musique Luba: (Shaba, Zaïre).* Tervuren: Musée royal de l'Afrique centrale, 1980. 100pp. (Annalen. Series in-8°. Menselijke wetenschappen, no. 103 = Annales. Série in-8°. Sciences humaines, no. 103)
Music and musical instruments of the Luba people of Shaba, Zaïre. Bibliography.

608. Gansemans, Jos. DE JACHTLIEDEREN DER LUBA-SHANKADI. Graduate Paper, University of Louvain, 1967. 230pp.

609. Gansemans, Jos. "De Jachtliederin der Luba-Shankadi [Hunting songs of the Luba-Shankadi]." AFRIKA-TERVUREN 14, no. 2 (1972): 2-5.

610. Gansemans, Jos. "La morphologie des chants Luba (Shaba-Zaïre)." AFRICAN MUSICOLOGY 1, no.1 (1983): 34-40.
In French. Illustrations, music, bibliography.

Gansemans, Jos. *La musique et son rô le dans la vie sociale et rituelle Luba.*
See: **Banje, Han.** *Kaonde song and ritual*, **181.**

611. Gansemans, Jos. *Volksmuziekinstrumenten, getuigen en resultaat van een interetnische samenleving: een organologische studie met betrekking tot Aruba, Bonaire en Curaçao.* Tervuren, Belgium: Koninklijk Museum voor Midden-
continued

Afrika, 1989. 185pp. (Annales Sciences humaines, 128)
This work is an organology (i.e., description of instruments) of the Caribbean islands of Aruba, Bonaire, and Curaçao, and is written in Flemish. Instruments of African derivation are not the only ones described, but they certainly make up the bulk of the book. Some 84 photographs of instruments and instrumentalists from the three islands are included, with detailed accompanying information and often photos of their African equivalents in use. (The barrel piano, a decidedly non-African instrument found in Aruba and Curaçao, gets a chapter.) Maps, line drawings, and a fine bibliography that incorporates articles from lesser-known journals.

612. **Gansemans, Jos.** *Zentralafrika.* [A collaboration by Simha Arom, Geneviève Dournon, Benoit Quersin, Pierre Sallée, Paul van Thiel and Daniel Vangroenweghe]. Leipzig: VEB Deutscher Verlag für Musik, 1986. (Musikgeschichte in Bildern: Musikethnologie, Part 9)

613. **Garfias, Robert.** "Die Rolle der Träume und Geisterbesessenheit in der Mbira Dza Vadzimu - Musik der Shona in Zimbabwe." In *Musikkulturen in Afrika.* Edited by Erich Stockmann, 221-245. Berlin: Verlag Neue Musik, 1987.
The role of dreams and spirit possession in *mbira dza vadzimu* music of the Shona of Zimbabwe is the subject. A few headings (translated from the German) are: Music in Ritual, Compositional Structure, The Music of *Nngororombe*-Ensembles. Transcriptions by several researchers are included. Several black and white photos show pan-pipes, drums, and rattles in use, and, of course, the *mbira dza vadzimu.* There are five bibliographic entries.

614. **Gaskin, L. J. P.** *A select bibliography of music of Africa.* Compiled at the International African Institute by L. J. P. Gaskin, under the direction of K. P. Wachsmann. London: International African Institute, 1965. 83pp. (Africa bibliography series B)
Researchers are referred to this superlative, primary source for coverage of "all known works...of relevance and significance" prior to 1965. Especially valuable is the inclusion of earlier European periodicals. (It did not hurt at all that this was directed by Klaus Wachsmann!) Entries, totalling 3370, are organized into: General, Africa (General), African Music Geographically Arranged, Musical Instruments, Dance, Catalogues, and Indexes. This is the first bibliography of its kind to include both dance, and African countries north of the Sahara. Includes a brief section on Cuba. Excellent cross-referencing. No annotations.

615. **Gaudet, Mary Marcia Gendron.** THE FOLKLORE AND CUSTOMS OF THE WEST BANK OF ST. JOHN THE BAPTIST PARISH. Dissertation, University of Southern Louisiana, 1980. 184pp.
This dissertation is included because various aspects of a rich Louisianian folk life, including songs, are traced to their origins in France, Germany and Africa. Information was gathered from taped interviews. Holidays with their associated rituals are described. Tales of slavery and other black experiences are included,

some interviews being in French with English translation. The presence of a large black population in an isolated part of Louisiana that is one of the oldest populated areas of the state, yet relatively untouched by industrialization, make this a likely site for research into African retentions.

Gay, Geneva
See: **Expressively Black, 571.**

616. **Gayle, Addison.** *The Black aesthetic.* Garden City, New York: Doubleday, 1971. 432pp.
Treats a number of African-American arts, though somehow dance was not included. There is a music section from which the following essay was extracted, not so much because of its comments about African music, though they are interesting, but because of its perceptive and enormously humorous analysis of a Western orchestral performance seen through African eyes.
•**Walton, Ortiz M.** "A comparative analysis of the African and the Western aesthetic," 154-164.

617. **Gbàdàmósí, Bákàrè, and Ulli Beier**, trans. "Yorùbá funeral songs." **BLACK ORPHEUS** no. 22 (1967): 5-7.
Words to three songs are included.

618. **Gbomba, Lele.** *The bossy wife.* Freetown: People's Educational Association of Sierra Leone, 1987. 91pp. (Stories and songs from Sierra Leone, 23)
Short stories and songs.

Gerson-Kiwi, Edith
See: **Lachmann, Robert.** *Posthumous works*, **938.**

619. **Geschichten und Lieder der Afrikaner.** Edited by August Seidel. Nendeln, Liechtenstein: Kraus Reprint, 1970. 340pp.
Originally published by Schall and Grund, Berlin, 1896. Songs, tales and folklore of Africa. Includes bibliographical references.

620. **Gessain, Monique.** "Les Malinke des chants de chasseurs Bassari." **OBJETS ET MONDES** 12, no. 4 (1972): 355-360.

621. **Ghana praise: tunes from Ghana, Africa, and the world.** Designed and illustrated by Charles Enning. Accra, Ghana: Asempa Publishers, 1979.
This hymn book containing music is cross-referenced to **Asempa hymns**, which contains the words, **142**. The foreword explains that with the publication of these books, a situation has been corrected in which Western hymnody was favored at the expense of other sources. For the first time in print are compositions of several generations of Ghanaian hymn-writers, and "fresh material" from other countries in Africa and Asia. Included are 144 songs by Ghanaian composers, 19

from other parts of Africa, and 33 from other parts of the world. Several indexes make searching easier. See also: **Good News Hymns, 632.**

622. **Gibson, Gordon D.** "The Himba trumpet." [Angola] MAN 62, no. 258 (1962): 161-163.

623. **Gĩkũyũ**. Compiled by John Kamenyi Wahome. Kampala: East African Literature Bureau, 1974. 40pp. (Traditional music and songs for adult education)
(First published in 1970 by Equatorial Publishers of Nairobi, and designed for teaching in the primary school.) One song (of 40 total) is on each page, with a charming illustration at the top, and notated melody on the treble staff below. Gĩkũyũ syllables match notes (the latter identified by a solmization system with fixed do). A few explanatory sentences about each song occur at the end of the book. The work represents a much needed gathering together of music from the past that had been eclipsed or replaced by western forms. Foreword by R. D. Wambũgũ, Senior Inspector of Schools (Music).

624. **Gildenhuys, Cecilia**. "Musical instruments of South West Africa/Namibia." In **Symposium on Ethnomusicology**. (2nd: 1981: Rhodes University) *Papers presented at the Second Symposium on Ethnomusicology, Music Department, Rhodes University, 24th to 26th September, 1981.* Edited by Andrew Tracey, 28-33. Grahamstown: International Library of African Music, Institute of Social and Economic Research, Rhodes University, 1982.

624a. **Gillis, Frank**. "Hot rhythm in piano ragtime." In **Music in the Americas**. Edited by George List and Juan Orrego-Salas, 91-104. [Bloomington]: Indiana University Research Center in Anthropology, Folklore and Linguistics, 1967.
Notes, and many musical notations.

625. **Gillis, Frank, and Alan P. Merriam**, comps. *Ethnomusicology and folk music: an international bibliography of dissertations and theses.* Middletown, Connecticut. Published for the Society for Ethnomusicology by the Wesleyan University Press, 1966. 148pp.
A useful guide that is cross-indexed. Many references are found in the index under African Music and associated words, such as names of specific countries, instruments, etc. Annotations are added "whenever possible." This would be a good source for those researching dissertations or theses on African music *before* 1960 (with few exceptions, the earliest year included in the present bibliography).

626. **Gilombe, Mudiji-Malamba.** "Community life and the Church: selected perspectives and points of contact as exemplified in the Phende society of Zaïre." In **Symposium musico-ethnologicum.** Edited by Johannes Overath, 56-69. MUSICES APTATIO 1980 (Roma: CIMS, 1980).
The work is trilingual, in English, French, and German. Bibliography. Abstracted in **RILM**, 1965.

627. **Godsey, Larry Dennis.** MUSICAL FORM IN SANDAWE *GÓŨ* AND *KEREM'TA* SONGS. Master's Thesis, University of California, Los Angeles, 1975. 175pp.
The Sandawe are people of Tanzania. This is about circumcision music used during and after the ceremony.

628. **Godsey, Larry Dennis.** THE USE OF THE XYLOPHONE IN THE FUNERAL CEREMONY OF THE BIRIFOR OF NORTHWEST GHANA. Dissertation, University of California, Los Angeles, 1980. 332pp.
Maps, music, bibliography.

629. **Godsey, Larry Dennis.** "The use of variation in Birifor funeral music." In **Studies in African music**. Co-editors, J. H. Kwabena Nketia, and Jacqueline Cogdell DjeDje, 67-80. [Los Angeles]: Program in Ethnomusicology, Department of Music, University of California, Los Angeles, 1984.
Notated examples, one of a complete performance of *Darafo* by Belimbee Deri. Bibliography, discography, map, photographs.

630. **Goines, Leonard.** "Music of Africa south of the Sahara." In **Music in world cultures.** Edited by Margaret Mead. MUSIC EDUCATORS JOURNAL 59, no. 2 (1972): 46-51.
Photos of instruments and instrumentalists are included in the essay.

631. **Gomi, Nâ Nasia.** *Finasons.* Tomé Varela da Silva. Praia: Institutu Kauberdianu di Libru, 1985. 117pp. (Kuleson Tradisons oral di Kauberdi)
Written in the Portuguese Creole of Cape Verde. Includes information on the songs and oral tradition of the island. Illustrations.

632. **Good news hymns: (Asɛmpa hymns).** Drawings and cover design by Abraham Yeboah. Accra, Ghana: Asɛmpa Publishers, 1978. 176pp.
Words only are included in this book, cross-referenced to its companion book that has the music, **Ghana praise, 621.** (In the latter entry, the uniqueness of these publications is explained.) The hymns are translated into English from Ewe, Fante, Ga, and Twi. "Asɛmpa" means "good news" in Twi. There is also a foreword, a list of subjects, notes on tunes and references, an authors' and

translators' index with brief biographies, and a words index. This edition does not contains Protestant and Catholic communion services. Another edition designed for schools and colleges, entitled **Asempa hymns**, does, **142**.

633. Gosebrink, Jean E. Meeh, ed. *African studies information resources directory*. Oxford: Hans Zell, 1986. 572pp.
"Published for the African Studies Association." An important, comprehensive reference tool. Covers the United States only. Over 100 entries relate to subSaharan African music. In the index, music references are dispersed under the following subject headings: Music & Musical Instruments; Phonorecordings & Phonorecording Collections; Phonorecordings, Sellers of; Oral Data Collections, and also listed under a few African areas or specific countries having a subheading Music. A meticulously executed and informative book.

Gosebrink, Jean E. Meeh
See also: •**Africa, 20.**
•**Africa**, 2d ed., **21.**

634. Gottheim, Vivian I. "*Bumba-meu-boi*, a musical play from Maranhão." THE WORLD OF MUSIC 30, no. 2 (1988): 40-66.
Bibliography, notes, photographs. (Brazil)

635. Gourlay, K. A. *The making of Karimojong' cattle songs*. [Nairobi]: University of Nairobi, Institute of African Studies, [1971]. 13pp. (Discussion paper - University of Nairobi, Institute of African Studies, no. 18)
Bibliography.

636. Gourlay, K. A. "Songs of the *Karimojong*: a talk with slides." In **Symposium on Ethnomusicology**. (3rd: 1982: University of Natal) [4th: 1983: Rhodes University] *Papers presented at the Third and Fourth Symposia on Ethnomusicology*, Music Department, University of Natal, Durban, 16th to 19th September 1982, 2-8; Music Department, Rhodes University, 7th to 8th October 1983. Grahamstown, South Africa: International Library of African Music, 1984.
Note that this paper is in the 3rd Symposium. (The 3rd and 4th Symposia are bound in one volume.)

637. Gourlay, K. A. STUDIES IN KARIMOJONG MUSICAL CULTURE. 2 vols. Dissertation, University of East Africa, 1971. 523pp.

638. Graham, Ronnie. *The Da Capo guide to contemporary African music*. New York: Da Capo Press, 1988. 315pp.
An outstanding pioneer work, and a mandatory reference tool. Essentially a giant discography of subSaharan urban (i.e., "popular," "modern," "contemporary," "commerical") music. Some information on traditional music. Biographies of key

key African musicians, information about groups, dance and music forms (by country), historical data, a penetrating analysis of the music industry, (with compassionate understanding of the African musician's particular struggles), over twenty political, linguistic and geographical maps, and a well-executed index. Hardly a recording group is not mentioned, though, as Graham acknowledges, this means that hundreds of fine unrecorded musicians are unavoidably eliminated. A select bibliography with a few inaccuracies in names and spellings.

639. **Graham, Ronnie.** *Stern's guide to contemporary African music.* London: Zwan: "Off the Record Press," c1988. 315pp.
This represents the first publication of the immediately preceding entry. It would appear to be identical in content.

640. **Gray, John.** *African music: a bibliographic guide to the traditional, popular, art, and liturgical musics of sub-Saharan Africa.* New York: Greenwood Press, 1991. 499pp. (African special bibliographic series, no. 14)
Contains 5,802 entries classified according to: Cultural History and the Arts, Ethnomusicology, Traditional Music, Popular Music, Art Music, and Church Music. Appendixes include Reference Works, Archives and Research Centers, and a Selected Discography. There are indexes for: Ethnic Groups, Subjects, Artists, and Authors. The book is strong in periodical articles, with a large number on contemporary African music and performing musicians. Primarily a data base, with occasional brief annotations.

641. **Green, Doris.** "The liberation of African music." JOURNAL OF BLACK STUDIES 8, no. 2 (1977): 149-167.
The word "liberation" has nothing to do with freedom songs or new urban music but refers instead to a music notation system the author has devised that she feels "actually liberates African music." Though Green agrees with Hood's and Ekwueme's ideas about transcribing African music, she feels that a notational system should combine more elements of culture, such as dance, and should also be comprehensible to both the literate and illiterate "because many griots are excellent musicians who cannot read music." The MUZIKI WAKIAFRIKA system she uses is based upon mnemonics of, and symbols for, instruments. Green says it is parallel in some ways to the Laban approach. Technical illustrations.

642. **Griot sings: songs from the black world.** Collected and adapted by Edna Smith Edet. [Brooklyn, N.Y.]. Medgar Evers College Press, 1978. 94pp.
Children's songs. Illustrations. (This woman has also published under the name Edna Marilyn Smith.)

643. **Griots de Samatiguila.** Text by Karamogo Kamara. Collected by M. J. Derive and Anot N'Guessan. Transcribed and translated by C. Braconnier and S. Diaby. [Abijan]: Institut de linguistique appliquée: Agence de coopération culturelle et technique, 1982. 40pp. *continued*

The introduction is in French; the text is in Dyula (Côte d'Ivoire) and French. Although there is no mention of music, an educated guess is that the "griot" either sings or chants the text, and likely accompanies himself on a musical instrument.

Grove's dictionary of music and musicians
See: **The new Grove dictionary of music and musicians, 1161.**

Guarisma, Gladys
See: **Tons et accents dans les langues africaines, 1568.**

644. **Guettat, Mahmoud**. *La musique classique du Maghreb* [al-Maghrib]. Paris: Sindbad, c1980. 398pp. (Bibliothèque arabe. Collection Hommes et sociétés)
On Arab music of Northern Africa. Bibliography. Discography.

645. **Guignard, Michel**. *Musique, honneur et plaisir au Sahara: étude psycho-sociologique et musicologique de la société maure*. Paris: P. Geuthner, [1975]. 232pp. (Bibliothèque d'études islamiques, t. 3)
Bibliography and discography. Accompanied by 45 rpm disc.

646. **Guillermoprieto, Alma**. *Samba*. New York: Knopf, 1990. 244pp.
An enthralling narrative that describes a season spent with the Mangueira samba school by a former professional dancer who became a journalist. Guillermoprieto, Mexican by birth, gives the inside story in a vivid, personalized account that also incorporates history, and astute sociological observations. Reads like a good novel.

647. **Günther, Robert**. *Musik in Rwanda: ein Beitrag zur Musikethnologie Zentralaf2rikas*. Tervuren, Musée royal de l'Afrique centrale, 1964. 128pp. (Musée royal de l'Afrique centrale, Tervuren, Belgium. Annales. Série in-8°. Sciences humaines no. 50, 1964)
Rwandan music. Bibliography, discography, summary in French.

648. **Günther, Robert**. VOKALE MUSIZIERFORMEN IM SUDAN UND IN DEN SAHARA: STILSCHICHTEN UND STILPROVINZEN. Dissertation, Universität Köln, 1968.

Günther, Robert
See also: •**Musikkulturen Asiens, Afrikas und Ozeaniens im 19. Jahrhundert, 1137.**
•**Die Musikkulturen Lateinamerikas im 19. Jahrhundert, 1139.**

Gwangwa, Jonas
See: **Makeba, Miriam**. *Makeba: my story*, **1009.**

649. **Gyimah, Cynthia**. THE HOMOWO FESTIVAL OF THE GA MASHI PEOPLE OF ACCRA. Master's Thesis, York University (Canada), 1985. 167pp.

650. **Hall-Alleyne, Beverley, Garth White, and Michael Cooke.** *Towards a bibliography of African-Caribbean studies, 1970-1980.* Kingston: African-Caribbean Institute of Jamaica, c1982. 37pp.

Treats the effects of African culture on Caribbean culture. There are sections on art, dance, folklore, family structure, language, literature, religion. The 4-page, excellent music section has a preponderance of periodical articles, many of which are not frequently encountered in similar or related bibliographies.

651. **Hamm, Charles.** *Afro-American music, South Africa, and apartheid.* Brooklyn, N.Y.: Institute for Studies in American Music, Conservatory of Music, Brooklyn College of the City University of New York, c1988. 42pp. (I.S.A.M. monographs, no. 28)

The author examines historically the parallel experiences of South Africans and American blacks with regard to discrimination, but is particularly interested in musical interaction between the two countries. Contact began at least as early as the tours of South Africa by American minstrel shows and has been maintained, though sometimes intermittently, throughout the years. The influence of countless black American forms on black South African music is examined in some detail. Hamm believes that Paul Simon's hybrid recording, *Graceland*, begins a new era in relations between South Africa and the United States. Bibliography.

652. **Hamm, Charles, Bruno Nettl, and Ronald Byrnside.** *Contemporary music and music cultures.* Englewood Cliffs, New Jersey: Prentice-Hall, 1975. 270pp.

The following essay has been selected for listing:

•**Nettl, Bruno.** "The Western impact on world music: Africa and the American Indians," 101-124.

653. **Hampton, Barbara L.** ADOWA LALA: A SYNCHRONIC ANALYSIS OF GA FUNERAL MUSIC. Master's Thesis, University of California, Los Angeles, 1972.

654. **Hampton, Barbara L.** "The contiguity factor in Ga music." **THE BLACK PERSPECTIVE IN MUSIC** 6, no. 1 (1978): 32-48.

655. **Hampton, Barbara L.** THE IMPACT OF LABOR MIGRATION ON MUSIC IN URBAN GHANA: THE CASE OF KPEHE GOME. Dissertation, Columbia University, 1977. 416pp.

656. **Hanna, Elaine S. Harambee.** LET'S PULL TOGETHER: MUSIC AND NATION BUILDING IN KENYA. Master's Thesis, University of Iowa, 1986.

657. Hanna, Judith Lynne. THE ANTHROPOLOGY OF DANCE RITUAL: NIGERIA'S UBAKALA NKWA DI ICHE ICHEN. Dissertation, Columbia University, 1976. 258pp.

This is a study of the dance-plays of Ubakala (one of about 200 Igbo groups located in the former Eastern Region of Nigeria). The author's main thesis is that "dance reflects, influences, and is constitutive of other sociocultural aspects of the system of which it is a part." The context and text for six dance-play genres are analyzed. For each there is a section called, Accompaniment, divided into Song (Structure, Content), and Instruments (Musicians and their Roles). Song texts are in Igbo and English. Chapter 9 summarizes the Ubakala dance-play. Figures, diagrams, tables, maps, plates, and bibliography.

658. Hanna, Nabil Iskandar. CONTEMPORARY EGYPTIAN MUSIC. Master's Thesis, California (Los Angeles), 1971. 144pp.

659. Hansen, Deirdre Doris. "The categories of Xhosa music." In **Symposium on Ethnomusicology.** (2nd: 1981: Rhodes University) *Papers presented at the Second Symposium on Ethnomusicology, Music Department, Rhodes University, 24th to 26th September, 1981.* Edited by Andrew Tracey, 34-52. Grahamstown: International Library of African Music, Institute of Social and Economic Research, Rhodes University, 1982.

660. Hansen, Deirdre Doris. *The life and work of Benjamin Tyamzashe; a contemporary Xhosa composer.* Grahamstown, Rhodes University, Institute of Social and Economic Research, 1968. (Rhodes University, Grahamstown, South Africa. 33pp. Institute of Social and Economic Research. Occasional papers no. 11)

Includes bibliographical references.

661. Hansen, Deirdre Doris. THE MUSIC OF THE XHOSA-SPEAKING PEOPLE. Dissertation, University of the Witwatersrand, Johannesburg (South Africa), 1982.

Hansen uses research techniques and methods proposed by Merriam (1964), with certain extensions and innovations of John Blacking's. She quotes Merriam's definition of ethnomusicology as "the study of music in culture," and divides her research on Xhosa music into three analytical levels accordingly: (1) conceptualization about music; (2) behavior in relation to music, and (3) music sound itself. She says that the aim of her thesis is to give a description of Xhosa music as it was practiced in the period 1969-1972, and to generalize about the processes which the Cape Nguni use to produce musical sound. **(UMI)**

662. Harper, Peggy. "The role of dance in the *Gẹ̀lẹ̀dẹ́* ceremonies of the village of Ìjìó." ODÙ New Series no. 4 (1970): 67-94.

Description of the entire ceremony, the drumming, the clothing, the order of procedure. Notes, bibliography, song texts, photographs.

663. **Harrev, Fleming**. "Jambo records and the promotion of popular music in East Africa: The Story of Otto Larsen East African Records Ltd. 1952-1963." In *Perspectives on African music*. Edited by Wolfgang Bender, 103-137. Bayreuth, Germany: Bayreuth University, c1989.

664. **Harrison, Daphne**. "Aesthetics and social aspects of music in African ritual settings." In **More than drumming: essays on African and Afro-Latin music and musicians**. Edited by Irene V. Jackson, 41-48. Westport, Connecticut: Greenwood Press, c1985.
This is abstracted in **RILM**, 1985.

665. **Hartigan, Royal James**. BLOOD DRUM SPIRIT: DRUM LANGUAGES OF WEST AFRICA, AFRICAN-AMERICA, NATIVE AMERICA, CENTRAL JAVA AND SOUTH INDIA. Dissertation, Wesleyan University, 1986. 1705pp.
This multi-cultural study is of particular interest because of the West African and African-American component. Research was conducted through the eyes of master drummers of each tradition, interviews and performances providing the basis for research. Music sessions were tape recorded, transcribed and analyzed. (Included is a section on the stylistic history of the drum set in African-American music.) Additional sections treat Native American, Javanese, and South Indian drumming. **(UMI)**

666. **Hartigan, Royal James**. THE DRUM: CONCEPTS OF TIME AND NO TIME, FROM AFRICAN, LATIN AMERICAN, AND AFRICAN-AMERICAN ORIGINS. Master's Thesis, Wesleyan University, 1983. 394pp.

667. **Hartwig, Charlotte Mae**. "Music in Kerebe culture." **ANTHROPOS** 68, no. 3/4 (1972): 449-464.
The Kerebe are an interlacustrine people of East Africa. Prior to this essay, only Klaus P. Wachsmann and Hugh Tracey had given their music serious attention. Bibliography.

Harvard dictionary of music
See: **The new Harvard dictionary of music, 1163.**

668. **Hasthorpe, Elizabeth**. GIRLS CIRCUMCISION SONGS AMONG THE POKOT OF EAST AFRICA. Master's Thesis, University of Washington, 1974. 135pp.

669. **Hasthorpe, Elizabeth**. A STUDY OF POKOT SONGS. Dissertation, London University, 1983. 280pp.
The Pokot are a Suk people of western Kenya.

Haydon, Geoffrey
See: **Repercussions: a celebration of African-American music, 1366.**

670. **Hebidge, Dick**. *Cut 'n' mix: culture identity and Caribbean music*. New York: Methuen & Co., 1987. 77pp.
Packed with information on Africa in Caribbean culture - religion, myth, rhythm; Trinidad music (carnival, steel pan, calypso); the record industry in Jamaica; reggae, mento and ska through dub to lovers' rock and talk over; Rastafari, the music and the spiritual aspects; and "today's scene - black British reggae, white 'jamaican' music, Two Tone, and the legacy of punk; 'slack style'and the links between New York rap and MC reggae." Map, notes and references, a general index, an index of musicians, singers, disc jockeys, record producers, and sound system operators, and an index to song and record titles.

671. **Hecht, Dorothea**. *The material culture collection of the National Museum of Kenya*. [s.l.: s.n., 1980] 22pp. (Paper - University of Nairobi, Institute of African Studies, no. 140)
The author gives a vivid third-dimensional picture of the National Museum of Kenya. She selects four of the better collections, and gives an inventory of items in them. Two, the Kamba and Kikuyu [Gĩkũyũ], contain a few musical instruments - some worn for dancing - which are listed though not described. She calls the latter collection "the richest" of all. The classification catalogue is divided into language groups, sub-groups, and into what the author calls, "sectors of culture." Music and dance is the likely heading here. Hecht paints a dismal picture of serious museum inadequacies because of lack of funding. Bibliography.

671a. **Hefele, Bernhard**. *Jazz-bibliography: international literature on jazz, blues, spirituals, gospel and ragtime music with a selected list of works on the social and cultural background from the beginning to the present = Jazz-Bibliographie: Verzeichnis des internationalen Schrifttums über Jazz, Blues, Spirituals, Gospel und Ragtime mit einer Auswahlbibliographie über den sozialen und kulturellen Hintergrund von den Anfängen bis zur Gegenwart*. Münich; New York; London; Paris: Saur, 1980. 368pp.
This is an impressive bibliography of music forms created by black Americans. An early section, (49 - 73) is of particular interest because it presents the socio-historical background of these forms, and includes a bibliography with occasional relevant entries on the African connection. Range is as far back as Mungo Park's African travels (1903) to recent works by Francis Bebey. Text in German and English.

672. **Hen, Ferdinand J. de**. *Beiträge zur Kenntnis der Musikinstrumente aus Belgisch Kongo und Ruanda-Urundi*. [Tervuren], 1960. 259pp.
Bibliography.

673. **Henning, C. G.** "Indian musical instruments." In **Symposium on Ethnomusicology**. (5th: 1984: University of Cape Town). *Papers presented at the fifth Symposium on Ethnomusicology:*

Faculty of Music, University of Cape Town, August 30th-September 1st, 1984, 57-61. Grahamstown: International Library of African Music, 1985.

Henning makes the point at this conference that there has been very little researched or published on Indian music in South Africa. (But see also Melveen Jackson's paper (**751**) presented at the 7th Symposium, on the "Indian" orchestra, and an Indian South African record company. Since 1985, there have been other publications on South African Indian music, as well. Things are looking up!)

674. The heritage of African poetry: an anthology of oral and written poetry. Edited by Isidore Okpewho. Burnt Mill, Essex, England: Longman, 1985. 279pp.

The 32-page introduction is packed with important information on the oral tradition in Africa. Okpewho speaks of the emotional delight of oral poetry that comes from the musical quality contained in the song or chant. He mentions the two kinds of music generally heard in poetry performance, one involving various instruments, hand-clapping or foot stamping; the other, vocal or tonal. An historical overview is given of the training and role of the traditional African poet, as contrasted with the more widespread category, the freelance entertainer, whose training has been less formal. One hundred poems are included. Index.

675. HERSKOVITS, MELVILLE JEAN

This world famous anthropologist established one of the first African Studies Centers of its kind - the Program of African Studies at Northwestern University, 1948. Though most of his publications predate the scope of this bibliography, Herskovits' writings always revealed a keen interest in African music and dance, and he was early to point out the indivisibility of both arts. A bibliography of his complete works can be found in: **AMERICAN ANTHROPOLOGIST** 66, no. 1, (1964): 91-109. A memorial essay, by Alan P. Merriam, is followed by the bibliography, compiled by Anne Moneypenny and Barrie Thorne (**1099**). There are 479 entries.

676. Herskovits, Melville J. *The myth of the Negro past*. With a new introduction by Sidney W. Mintz. Boston, Massachusetts: Beacon Press, 1990. 368pp.

This is a reprint of the frequently quoted classic that originally appeared in 1958. For purposes of this book, Chapter 8, The Contemporary Scene: Language and the Arts, is rich in information on the tie-in of music and dance of the New World to Africa, as is also Chapter 7, The Contemporary Scene: Africanisms in Religious Life. There are notes for each chapter, a bibliography, a supplement to the latter, and an index.

Herskovits, Melville J.
See also: **Melville J. Herskovits Library of African Studies, 1063.**

677. Hesse, Axel. DAS TRANSMISSIONEN-SINGEN IN KUBANISCHEN SPIRITISMUS: MUSIKETHNOLOGISCHE UND SOZIOLOGISCHE UNTERSUCHUNG ZUR TRANSKULTURATIONS-PROBLEMATIK IM

STÄDTISCHHALBPROLETARISCHEN KONTAKTBEREICH DER AFROIDEN UND EUROPÄIDEN GRUPPENKULTUREN KUBAS. Dissertation, University of Berlin, 1971. 538pp.

678. **Hickmann, Hans.** *Ägypten.* Leipzig: Deutscher Verlag für Musik [1961]. 185pp. (Musikgeschichte in Bildern 2: Musik des Alterums, Part 1)
Egyptian music as portrayed in pictorical works of art. Bibliography.

679. **Hickmann, Hans.** *Musicologie pharaonique: études sur l'évolution de l'art musical dans l'Égypte ancienne.* Baden-Baden: Koerner, 1987. 165pp. (Collection d'études musicologiques = Sammlung Musikwissenschaftlicher Abhandlungen, v. 34).
In French. On the evolution of Pharaonic music of ancient Egypt. Bibliographical references.

680. **Hickmann, Hans.** *La trompette dans l'Égypte ancienne.* Nashville: Brass Press, 1976. 75pp. (Brass research series, no. 4)
This is a reprint of the 1946 edition published by l'Institut français d'archéologie orientale, Cairo, which was issued as no. 1 of Supplément aux Annales du Service des antiquités de l'Égypte. Egyptian music to 500. The history of the trumpet. Bibliographical references.

681. **Hill, Errol.** THE TRINIDAD CARNIVAL: A STUDY OF ITS FORMS AND CONTENT AS THE BASIS FOR A NATIONAL THEATRE. Dissertation, Yale University, 1966.
See **682** below.

682. **Hill, Errol.** *The Trinidad carnival: mandate for a national theatre.* Austin, University Press, [1972]. 139pp.
Would *have* to be, and *is*, breathtaking. But the dazzling visuals are matched by solid scholarship. (Much of the material must have come from Hill's earlier Yale dissertation entered above.) Sections are: The Historical Background; Sources and Attitudes; Canboulay: A Ritual Beginning; The Carnival Tent: Backyard Theatre; Rise of the Steel Band: Carnival Music; The Calypso: Form and Function, Calypso Drama, The Masquerade, Theatre of the Streets, Carnival Stage Spectacles, and Towards a National Theatre. Includes 50 famous calypsos classified by subject, a bibliography, index. Merits are too numerous to list here, alas. Certainly on music, and on African retentions.

Hilleström, Gustaf
See: **Festschrift to Ernst Emsheimer, 586.**

683. **Himmelheber, Hans.** *Masken, Tänzer und Musiker der Elgenbeinküste.* Göttingen, Institut für den Wissenschaftlichen Film, 172. 178pp. (Publikationen zu wissenschaftlichen Filmen.
continued

Sektion B: Völkerkunde- Völkskunde. Ergänzungsband, 2) "Dokumentationsfilm-Expeditionen des Instituts für den Wissenschaftlichen Film."
Masks, dancing and music of the Ivory Coast. Bibliography.

Hinzen, Heribert
See: **Stories and songs from Sierra Leone, 1513.**

684. **HISTORICAL ABSTRACTS. PART B: TWENTIETH CENTURY ABSTRACTS.** 1955- . Santa Barbara, California.
A publication appearing quarterly, and covering 1914 to the present. Listed here because it abstracts several included periodicals. Available on a service basis. Available online; issues a cumulative index every 5 years.

685. **Hlabelela mntwanami = Sing, my child!: Zulu children's songs.** Collected and transcribed by Pessa Weinberg. Illustrated by Gamakhulu Diniso and Rose Crass-Striebel. Johannesburg, South Africa: Ravan Press, 1984. 140pp.
Contains unaccompanied melodies, some of which are in two to three parts. The songs were recorded from 1976 to 1978, mainly in Edendale, a semi-urban residential and business area bordering on Pietermaritzburg. Zulu words are also printed as text with English translation preceding each song. Bibliographical references. See also Pessa Weinberg's dissertation, **1662.**

Hodza, A. C.
See: **Shona praise poetry, 1450.**

686. **Hommage à Grand Kallé.** [Kinshasa, Zaïre?]: Editions Lokole, c1985. 118pp. (Collection "Temoignages")

687. **HOMME: REVUE FRANÇAISE D'ANTHROPOLOGIE.** 1961- . Paris, France: Éditions de l'ecole des Hautes Études en Sciences Sociales.
(Formerly spelled, **"L'HOMME."**) In French, issued quarterly, indexed in **CURRENT CONTENTS, AICP, SSCI.** Though the following were the only two found, there might be others.
- **Muller, Jean-Claude.** "Interlude pour charivari et tambour silencieux: l'intronisation des tambours chez les Rukuba (Plateau State, Nigeria)," vol. 16, no. 4 (1976): 77-95.
- **Rouget, Gilbert.** "Une convergence remarquable entre langages tambourinés, codes nerveux, et langages machines," vol. 17, no. 1 (1977): 117-121.

688. **Honore, Jasmine.** "A transcription system for Xhosa dance-songs." In **Symposium on Ethnomusicology.** (7th: 1988: Venda, South Africa). *Papers presented at the 7th Symposium on Ethnomusicology: Department of Anthropology and*

Ethnomusicology, University of Venda, 3rd to 5th September 1988. Edited by Andrew Tracey, 14-21. Grahamstown, South Africa: Rhodes University, 1989.

689. **Hood, Mantle.** *The ethnomusicologist.* New edition. Kent State University Press, c1982. 400p.
An authoritative, thorough guide written by a highly respected scholar. Almost everything one needs to be a crackerjack ethnomusicologist is included. Unlike the first edition, this one has a preface and a bibliography. The comprehensive new introduction gives a keen analysis, with updating, of the myriad changes in ethnomusicology since 1971, and how these developments have affected Hood's approach to the new edition. The older introduction is retained, as is Charles Seeger's original essay. Numerous photographs of instruments appear, with their symbolic diagrams known as *organograms*. Ghana gets considerable attention. Three pocket disks include African examples: Lobi, Yorùbá, Ewe, Fanti.

690. **Hooker, Naomi W.** "Popular musicians in Freetown." **AFRICAN URBAN STUDIES** vol. 5, no. 4 (1970): 52-62.

Hoover Institution bibliographic series
See: **Duignan, Peter, 483.**

691. **Hornbostel, E. M. von, and Curt Sachs.** "Classification of musical instruments." Translated by Anthony Baines and Klaus P. Wachsmann. **THE GALPIN SOCIETY JOURNAL** 14, (1961): 4-29.
(This originally appeared in **ZEITSCHRIFT FÜR ETHNOLOGIE** 46, Nos. 4-5 (1914): 553-590.) The Sachs-Hornbostel instrument classification system represents a revision and expansion of an earlier system developed in 1880 by Victor Mahillon, curator of the instrumental collection of the Brussels Conservatory. (Mahillon had based his own system on an Indian classification system described in the *Natyashastra*, dating from the first century.) Although there are valid criticisms of the Sachs-Hornbostel system, it has generally had wide endorsement. Despite Jaap Kunst's fault-finding, he had to admit that "only in extremely rare cases does it let the investigator down."

692. **Horton, Christian Dowu.** INDIGENOUS MUSIC OF SIERRA LEONE: AN ANALYSIS OF RESOURCES AND EDUCATIONAL IMPLICATIONS. Dissertation, University of California, Los Angeles, 1979. 429pp.
Illustrations, music, bibliography.

693. **Horton, Christian Dowu.** THE SUITABILITY OF THE INDIGENOUS MUSIC OF SIERRA LEONE FOR USE IN THE PUBLIC SCHOOLS. Master's Thesis, Howard University, 1967. 80pp.

694. **Howard, Joseph H.** *Drums: from the tropics to the Arctic Circle.* Los Angeles, California: Howard's Drum Collection

Committee, c1982. 214pp.
An extremely fine resource. Contains 140 plates of instruments. Divided into an Introduction, Early Drum Records, Classification of Drums, Drumming Styles and Techniques, Drums from Around the World, African Drums, Afro-American Drums, Signal Drums, Cross Cultural Blendings. The latter chapter includes a section on Drums of the Caribbean and Latin America, and another on Central American Drumming. Contains a Catalog of Instruments and Artifacts Included in the Howard Collection of Instruments. The brief index has many roads leading to Africa.

695. **Howard, Joseph H.** *Drums in the Americas.* New York: Oak Publications, 1967. 319pp.
Contains chapters on African and Aframerican [*sic*] Influences, Afro-American Drums, African Drums, Rhythm and Drumming, Drumlore, Drum Accessories and Auxiliary Instruments - all of which contain information pertinent to this bibliography. There are 244 text figures, 29 plates, notes, an index, and a bibliography. Includes a glossary of unusual drumming terms.

696. **Hsu, Francis L. K.** "Rethinking the concept 'primitive.'" **CURRENT ANTHROPOLOGY** 5, no. 3 (1964): 169-178.
Last paper in a series honoring Herskovits. Not specifically on African music, but considered too relevant not to be included. To quote from the abstract, "This article shows the empirical, theoretical, and practical obsolescence of the concept 'primitive' except in some most restricted sense, such as application to peoples and cultures in prehistory times...The reasons for this insistent use of the concept by anthropologists despite its obsolescence are discussed...One of the reasons is the seeming reluctance of anthropologists to examine their own societies and culture..." Comprehensive documentation, extensive bibliography.

697. **Huet, Michel.** *The dance, art, and ritual of Africa.* Introduction by Jean Laude. Text by Jean-Louis Paudrat. Translated from the French. 1st American ed. New York: Pantheon Books, c1978. 241pp.
Translation of *Danses d'Afrique.* The Guinea Coast, Western Sudan, and Equatorial Africa are the regions covered. There are ethnographic notes, but the book is essentially pictorial. Huet's large photographs in full color show spectacularly-dressed dancers spinning, stomping, swirling, leaping across the pages, as musicians beat or coax their xylophones, gourd trumpets, bows, drums, slit-gongs - all participants caught up in the emotion, the surging energy of events set in natural surroundings. These photos say as no words can something about the beauty, the excitement, and mostly, the indivisibility of the arts in Africa. Includes bibliographies.

698. **Huet, Michel.** *Danses d'Afrique.* [Photographies de] Michel Huet. Notes ethnographiques de Jean-Louis Paudrat. Préface de Jean Laude. Paris: Chêne, 1978. 241pp.
This French version was the original. See the preceding entry (**697**) for the English translation.

699. **Hughes, Langston.** *An African treasury: articles, essays, stories, poems, by black Africans.* New York: Crown Publishers, [1969]. 207pp.
There are two important essays in the collection that have to do with African music. They also appear as separate entries in this bibliography:
•**Makiwane, Tennyson.** "African work songs," 95-97.
•**Nketia, J. H. Kwabena.** "Akan poetry," 102-109.

700. **Hulstaert, G.** *Berceuses mongo: Supplément de numération mongo.* Bandundu, République du Zaïre: Ceeba, c1977. 96pp. (Publications Ceeba, Série 2, vol. 36)
French and Mongo. Bibliography and index.

701. **Hulstaert, G.** *Chansons de danse mongo (Rép. du Zaïre).* Bandundu, République du Zaïre: Ceeba, 1982. 127pp. (Publications Ceeba, Série 2, vol. 78)
On Mongo (Zaïre) dance, song, and poetry. Song texts are in French and Mongo. Critical material in French. Bibliography.

Hulstaert, G.
See also: **Chants mongo, 339.**

702. **Hürter, Friedegard.** *Heilung und Musik in Afrika.* Frankfurt am Main; New York: P. Lang, c1986. 151pp. (Europäische Hochschulschriften. Series 36, Musikwissenschaft; Volume 21 = Publications universitaires européennes. Série 36, Musicologie; Volume 21 = European Studies. Series 36, Musicology; v. 21)
Music therapy in sub-Saharan Africa. Healing and folk medicine. Bibliography, illustrations.

703. **Hurwitz, Joseph.** A PLAN FOR THE IMPLEMENTATION OF TRADITIONAL INSTRUMENTAL GHANAIAN ENSEMBLE IN SECONDARY SCHOOLS. Master's Thesis, University of California, Los Angeles, 1971. 104pp.

704. **Huskisson, Yvonne.** *The Bantu composers of Southern Africa. Die Bantoe-komponiste van Suider-Afrika.* Johannesburg: [South African Broadcasting Corporation, 1969]. 335pp.
There is a long introduction followed by double-columned pages in English and Afrikaans. Photographs and biographies of 318 black composers are included. (Alas, they are amassed in the title by the pejorative South African designation, "Bantu." Only 4 of this large group of composers, many of them exceedingly accomplished and distinguished, "made it" into the four volumes of the *South African Music Encyclopedia.*) A supplement to this work follows as the next entry.

H

705. **Huskisson, Yvonne.** *The Bantu composers of Southern Africa. Supplement.* [Johannesburgh]: South African Human Services Research Council, [1974?]. 28pp.
The reason for this brief supplement is never given, but it is inferior in quality to the original work. Though it, too, includes many photographs, the results are amateurish, and the information reads like a high school annual. The next-to-last page of the book lists births and deaths of the included musicians by month. Book entirely in English.

706. **Huskisson, Yvonne.** *Music of the Bantu.* Sovenga, Pietersburg: University College of the North, 1969. 15pp.
The author's writings exemplify the white paternalistic approach to African music. Despite the title, this pamphlet contains very little about music, the emphasis being placed on rites of passage and other aspects of black South African life. Cursory summaries show very little ethnological understanding or sensitivity. There are strange subject headings such as: Literary Inclination [on story-telling]; Integral Part [i.e., music as inseparable from life]; and "The Bantu Boy." Two pages of excellent drawings of indigenous African instruments also include a saxophone. The word "Bantu," used in this pejorative sense, must go!

707. **Huskisson, Yvonne.** "Music of the Pedi." In *South African music encyclopedia.* Vol. 2. Edited by Jacques P. Malan, 345-374. Cape Town: Oxford University Press, 1979-1986.

708. **Huskisson, Yvonne.** "A note on the music of the Sotho." In *South African music encyclopedia.* Vol. 2. Edited by Jacques P. Malan, 375-376. Cape Town: Oxford University Press, 1979-1986.

709. **Huskisson, Yvonne.** *Traditional instruments and folk-song of the Bantu = tradisionele instrumente en volksang van die Bantoe.* [s:.l.: s.n., 1968?].
A kind of general, non-technical survey of the song style and instruments of black South Africans, whom Huskisson consistently calls "the Bantu," or even, as did Kirby on occasion, "*our* Bantu." She mentions how traditional songs are used for every phase of living, describes a number of instruments, how they are used, and with which peoples they are associated. The Western orchestra classification is used throughout, which somehow causes the *mbira* to end up a "keyboard instrument." But this book is not directed to musicologists. No bibliography. In English and Afrikaans.

710. **Hyslop, Graham.** *Musical instruments of East Africa: notes.* Nairobi: Nelson, 1975- .
Volume 1 is on Kenya. Illustrations, music.

711. **ISME YEARBOOK**. 1973- . Mainz, New York: B. Schott's Sohne. (International Society for Music Education)
Issued annually. Also called **INTERNATIONAL MUSIC EDUCATION**. Supersedes **INTERNATIONAL MUSIC EDUCATOR**. Selected examples follow:
- **Mbuyamba, L.** "The training of the virtuoso in traditional Africa," vol. 13 (1986): 136-142.
- **Nketia, J. H. Kwabena**. "Community-oriented education of musicians in African countries," vol. 2 (1974): 38-42.
- **Twerefoo, Gustav Oware**. "Music educators' materials for a changing African society," vol. 8 (1981): 74-79.

712. **ÌBÀDÀN**. 1957-1975. Ìbàdàn, Nigeria, Ìbàdàn University Press.
Issued three times a year, and was continued by **ÌBÀDÀN REVIEW**, from 1977 until when it ceased publication, 19??.
At least three articles on African music appeared during its tenure, possibly more:
- **Ames, David W.** "Hausa drums of Zaria," vol. 21 (1965): 62-79
- **Euba, Akin**. "Preface to a study of Nigerian music; in the light of references which made it what it is," vol. 21 (1965): 53-62.
- **Thieme, Darius L.** "Style in Yorùbá music, "24 (1967): 33-39.

713. **Ibrahim, Mustafa Fathy** [Ibrahīm Muṣṭafa Fatḥī], **and Armand Pigol**. *L'extase et le transitor: aperçus sur la chanson égyptienne contemporaine de grande audience*. Le Caire: Centre d'études et de documentation économique juridique et sociale, c1987.
Egyptian songs. In Arabic and French. Bibliography.

714. **Ìdòwú, Mábinúorí Káyọ̀dé**. *Fẹlá: why blackman carry shit*. Kaduna [Nigeria]: Opinion Media, 1986. 186pp.
A comprehensive biography of the famous Nigerian musician, Fẹlá Aníkúlápó-Kútì. This is a serious and informative book that gives interesting and little-known facts about Fẹlá's life, with many fascinating old photos. Music is not the main concern. There are direct quotations by Fẹlá himself, and a transcription of his entire lecture at the University of Ifẹ̀ entitled, The Essence of Culture in Development. We learn of Fẹlá, the intellectual, who gave over 60 public lectures at institutions of higher learning from 1980-81. Idowu sees Fẹlá's artistic creation as a mass expression of the oppressed of the earth.

715. **Ifẹ̀: annals of the Institute of Cultural Studies**. Ilé-Ifẹ̀, Nigeria: Institute of Cultural Studies, University of Ifẹ̀. 1986- .
Volumes 1 and 2, published as separate hard covers, yield only the following two articles on music:
- **Vidal, Túnjí**. "The Westernization of African music: a study of Yorùbá liturgical church music," 70-82 (Vol. 1).
- **Vzoigwe, Joshua**. "Operational and hierarchial forms of creativity in Igbo music: the *Ukom* music system as a case study," 65-83 (Vol. 2).

I

716. **Ifẹ̀ Festival of the Arts (3rd: 1970: University of Ifẹ̀).** *Third Ifẹ̀ Festival of the Arts: Ilé-Ifẹ̀, 4th-18th December, 1970.* [Ìbàdàn]: University of Ifẹ̀, Institute of African Studies, c1970. 46pp.

This is a splendid program for a key event. Information and impressive photos are given for dancers, musicians, artists, poets, playwrights, scholars. Pictured also are world famous dignitaries who gave addresses or had works performed. To give an idea of the magnitude of this Festival, the following names appear on one program: Léopold Sédar Senghor, Aimé Césaire, Francis Bebey, Edward Braithwaite, Akin Euba, John Akar (Ambassador to the United States, from Sierra Leone), Peggy Harper, Samuel Akpabot. The Senegalese National Theatre was represented; there was a lecture on Modern Art in Senegal; a one-act play in Yorùbá, and more.

Ifill, Max B.
See: **Proceedings of a sesquicentennial conference on human development, 1346.**

717. **Ifionu, Azubike Obed.** IFO: A STUDY OF AN IGBO VOCAL GENRE. Dissertation, University of London, 1979.

718. **Igbo poems and songs.** [Collected] by F. Chidozie Ogbalu. Onitsha [Nigeria]: University Publishing Company, [1974?]. 198pp. (Igbo oral traditional literature series.)

The poems and song texts are in Igbo and gathered from all parts of Igbo-speaking areas of Nigeria. Preface in English. Ogbalu says this is the first attempt at recording Igbo oral/traditional literature in writing. Included are incantations, lullabies, songs for assorted rites of passage, songs for war, for festivals, and more. The categories are explained in a three-page section at the beginning of the book. A few black and white drawings give interest.

719. **Igoil, Iyortange.** THE CULTURAL ASPECTS OF TIV MUSIC. Master's Thesis, Ahmadu Bello University (Zaria), 1985.

720. **IKENGA.** 1972- . Nsukka, Nigeria: Institute of African Studies, University of Nigeria.

A cursory examination of various issues from 1972 through numbers 1/2, 1985 yielded the following two articles on music (briefly described in entries under author's names):

- **Amankulor, Jas. N.** "Ekpe festival as religious ritual and dance drama," vol. 2, no. 2 (1972): 37-47.
- **Nzewi, Meki.** "Some reflections on research methodology in ethnomusicology," vol. 4, no.2 (1980): 66-70.

721. **IKOROK.** 1971- . Nsukka, Nigeria.

The other title of this journal is **IKORO**. Both names indicate the same huge wooden talking drum made from a large tree trunk, traditionally used in

southeastern Nigeria for disseminating information. In those copies examined, only one article had to do with music:
•**Uka, N.** "The *ikoro* and its cultural significance," Vol. 3, No. 1 (1976): 21-27.

722. **Inanga, Amorelle Eugenie.** THE BEMBE ENSEMBLE AMONG THE EGBE: AN ETHNOMUSICOLOGICAL STUDY. Master's Thesis, Institute of African Studies, University of Ìbàdàn, 1983.

723. **Indiana University, Bloomington. Archives of Traditional Music.** *Catalog of African music and oral data holdings.* [Compiled by Philip M. Peek. Bloomington, Indiana University Archives of Traditional Music and African Studies Association Center for African Oral Data, 1970]. 18pp.
A discography pertaining to "the continent of Africa."

724. **Indiana University, Bloomington. Archives of Traditional Music.** *Catalog of Afroamerican music and oral data holdings.* [Compiled by Philip M. Peek. Bloomington], 1970. 28pp.
Sound recordings of African-Americans in the Western Hemisphere. There are strongly Africa-related music entries to be found under Caribbean, Central America, South America, and a few under U.S.: General.

725. **Indiana University, Bloomington. Archives of Traditional Music.** *A catalog of phonorecordings of music and oral data held by the Archives of Traditional Music.* Archives of Traditional Music, Folklore Institute, Indiana University, Bloomington, Indiana. Boston: G. K. Hall, [1975]. 541pp.

726. **Innes, Gordon.** "Mandinka circumcision songs." **AFRICAN LANGUAGE STUDIES** 13 (1972): 88-112.

Innes, Gordon
See also: •**Kaabu and Fuladu, 800.**
•**Sunjata: three Mandinka versions, 1517.**

726a. **Institut für neue Musik und Musikerziehung Darmstadt.** *Musik fremder Kulturen: 5 einfuhrende Studien.* Edited by Rudolf Stephan. Mainz: Schott, 1977. 108pp. (Veröffentlichungen des Instituts für Neue Musik und Musikerziehung Darmstadt, vol. 17)
On ethnomusicology. This is a collection of papers presented at the meeting in Darmstadt in 1976 (April 5-10) of the Institut für Neue Musik und Musikerziehung. The following paper was included:
•**Raab, Claus.** "Afrikanische Musik," 66-108.

I

727. **Instruments de musique de Gandajika: (République du Zaïre).** Katende Cyovo. Bandundu, République du Zaïre: Ceeba, 1978. 102pp. (Publications Ceeba, Série 2, vol. 35/2)
Bibliography. Index.

727a. **Intercultural music studies.** Wilhelmshaven: F. Noetzel, 1990- . Max Peter Baumann, Editor. (International Institute for Comparative Music Studies and Documentation, Berlin)
The first two volumes of this ethnomusicology book series have been announced, and should be appearing soon enough to warrant their inclusion in this bibliography. Volume 1, entitled "Music, Gender, and Culture" will incorporate essays on women's music of Southern Algeria (Edda Brandes), and women's music of Liberia (Cynthia Schmidt). Volume 2, entitled "Music in the Dialogue of Cultures: Traditional Music and Cultural Policy," will contain at least two essays on African music (J. H. Kwabena Nketia, and Artur Simon). Volumes 3/4, are entitled, "Theory of African Music" (Gerhard Kubik), and should have two accompanying music cassettes.

728. **INTERNATIONAL AFRICAN BIBLIOGRAPHY: CURRENT BOOKS, ARTICLES, AND PAPERS IN AFRICAN STUDIES.** 1971- . London, England: Mansell Publishing, Ltd. (University of London, School of Oriental and African Studies)
Issued quarterly. This is an excellent resource for researching African music. It continues: **AFRICA, BIBLIOGRAPHY OF CURRENT PERIODICALS**. It is indexed in **AICP**, and **CURRENT CONTENTS AFRICA**. (Check **ULRICH'S** for other indexing periodicals.)

729. **INTERNATIONAL AFRICAN BIBLIOGRAPHY, 1973-1978: BOOKS, ARTICLES AND PAPERS IN AFRICAN STUDIES.** Edited by J. D. Pearson. London: Mansell, 1982. 343pp.
A reference tool that represents the merging of twenty-four issues of **INTERNATIONAL AFRICAN BIBLIOGRAPHY**, plus some 3,000 additional entries. One reads that the book is "directly in line with Ruth Jones' **CUMULATIVE BIBLIOGRAPHY OF AFRICAN STUDIES** (Boston, G. K. Hall, 1973, 5 volumes)," and that the two form a continuous sequence, from 1929-1978. In this volume, eight pages that have musical references can be found if one follows instructions at the beginning, and looks for Music in the general and regional sections.

International African Institute
See: •**AFRICA BIBLIOGRAPHY, 22.**
•**Baker, Philip, 172.**
•**Gaskin, L. J. P., 614.**

730. **INTERNATIONAL BIBLIOGRAPHY OF SOCIAL AND CULTURAL ANTHROPOLOGY.** 1955-1986. London: Tavistock.
Was issued annually in English and French. At one time this was cosponsored by UNESCO. Contains an author and subject index. The prefix "musi" and the word "Africa" bring results, as could other geographical terms. There might be only one

useful entry under a heading, but sometimes there are surprisingly more. As a workable reference tool, this bibliography leaves something to be desired, but worthwhile information is obtainable with persistence. Volumes begin with a preface, a chart showing criteria for inclusion, a list of other bibliographical journals, and a list of periodicals consulted for that year's bibliography. Coverage is impressively global.

731. **INTERNATIONAL COMMITTEE ON URGENT ANTHROPOLOGICAL AND ETHNOLOGICAL RESEARCH. BULLETIN.** 1958- . Austria.
Listed as being published under the auspices of UNESCO upon recommendation of the International Committee on Urgent Anthropological and Ethnological Research. Text is in English, French and German. Indexed in **CURRENT CONTENTS AFRICA**, and **AICP**. Back issues are available. Examples follow:
- **Butumweni, Nlandu Yambula**,"Perspectives d'avenir des musiques africaines," vol. 24 (1982): 83-88.
- **Eno Belinga, Samuel-Martin**. "Musique traditionelle et musique moderne au Cameroun," vol. 11 (1969): 83-90.
- **Mensah, Atta Annan**, "Performing arts in Zambia," vol. 13 (1971): 67-82.
- **Omibìyí, Mosúnmọ̀lá Àyìnkẹ́**. "Human migration and diffusion of musical instruments in Nigeria," vol. 25 (1983): 77-93.

732. **International Congress of Africanists, 1st, Accra, 1962.** *The proceedings of the First International Congress of Africanists, Accra, 11th-18th December 1962.* Foreword by K. Onwuka Dike. Edited by Lalage Brown and Michael Crowder. Evanston, Ill.: Northwestern University Press, 1964. 368pp.
- **Nketia, J. H. Kwabena**. "Unity and diversity in African music: a problem of synthesis," 256-263.

733. **International Congress of Americanists, 29th, New York, 1949.** *Acculturation in the Americas: proceedings and selected papers.* Edited by Sol Tax. With an introduction by Melville J. Herskovits. New York, Cooper Square Publishers, 1967 [c1952]. 329pp.
- **Waterman, Richard Alan**. "African influence on the music of the Americas," 207-218.

734. **INTERNATIONAL FOLK MUSIC COUNCIL. JOURNAL.** 1949-1968. New York: Columbia University.
Annual. Superseded by: **INTERNATIONAL FOLK MUSIC COUNCIL. YEARBOOK, 735.** The latter in turn was superseded by the **YEARBOOK FOR TRADITIONAL MUSIC, 1695.** During the tenure of the this journal, a number of articles were published on African music. Only three are listed below, but there are many more to be found.
- **England, Nicholas M.** "Bushman counterpoint," vol. 19 (1967): 58-66.
- **Nketia, J. H. Kwabena**. "The hocket technique in African music," vol. 14 (1962a): 44-52.
- **Rycroft, David**. "Nguni vocal polyphony," vol. 19 (1967): 88-103.

I

735. INTERNATIONAL FOLK MUSIC COUNCIL. YEARBOOK. 1969-1980. New York: Columbia University.

Annual. Supersedes **INTERNATIONAL FOLK MUSIC COUNCIL,** continued by **YEARBOOK FOR TRADITIONAL MUSIC.** Though only two articles on African music are listed below, there are probably others. Volumes are numbered from 1-12. **MUSIC INDEX** seems to have indexed the publication for the years 1979 and 1980, and then continued to index it under the current title, **YEARBOOK FOR TRADITIONAL MUSIC. RILM** included the earlier numbers, but only later listed them as qualifying to be fully abstracted. Since the publication became the **YEARBOOK FOR TRADITIONAL MUSIC,** however, it has been fully abstracted in **RILM.**

- •**Kauffman, Robert.** "Shona urban music and the problem of acculturation," vol. 4 (1972): 47-56.
- •**Mapoma, Mwesa Isaiah.** "The use of folk music among some Bemba church congregations in Zambia," vol. 1 (1969): 72-88.
- •**Omibìyí, Mosúnmọ́lá Àyìnkẹ́.** "Folk music and dance in African education," vol. 4 (1972): 87-94.

International Library of African Music

See: •**AFRICAN MUSIC: Journal of the African Music Society, 38.**
•**Symposium on Ethnomusicology, 1522-1528.**
•**Tracey, Andrew T. N.** (assorted entries under his name).
•**Tracey, Hugh, 1577, 1579, 1581.**

736. INTERNATIONAL MUSICOLOGICAL SOCIETY. CONGRESS. REPORT. 1949- . Kassel, Barenreiter.

Reports from this society appear irregularly. The following entries were obtained from **RILM's** listing (and in some cases abstracting) of the papers from the 1977 Congress (Berkeley, California), and the 1981 Congress (Bayreut). (For future reference, Congresses are found in **RILM** under **Collected Writings,** subheading, "Congress Reports, Symposium Proceedings.")

1977 (Listed in **RILM,** 1981)

Gerard Béhague was Chairperson of the panel entitled, "African Roots of Music in the Americas."

- •**Aretz, Isabel.** "African characteristics in the folkloric music of Venezuela: Afro-Venezuelan instruments and acculturation and change," 53-54.
- •**Evans, David.** "African elements in twentieth-century United States black folk music," 54-66.
- •**Kubik, Gerhard.** "Angolan traits in black music of Brazil," 64-74.
- •**Maultsby, Portia K.** "Africanisms retained in the spiritual tradition," 75-82.
- •**Nketia, J. H. Kwabena.** "African roots of music in the Americas: an African view," 82-88.
- •**Southern, Eileen.** "African retentions in Afro-American music in the nineteenth century," 88-98.
- •**Wilson, Olly.** "The association of movement and music as a manifestation of a black conceptual approach to music making," 98-105.
- •**Witmer, Robert.** African roots: the case of recent Jamaican popular music," 105-113.

1981 (Listed in **RILM,** 1984)

- •**Nketia, J. H. Kwabena.** "On the historicity of music in African cultures," 48-57.

INTERNATIONAL SOCIETY FOR MUSIC EDUCATION
See: **ISME YEARBOOK, 711.**

737. **Ismail, Mahi**. "Musical traditions in the Sudan." In **African music: meeting in Yaoundé (Cameroon) 23-27 February 1970, organized by UNESCO**, 89-94. Paris: *La revue musicale*, 1972.
Bibliography. See following entry, **739**, for the original French version.

738. **Ismail, Mahi**. "Traditional music in the Sudan." In **Creating a wider interest in traditional music: proceedings of a conference held in Berlin in cooperation with the International Music Council, 12th to the 17th June, 1967**. [Edited by Alain Daniélou and others], 104-111. Berlin: International Institute for Comparative Music Studies and Documentation, [1967?].

739. **Ismail, Mahi**. "Les traditions musicales du Soudan." In **La musique africaine, réunion de Yaoundé (Cameroun)** [sur les traditions musicales de l'Afrique subsaharienne], **23-27 février 1970, organisée par l'UNESCO**, 87-93. Paris: *La revue musicale*, Richard-Masse, 1972.
Bibliography. See preceding entry, **737**.

740. **Ìṣọ̀lá, Akínwùmí**. "The artistic aspects of Ṣàngó-pípè." ODÙ New Series no. 13 (1976): 80-103.
Ṣàngó-pípè refers to a chant for invoking and singing the praises of the Yorùbá deity, Ṣàngó. Ṣàngó-pípè singers, who are more apt to be female, begin their arduous training when they are approximately 8 years old. Several years, and a great deal of effort, go into this instructive period, but study can continue for a lifetime. To excel at the art, a good memory and mellifluous voice are mandatory. There is a useful section at the end of the paper, entitled "References," that is virtually a glossary.

741. **Ita, Bassey**. *Jazz in Nigeria: an outline cultural history*. [Chief Bassey Ita]. Lagos: Radical House, c1984. 99pp.
Popular music in Nigeria, not just jazz.

742. **Ìwàlewà-Haus Bayreuth. Archiv Moderner Afrikanischer Musik**. *Musik aus Äthiopien: ein kommentierter Katalog zu einer Auswahl traditioneller und moderner Musik aus Äthiopien*, by Wolfgang Bender. [Bayreuth, Germany]: Archiv Moderner Afrikanischer Musik, ÌWÀLEWÀ, Universität Bayreuth, 1982. 18pp. (Kommentierte Kataloge zur afrikanischen Musik, no. 1)
A catalog with commentary on recorded Ethiopian music classified as Traditional, Modern, and "Modern Classical." There is brief information preceding each

section. A one-page bibliography of books and articles follows. There are a few sketches of instruments alone and being played, and a dramatic, Ethiopian-style, cover drawing of a huge-eyed musician playing a *mansinqo*.

743. **Ìwàlewà-Haus Bayreuth. Archiv Moderner Afrikanischer Musik.** *Waka, Sakara, Apala, Fuji: islamisch beeinflusste Musik der Yorùbá in Nigeria und Benin: ein kommentierter Katalog*, by Wolfgang Bender. [Bayreuth, Germany]: ÌWÀLEWÀ, Universität Bayreuth, 1983. 25pp. (Kommentierte Kataloge zur afrikanischen Musik, no. 4)
A catalog with commentary on recorded Yorùbá music in Benin and Nigeria showing Islamic influence. Information on musical styles mentioned in title. Bibliography with three entries. Cover shows a *goje* (a one-string fiddle of the Savannah belt, West Africa). A few other illustrations are inside, including a photo of a Sakara group.

744. ***Ìyẹ̀rẹ́ Ifá*: the deep chants of Ifá.** Transcribed and translated by Robert G. Armstrong...*et al.* [Ìbàdàn, Nigeria]: Institute of African Studies, University of Ìbàdàn, 1978. 141pp. (University of Ìbàdàn, Institute of African Studies, Occasional Publication no. 32)
The text, in Yorùbá and English, is taken from a performance recorded in 1965 by Curt Wittig in the Ilé Awo (the House of Secrets) of Òsogbo. The *Ìyèré* is the cycle of the great classical chants and songs for the principal Odù of Ifá, and involves complex symbolism. It incorporates dancing, chants and song-codas, and may be accompanied by gongs and drums. Entrances are indicated in the text. Call-response prevails. According to the Preface, "the whole performance ends in a great blaze of singing and dancing."

745. **Ize-Senze, Kabulampuka Kanyinda**, *et al. Symbolique verbale et rituelle chez les Sakata, Lele, Wongo, Kuba, Lulua, Mbole et Vira (Rép. du Zaïre).* Bandundu, République du Zaïre: Ceeba, 1984. 125pp. (Publications Ceeba, Série 2, vol. 93)
The book contains various essays having to do with the ethnology of Zaïre, rites and ceremonies, social life and customs, and folk literature. One of them pertains to music:
•**Makuta-Nyim, and Minga Shanga.** "Les chansons traditionnelles Lele et leur signification socioculturelle."

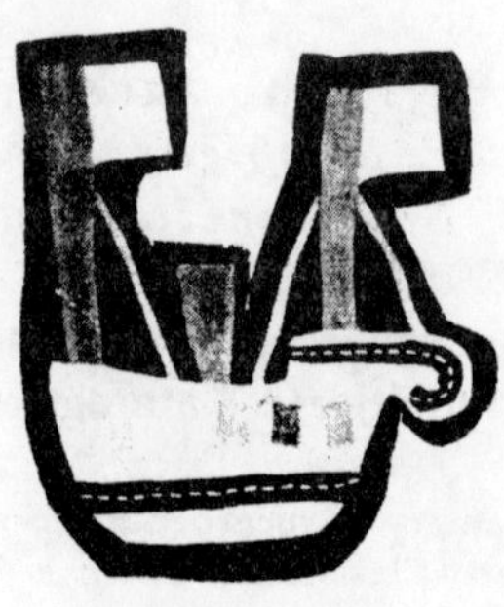

746. **"J. H. Kwabena Nketia: a biobibliographical portrait."** In **African musicology: current trends: a festschrift presented to J. H. Kwabena Nketia.** Edited by Jacqueline Cogdell DjeDje, and William G. Carter, 3-39. [Atlanta, Georgia: Crossroads Press, 1988]- .

A biographic essay that focuses primarily on Nketia's professional life. This is followed by a comprehensive bibliography of his works.

747. **Jackson, Bruce**, ed. *The Negro and his folklore in nineteenth-century periodicals.* Austin: Publication of the American Folklore Society by the University of Texas Press, 1969. 374pp. (Publication of the American Folklore Society, bibliographical and special series, vol. 18)

Folksongs, beliefs, speech, customs, and tales of early African-Americans are documented in 35 articles written between 1838 and 1899. The book consists of letters, and reviews extracted from nineteenth-century periodicals. References to music, dance and other performance practices having built-in Africanisms are too numerous to mention. Jackson writes informed and compassionate introductions to each excerpt. There are transcriptions, illustrations, an index, and abundant bibliographical references. Includes the famous article on slave dancing in Place de Congo, New Orleans, but without the dramatic illustrations. (See: **Cable, George W., 305,** for the source of the original article.) Powerful. Poignant.

748. **Jackson, Bruce**, ed. *Wake up dead man: Afro-American worksongs from Texas prisons.* Cambridge, Massachusetts: Harvard University Press, 1972.

Jackson says that the prison worksongs he studies are sung by Americans, but are African in style and function. He refers the reader to earlier works by four Africanist musicologists. Most of the songs in this chilling book with its chilling photographs do not exist in the outside world. Hence, this represents an important body of music for researching African connections. (Prisoners coming from different cultures, for example, do not have equivalent collections of music for similar use.) There are transcriptions, texts, predominantly in call-response form, plates, and a bibliography.

749. **Jackson, George S.** *Music in Durban: an account of musical activities in Durban from 1850 to the early years of the present century.* Johannesburg: Witwatersrand University Press, 1970. 166pp.

Overall impression is given that there were no black people anywhere in South Africa. With a little probing, however, we find passing reference to the African-American minstrel, Orpheus McAdoo (see Erlmann's, *A feeling of prejudice,* **540**), including comments on his excellent voice and that of a woman in his company. (His troupe is rated higher than Christy's minstrels.) There is also mention of a little-known Zulu choir of 1891, "the forerunner of many African choirs," that was trained to sing "not their own songs, but English glees, part-songs, and ballads."

J

750. **Jackson, Irene V.**, comp. *Afro-American religious music: a bibliography and a catalogue of gospel music.* Westport, Connecticut: Greenwood Press, 1979. 210pp.

This excellent compendium also incorporates a number of entries specifically on African music, or on the African component in black music and culture of the New World. Nine separate, smaller bibliographies are listed under the main heading, Bibliography. Although there might be something relevant in any of them, the most promising are entitled: Ethnomusicology; Dance and Folklore; African and African-American Folksong; and, Caribbean: Religion, Music, Culture, Folklore, and History. The index has many entries under African, and - to name but a few: Candomblé, Caribbean, Dance, Drums, Drumming, Brazil, Bermuda, and the like. No annotations.

Jackson, Irene V.
See also: •**More than dancing, 1109.**
•**More than drumming, 1110.**

751. **Jackson, Melveen**. "The advent of the 'Indian' orchestra and a local Indian record company: music into the Indian South African economy." In **Symposium on Ethnomusicology**. (7th: 1988: Venda, South Africa). *Papers presented at the 7th Symposium on Ethnomusicology: Department of Anthropology and Ethnomusicology, University of Venda, 3rd to 5th September 1988.* Edited by Andrew Tracey, 22-27. Grahamstown, South Africa: Rhodes University, 1989.

See also C. G. Henning's paper on Indian music published in the 5th Symposium, 673.

752. **Jacobs, Virginia Lee.** *Roots of Rastafari.* San Diego, California: Avant Books, 1985. 130pp/

On reggae music, history of the Ras Tafari movement, and Haile Selassie I. Bibliography.

753. **Jahn, Janheinz.** "Residual African elements in the blues." In **Mother wit from the laughing barrel: readings in the interpretation of Afro-American folklore**. Edited by Alan Dundes, 95-102. New Printing with addendum. New York: Garland, 1981.

Jahn has his own unique ideas on the subject of the blues, one being that the blues "do not arise from a mood but produce one." He believes that, as in all African art forms, song too is "an attitude that effects something." Footnotes.

754. JAMAICA BEAT. 1969- . Newshound Pub., Kingston, Jamaica.

Described as providing news and information on sports, arts, real estate, business investment, tourism, and reggae music.

755. **James, Debba**. "Some inter-disciplinary problems in the teaching of African music." In **Symposium on Ethnomusicology**. (3rd: 1982: University of Natal) [4th: 1983: Rhodes University] *Papers presented at the Third and Fourth Symposia on Ethnomusicology*, Music Department, University of Natal, Durban, 16th to 19th September 1982; Music Department, Rhodes University, 7th to 8th October 1983, 59-60. Grahamstown, South Africa: International Library of African Music, 1984.
Note that this paper is in the 4th Symposium. The 3rd and 4th Symposia are in one volume.

Jara, Mamadu
See: **Chants de chasseurs du Mali, 335.**

756. **Jatta, Sidia**. "Born musicians: traditional music from the Gambia." In **Repercussions: a celebration of African-American music**. Edited by Geoffrey Haydon and Dennis Marks, 14-29. London: Century Publications, 1985.
Qualifying himself as neither musician nor musicologist but one who has known music of the Gambia from childhood, Jatta presents an illuminating study of Mandinka music. We learn how inadequate the terms "griot" or "bard" are to explain "jali" or "jaliyaa." Countless misconceptions about the *jali* and Mandinka social structure are corrected. We learn of instruments, their repertoires, of women *jali*, and contemporary changes. Invention of the *kora* (spelled *koora*) is unequivocally claimed for Africa. Westerners get their wrists slapped for using ethnocentric terms and concepts. Jatta believes, nonetheless, in music's power to transcend barriers between peoples.

757. **JAZZFORSCHUNG/JAZZ RESEARCH**. 1969- . Graz, Austria. (International Society for Jazz Research)
Issued annually. Indexed in **MUSIC INDEX** (under the English title), and in **RILM**. Only a few essays have been selected for listing below.
- **Kubik, Gerhard**. "Afrikanische Elemente im Jazz: Jazzelemente in der populären Musik Afrikas," 1, 1969.
- **Kubik, Gerhard**. "Der Verarbeitung von Kwela, Jazz und Pop in der modernen Musik von Malaŵi," 3, 4, 1971-72.
- **Mensah, Atta Annan**. "Jazz - the round trip," 3, 4, 1971-72.

758. **Je désire danser!: chansons populaires de la Zone de Gandajika (Rép. du Zaïre)**. Katende Cyovo. Bandundu, République du Zaïre: Ceeba, 1979. 120pp. (Publications Ceeba, Série 2, vol. 49)
Sequel to: **Voilà la nouvelle lune! Dansons! (1629)** In French and Luba. Includes texts of popular songs of Zaïre.

J

759. **Jẹ́gẹ́dẹ́, Délé**. "Popular culture in urban Africa." In *Africa.* 2d ed. Edited by Phyllis M. Martin, and Patrick O'Meara, 265-277. Bloomington Indiana University Press, c1986.
References to music under Theater; and Music and the Mass Media. Comic theater in Africa, and the close association of music and theater in South Africa are discussed. A few big name performers, groups and music types are given historical perspective. Music of the Alàdúrà Church of Nigeria is touched on briefly, page 274. Short bibliography with three entries specifically on music.

760. **Jessup, Lynne.** AFRICAN CHARACTERISTICS FOUND IN AFRO-AMERICAN AND ANGLO-AMERICAN MUSIC. Master's Thesis, University of Washington, 1971. 340pp.

761. **Jessup, Lynne.** *Afro ensemble: a beginning book.* Fort Worth, Texas: Harris Music Publications, 1975. [28pp.]
An attractively-designed handbook that uses - and explains - the symbols used in *adinkra* (an African fabric of special design), and distills an enormous amount of Jessup's considerable knowledge into a few pages of information, well-explained, easily-comprehensible. Intended for use by both teacher and student. Includes a culture area map of Africa, six density referent charts that teach basic rhythms, information on equipment, costumes, dancing, how to construct a drum. Several films are listed, and sources for obtaining "Afro-percussion" scores. In an innocuous way, the book conveys vital information, and even does corrective work, i.e., "Africa is - a continent, not a country...not just drumming..." etc. Excellent.

762. **Jessup, Lynne.** *The Mandinka balafon: an introduction with notation for teaching.* Illustrations by Mary McConnell. La Mesa, California: Xylo Publications, c1983. 191pp.
Bibliography and discography. Illustrations, music.

763. **Jessup, Lynne.** *World music: a source book for teaching.* Illustrations by Mary McConnell. Danbury, Connecticut: World Music Press, c1988. 64pp.
A tidy, attractive little reference book. Included in the bibliography is a several-page section on Africa. The discography and audio-visual sections treat Africa and North Africa as separate entities.

764. **JEUNE AFRIQUE**. 1960- . Paris: Societé africaine de presse.
Appears weekly, formerly known as **J.A.** In French. Features African politics and culture. Includes articles on events taking place in Africa, and on important figures of African descent. Said to be the most widely read journal in francophone Africa. Has a music section that is more apt to focus on popular music of Africa. Indexed in **CURRENT CONTENTS AFRICA**. Also available in microform and as reprints from **UMI**.

765. **Johnson, Alex**. "Transcription and translation of Ebenezer Calender's repertoire list." In *Perspectives on African music*. Edited by Wolfgang Bender, 70-90. Bayreuth, Germany: Bayreuth University, c1989.

766. **Johnson, John William**. THE EPIC OF SUN-JATA: AN ATTEMPT TO DEFINE THE MODEL FOR AFRICAN EPIC POETRY. 3 vols. Dissertation, Indiana University, 1978.
Text of the epic poem in volumes 2 and 3 is in English and Mandingo. Contents are: Volume 1.: The epic of Sun-jata; Volume 2.: The epic of Son-Jara (according to Fa-Digi Sisoko), translated and annotated by J. W. Johnson, with the assistance of Charles S. Bird...*et al.*; Volume 3. The epic of Sun-Jata (according to Magan Sisoko), collected, translated, and annotated by J. W. Johnson, with the assistance of Cheick Omar Nara...*et al.* Illustrations, genealogy tables, maps, bibliography.

767. **Johnson, Joyce Marie**. "The black American folk preacher and the chanted sermon: parallels with a West African tradition." In **A tribute to Alan P. Merriam**. Edited by Caroline Card, *et al.*, 205-222. Bloomington, Indiana: Indiana University. (Archives of Traditional Music), c1981.
Johnson finds parallels to the African "griot" (*jali*).

768. **Johnson, Rótìmí**. "The language and content of Nigerian popular music." In *Perspectives on African Music*. Edited by Wolfgang Bender, 91-102. Bayreuth, Germany: Bayreuth University, c1989.

769. **Johnson, Sheila J.** *Non-Western music: a selected bibliography*. 2d ed. [Sacramento] Library. California State University, Sacramento, 1973. 40pp. (California State University, Sacramento. Library. Bibliographic series, no. 10)
This series was begun in 1969 to assist patrons to use the Sacramento Library. All materials listed in the Bibliography are part of the Library holdings. Part One includes General Works; Part Two covers specific geographical areas - Africa on pages 10-15, the Middle East on pages 16-18. The latter section has a few entries that includes the music of Egypt and the Western Sudan. Short annotations accompany each entry. Johnson compiled the first edition in 1973. The later, third edition, is listed in this bibliography under **Smith, Donna Ridley, 1470.**

770. **Johnston, Thomas F.** "Aspects of Tsonga history through song." **AFRICANA MARBURGENSIA** 6, no. 1 (1973): 17-36.

771. **Johnston, Thomas F.** Hand pianos, xylophones and flutes of the Shangana-Tsonga." **AFRIKA UND ÜBERSEE** 57, no. 3 (1974): 186-192.

J

772. Johnston, Thomas F. "Humanized animal and bird figures in Tsonga songtexts." **AFRICANA MARBURGENSIA** 14, no. 2 (1981): 55-71.

773. Johnston, Thomas F. "Music of the Shangana-Tsonga." In *South African music encyclopedia*. Vol. 2. Edited by Jacques P. Malan, 381-418. Cape Town: Oxford University Press, 1979-1986.

774. Johnston, Thomas F. THE MUSIC OF THE SHANGANA-TSONGA: A STUDY, IN CULTURAL CONTEXT, OF THE VOCAL AND INSTRUMENTAL MUSIC OF A PEOPLE OF MOZAMBIQUE AND THE NORTHERN TRANSVAAL. 2 vols. Dissertation, University of the Witwatersrand, 1972. 525pp.
Illustrations, music, two phonotapes (7 inches), bibliography.

775. Johnston, Thomas F. "Musical instruments and dance uniforms in Southern Africa." **OBJETS ET MONDES** 13, no. 2 (1979): 81-90.

776. Johnston, Thomas F. "Notes on the music of the Tswana." In *South African music encyclopedia*. Vol. 2. Edited by Jacques P. Malan, 376-381. Cape Town: Oxford University Press, 1979-1986.

777. Johnston, Thomas F. THE STRESS-REDUCING FUNCTION OF TSONGA BEER SONGS. Master's Thesis, California State University, Fullerton, 1972. 220pp.

778. Johnston, Thomas F. "Structure in Tsonga music: an analysis in social terms." **JOURNAL OF AFRICAN STUDIES** 3, no. 1 (1976): 51-81.
Song texts, 16 tables.

779. Johnston, Thomas F. "Tsonga children's folksongs." **JOURNAL OF AMERICAN FOLKLORE** 86, no. 341 (1973): 225-240.

780. Johnston, Thomas F. "Tsonga musical performance in cultural perspective." **ANTHROPOS** 70, no. 5/6 (1975): 761-799.
Illustrations, music, bibliography.

781. Jones, A. M. "Africa and Indonesia: an ancient colonial era?" In *Essays on music and history in Africa*. Edited by Klaus P. Wachsmann, 81-92. Evanston: Northwestern University Press, 1971.
Even though Jones' ideas about an African-Indonesian connection have by now been largely discounted by musicologists - though not totally explained away - he is to be remembered particularly for his *magnum opus*, *Studies in African music* (**785**) which represented a major breakthrough in its day. There are in fact

some musicologists even now who have not caught up with the information resulting from Jones' careful and unprecedented research. Fage, the historian, treats the Indonesian ideas of Jones with respectful consideration in his own essay in Wachsmann's collection (**575**), but also adds his doubts to those of others. Footnotes.

782. Jones, A. M. *Africa and Indonesia: the evidence of the xylophone and other musical and cultural factors.* Photomechanical reprint with an additional chapter "More evidence on Africa and Indonesia." 2d ed. Leiden: E. J. Brill, 1971. 286pp.
A significant work, though controversial. First published by Brill in 1964. Bibliography.

783. Jones, A. M. *African hymnody in Christian worship: a contribution to the history of its development.* Gwelo, Rhodesia [Zimbabwe]: Mambo Press, 1976. 64pp. (Mambo occasional papers. Missio-pastoral series, no. 8)
After the introduction, the three chapters are entitled: Hymns in the Early Days, The Rise of Dissatisfaction, and The Beginning of African Hymnody. A chronological bibliography covers 1871-1967, and includes hymn books with varying degrees of African music content and varying degrees of African involvement in their creation. Some works are in African languages. A useful book by a dedicated scholar.

784. Jones, A. M. "Instruments de musique africains." PRÉSENCE AFRICAINE 6-7, nos. 34-35 (1961): 132-150.
An essay, written in French, that surveys African instruments from their origins up to the time of writing.

785. Jones, A. M. *Studies in African music.* 4th printing. 2 vols. London: Oxford, [1959] 1971.
A major, pioneer work by an early luminary. Father Jones' meticulous, scientific approach, along with his sensible and respectful idea of working closely with a highly-skilled Ewe drummer (Desmond K. Tay) resulted in a significant breakthrough in concepts about African music. His book continues to be reprinted and is still well worth reading. Volume 1 is essentially textual. Volume 2 is oblong and protrudes from the shelf, filled with impressive and detailed musical transcriptions, careful in a way no transcriptions had been before this time. Photographs, folding map, charts, music notations, diagrams, song texts, index.

786. Jones, Bessie, and Bess Lomax Hawes. *Step it down: games, plays, songs, and stories from the Afro-American heritage.* New York: Harper and Row, 1972. 232pp.
A "national treasure" that preserves the rich African-American traditions of the South. When Bessie Jones moved to the Georgia Sea Islands, she had already acquired an extraordinary repertoire of songs and games, and this, coupled with her vibrant personality and singing style, endeared her to the Georgia Sea Island

Singers who asked her to join their group. In 1964, she, the Singers, and folklorist, Bess Lomax Hawes, presented a two-week teaching workshop in California, and out of this grew the present book. Africa is ever-present in its pages. Music notations, song texts, stories, games. Index, bibliography, discography.

787. Jones, Lura Jafran. THE 'ISAWIYA OF TUNISIA AND THEIR MUSIC. Dissertation, University of Washington, 1977. 314pp.

788. JOURNAL DES AFRICANISTES. 1931- . Paris: Société des Africanistes.

Issued semi-annually, text in French and English. Formerly this was called **SOCIÉTÉ DES AFRICANISTES. JOURNAL**. Indexed by **AICP**. Two examples follow:

- **Kabore, Oger.** "Chants d'enfants Mossi," vol. 51, no. 1/2 (1981): 183-200.
- **Koudjo, Bienvenu.** "Parole et musique chez les Fon et les Gun du Benin, pour une nouvelle taxonomie de la parole littéraire," vol. 58, no. 2 (1988): 73-97.

JOURNAL FOR ETHNOMUSICOLOGY

See: **ETHNOMUSICOLOGY: JOURNAL OF THE SOCIETY FOR ETHNOMUSICOLOGY, 551.**

789. JOURNAL OF AFRICAN STUDIES. 1974-1989. Washington D.C. Heldref Publications.

This journal was issued quarterly. During its tenure, it occasionally had fine articles on African music. Three have been selected for listing, but there are others. (Volume 9, no. 3, 1982, was an issue that focused entirely on African music. It is treated separately, and its contents indicated. See next entry (**790**) for information on this issue.) Indexed in **CURRENT CONTENTS AFRICA**.

- **Ekwueme, Lazarus.** "Linguistic determinants of some Igbo musical properties," vol. 1, no. 3 (1974): 335-353.
- **Johnston, Thomas F.** "Structure in Tsonga music: an analysis in social terms," vol. 3, no. 1 (1976): 51-81.
- **Ọlátúnjí, Olátúndé O.** "Issues in the study of oral poetry in Africa," vol. 6, no. 1 (1979): 112-119.

790. JOURNAL OF AFRICAN STUDIES. Vol.9, no. 3, 1982.

This special issue on African music has a foreword by Jacqueline Cogdell DjeDje and J. H. Kwabena Nketia. It contains the following essays, arranged here alphabetically:

- **Aning, B. A.** "Tuning the *kora*: a case study of the norms of a Gambian musician," 164-175.
- **DjeDje, Jacqueline Cogdell.** "The concept of patronage: an examination of Hausa and Dagomba one-string fiddle traditions," 116-127.
- **Martin, Stephen H.** "Music in urban East Africa: five genres in Dar es Salaam," 155-163.
- **Mensah, Atta Annan.** "*Gyil*: the Dagara-Lobi xylophone," 139-154.
- **Monts, Lester P.** "Music clusteral relationships in a Liberian-Sierra Leonean region: a preliminary analysis," 101-115.

continued

•**Nketia, J. H. Kwabena**. "On the historicity of music in African cultures," 91-99.
•**Shelemay, Kay Kaufman**. "The music of the Lablibeloč: music mendicants of Ethiopia," 128-138.
(See also the main entry for this periodical, **789**.

791. **JOURNAL OF AMERICAN FOLKLORE**. 1988- . (American Folklore Society) American Anthropological Association, Washington, D.C.
Described as having articles on all areas of folklife and folklore. Occasionally there are articles on African or African-related musics. It is recommended that the Journal's indexes be examined for pertinent articles. Also indexed in: **CURRENT CONTENTS, HISTORICAL ABSTRACTS, ARTS AND HUMANITIES CITATION INDEX, MLA,** and others.
•**Johnston, Thomas F.** "Tsonga children's folksongs," vol. 86, no. 341 (1973): 225-240.
•**Kratz, Corinne A.** "Persuasive suggestions and reassuring promises: emergent parallelism and dialogic encouragement in song," vol. 103, no. 1 (1990): 42-67.
•**Merriam, Alan P.** "The African idiom in music," vol. 75, no. 296 (1962): 120-130.

792. **JOURNAL OF BLACK STUDIES**. 1970- . Newbury Park, Califiornia: Sage Publications.
Issued quarterly. Indexed in **RILM, CURRENT CONTENTS, HISTORICAL ABSTRACTS,** and others. Volume 15, no. 4 is devoted to African and African-American Dance, Music, and Theater. Following are a few randomly selected articles:
•**Abarry, Abu**. "A traditional poetry of the Ga of Ghana," vol. 14, No.4 (1984): 493-506.
•**Ekweume, Lazarus Edward Nnanyelu**. "Concepts of African musical theory," vol.5, no. 1 (1974): 35-64.
•**Green, Doris**. "The liberation of African music," vol. 8, no. 2 (1977): 149-167.

793. **JOURNAL OF CARIBBEAN STUDIES**. 1980- . Lexington, Kentucky, Association of Caribbean Studies.
Issued three times a year. In English, French, or Spanish. Contains book reviews, bibliographies. Cumulative index. Indexed in **MLA (1003).**

794. **JOURNAL OF THE FOLKLORE INSTITUTE**. 1964-1982. [The Hague]: Mouton and Company.
This journal superseded **MIDWEST FOLKLORE**, and was continued by **JOURNAL OF FOLKLORE RESEARCH**. It was issued three times a year, edited and published at Indiana University. The following paper is listed in this bibliography:
•**Elder, Jacob D.** "*Kalinda* - song of the battling troubadours of Trinidad," vol. 3, no.2 (1966): 192-203.

795. **JOURNAL OF THE PERFORMING ARTS**. 1980- . Accra, Ghana: School of Performing Arts, University of Ghana.
Listed as semi-annual, but only volume 1, number 1 (January 1980) has been available for examination. It contains the following essays:

- •**Adinku, William Ofotsu**. "The *kpatsa* dance of the Dangme," 66-82.
- •**Fiagbedzi, Nissio**. "On signing and symbolism in music: the evidence from among an African people," 54-65.
- •**Fiagbedzi, Nissio**. "A preliminary inquiry into inherent rhythms in Anlo dance drumming," 83-92.

796. **Jules-Rosette, Benetta**. *African apostles: ritual and conversion in the church of John Maranke*. Ithaca, New York: Cornell University Press, 1975. 302pp.
Bibliography, glossary, index, music, photos.

797. **Jules-Rosette, Benetta**. "Ecstatic singing: music and social integration in an African church." In **More than drumming: essays on African and Afro-Latin music and musicians**. Edited by Irene V. Jackson, 119-143. Westport, Connecticut: Greenwood Press, c1985.
Notes, bibliography, song texts, photographs. Abstracted in **RILM**, 1985.

798. **Junod, Henri Alexandre**. *Cantos e contos dos Rongas*. [s.l.: Instituto de Investigação Científica de Moçambique, 1975]. 187pp.
Portuguese translation of *Les chants et les contes des Ba-Ronga de la baie de Delagoa*. (See following entry, **799**.) Includes bibliographical references.

799. **Junod, Henri Alexandre**. *Les chants et les contes des Ba-Ronga de la baie de Delagoa*. Nendeln: Kraus Reprint, 1970. 327pp.
The first part includes songs of the Thonga of Mozambique, the musical instruments, the music system. There are notated melodies of songs used for different purposes. Words are in the original language and translated into French. The second part of the book has to do with folk tales. A few charming sketches will delight children. This is a reprint of the 1897 edition published by G. Bridel, Lausanne.

800. **Kaabu and Fuladu: historical narratives of the Gambian Mandinka.** [Transcribed by B. K. Sidibe]. [Translated and edited by Gordon Innes]. London: University of London School of Oriental and African Studies, 1976. 310pp.
Includes song texts in English and Mandinka. Bibliography.

801. **Kabira, Wanjikũ Mũkabi, and Karega Mũtahi.** *Gĩkũyũ oral literature.* Nairobi: Heinemann Kenya, 1988. 167pp.
In English and Gĩkũyũ. There are oral narratives, proverbs, riddles, poetry and 167 song texts, scattered throughout the book. Oral literature is classified, and song described as the most flexible genre. Songs are categorized as to their assorted uses. Their texts appear throughout the book, but there are no transcriptions.

802. **Kabore, Oger.** "Chants d'enfants Mossi." JOURNAL DES AFRICANISTES 51, no. 1/2 (1981): 183-200.
Children's songs of the Mossi of Burkina Faso and Ghana.

803. **Kaemmer, John E.** "Changing music in contemporary Africa." In *Africa.* Edited by Phyllis M. Martin, and Patrick O'Meara, 367-377. Bloomington: Indiana University Press, c1977.
Discussed are changing attitudes towards music, as affected by sociological and political factors, as well as the economic impact of the advent of the music industry with its concomitant technology. Influences of Arabic music, Western music, and the dance rhythms of Latin America (themselves, already Africanized) are touched on. Kaemmer contrasts the guitar-based urban music of West Africa, black South Africa, and Zaïre, as well as concert-type African music by Western-trained composers. Highlife is examined, along with other hybrid forms (though much has happened subsequent to 1977). Notes, bibliography.

804. **Kaemmer, John E.** THE DYNAMICS OF A CHANGING MUSIC SYSTEM IN RURAL RHODESIA. Dissertation, Indiana University, 1975. 224pp.
Illustrations, maps, bibliography.

805. **Kakoma, George W.** "Musical traditions of East Africa." In **African music: meeting in Yaoundé (Cameroon) 23-27 February 1970, organized by** UNESCO, 77-88. Paris: *La revue musicale*, 1972.
Music notations. Next entry (**806**) is the original French version.

806. **Kakoma, George W.** "Les traditions musicales de l'Afrique orientale." In **La musique africaine, réunion de Yaoundé (Cameroun)** [sur les traditions musicales de l'Afrique subsaharienne], **23-27 février 1970, organisée par l'**UNESCO, 75-86. Paris: *La revue musicale*, Richard-Masse, 1972.
Music notations. Preceding entry (**805**) is the English translation of this one.

K

807. **Kalanzi, Benny A.** *The Bantu and you: African songs of yesterday and today = Afrikanische Musik von gestern und heute = La musique traditionelle et moderne africaine.* Text by B. A. Kalanzi. Music by B. A. Kalanzi and J. M. Sendaula. Zürich: Eulenberg, c1969. 93pp. (General music series, no. GMS 3)
Written information is in English, French and German; song lyrics are in Ganda. The cover describes the contents as "Sweet melodies and rich rhythms in Western notation with accompaniment on: piano, guitar, bowl-lyre, fiddle, harp, flute, maracas and drum." Kalanzi, a versatile Ugandan scholar and musician with a good deal of Western music training, divides textual material by language into three columns. There are notes about Uganda, its music, the instruments used. The 24 song texts are translated into English. Music scores are complete, and indicate voice and instrumental parts. The title, used in this way, is offensive.

808. **Kalanzi, Benny A.** *The Mysteries of African music.* Dayton, Ohio: McAfee Music Corporation, 1974. 48pp.
Twelve African songs are scored in Western notation, with indications for accompanying instruments. Languages of song texts and names of associated countries are not given, though all songs are translated into English. Generalities occur frequently in an essay on African music that seems to extend primarily from Kalanzi's acquaintance with music of Uganda, his birthplace. Some information is factual, but one must constantly be on guard to separate chaff from wheat. The statement, "African music abounds in syncopation," and use of the word "Bantu" reveal just how far Kalanzi's point of view has been affected by study abroad.

Kamara, Karamoga
See: **Griots de Samatiguila, 643.**

809. **Kamara, Seyidu**. *Kambili: Seyidu Kamara ka donkiliw.* Bourama Soumaoro...[*et al.*] y'a sèbèn. [Bloomington: African Studies Center, Indiana University, 1976. 101pp.
In Mandingo. English translation published under title: *The songs of Seydou Camara: Kambili* (entered under "Kamara," not "Camara)."

810. **Kamara, Seyidu**. *Nyakhalen la forgeronne: chant récit de chasseurs du Mali.* [Paris]: Annik Thoyer, 1986. 69pp. (Paris: Mathey), 69pp.
The tale is performed by the esteemed *jali*, Seyidu Kamara, whose music honors the hunter. Besides the text itself (in Bambara on one side, and French on the other) there are several pages on Kamara, the musician, and his role in recruiting hunters, inspiring the hunt, and participating in festivals. His instrument is the harp-lute. There is one standing photo of him, and 52 notes.

811. **Kamara, Seyidu**. *The songs of Seydou Camara.* Translated by Charles S. Bird, Mamadou Koita and Bourama Soumaoro. Bloomington: African Studies Center, Indiana University, 1974. 120pp. (Occasional papers in Mande studies, no. 1)
This is a translation of the epic, Kambili, as brought to life by Seyidu Kamara, a

Maninka of the blacksmith caste. Kamara has devoted his life to honoring the hunter in poetry and song, accompanying himself on the harp-lute. In 1953, he won the *jali*'s competition in Sikasso for his singular artistry. Bird's painstaking work and highly developed translating skill capture the beauty and flow of the poetry. At the end of the book are over 155 notes that give specific points of information on the epic itself. A beautiful and resplendent portrait of Kamara launches the text.

812. **Kamenyi, John W.** *Musical instruments: a resource book on traditional instruments of Kenya.* Nairobi: Jemisik Cultural Books, 1986. 71pp.
See the Author Index for other works of Kamenyi's.

Kamenyi, John W.
See also: •**Gĩkũyũ, 623.**
•**Songs of Kenya, 1481.**

813. **Kanza Matondo ne Mansangaza.** *Musique d'animation politique & culturelle: Festival de Kinshasa du 2 au 14 octobre, 1979: critique descriptive.* Kinshasa: Édition "Dialogue," Secrétariat permanent urbain mouvement populaire de la révolution, [1979?]. 31pp.
A booklet concerned with the political aspects of music in Zaïre during the 1979 Festival. The orchestra and participants are discussed. Choral music is compartmentalized (in good old Western style) into melody, harmony, rhythm and interpretation. *Folklorique* songs and *Chansons d'animation* are mentioned. Slogans as well. Inexpensively produced, but a handy small size with unusually good photocopies of photographs.

814. **Kanza Matondo ne Mansangaza.** *Musique zaïroise moderne [situation actuelle & perspectives d'avenir] extrait d'une conférence illustrée donnée en 1969 au campus universitaire de Kinshasa.* Kinshasa, Publications du C.N.M.A., 1972. 86pp.
Following the foreword and introduction, Zaïrian music is analyzed as to the pre-colonial period, the colonial period, the present, and perspectives for the future. Pages 75-83 are called, "The author's 'Discours prononcé...[devant la] Réunion d'experts de l'UNESCO sur l'utilisation des techniques audio-visuelles pour l'étude des traditions africaines, Porto-Novo (Dahomey) 14-20 novembre 1969." Bibliography.

815. **Kapalanga Gazungil Sang'Amin.** *Les spectacles d'animation politique en République du Zaïre: analyse des méchanismes de reprise, d'actualisation et de politisation des formes culturelles africaines dans les créations spectaculaires modernes.* Louvain-la-Neuve, Belgium: Éditions des Cahiers
continued

Théâtre Louvain, c1989. 262pp. (Cahiers Théâtre Louvain, 63-65) (Arts du spectacle)
A "spectacle," in this context, is a time for honoring and singing praise songs for a political leader. New words are commonly added to traditional songs. Kapalanga Gazungil Sang 'Amin says that the spectacle has three elements: 1. presence of certain personages from the African world, such as the "griot," to entertain the public, 2. use of specific means of expression, such as music and dance [in which those present actively participate], and 3. utilization of space, comparable to the village, in order to recreate the environment. Bibliographic references. No photographs or illustrations.

816. **Kartomi, Margaret J.** *On concepts and classification of musical instruments.* Chicago: University of Chicago Press, 1990. 329pp. (Chicago studies in ethnomusicology)
Chapter 16 is entitled, The Personification of Instruments in some West African Classifications. The essay is 12 pages long. The author says that the typically West African way of classifying instruments rests on the West African inclination to personify instruments. She backs-up this statement with charts, drawings, results of her own research, and the findings of others in the field. (The rest of the book does not appear, upon cursory examination, to have anything else specifically on African music. It does contain illustrations, bibliographic references, and an index.)

Katende Cyovo
See: •**Instruments de musique de Gandajika, 727.**
•**Je désire danser! 758.**
•**Voilà la nouvelle lune! 1629.**

817. **Katzenellenbogen, Edith H.** *South African dances in folk idiom.* Pretoria, Republic of South Africa: South African Association for Physical Education and Recreation, c1981. 29pp.
A booklet that includes descriptions of the sequencing of 12 dances correlated to appropriate music. Details of recordings that might accompany the dances are also given. Of particular interest are several songs of black South Africa: *Dingaka* [Sotho people]; *Pata-Pata*; a lullaby, and *Ipi Tombi.* The latter can be used synonymously to mean the name of a particular South African performance group, the name for their dramatic performance that includes dance and music, or the musical theme from the latter musical. Words and melody lines of songs are provided. The glossary describes steps, formations, and holds in more detail.

818. **Kauffman, Robert.** "Multipart relationships in Shona vocal music." In **Studies in African music.** Co-editors, J. H. Kwabena Nketia, and Jacqueline Cogdell DjeDje, 145-159. [Los Angeles]: Program in Ethnomusicology, Department of Music, University of California, Los Angeles, 1984.
Fourteen notated examples of songs for assorted purposes, some of them contemporary. Three references cited.

819. **Kauffman, Robert.** MULTI-PART RELATIONSHIPS IN THE SHONA MUSIC OF RHODESIA. Dissertation, University of California, Los Angeles. 1970, c1971. 333pp.
Illustrations, maps, music, bibliography.

820. **Kauffman, Robert.** "Shona urban music and the problems of acculturation." **INTERNATIONAL FOLK MUSIC JOURNAL. Yearbook.** 4 (1972): 47-56.

821. **Kauffman, Robert.** "Tactility as an aesthetic consideration in African music." In **The performing arts: music and dance.** Edited by John Blacking, and Joann W. Kealiinohomoku, 251-253. New York: Mouton, c1979.
A fascinating view of the *mbira* as a "personal instrument" played more for the performer's satisfaction than for the benefit of others. (Often the *mbira* cannot even be heard during a ritual.) Kauffman believes that this satisfaction comes from the tactility of the instrument rather than from its sound-producing characteristics, and refers to the pleasant sensation produced by the *mbira*'s "vibration complex." The concept of a possible tactility component to music performance suggests interesting avenues of research. (But also to be remembered is the joy of being a part of a music-making group, heard or not.)

822. **Kaufman, Fredrich, and John P. Guckin.** *The African roots of jazz.* [Sherman Oaks, California]: Alfred Publishing Company, c1979. 147pp.
Bibliography, discography, index, recordings.

823. **Kavyũ, Paul N.** *The development of guitar music in Kenya.* [Nairobi]: University of Nairobi, Institute of African Studies, 1978. 7pp. (Discussion paper - University of Nairobi, Institute of African Studies, no. 90)

824. **Kavyũ, Paul N.** *Drum music of Akamba: a study of the vocal and instrumental aspects in an ethnic community of Kenya.* Hohenschäftlarn: Klaus Renner Verlag, 1986. 258pp. (Studien zur Musik Afrikas, vol. 2)
This was originally a doctoral dissertation accepted by the Universität zu Köln. The author explains that the main title really refers to *mũkanda*, the most important music and dance entertainment form in the community. At the time of writing, Kavyũ says that there was no scientific work published on Akamba music. This book certainly corrects that situation. Maps, plates, bibliography. (Surprising that not more editorial guidance in English was provided for such an impressive example of scholarship.)

825. **Kavyũ, Paul N.** *An introduction to Kamba music.* [Kenya] Kampala: East African Literature Bureau, 1977. 119pp.
Includes music scores, bibliographical references and index.

K

826. **Kavyũ, Paul N.** *Problems of continuity in Kenya music education.* [Nairobi]: University of Nairobi, Institute of African Studies, 1974. (Discussion paper - University of Nairobi, Institute of African Studies, no. 59)
Bibliographical references.

827. **Kavyũ, Paul N.** "The role of traditional instruments in music." In **The arts and civilization of Black and African peoples**. Edited by Joseph Ohiomogben Okpaku, Alfred Esimatemi Opubor, and Benjamin Ọlátúnjí Ọlọ́runtìmẹhìn, Volume 1: 152-165. Lagos: Centre for Black and African Arts and Civilization, c1986.
In this short paper Kavyu, examines the significance of traditional instruments in African music, reaffirms the *originality* of African instruments, often erroneously assumed to be only imitative, remarks on the importance of music and musical instruments as communication media, and has kind words to say about creative Hungarian methods of teaching music and musical instruments. Heavily footnoted with a long song text, local names and descriptions of instruments used by various ethnic groups, notated nonsense syllables, and sketches of several instruments. Bibliography.

828. **Kavyũ, Paul N.** *Some Kamba dance songs.* 2 vols. [Nairobi]:University of Nairobi, Institute of African Studies, 1972-1973. (Discussion paper - University of Nairobi, Institute of African Studies, no. 36, 43)
This paper is concerned with Kamba dance songs of Kenya which existed up to about 50 years ago in both Kitui and Machakos Districts. Includes bibliographical references.

829. **Kavyũ, Paul N.** *Traditional musical instruments of Kenya.* Nairobi: Kenya Literature Bureau, 1980. 53pp.
Includes bibliographical references and illustrations.

830. **Kayo, Patrice.** "La chanson dans la société traditionelle bamiléké." In **Chansons d'Afrique et des Antilles**, 77-80. Paris: Harmattan, c1988.

831. **Kayo, Patrice.** *Chansons populaires bamiléké.* [Cameroon] [s.l.: s.n.,1975?] [Yaoundé Imp. St.-Paul]. 21pp.
Bamiléké songs translated into French.

832. **Kazadi, Ntole M'Bay.** *Chants, mariage et société au Bushi: textes littéraires et contexte.* Lubumbashi: Centre de linguistique théorique et appliquée, 1978. 77pp. (Collection "Travaux et recherches")
Six songs of the Bashi people of Zaïre are analyzed from the standpoint of oral tradition rather than as music. Wedding songs are included. No music

transcriptions, no photos, no index. Texts in the Shi language, translations into French. Small regional maps.

833. **Kazadi, Ntole M'Bay.** ESSAI D'ÉTUDE ETHNOLINGUISTIQUE DES CHANTS DES CULTES DU BÚTEMBÓ ET DES MÍKENDÍ (CHEZ LES BÁHÉMBA ET LES BÁLÚBA DU ZAÏRE). Dissertation, Université de la Sorbonne Nouvelle Paris III, 1982. 400pp.
An in-depth ethnological and linguistic study of Zaïrian songs. Many explanatory remarks. There are 20 Bútembó songs, and 18 Mikendi. Almost nothing about the music *per se*, though the texts show the traditional call-response structure. Written in the Luba-Katanga language with French translation. Three maps, bibliography.

834. **Kazadi, Pierre Cary.** *The characteristic criteria in the vocal music of the Luba-Shankadi children.* Tervuren, Musée royal de l'Afrique centrale, 1972. 93pp. (Musée royal de l'Afrique centrale. Annales. Sér. in 8. Sciences humaines, no. 75)
Children's songs of Zaïre.

835. **Kazadi, Pierre Cary.** "Congo music: Africa's favorite beat." **AFRICA REPORT** 16, no. 4, 1971.

836. **Kazadi, Pierre Cary.** GAME SONGS OF THE LUBA-SHANKADI CHILDREN. Master's Thesis, University of California, Los Angeles, 1971.

837. **Kazadi wa Mukuna.** *African children's songs for American elementary schools.* East Lansing, Michigan: African Studies Center and Music Department, Michigan State University, c1979. 40pp. (Resources for teaching and research in African studies, no. 2)
Includes 10 African songs designed for American children to learn. These come from the Luba, in the Kasai and Shaba regions of Zaïre. Lesson plans go by step. The author says that the procedures suggested for teaching are suitable for all ages, and can be scaled up or down, depending upon the individual or group involved. Phonetic pronunciation is given for song texts in Luba, but texts are also translated into English. Instructions are given for fabricating four African-type percussion instruments from readily available home materials, such as bottle caps. Sound sheet in back pocket. Spiral bound.

838. **Kazadi wa Mukuna.** O CONTATO MUSICAL TRANSATLANTICO: CONTRIBUIÇÃO BANTO A MÚSICA POPULAR BRASILEIRA. Dissertation, University of California, Los Angeles, 1978. 291pp.
The text is in Portuguese. (University Microfilms lists under **Mukuna, Kazadi wa**, but it would seem that he is in good company with the other Kazadi's.)

K

839. Kazadi wa Makuna. *Contribuição bantu na música popular brasileira.* [São Paulo]: Global Editora, [1978?]. 230pp.
On popular Brazilian music created by people of African descent. Bibliography, and abundant music notations, especially of short rhythmic patterns. Somewhat blurry photographs one has seen elsewhere - but which are honorably credited to their sources - primarily of African musicians. A few from Brazil. Informative.

840. Kazadi wa Mukuna. "The origins of Zaïrean modern music: a socio-economic aspect." **AFRICAN URBAN STUDIES** vol. 6 (1979-1980): 31-39.

841. Kebede, Ashenafi. "African music in the Western Hemisphere." In **African music: meeting in Yaoundé (Cameroon) 23-27 February 1970, organized by UNESCO**, 131-135. Paris: *La revue musicale*, 1972.
Bibliography. This is a translation of Kebede's, "La musique africaine dans l'hémisphère occidentale," **846.**

842. Kebede, Ashenafi. *Äthiopien: Musik der koptischen Kirche.* [Berlin: E. Blaschker], 1969. 19pp. (Veröffentlichung des Internationalen Instituts für Vergleichende Musikstudien und Dokumentation)
Music of the Ethiopian Orthodox Church. Contents:
•**Kebede, Ashenafi.** "Die geistliche Musik der orthodoxen Kirche Äthiopiens."
•**Suttner, Karl.** "Musik und Tanz im Reich des Löwen von Juda."
See the following entry, **843**, which is a French translation of this German version.

843. Kebede, Ashenafi. *Éthiopie: musique de l'Église copte.* Berlin: Institut International d'Études Comparatives la Musique, 1969. [33]pp.
This is a French translation of *Äthiopien: Musik der koptischen Kirche*, a study concerned with the music of the Ethiopian Orthodox Church. Contains the following two sections:
•**Kebede, Ashenafi.** "La musique sacrée de l'Église orthodoxe de l'Éthiope."
•**Suttner, Karl.** "Musique au royaume du lion de Juda."
See the preceding entry, **842.**

844. Kebede, Ashenafi. THE MUSIC OF ETHIOPIA: ITS DEVELOPMENT AND CULTURAL SETTING. Dissertation, Wesleyan University, 1971. 298pp.

845. Kebede, Ashenafi. "Musical innovation and acculturation in African music." In **Explorations in ethnomusicology: essays in honor of David P. McAllester**. Edited by Charlotte J. Frisbie, 59-67. Detroit: Information Coordinators, 1986.
Notes, bibliography.

846. Kebede, Ashenafi. "La musique africaine dans l'hémisphère occidentale. La musique noire des Amériques." **In La musique africaine, réunion de Yaoundé (Cameroun)** [sur les traditions musicales de l'Afrique subsaharienne], **23-27 février 1970, organisée par l'UNESCO**, 129-134. Paris: *La revue musicale*, Richard-Masse, 1972.
Bibliography. This is a translation of "African music in the Western Hemisphere," **841**.

847. Kebede, Ashenafi. *Roots of Black music: the vocal, instrumental, and dance heritage of Africa and Black America.* Englewood Cliffs, New Jersey: Prentice-Hall, c1982. 162pp.
Includes bibliographies, discographies, and index.

848. Kebede, Ashenafi. SECULAR AMHARIC MUSIC OF ETHIOPIA. Master's Thesis, Wesleyan University, 1969. 132pp.

849. Keil, Charles. TIV SONG. Dissertation, University of Chicago, 1979.
Listed by University Microfilms as not available, but the book by the same name, is.

850. Keil, Charles. *Tiv song.* Chicago: University of Chicago Press, 1979. 301pp.
An important work that is often quoted. Bibliography, indexes, illustrations, plates, music. The Tiv are identified by Murdock (**1120a**) as "Plateau Nigerians."

851. Kelefa Saane: his career recounted by two Mandinka bards. Edited and translated by Gordon Innes. London: School of African and Oriental Studies, University of London, 1978.
Two highly respected Gambian *jali*, Bamba Suso and Shirif Jebate, present the story of Kelefa Saane, a man largely ignored by historians because he had no discernible effect on history. Nevertheless, the story of his career, which has become an important part of the *jali* repertoire, is widely-known and cherished. It represents an example of Mandinka heroic literature, and shows the distinctiveness of the Mandinka warrior aristocracy of the 19th century. Lucy Duran treats the music on pages 16-26. Bibliography, discography, maps, music. Texts in English and Mandingo.

852. Kennedy, Scott. *In search of African theater.* New York: Scribner, [1973]. 306pp.
An interesting narrative, over and beyond any mention of music. Kennedy, an African-American, and both academician and creative artist, studied theater in Ghana. Because of his perspicacious observations and conscientious research, he became particularly qualified to interpret much of Ghanaian culture to the Westerner. After attending major festivals in Dakar, 1966, and Algeria, 1969, Kennedy presents brief but good accounts of these events. Description of a

number of Ghanaian happenings that incorporate music, and descriptions of Ghanaian "concert party theater" are important. Index includes music and dance. Bibliography, photographs, 4 maps of Ghana (one, of dubious reliability, shows instrument localities). Kennedy's poems are included.

853. **Kerkhof, Ian**. "Music in the revolution." **KESKIDEE: A JOURNAL OF BLACK MUSIC TRADITIONS** 1 (1986): 10-21.

854. **KESKIDEE: A JOURNAL OF BLACK MUSIC TRADITIONS**. 1986 - . Essex: United Kingdom.

The second issue of this magazine appeared three years later than the first, owing to assorted misfortunes of the editor, Keith Summers, but today things looks brighter. It is difficult to convey in a small space the worth, the broad perspective of this publication other than to say that besides having keen articles (two selected for listing below), occasional book reviews, and abundant, informed record reviews, it is handsomely designed and contains rare historical photographs of people and significant documents, along with more recent ones of eminent black musicians from Africa, the Caribbean, and the United States. May the journal thrive.

•**Deroff, Doug**. "The Zulu choirs: a brief introduction." 1 (1986): 20-21.
•**Kerkhof, Ian**. "Music in the revolution." 2 (1990): 10-21.

Khatchi, K.
See: **Die tunesische Nuba ed Dhil, 1593.**

855. **Kilson, Marion**. *Kpele lala: Ga religious songs and symbols.* Cambridge: Harvard University Press, 1971. 313pp.

Bibliography, illustrations.

856. **Kimberlin, Cynthia Tse**. "The music of Ethiopia." In **Musics of many cultures: an introduction**. Edited by Elizabeth May, 232-252. Berkeley: University of California Press, c1980.

Map, beautiful line drawings of instruments, by Jerome Kimberlin, glossary, bibliography, discography, films, tables, many notations, chart showing modes.

857. **Kimberlin, Cynthia Tse**. "Ornaments and their classification as a determinant of technical ability and musical style." In **African musicology: current trends: a festschrift presented to J. H. Kwabena Nketia**. Edited by Jacqueline Cogdell DjeDje, and William G. Carter, 265-305. [Atlanta, Georgia: Crossroads Press, 1988]- .

The ornaments studied were those played by *azmari*, professional *mansinqo* players of Ethiopia. The intention was to define a standard by which ability and style might be objectively quantified. (The *mansinqo* is a single-stringed, bowed spike fiddle with a diamond-shaped sound box.) Included are notations, tables, (one quite lengthy entitled, Classification of Ornaments), an appendix, with musical transcriptions of seven songs, notes, and bibliography.

858. **King, Anthony**. *Children's songs of Nigeria*. Lagos: African Universities Press, 1967. 96pp.
Pupil's Edition only contains the words. The Teacher's Edition has words and music.

859. **King, Anthony**. "The construction and tuning of the *kora*." **AFRICAN LANGUAGE STUDIES** 13 (1972): 113-136.

860. **King, Anthony**. MUSIC AT THE COURT OF KATSINA (*GANGUNA* AND *KAKAKAI*). Dissertation, University of London, 1969.

861. **King, Anthony**. *Songs of Nigeria*. London: University of London Press, 1973. 47pp.
A song book designed for school-use, apparently the first of its kind to reflect the musical variety of Nigeria. Twenty songs are staff-notated, with sol-fa indications, texts in any one of seven Nigerian languages, English translations, and notes. Includes pronunciation aids for Hausa, Igbo, Yorùbá and Ijọ. Songs range from easy to advanced.

862. **King, Anthony**. *Yorùbá sacred music from Èkìtì*. [Nigeria]: Ìbàdàn University Press, 1961.
Music, illustrations.

863. **King, Roberta Rose**. PATHWAYS IN CHRISTIAN MUSIC COMMUNICATION: THE CASE OF THE SENUFO OF CÔTE D'IVOIRE. Dissertation, Fuller Theological Seminary, School of World Mission, 1989. 451pp.
"This dissertation addresses the problem of contextualization of Christianity in Africa with the use of indigenous music. It focuses on 'how' and 'why' the use of culturally appropriate songs makes a significant difference in effective communication of the Gospel within the African context." **(UMI)**

864. **Kippen, Jim**. "John Blacking (1928-1990): a personal obituary." **ETHNOMUSICOLOGY** 34, no. 2 (1990): 263-270.
A bibliography of Blacking's works follows a beautifully written memorial essay.

865. **KIRBY, PERCIVAL ROBSON**
For a bibliography of publications by this renowned South African musicologist, see **Bryer, Valerie, 295**.

866. **Kirby, Percival Robson**. "The changing face of African music south of the Zembezi." In *Essays on music and history in Africa*. Edited by Klaus P. Wachsmann, 243-254. Evanston: Northwestern University Press, 1971.
There is no doubt that Kirby was a dedicated and knowledgeable researcher who studied indigenous South African music with a seriousness no one before him had shown. As a man well acquainted with various peoples of South Africa, who even

lived among them when studying their music and playing it, he could precisely describe their instruments and music practices. In this he is unsurpassed. But it is his conclusions and the faulty attitudes and assumptions they display that exemplify the eurocentric, condescending, unenlightened thinking of a bygone era. Terminology, too, is no longer acceptable. Careful interpretation is required. Footnotes.

867. Kirby, Percival Robson. *The musical instruments of the native races of South Africa.* 2d ed. Johannesburg, Witwatersrand University Press, 1965. 293pp.

Though decades have passed, this remains an awe-inspiring masterpiece. Originally published in 1934, the second edition has only minor changes. Kirby went on nine special expeditions in South Africa, setting an example for future musicologists by frequently living with, and participating in, music of the people he studied. Abundant photographs of musicians, comprising some 13 separate peoples, are remarkable. Chapters, organized by instrument, demonstrate vast knowledge. One must be on guard for *a priori* convictions regarding evolutionary "stages" of civilizations, and a dated, patronizing (if sometimes admiring) stance that sees the African essentially as an imitator. Notes, no bibliography.

868. Kirby, Percival Robson. "The musics of the Black races of South Africa." In *South African music encyclopedia.* Vol. 2. Edited by Jacques P. Malan, 267-294. Cape Town: Oxford University Press, 1979-1986.

869. Kirby, Percival Robson. *Wits end: an unconventional autobiography.* Cape Town: H. Timmins, 1967. 371pp.

...and also a disappointing and *uninteresting* autobiography...Stuffy, and contains almost nothing about Kirby's remarkable experiences among the indigenous South African peoples whose music he studied (and even played!) - the main reason, in fact, why he is known to Africanists, and why he is in this bibliography. One learns of Kirby's many honors and achievements in Western art music (documented by stilted photographs), but one would never guess he even knew the *word*, Zulu.

Kirby, Percival Robson
See also: **Africana Museum (Johannesburg, South Africa), 48.**

870. Kissi stories and songs. Collected by Charles Manga, *et al.* Freetown: People's Educational Association of Sierra Leone, 1987. 95pp. (Stories and songs from Sierra Leone, 31)

871. Kivnick, Helen. "Singing in South Africa: a conversation with Victoria Mxenge." SING OUT: THE FOLK SONG MAGAZINE 31, no. 2 (1985): 12-19.

Victoria Mxenge was a prominent South African civil rights attorney who was murdered shortly after this interview.

872. **Kivnick, Helen**. *Where is the way: song and struggle in South Africa*. New York City, New York: Penguin Books, 1990. 378pp.
"Nobody writes about us and gets it right, as she does," says Joseph Shabalala, leader of Ladysmith Black Mambazo." Chapters headings are: People Who Sing; In Church; In the Country; Migrants; In the City; In Protest. Appendixes have chapter notes, an itemization of contents of two recordings (*Let Their Voices be Heard*, and *Mbube! Zulu Men's Singing Competition*), a section on recordings correlated to chapters, and a concluding section, Background and Related Recordings. A probing analysis of music and politics in South Africa by one who knows and cares. A detailed map shows black homelands and townships. Photographs.

873. **Klotman, Phyllis, and Robert H. Klotman**. "Impression of music education in East Africa." In **Music in world cultures**. Edited by Margaret Mead. **MUSIC EDUCATORS JOURNAL** 59, no. 2 (1972): 105-106.

874. **Knappert, Jan**. "Swahili songs with double entendre." **AFRIKA UND ÜBERSEE** 66, no. 1 (1983): 67-76.

875. **Knight, Roderic.** AN ANALYTICAL STUDY OF MUSIC FOR THE KORA, A WEST AFRICAN HARP LUTE. Master's Thesis, University of California, Los Angeles, 1968. 264pp.

876. **Knight, Roderic**. "Mandinka drumming." **AFRICAN ARTS** vol. 7, no. 4 (1974): 24-35.

877. **Knight, Roderic.** MANDINKA JALIYA: PROFESSIONAL MUSIC OF THE GAMBIA. 2 vols. Dissertation, University of California, Los Angeles, 1973. 435pp.
Illustrations, music, bibliography.

878. **Knight, Roderic**. "Music in Africa: the Manding contexts." In **Performance practice: ethnomusicological perspectives**. Edited by Gerard Béhague, 53-90. Westport, Connecticut: Greenwood Press, c1984.
Detailed studies of the *jali* and the drummer, their roles in Manding society, and performance practices. Notes and bibliography.

879. **Knight, Roderic**. "Music out of Africa: Mande *jaliya* in Paris." **THE WORLD OF MUSIC** 33, no. 1, 1991.

880. **Knight, Roderic**. "The style of Mandinka music: a study in extracting theory from practice." In **Studies in African music**. Co-editors, J. H. Kwabena Nketia, and Jacqueline Cogdell DjeDje,

3-66. [Los Angeles]: Program in Ethnomusicology, Department of Music, University of California, Los Angeles, 1984.
An informative study of Mandinka music, focusing primarily on *jaliya*, or "the profession of the *jali*." Many examples and figures are given. One of Knight's objectives is to focus more attention on the vocal aspects of this music. Two fold-out melograms are included. Transcriptions, charts, a few brief song texts, notes, bibliography, discography, photographs.

881. **Kochman, Thomas,** comp. *Rappin' and stylin' out: communication in urban black America.* Urbana: University of Illinois Press [1972]. 424pp.
Included because of the following essay:
•**Sithole, Elkin M. T.** "Black folk music," 65-82.

882. **Koetting, James T.** "Analysis and notation of West African drum ensemble music." In **SELECTED REPORTS IN ETHNOMUSICOLOGY** 1, no. 3 (1970): 115-147.
TUBS (Time Unit Box System) was chosen for notational purposes because of inherent inadequacies in the Western system. TUBS was developed by Philip Harland in 1962 for teaching purposes with the UCLA African Study Group, and according to Koetting, represents music on "approximately the same level of precision that a trained observer hears." He agrees, however, that for more difficult music the system has its limitations, and then would suggest the Seeger Mode C and the Stroboconn as more appropriate. (Visually, TUBS looks like from one to several tiers of box-chains, some boxes of which contain dots.)

883. **Koetting, James T.** AN ANALYTICAL STUDY OF ASHANTI KETE DRUMMING. Master's Thesis, University of California, Los Angeles, 1970.

884. **Koetting, James T.** CONTINUITY AND CHANGE IN GHANAIAN KASENA FLUTE AND DRUM ENSEMBLE MUSIC: A COMPARATIVE STUDY OF THE HOMELAND AND NIMA/ACCRA. Dissertation, University of California, 1980. 316pp.
This is a study of the influences of migration and urbanization on Kasena flute and drum ensembles that regularly perform in Nima, a migrant quarter in the city of Accra, Ghana. Illustrations, maps, music, bibliography. **(UMI)**

885. **Koetting, James T.** "Hocket concept and structure in Kasena flute ensemble music." In **Studies in African music.** Co-editors, J. H. Kwabena Nketia, and Jacqueline Cogdell DjeDje, 161-172. [Los Angeles]: Program in Ethnomusicology, Department of Music, University of California, Los Angeles, 1984.
Notated examples, map.

886. **Kofie, Nicodemus Nicholas.** AUSSERMUSIKALISCHE BEDEUTUNGEN AFRIKANISCHER MUSIK: EIN BEITRAG ZUM

VERSTÄNDNIS AFRIKANISCHER MUSIK. Dissertation, University of Hamburg, 1978. 144pp.

887. **Kòfowórọlá, E. O.** *Functions and concept in performing arts culture: a case study of the palace traditions in the Northern states of Nigeria: an interim report to Ahmadu Bello University Central Board of Research, Humanities Complex A.B.U., Zaria, Nigeria.* [Zaria, Nigeria: Centre for Nigerian Cultural Studies, Ahmadu Bello University, 1987]. 28pp.
Kòfowórọlá studies pre-Emirate and Emirate palace systems from the standpoint of the performing arts, which he regards as "total theater." He is concerned with the cultural, religious, social, political and economic aspects of the performing arts. Although music is not featured, it is occasionally mentioned with regard to the place of instruments - particularly the royal band - in certain palace events. There is casual mention of the use of the *dùndún* for praise songs. No index or bibliography.

888. **Kòfowórọlá, Ziky, and Yusef Lateef.** *Hausa performing arts and music.* Lagos, Nigeria: Department of Culture, Federal Ministry of Information and Culture, c1987. 330pp.
This is a Nigeria Magazine publication, an interesting collaboration of two scholars born an ocean apart. The first section, by Ziky Kòfowórọlá and Yusef Lateef, is entitled, Hausa Performing Arts. The second section, by Lateef, is entitled, The Musician, Music, and Musical Instruments of Northwestern Nigeria. There are illustrations and music notations. Bibliographies for each section appear at the end of the book. This work provides comprehensive and scholarly coverage of the music of an important area of Nigeria. An excellent resource.

889. **Konaté, Yacouba.** *Alpha Blondy: reggae et société en Afrique noire.* Abidjan: CEDA; Paris: Karthala, c1987. 295pp.
Alpha Blondy, possibly the most popular star of Côte d'Ivoire at the time of writing, is noted for his strong reggae beat. Biographies of other reggae musicians of Côte d'Ivoire also appear. Bibliography.

890. **Koroma, Salia.** *Salia Koroma: my life story.* Interviewed by Heribert Hinzen. Freetown: People's Educational Association of Sierra Leone, 1985. 27pp. (Stories and songs from Sierra Leone, 5)
A service has been rendered by recording this outstanding musician's songs, stories, life. Born in 1903, Salia Koroma was forced, through fear of his father's curse, to become an accordionist (when he wanted only to learn reading and writing). Despite this, he became a top singer, composer, instrumentalist, and story teller who travelled extensively in Sierra Leone and was often a court musician. As an elder, he underrates his own brilliance, yet is embittered by his country's lack of appreciation for the indigenous singer. At the time of the interview, Koroma wanted his only child to have the European education denied him. Poignant. Many absorbing photographs.

K

891. **Koroma, Salia**. *The spider's web*. Collected by M. B. Lamin and Heribert Hinzen. Freetown: People's Educational Association of Sierra Leone, 1986. 134pp. (Stories and songs from Sierra Leone, 14)
Illustrations.

892. **Kotchy, B. Nguessan**. "Fonction sociale de la musique traditionelle." **PRÉSENCE AFRICAINE** no. 93 (1975): 80-91.
Notes follow the essay.

893. **Koudjo, Bienvenu**. "Parole et musique chez les Fon et les Gun du Benin, pour une nouvelle taxonomie de la parole littéraire." **JOURNAL DES AFRICANISTES** 58, no. 2 (1988): 73-97.

894. **Kratz, Corinne A.** "Persuasive suggestions and reassuring promises: emergent parallelism and dialogic encouragement in song." **JOURNAL OF AMERICAN FOLKLORE** 103, no. 1 (1990): 42-67.
About the Okiek people of Kenya.

895. **Krehbiel, Henry Edward.** *Afro-American folk songs: a study in racial and national music*. New York: Frederick Ungar, 1962. 176pp.
An historically important book, first published in 1913, republished in 1962, reprinted in 1971. In his day, Krehbiel was a distinguished music critic, and this work represents one of the earliest research studies on the subject of African-American song - particularly early slave music. Documentation is detailed, with some insights into the African connection, but with some concomitant misconceptions as well. At the very least, Krehbiel's hypotheses make interesting reading. He attempted to be objective, did gather together a great deal of valuable data, and obviously took the subject seriously. Many transcriptions, quotations from old sources, footnotes, index.

896. **Krige, Eileen Jensen**. "Girl's puberty songs and their relation to fertility, health, morality, and religion among the Zulu." **AFRICA** 38, no. 2 (1968): 173-198.

897. **Kruger, Duane Robert**. AN INVESTIGATION INTO INDIGENOUS SACRED HYMNODY AS APPLIED TO THE ZULU CHURCH OF SOUTH AFRICA. Master's Thesis, Columbia Bible School, 1977. 104pp.

898. **Kruger, Jaco**. "Introduction to the social context of two Venda dances: *Tshikona* and *Tshigombela*. In **Symposium on Ethnomusicology**. (7th: 1988: Venda, South Africa). *Papers presented at the 7th Symposium on Ethnomusicology: Department of Anthropology and Ethnomusicology, University of Venda, 3rd to 5th September 1988*. Edited by

Andrew Tracey, 28-31. Grahamstown, South Africa: Rhodes University, 1989.
Very little written on music here. There is mention that women are usually the drummers in the *Tshikona* dance, and reference to "reedpipes."

899. **Kruger, Jaco.** "The state of Venda chordophones." In **Symposium on Ethnomusicology**. (5th: 1984: University of Cape Town). *Papers presented at the fifth Symposium on Ethnomusicology: Faculty of Music, University of Cape Town, August 30th-September 1st, 1984*, 8-12. Grahamstown: International Library of African Music, 1985.

900. **Kruger, Jaco.** VENDA INSTRUMENTAL MUSIC WITH REFERENCE TO CERTAIN CHORDOPHONES AND IDIOPHONES. Master's Thesis, University of Cape Town, 1986.

901. **KUBIK, GERHARD**
The production rate of this excellent musicologist has been so exceptional for three decades that there regrettably has to be a limit to how many items can be included in this bibliography. Upon consultation with Dr. Kubik, however, it seems that he might be willing to forward a mimeographed copy of his complete publications list upon request from: Institut für Völkerkunde, Universität Wien, Universitätsstrasse 7, A - 1010. Vienna, Austria. (This writer suggests that a self-addressed, stamped envelope be included as a courtesy.)

902. **Kubik, Gerhard.** "African music: the dimensions of cross-cultural understanding." **SOUTH AFRICAN JOURNAL OF MUSICOLOGY** 5, no. 1 (1985): 1-5.
Brief abstract in **RILM**, 1985.

903. **Kubik, Gerhard.** "Afrikanische Elemente im Jazz: Jazzelemente in der populären Musik Afrikas." **JAZZFORSCHUNG/JAZZ RESEARCH** 1, 1969.
With English summary.

904. **Kubik, Gerhard.** "Afrikanische Musik, ideologischer Kolonialismus und Identitätskrise der Zöglingsgeneration 1945-1970." In *Perspectives on African music*. Edited by Wolfgang Bender, 7-24. Bayreuth. Germany: Bayreuth University, c1989.

905. **Kubik, Gerhard.** "Àlọ́ - Yorùbá chantefables: an integrated approach towards West African music and oral literature." In **African musicology: current trends: a festschrift presented to J. H. Kwabena Nketia**. Edited by Jacqueline Cogdell DjeDje, and

William G. Carter, 129-182. [Atlanta, Georgia: Crossroads Press, 1988]- .
Many transcriptions, song texts in Yorùbá, notes, bibliography.

906. Kubik, Gerhard. "Angolan traits in black music of Brazil." In **INTERNATIONAL MUSICOLOGICAL SOCIETY. Congress. Reports,** 64-74, 1977. Berkeley, California.
Source is **RILM**, 1981.

907. Kubik, Gerhard. *Angolan traits in Black music, games and dances of Brazil: a study of African cultural extensions overseas.* Lisbon: Junta de Investigações Científicas do Ultramar, 1979. 55pp. (Estudos de Antropologia Cultural, no. 10)
Bibliography, plates.

908. Kubik, Gerhard. *Boys' circumcision school of the Yao, Malawi, southeast Africa.* Göttingen [Germany]: Institute für den Wissenschaftlichen Film, 1979. 19pp. (Publikationen zu wissenschaftlichen Filmen. Sektion Ethnologie. Serie 9, no. 1: 1978)
This is commentary to accompany a film on aspects of traditional education for boys among the Yao, and a result of research carried out in Malawi in 1967. The first section is called, "Circumcision and construction of a *Jando* school," the second section, "Customs and educational processes in another *Jando* already established." Drums, rattles and song figure in the associated rituals, as well as an unusual instrument made of bamboo, called a "percussion beam," on which the boys strike the same pattern in unison. In English. Bibliography.

909. Kubik, Gerhard. "The emics of African musical rhythm." In **Cross rhythms** 2 (1985): 26-66.
Kubik finds many indications that what actually is learned in Africa by what he calls "music/dance apprentice" is more the abstract structural content of a pattern, defined by a numerical relationship or configuration, than an audible or visible representation of a pattern alone. He believes that this is why motion patterns in African cultures are *convertible*, and may be "recast and transformed from spatial/temporal into aural/temporal phenotypes and the reverse." This is an exciting theory. (Thompson speaks of "rhythmized" African textiles, **1556.**) Many notes and references follow.

910. Kubik, Gerhard. "How my research developed from 1959 to now." In **Symposium on Ethnomusicology**. (3rd: 1982: University of Natal) [4th: 1983: Rhodes University] *Papers presented at the Third and Fourth Symposia on Ethnomusicology,* Music Department, University of Natal, Durban, 16th to 19th September 1982; Music Department, Rhodes University, 7th to 8th October 1983, 48-51. Grahamstown, South Africa: International Library of

African Music, 1984.
Note that this paper is in the 4th Symposium. (The 3rd and 4th Symposia are in one volume.)

911. **Kubik, Gerhard.** *The Kachamba Brothers' Band: a study of neo-traditional music in Malaŵi.* Manchester: Manchester University Press for University of Zambia Institute for African Studies, 1974. 65pp. (Zambian papers, no. 9) (Original published in German in Acta ethnologica et linguistica, no. 27)
Kubik studies the music of the Malaŵian Kachamba brothers from the dual standpoint of vocalist and rattle player *in* the band, touring through East Africa and Europe, and as objective, exceptionally well-informed ethnomusicologist. This reads like a fascinating adventure story. The Brothers make music, interact with the author, with each other, with assorted audiences. Much enlightening information is given regarding Malaŵian music and dance, the resourcefulness of constructing instruments from scratch, performance techniques, tuning systems, popular music and styles in Malaŵi, and even in South Africa of that time. Linguistic information, bibliography, disc. (Kachamba recordings listed in Graham's *Da Capo guide*, **638.**)

912. **Kubik, Gerhard.** *The Kachamba Brothers' Band: Text zur Schallplatte AEL Series Phonographica No. 1.* Vienna: [E. Stiglmayr], 1972. 91pp. (Acta ethnologica et linguistica, no. 27. Series phonographica, 1)
This is the German original of the immediately preceding entry (**911**) which is in English. The book is to accompany a phonodisc with the title: *The Kachamba Brothers' Band (in Poetry and Listening).*

913. **Kubik, Gerhard.** "Das Khoisan-Erbe im Süden von Angola." In *Musikkulturen in Afrika.* Edited by Erich Stockmann, 82-196. Berlin: Verlag Neue Musik, 1987.
A stunning, comprehensive monograph on the Khoisan legacy in the south of Angola, and particularly the music of the !Kung' people. The history and culture of the region is examined, but the main concentration is on various musical bows and how they are used. Kubik gives detailed information on the physics of sound in the form of charts, tables, drawings, notations. He is also concerned with the evolution of the !Kung' tonal system. The *likembe* (plucked idiophone) is discussed. Bibliography, large, fold-out tables in back of book. Photographs of musicians reveal performance techniques. 1719 manuscript reproduction shows "Khoi-Khoi" music practices.

914. **Kubik, Gerhard.** *Malaŵi, southeast Africa: Daniel Kachamba's guitar songs.* Göttingen: Institut für den Wissenschaftlichen Film, c1977. 16pp. (Publikationen zu Wissenschaftlichen Filmen. Sektion Ethnologie. Serie 7, no. 32: 1977)
continued

This is commentary about a film that documents the neo-traditional style of singing and guitar-playing of Daniel Kachamba, from Chileka. Three songs composed by Kachamba are sung in Chickeŵa and Kiswahili. (Kubik has published a number of other works on the Kachamba brothers, and also toured as a performing member of their ensemble.) Text in English. Bibliography and "filmography."

915. **Kubik, Gerhard**. *Malaŵi, southeast Africa: Daniel Kachamba's solo guitar music*. Göttingen [Germany]: Institut für den Wissenschaftlichen Film, 1977. 14pp. (Publikationen zu wissenschaftlichen Filmen. Sektion Ethnologie. Serie 7, No. 33: 1977)
This is also associated with a film, and is described as: "Documentation of neo-traditional techniques of playing the guitar by an excellent African musician. Daniel Kachamba from Chileka demonstrates the manner of playing the rumba and the *Sinjonjo* and a special technique called *Putugizi*." Bibliography and "filmography." Includes bibliographical references.

916. **Kubik, Gerhard**. *Malaŵian music: a framework for analysis*. Gerhard Kubik assisted by Moya Aliya Malamusi, Lidiya Malamusi, and Donald Kachamba. Zomba: University of Malaŵi, 1987. 93pp.
Covers roughly 1967 to 1984. A technical but also highly readable booklet. Five genre studies focus on the mouth-bow, *kwela* flute "jive music," music of two kinds of log xylophones meant to be played by partners, a tradition of didactic songs for girls' initiation ceremonies, and community-oriented oral literature that incorporates song. The reader is directed to sources for recordings and videos mentioned in the book. Kubik distills with skill the work of others, and presents updated information along with his own insights for consideration. There are marvelous photos and a 7 page bibliography.

917. **Kubik, Gerhard**. *Mehrstimmigkeit und Tonsysteme in Zentral- und Ostafrika: Bemerkungen zu den eigenen, im Photogrammarchiv der Österreichischen Akademie der Wissenschaften archivierten Expeditionsaufnahmen*. Vienna: H. Böhlaus Nachf., K1ommissionsverlag der Österreichischen Akademie der Wissenschaften, 1968. 64pp. (Österreichische Akademie der Wissenschaften. Philosophisch-Historische Klasse. Sitzungsberichte, 254. Volume 4. Abh. 83.) (Mitteilung der Phonogrammarchivs-Kommission)
African choral music. Bibliography. Illustrations. Music.

918. **Kubik, Gerhard**. *Música tradicional e aculturada dos !Kung' de Angola: uma introdução ao instrumentário, estrutura e técnicas de execução da música dos !Kung', incidindo em especial nos factores psicológico-sociais da actual mudança na cultura dos povos Khoisan*. Translated by João de Freitas Branco. Lisbon, 1970. 88pp. (Estudos de antropologia cultural,

no. 4). At head of title: Junta de Investigações do Ultramar. Centro de Estudos de Antropologia Cultural.
Music and musical instruments of the !Kung' people of Angola. In Portuguese. Bibliography.

919. **Kubik, Gerhard**. "Musikaufnahme in Malaŵi: Probleme der Durchführung." **AFRIKA HEUTE**, No. 4, 1968.

920. **Kubik, Gerhard**. *Natureza e estrutura de escalas musicais africanas*. Translated by João de Freitas Branco. Lisbon, [Junta de Investagações do Ultramar], 1970. 36pp. Centro de Estudos de Antropologia Cultural. At head of title: Junta de Investigações do Ultramar. Centro de Estudos de Antropologia Cultural.
Translated into Portuguese from the German. Bibliography.

921. **Kubik, Gerhard**. "Neue Musikformen in Schwarzafrika. Psychologische und musikethnologische Grundlagend." **AFRIKA HEUTE** 4, no. 1, 1965.

922. **Kubik, Gerhard**. *Ostafrika*. [With collaboration of Jim de Vere Allen...*et al*. Leipzig: VEB Deutscher Verlag für Musik, c1982. 250pp. (Musikgeschichte in Bildern 1: Musikethnologie, Part 10)
East African music: instruments, pictorial works, history and criticism. Includes bibliographical references.

923. **Kubik, Gerhard**. "Pattern perception and recognition in African music." In **The performing arts: music and dance**. Edited by John Blacking, and Joann W. Kealiinohomoku, 221-249. New York: Mouton, c1979.
Kubik explores pattern psychology as it relates to African music. Considering the field still only to be in its infancy, and the paper merely to be an introduction, he proposes to explore "in what manner auditory complexes in Black Africa can be perceived, recognized, interpreted, and understood by musicians and participants of the most varied ethnic, linguistic, and cultural heritages." Weighing observations stemming from his own research and that of others, he summarizes his findings as being "a further example which shows how the coherence of patterns as a perception-determining force can be stronger than physical facts." Bibliography.

924. **Kubik, Gerhard**. "Patterns of body movement in the music of boy's initiation in South-east Angola." In **The anthropology of the body**. Edited by John Blacking, 253-274. New York: Academic Press, 1988.
Kubik writes again on the *Mukanda*, the most important educational institution for a number of peoples throughout Central Africa. Though dance is the primary concern, there is considerable information on song, instruments, and associated

rituals and dance patterns. In one place, when considering a secret instrument known as *tutanga*, Kubik describes the music in terms of body movement rather than sound. (He says that the *tutanga* has probably not been seen by earlier musicologists unless they stayed in the initiation lodge that is burned down with its contents on the final day of *Mukanda*. Kubik fortunately got out in time.) Meticulous graphs, drawings, charts. Bibliography.

925. **Kubik, Gerhard**. "Probleme der Tonaufnahme afrikanischer Musiker." **AFRIKA HEUTE** No. 15-16, 1966.

926. **Kubik, Gerhard**. "The Southern Africa periphery: banjo traditions in Zambia and Malaŵi." **THE WORLD OF MUSIC** 31, no. 1 (1989): 3-29."
Bibliography, notes, illustrations, photographs.

927. **Kubik, Gerhard**. "Subjective patterns in African music." **Cross rhythms** 3 (1989): 129-154.
A fascinating exploration having to do with the creation by musicians of instrumental patterns that break up into subjective components. A number of separate disciplines are used as resources for the study.

928. **Kubik, Gerhard**. "Der Verarbeitung von Kwela, Jazz und Pop in der modernen Musik von Malawi." **JAZZFORSCHUNG/JAZZ RESEARCH** 3, 4, 1971-72.

929. **Kubik, Gerhard**. *Westafrika.* [With collaboration of Danhin Amagbenyõ...*et al.]* Leipzig: Deutscher Verlag für Musik, c1989. 221pp. (Musikgeschichte in Bildern 1: Musikethnologie, Part 11)
Bibliographical references.

930. **Kubik, Gerhard**. *Zum Verstehen afrikanischer Musik: ausgewählte Aufsätze.* Leipzig: P. Reclam, 1988. 367pp. (Reclams Universal-Bibliothek, vol. 1251)
Written entirely in German. This work is essentially a collection of essays on various aspects of African music, some published earlier by Kubik. It is packed with information. There are notes, a comprehensive bibliography, a number of illustrations, music notations, a map of Africa, and a stunning mid-section with 60 photographs, many in color, of musical instruments, performing musicians, illustrations from old books, reproductions of museum items of antiquity, album covers. Following, in order as they appear in the book, are essay titles:
•Einführung in das Studium von Musik und Tanz in Afrika.
•Einige Grundbegriffe und -konzepte der afrikanischen Musikforschung.
•Ikonologie der afrikanischen Musik.
•Xylophonspiel im Süden von Uganda.
•Harfenmusik der Azande und verwandter Populationen in der Zentralafrikanischen Republik.
•Àló - Yorùbá Märchen mit Liedern.
continued

•Afrikanische Elemente im Jazz - Jazzelemente in der populären Musik Afrikas.
•Afrikanische und europäische Transkulturation im Umfeld expressiver Kultur.

931. **KUNST, JAAP**
A mimeographed bibliography of Kunst's works was issued by the Royal Tropical Institute of Amsterdam, in 1961. (It is not known whether or not this is still available.)

932. **Kunst, Jaap**. *Ethnomusicology*. 3d ed. The Hague: Martinus Nijhoff, 1959. 303pp.
This is without doubt Kunst's *magnum opus* - featuring an enormous bibliography that, with the Supplement, comprises over 5,000 items, including many entries on African music by musicologists whose primary research was on that continent. Of particular interest is the extensive collection of photographs of a number of these scholars, dead and living, whose names have been known for decades, but who might never before have been seen in photographs as living, breathing, and even vulnerable human beings. Despite its early date, the book has a certain timeless quality. Certainly it includes one of the finest bibliographies available on world music. *Supplement* listed below.

933. **Kunst, Jaap**. *Supplement to the third edition* [of *Ethnomusicology*]. The Hague: Martinus Nijhoff, 1960. 45pp.
See **932** above.

Kunst, Jaap
See also: **Sachs, Curt**. *The wellsprings of music*, **1405**.

934. **Kyaagba, H. A.** THE TIV POPULAR SONG: TWO CASE STUDIES (A LITERARY STUDY OF SONG TEXTS. Master's Degree, University of Ìbàdàn, 1982.

L

935. **Laade, Wolfgang.** *Gegenwartsfragen der Musik in Afrika und Asien: eine grundlegende Bibliographie.* Baden-Baden, V. Koerner, 1971. 110pp. (Collection d'études musicologiques = Sammlung musikwissenschaftlicher Abhandlungen, 51)

The bibliography is in German, with occasional annotations in German and English. Some 874 entries, most of which come from periodicals, are organized by region, and go as far back as 1900, though most entries are from 1945 on. Dance is incorporated, as well as a section on church music. The book also furnishes information on institutions and societies involved in the study of African or Asian music. Subject index.

936. **Laade, Wolfgang.** *Neue Musik in Afrika, Asien and Ozeanien: Diskographie und historisch-stilistischer Überblick.* Heidelberg: Wolfgang Laade, 1971. 463pp.

Primarily a discography in which Africa shares equal time with Asia and Oceania. The essay, that runs from page 57 to 102, has as its subjects: church music; choral music; the influence of military music; freedom songs; modern dance and entertainment music; and a section on national ballet and neo-African music. Bibliographic references.

937. **Laade, Wolfgang.** *Die Situation von Musikleben und Musikforschung in den Ländern Afrikas und Asiens und die neuen Aufgaben der Musikethnologie.* Tutzing: H. Schneider, 1968. 227pp.

There is an English summary. Bibliography.

Laade, Wolfgang
See also: **Musik der Götter, Geister und Menschen, 1134.**

Labatut, Roger
See: **Chants de vie et de beauté, 337.**

938. **Lachmann, Robert.** *Posthumous works.* 2 vols. Edited by Edith Gerson-Kiwi. Jerusalem: Magnes Press, Hebrew University, 1974. (Yuval monograph series 2, 7)

In the first volume, pages 11-28, the following old essay appears, "Die Musik im Volksleben Nordafrikas." In the center of this same volume there are a number of original photographs taken by Lachmann, some static and formally posed, others showing people dancing and playing musical instruments.

939. **Ládipọ̀ *[Ládiípọ̀], Dúró.** *Ẹ̀dá: opera.* Transcribed and translated by Val Ọláyẹmí [Ìbàdàn] Institute of African Studies [c1970]. 128pp. (Institute of African Studies, University of Ìbàdàn. Occasional publication, no. 24)

This is the opera libretto, with words by the composer. Drums and singing entrances only are indicated. (Yorùbá consultant, Rótìmí Ògúnṣuyì, advises that **Ládiípọ̀** is the correct spelling of the artist's name.)

940. **Ládipọ̀ [Ládiípọ̀], Dúró.** *Morèmi: a Yorùbá opera.* Translated with an introduction and a glossary by Joel Adéyínká Adédèjì. Ìbàdàn, Nigeria: School of Drama, University of Ìbàdàn, 1973. 207pp.
A product of cultural nationalism at the turn of the century. In English and Yorùbá. In a bibliography of Adédèjì's, this work is also listed as a UNESCO Publication, Centre for Oral Documentation, Niamey, Niger (1972).

941. **Ládipọ̀ [Ládiípọ̀], Dúró.** *Ọba kò so = The king did not hang: opera.* Rev. ed. Transcribed and translated by R. G. Armstrong, Robert L. Awujọola, and Val Ọláyẹmí; from a tape recording by R. Curt Wittig. [Ìbàdàn, Nigeria: Institute of African Studies, University of Ìbàdàn, 1972, c1964. 149pp. (Bi-lingual literary works - Institute of African Studies, University of Ìbàdàn, no. 1)
Poetic drama with praise songs, prayers, hymns. In Yorùbá and English.

942. **Ladzekpo, Alfred Kwashie, and Kọbla Ladzekpo.** "Anlo-Ewe music in Anyako, Volta Region, Ghana." In *Musics of many cultures: an introduction.* Edited by Elizabeth May, 216-231. Berkeley: University of California Press, c1980.
Map, bibliography, glossary, footnotes, scale notations, illustrations, excellent line drawings by Leonice Shinneman, chart of dance clubs of Anyako.

943. **Laffont, Elisabeth.** "Les cordophones congolaise: survie des harpes de l'antique Egypte dans les cordophones Zande et Mangbetu." **ARTS D'AFRIQUE NOIRE** 6 (1973): 16-23.
Laffont claims that the Zande and Mangbetu harps bear a close resemblance to the harps of ancient Egypt, and shows many pictorial examples, reinforced by comparative analysis, to back her hypothesis that these harps are survivals from Egyptian days. Many photographs of magnificently sculptured, anthropomorphic harps.

944. **Laguerre, Michel S.** *The complete Haitiana: a bibliographic guide to the scholarly literature, 1900-1980.* 2 vols. Millwood, New York: Kraus International Publications, 1982.
In Volume 1, the major section entitled, Haitian Culture, runs from page 627 to page 806. The most important subdivision, Chapter 29, is called, Music and Dance. This is further broken down into: History of music; musical performers; musical instruments; secular folk dance; Voodoo dances; folk songs; meringue. The reader is also referred to Chapter 24, Creative Arts and Recreation; Chapter 25, Religion: Catholicism, Protestantism, and Voodoo; and Chapter 26, Folklore. Worth examining carefully.

945. **Laing, Ebenezar.** "Regulative beat and phrase duration in Ghanaian songs." In **Papers in African studies**, 57-63. Legon:
continued

University of Ghana, Institute of African Studies, 1968.
The author presents a table showing rhythmic patterns (from Nketia's book, *Music in Ghana*) and treats them algebraically. The results of his study are summarized.

Lamin, M. B.
See: **Koroma, Salia**. *The spider's web*, **891**.

946. **Lamm, Judith A.** MUSICAL INSTRUMENTS OF SIERRA LEONE. Master's Thesis, University of Wisconsin, 1968.

947. **Lamp, Frederick John.** TEMNE ROUNDS: THE ARTS AS SPATIAL AND TEMPORAL INDICATORS IN A WEST AFRICAN SOCIETY. 2 vols. Dissertation, Yale University, 1982. 523pp.
A system of dual categories is seen as the main determinant in the way in which the Temne of Sierra Leone conceive of space and time. Lamp finds this system operating in "its most dramatic and crystallized form" in the ritual arts - music and dance being but two of those studied. **(UMI)**

948. **Landeck, Beatrice**, ed. *Echoes of Africa in folk songs of the Americas*. 2d rev. ed. Instrumental arrangements by Milton Kaye. English version of foreign lyrics by Margaret Marks. Drawings by Margaret Marks. New York: McKay, 1969. 184pp.
This excellent music education book contains competently written information on African music, and on black music of the New World, the latter organized by country. Almost 100 songs are scored for voice, piano, guitar, drum and other instruments that require little advanced technique. As might be expected, by converting these songs to Western musical notation (with its built-in limitations), something of the rhythmic subtlety of the music is lost. But perhaps this should be overlooked when one considers the broader cultural understanding the book must foster. (Words to African songs, however, might be improved.) Illustrations, discography, bibliography, index.

949. **Lange, Werner J.** *Domination and resistance: narrative songs of the Kafa Highlands*. East Lansing, Michigan: African Studies Center, Michigan State University, c1979. 90pp. (Ethiopian series, no. 8). (Language and linguistics, no. 2)
Ethiopian songs, including national songs.

949a. **Lapassade, Georges.** "Un art marginal (Essai sociologiques sur le dépérissement de l'art musical nègre dans le Maghreb [al-Maghrib]." In **Colloque sur l'art nègre**. Rapports. Vol. 2 (1971): 199-210. [Paris: Présence africaine]

Larby, Patricia M.
See: **New directions in African bibliography, 1160.**

950. **Larlham, Peter**. *Black theater, dance, and ritual in South Africa*. Ann Arbor, Michigan: UMI Research Press, c1985.
The book surveys indigenous black performance in South Africa in order to document performances and to investigate the impact of the socioeconomic and sociopolitical pressures of a predominantly Western way of life on African culture. There is much to be found on music, but not if one only looks under Music in the index. Chapter headings indicate the broad scope: 1. Traditional Zulu Rites and Ceremonies, 2. Zionist Ritual, 3. Festivals of the Nazareth Baptist Church, 4. Contemporary Folk Dance, and 5. Popular Theater. There is an Appendix of selected Zulu and dance/song terms, 47 plates, notes for each chapter, and a bibliography.

LATIN AMERICAN MUSIC REVIEW
See: **REVISTA DE MÚSICA LATINO AMERICANO, 1368.**

951. **Lauer, Joseph J., Gregory V. Larkin, and Alfred Kagan**. *American and Canadian doctoral dissertations and master's theses on Africa, 1974-1987*. Atlanta, Georgia: Crossroads Press, Emory University, c1989. 377pp.
A major resource for doctoral dissertations. Continues the book by Michael Sims and Alfred Kagan, *American and Canadian doctoral dissertations and master's theses on Africa, 1886-1974*, **1460**. Includes an index.

952. **Launching and reporting**. Edited by Heribert Hinzen, and Sheikh Ahmed Tejan Tamu. Freetown: People's Educational Association of Sierra Leone, 1986. 48pp. (Stories and songs from Sierra Leone, 10)
The event this booklet records is the Launching Ceremony for the Stories and Songs from Sierra Leone series (SAS), held on February 25th, 1986. One hundred people, including officials and dignitaries, attended. Their speeches and comments are recorded, along with excerpts from various reports and minutes written during the earlier formative period of PEA, June, 1984 to April, 1986. Six SAS publications "launched" that morning are listed. This publication, the 10th in the series, really amounts to a history of PEA (a number of whose other publications are listed in this bibliography under Stories and songs from Sierra Leone).

953. **Laurenty, Jean Sébastien**. *Les cordophones du Congo belge et du Ruanda-Urundi*. Tervuren, 1960. 230pp. (Annales du Musée royal du Congo belge. Nouvelle série in-4°. Sciences humaines, vol. 2)
Musical instruments of Zaïre and Ruanda-Urundi. History of stringed instruments. Illustrations, and atlas with 37 plates, 5 colored maps. Bibliography: pages, 227-230. (Urundi is an old colonial name for Burundi.)

954. **Laurenty, Jean Sébastien**. *Répartition géographique des aérophones de l'Afrique centrale*. Tervuren, Belgium: Musée royal de l'Afrique centrale, 1990. 377pp. (Annales. Sciences

humaines, v. 129)
In French. On the geographic distribution of aerophones in central Africa. In essence this is a methodical inventory of pieces in the Museum's collection. It includes maps, and many tables with details about the instruments, their dimensions, where gathered, by whom, size, composition. No photographs, but countless line drawings executed with great care as to the individual features of a given instrument. At the end are listed several conclusions resulting from the study. The variety and abundance of aerophones is impressive. Equally impressive is the care used in preparing this tome.

955. **Laurenty, Jean Sébastien.** *Les sanza du Congo.* 2 vols. [Tervuren], 1962. (Musée royal de l'Afrique centrale, Tervuren. Annales. Nouvelle série in-4°. Sciences humaines, no. 3)
Sanza is one of more than 100 names for a widespread African instrument composed of tuned metal or split-cane tongues fitted to a wooden board or other resonator, such as a gourd. The unattached ends of the lamellae vibrate freely when plucked by the fingers. Distant progeny of this African instrument are found today in several areas of the New World. Bibliography.

956. **Laurenty, Jean Sébastien.** *La systématique des aerophones de l'Afrique centrale.* 2 vols. Tervuren: Musée royal de l'Afrique centrale, 1974. (Musée royal de l'Afrique centrale. Annales. Nouvelle série in-4°. Sciences humaines, no. 7)
In French. On African wind instruments. Bibliography.

957. **Laurenty, Jean Sébastien.** *Les tambours à fente de l'Afrique centrale.* 2 vols in 1. Tervuren, Musée royal de l'Afrique centrale, 1968. (Musée royal de l'Afrique centrale. Annales. Nouvelle série in-4°. Science humaines, no. 6)
In French. Slit drums of Central Africa. Illustrations, maps, music, plates. Bibliography in first volume.

958. **Lawrence-McIntyre, Charshee.** "African and African-American contributions to world music." In **African-American Baseline Essays**. Rev. ed., 1990. Portland, Oregon: Multicultural/Multiethnic Education Office, Portland Public Schools.
The six components of the Baseline Essays are not divisible. The Music unit - the only one examined - comprises 105 pages, has been punched with three holes, and is undoubtedly designed for upper grade teachers. This is a well-researched monograph, including chapters entitled: Classical Africa's Influences on Other Civilizations [focus on ancient Egyptian music]; Migration and Evolution of Music Throughout Continental Africa; Islamic Influences; African Music in the Americas. The last and longest section on the African-American Tradition, has succinct paragraphs of special interest on worksongs, hollers, the ring shout, reggae, and more recent developments. Notes, glossary.

959. **Lee, Hélène.** *Rockers d'Afrique: stars et légendes du rock mandingue.* Paris: A. Michel, c1988. 216pp.
In French. Musically questionable. It is doubtful that all the included performers and composers of contemporary African music quite fall into the "rock musician" category. Fẹlá, for example, is referred to as the "father of all rockers" [translation]. The cover title mentions Alpha Blondy, Mory Kanté, Salif Keita, Touré Kunda, and "les autres," and there is a large map of West Africa showing the zones of Mandingo influence. Twenty-five promotional-type photos of African musicians augment the book. Discography. No index or bibliography.

960. **Lehuard, Raoul.** "Trompes anthropomorphiques du Bas-Congo." **ARTS D'AFRIQUE NOIRE** 4 (1973): 4-15.
The cover features what are called "super-puppets" by Olenka Darkowska-Nidzgorski, in *L'Afrique noire en marionettes*, **53**. Many more impressive photos of these huge wooden trumpets in human likeness are inside. Created by the Babembe [Bembe], they are graduated to resemble a family, carried in single file, and blown into by each person participating in the ritual. The eerie tone produced has a particular symbolic meaning. One resource (not presently verified) indicated that the sound was interpreted as the voice of an ancestor. Darkowska-Nidzgorska could not trace down any of these figures at Mouyondzi around 1988.

961. **Lems-Dworkin, Carol.** *Africa in Scott Joplin's music.* Evanston, Illinois: Carol Lems-Dworkin, 1991. 25pp.
(Expansion of a workshop presented at the African Study Association annual meeting in November, 1990, at Baltimore. Original title was, "African Retentions in the Music of Scott Joplin".) African retentions are demonstrated in Joplin's ragtime compositions, his opera, in his life-long preoccupation with dance, and in his vision of art as a totality. Musical and sociological explanations are offered as to why ragtime music is sometimes regarded - especially by the African-American community - as "white man's music." The "Scotch snap" (renamed the "black snap") receives detailed treatment as but one important indicator of the African connection. Bibliography.

962. **Lems-Dworkin, Carol.** *World Music Center: African and New World black music bibliography.* Evanston: Northwestern University, Program of African Studies, 1976. 14pp. (Reprint series, no. 23)
A brief pamphlet produced in one week. In place of annotations, asterisks indicate books of particular worth. Several fine related works outside the field of music are also included. Useful in its time.

963. **Leonard, Lynn.** THE GROWTH OF ENTERTAINMENTS OF NON-AFRICAN ORIGIN IN LAGOS FROM 1866-1920 (WITH SPECIAL EMPHASIS ON CONCERT, DRAMA AND THE CINEMA). Master's Thesis, University of Ìbàdàn, 1967.
The author attributes much of the European influence to Sierra Leonean emigrants who began to arrive in Lagos as early as 1839. The first public concert was held in 1866. The study is in three parts, each one covering a major

chronological period. Abstracted in **Nigerian universities dissertation abstracts, 1178.**

964. **Lestrade, A.** "La flute traditionelle au Rwanda." **AFRIKA-TERVUREN** 16, no. 1 (1970): 30.

965. **Let your voice be heard!: songs from Ghana and Zimbabwe: call-and-response, multipart, and game songs.** Arranged and annotated for grades K-12 by Abraham Kobena Adzinyah, Dumisani Maraire, and Judith Cook Tucker. Musical transcriptions by Judith Cook Tucker. Danbury, Connecticut: World Music Press, c1986. 116pp. (Songs from singing cultures, vol. 1)
This is an admirable cooperative effort containing abundant and useful teaching materials of all kinds. The 19 game songs, story songs and multipart recreational songs represent the Akan people of Ghana, and the Shona people of Zimbabwe. Words are in the Akan and Shona languages, but there are also texts with English translations. Included are pronunciation keys for both languages, a glossary, many drawings, photographs, maps, transcriptions. Index, and an excellent annotated bibliography. Companion tape available.

966. **Lewin, Olive.** *Forty-five songs of Jamaica.* Collected and transcribed by Olive Lewin. Washington, D.C., General Secretariat of the Organization of American States, 1973. 107pp.
Only the melody lines of songs are transcribed. Often several verses are included, many of them in Creole. A few explanatory sentences accompany each song, with indications of associated movements, games, or dances. Excellent explanatory notes - really a sort of glossary - are at the beginning of the book, and many of the terms listed often have African implications. If a word is in Creole, its English equivalent is given. Song indexes are by title, first line, and category. There are a few unclear photographs and a map.

967. **Lewin, Olive.** "Musical life of Jamaica in the 19th Century," **In Die Musikkulturen Lateinamerikas im 19. Jahrhundert.** Edited by Robert Günther, 277-297. Regensburg: Gustav Bosse, 1982.
This essay, written in English, with a Spanish summary, has a great deal to do with Africa, and covers a period not frequently encountered in musical references. There are also two sketches of instruments, one of a ceremony, and two of performing musicians. (The small print of this book makes for difficult reading.)

968. **Lewis, Ida.** "Songs with soul: Dorothy Masuka talks about her music." **AFRICA REPORT** 15, no. 6, 1970.

969. **Lewis, John Lowell.** SEMIOTIC AND SOCIAL DISCOURSE IN BRAZILIAN CAPOEIRA. Dissertation, University of Washington, 1986.
Capoeira is a ritualized Afro-Brazilian martial art and dance form, sometimes referred to as a "game" or "sport." Cultural patterns traceable to Africa and particularly to slavery are the focus. Fieldwork was centered in Salvador, Bahia. Movement interactions, musical structures, and song texts and oral traditions are

examined from the standpoint of both their independent and cooperative functions that give meaning to performance. **(UMI)**

970. **Leymarie, Isabelle.** THE ROLE AND FUNCTIONS OF THE GRIOTS AMONG THE WOLOF OF SENEGAL. Dissertation, Columbia University, 1978. 284pp.
Genealogy tables, maps, bibliography.

971. **Liberia. Department of Information and Cultural Affairs.** *Musical instruments of Liberia.* Monrovia, 1971. 29pp.
Illustrations.

972. **Liberian educational and cultural materials research project.** Monrovia, 1970. 296pp.
Sponsored by the United States Agency for International Development. Includes music and a 20 page bibliography.

973. LIBERIAN STUDIES JOURNAL. 1968- . Oak Park, Illinois: Liberian Studies Association.
Issued semiannually. Back issues are available. Indexed by **MLA** and **CURRENT CONTENTS AFRICA**. There may not be any more than the following two articles:
- **Moore, Bai T.** "Categories of traditional Liberian songs," vol. 2, no. 2 (1970): 81-82.
- **Stone, Ruth M.** "Meni-Pelee: a musical-dramatic folktale of the Kpelle." vol. 4 (1972): 31-46.

974. **Library of Congress. African Section.** *Africa south of the Sahara: index to periodical literature, 1900-1970.* 4 vols. Compiled in the African Section, General Reference and Bibliography Division, Reference Department, Library of Congress. Boston: G. K. Hall, 1971. 1st-3rd supplement. 1971-1977. 5 vols.

975. **Library of Congress. Music Division.** *African music: a briefly annotated bibliography.* Compiled by Darius L. Thieme. Washington, 1964. 55pp.
Another major bibliography of African music, especially useful because of the annotations. Though this work appeared a year before Gaskin's, the two are supplemental. Sub-Saharan African music is the subject. Separate sections are for "periodical and serial articles, and books." Thieme excludes references to music of people of "non-African extraction," and anything on African influence on music of other cultures and geographical areas, with few exceptions. Entries total 547, start with 1950; Gaskin's bibliography includes "all known works." Thieme wrote this to update bibliographies of Merriam and Varley that were not "sufficiently available" to meet requirements of the times.

L

976. **Limba stories and songs.** Collected by Samura Bockarie and Heribert Hinzen. Freetown: People's Educational Association of Sierra Leone, 1986. 36pp. (Stories and songs from Sierra Leone, 13)
There are songs and stories collected from "children, the young and the old." There are nine stories accompanied by drawings (art work by Maliki Koroma). Following are 17 song texts in English. Almost every page contains a black and white photograph.

976a. **List, George.** "The folk music of the Atlantic Littoral of Colombia, an introduction." In **Music in the Americas.** Edited by George List and Juan Orrego-Salas, 115-122. [Bloomington]: Indiana University Research Center in Anthropology, Folklore and Linguistics, 1967.
List says that his paper is based upon ongoing research in the Atlantic Littoral area of Colombia, but that because of the limited time frame assigned for writing the paper, he could only present a description of certain types of folk music of the region, specific elements of which seemed to be either Spanish, African, or Indian in origin. He speaks of the difficulty in determining the cultural origin of a "mestizo music," and cautions that any conclusions he might make are only tentative in light of the work lying before him. Map of the area.

977. **Littmann, Enno,** ed *Ägyptische Nationallieder und Königslieder der Gegenwart.* [Leipzig, 1938] Nendeln, Lichtenstein, Kraus Reprint Corporation, 1966. 39pp. (Abhandlungen für die Kunde des Morganlandes, Vol. 23, 4)
Includes Egyptian national songs and other categories of song. Transliterated Arabic text with German translation on opposite pages. Without music.

978. **Liverpool, Hollis.** *Calypsonians...to remember.* Juba Publications, Diego Martin, Trinidad, West Indies [19??]. 105pp.
Gleaned from a secondary source, **KESKIDEE**, 1990 (**854**), where it is reviewed by Norman Darwen. Liverpool is an historian, teacher, and calypsonian known as "The Mighty Chalkdust." (He writes an introduction for *Music in the Caribbean.* See **Sealey, John, and Krister Malm, 1432.**) The book contains a number of short essays that focus on the Twenties and Thirties. Song texts are included. Famous calypsonians get separate chapter treatment. (The title may not be exactly as it appears above)

979. **LIVING BLUES: A JOURNAL OF THE BLACK AMERICAN BLUES TRADITION.** 1970- . University of Mississippi: Center for the Study of Southern Culture.
Issued 6 times a year, features interviews with blues musicians, reviews of recordings, announcement of upcoming festivals, and more. Some years ago, there were particularly interesting articles on the Africa-connection (see listings below). The periodical may not be a rich source of pertinent items, but as recently as 1986 an article appeared on the blues in South Africa. Available on microfilm from **UMI**. Back issues are also available. Indexed in **MLA, RILM, MUSIC INDEX.**
•**Evans, David.** "Africa and the blues," no. 10, 1972.
continued

•**Oliver, Paul**. "African influence and the blues," no. 8, 1972.
•**Summers, Lynn S**. "African influence and the blues: an interview with Richard A. Waterman," no. 6, 1971.

980. **The living culture of Nigeria**. Edited by Sàbúrì O. Bíòbákú. Photographs by Peccinotti. Lagos: Nelson, 1976. 55pp.
Covers many aspects of Nigerian culture, with essays and brilliant photographs showing animated, vibrant people in full array. Contains a 4-page essay on Nigerian music by Akin Euba, followed by 11 plates showing musicians playing the following: raft zither, *alghaita*, xylophone, harp, *kora*, drums, and other instruments. Dynamic pictures of totally involved musicians and dancers will long be remembered. The book has an index.

981. **Lo-Bámijoko, Joy Ifeoma Nwosu**. "Music education in Nigeria." NIGERIA MAGAZINE no. 150 (1984): 40-47.

982. **Lo-Bámijoko, Joy Ifeoma Nwosu**. A PRELIMINARY STUDY OF THE CLASSIFICATION, TUNING AND EDUCATIONAL IMPLICATIONS OF THE STANDARDIZATION OF MUSICAL INSTRUMENTS IN AFRICA: THE NIGERIAN CASE. Dissertation, University of Michigan, 1981. 238pp.
This study discusses selected problems of music and music education in Nigeria. It also gives suggestions on how some of these problems can be alleviated. One problem mentioned is the lack of standardization of musical instruments. Illustrations, music, bibliography. **(UMI)**

983. **Locatelli de Pérgamo, Ana María**. "Raices musicales." In **América Latina en su música**. Edited by Isabel Aretz, 35-52. Paris: UNESCO, 1977.
This essay, which is Chapter 3, has a pertinent subsection entitled, "Aporte Africano."

984. **Locke, David**, comp. *A collection of Atsiagbeko songs, 1975-1977*. Institute of African Studies, University of Ghana, 1980. 119pp.
Music of the Ewe people of Ghana. Texts only, bibliography.

985. **Locke, David**. *Drum Damba: talking drum lessons from master drummers*. Crown Point, Indiana: White Cliffs Media Company, c1988. (Performance in world music series, no. 2)
Damba, the annual festival commemorating the birth of the Prophet Mohammed, is celebrated by the *Dagbamba* people of Ghana. This book concerns two types of dance drumming associated with the festival: *Damba* ("hard-driving and joyous") and *Damba Sachandi* (described as "smoother, elegant, refined"). Locke mentions that the substance of this book is based firmly on performance of *Damba* by Dagbamba musicians. Just about everything one would need to know on the subject can be found in this book. Comprehensive table of contents, index, bibliography, pronunciation and orthography guide, illustrative photographs. Cassette of the drumming.

986. Locke, David. *Drum Gahu!: a systematic method for an African percussion piece*. Crown Point, Indiana: White Cliffs Media Company, c1987. 142pp. (Performance in world music series, no. 1)
On Ewe dance music. Illustrations, music, bibliography, index, 3 sound cassettes. Locke says that this book is a "very personal synthesis of *Gahu*," in contrast to his later work, *Drum Damba*, that is based on Dagbamba musician performance. This is a part of an excellent series published by White Cliffs devoted to African traditional dance drumming.

987. Locke, David. THE MUSIC OF ATSIAGBEKO. Dissertation, Wesleyan University, 1979. 670pp.
This study concerns a highly complex dance-music of the Anlo-Ewe. Music, bibliography.

988. Locke, David. "The rhythm of Takai." **PERCUSSIVE NOTES** 23, no. 4 (1985): 51-54.

989. Lomax, Alan. *Cantometrics, a method in musical anthropology*. With Roswell Rudd, co-editor of the tapes, Victor Grauer, co-inventor of cantometrics, Norman Berkowitz, program design, Bess Hawes, song note research, and Carol Kulig, editorial assistant. Berkeley, California: Distributed by University of California Extension Media Center, c1976. 273pp.
Three particularly important statements (of many) are to be remembered: "Cantometrics was designed for the big picture, to help give every branch of the human family a sense of its place, its role, its special musical contribution."..."Cantometrics is concerned with singing, not songs"..."Much will come when formal musical textual and stylistic analyses are combined."...Africa and the New World figure prominently in cantometric studies. Bibliography, discography. Includes 7 cassettes. See also the next entry, **990.**

990. Lomax, Alan. *Folk song style and culture*. With contributions by the cantometrics staff and with the editorial assistance of Edwin E. Erickson. Washington, American Association for the Advancement of Science [1971, c1968]. 363pp. (AAAS publication no. 88)
Contains major information on Cantometrics. Though shock waves continue since the advent of this innovative research method, the idea of analyzing song style the world over into its component parts and applying the computer to the data, remains a brilliant insight. Perhaps Lomax's vision of "a science of social aesthetics which looks at all social processes in terms of stylistic continuity and change" represents a leap of the imagination, but when certain refinements of technique and interpretation are applied to cantometrics - which Lomax himself would encourage - who knows what possibilities might not still lie in the future?

991. Lomax, Alan. *The folk songs of North America, in the English language.* Melodies and guitar chords transcribed by Peggy Seeger, with one hundred piano arrangements by Matyas Seiber and Don Banks. Illustrated by Michael Leonard. Editorial assistant, Shirley Collins. Garden City, New York: Doubleday, 1975. 623pp. (Reissue of the first publication of 1960.)

In the Introduction Lomax says, "Two principal traditions gave rise to our hybrid music - the British and the West African." He contrast these styles, and elucidates those African characteristics that carried over into black song of North America. Chapter 4, The Negro South, has the most concentrated information on African-American music, and includes reels, work songs, ballads, and blues, preceded by a further elaboration of the Africanisms detectable in the music. Bibliography, discography, illustrations, much notated music, and background information on each song. Still an awe-inspiring work.

992. Lomax, Alan. "The homogeneity of African-African-American musical style." In *Afro-American anthropology: contemporary perspectives.* Edited by Norman E. Whitten, Jr., and John F. Szwed, 181-201. Foreword by Sidney W. Mintz. New York: Free Press, [1970].

Lomax studies Afro-American song style and finds it "considered as a whole...a sub-system of a continental Black African style tradition..." He reaches this conclusion after applying cantometrics to data from Africa, Western Europe and the New World, both white and black. Included is a table of the Cantometric Sample for Africa, a Cantometric Profile for African Hunters, a Cantometric Profile for the Sahara, a Table of Six World Style Regions, a figure showing African Cultural Traits Rated on 13 Cantometric Traits, and a Preliminary Sketch Map of African Song Style Areas. Provides detailed information on cantometrics techniques.

992a. Lomax, Alan. "Song structure and social structure." **ETHNOLOGY** 1, no. 4 (1962): 425-451.

An early presentation of cantometrics. Lomax explains the philosophy behind cantometrics theory, and techniques used in its implementation. At the time of writing, a Cantometric Coding Book of more than 50 pages was about to be published. Included are figures showing a sample cantometric coding sheet, a resultant: African and Afro-American Profile, Pygmy-Bushman and Western European Folk Song Profile, and profiles for other peoples and areas of the world. Bibliography, and "record bibliography."

993. Lonoh Malangi Bokelenge. *Essai de commentaire de la musique congolaise moderne.* [Kinshasa, S.E.I./A.N.C., 196-?]. 95pp.

A thorough coverage of modern Zaïrian music, written in French. The book is divided into four parts (with subdivisions in each) that treat the history of the music, its content, "La Grande Révolution et ses conséquences," and a final section on composers of Congolese song, and modern orchestras. Photographs, bibliography.

994. **Lonoh Malangi Bokelenge.** *Homage à Grand Kallé.* Kinshasa: Éditions LOKOLE, 1985. 118pp.

995. **Lonoh Malangi Bokelenge.** *Négritude et musique: regards sur les origines et l'évolution de la musique négro-africaine de conception congolaise.* République démocratique du Congo, 1971.
Published under the author's earlier name: Michel Lonoh. On black music, Zaïre in particular, and black identity. Bibliography.

996. **Lopes Filho, João.** *Cabo Verde, apontamentos etnográficos.* Lisbon: [s.n.], 1976. 54pp.
In Portuguese. Most of the book concerns rural housing in Santiago, Cape Verde, but there is a special section on instruments that are disappearing: the *berimbau* (along with other varieties of plucked or struck bows) and an instrument called a *cimbó*, a kind of one-stringed, bowed lute with a gourd resonator. There are six plates of instruments. Bibliography.

997. **Lopes, Helena Theodoro, José Jorge Siqueira, and Maria Beatriz Nascimento.** *Negro e cultura no Brasil.* Rio de Janeiro, Brazil: Unibrade/UNESCO, 1987. 136pp. (*Pequena enciclopédia da cultura brasileira*)
In Portuguese, and a fascinating book to read in entirety. Many aspects of the history and culture of Brazilian people of African descent are presented. The chapter on music, which is 12 pages long, is a kind of overview rather than an in-depth study. There is information on the Colonial Period, carnival, samba schools (and the musical diversification of the samba), notes on other dances, some mention of musical instruments. The African tie-in, though always implied, is indicated more specifically in the chapter on religion. Brief bibliographies follow each chapter.

998. **Lortat-Jacob, Bernard.** *Musique et fêtes au Haut-Atlas.* Paris; New York: Mouton; Paris: École des hautes études en sciences sociales, c1980. 152pp. (Cahiers de l'homme. Nouv. série, 20)
Information on fasts and feasts, social life and customs, and, happily, the music of the Atlas Mountains of Morocco. Bibliography, discography, plates, illustrations. Published with the concurrence of the Centre national de la recherche scientifique. Sound disc in pocket.

999. **Low, John.** *Shaba diary: a trip to rediscover the "Katanga" guitar styles and songs of the 1950s and '60s.* Wien-Föhrenau: E. Stiglmayr, 1982. 123 pp. (Acta ethnologica et linguistica, no. 54. Series musicologica, 4). (Acta ethnologica et linguistica, no. 54. Series Africana 16)
Bibliography, illustrations.

Lucia, Christine
See: **National Music Educator's Conference, 1151.**

1000. **Luneau, René.** *Chants des femmes au Mali.* Paris: Luneau Ascot, c1981. 175pp.
In French. Songs of women of Mali.

1001. **Lynn, Kwaku.** AMERICAN AFRIKAN MUSIC: A STUDY OF MUSICAL CHANGE. Dissertation, University of California, Los Angeles, 1987. 247pp.
An informed socio-musicological work that resulted from an individualized Ph.D program. The author uses the word "Afrikan" because be believes it to be more accurate historically, and because "American Afrikan music has Afrikan roots." He lists these shared characteristics. An historical overview is given, primarily of American (some Jamaican) black music. Having spent time in the music industry, plus a stint in Africa, the author is worried that American Afrikan music is not evolving naturally but is being controlled by the industry and directed away from its deeper African roots. He cautions that any legitimate future research into black music must incorporate this critical commercial component. Interviews with musicians. Bibliography.

1002. **Lystad, Robert A.** *The African world: a survey of social research.* Edited for the African Studies Association by Robert A Lystad. New York: Praeger, [1965]. 575pp.
A collection of essays on a variety of subjects. Bibliographies and literature cited appear at the end of the book for each chapter. The two essays relevant to African music are:
•**Bascom, William**. "Folklore and literature," 469-490.
•**Merriam, Alan P.** "Music and the dance," 452-468.

M

1003. **MLA INTERNATIONAL BIBLIOGRAPHY OF BOOKS AND ARTICLES ON THE MODERN LANGUAGES AND LITERATURES**. 1922- . New York: Modern Language Association of America.

This is an annual bibliographic index of scholarly and critical works. It lists journal articles, books, and dissertation abstracts. An attempt has been made to indicate those periodicals in this African music bibliography that are regularly indexed in **MLA**.

1004. **Machado Filho, Aires da Mata.** *O Negro e o Garimpo em Minas Gerais.* Belo Horizonte: Itatiaia, 1985. 141pp. (Coleção Reconquista do Brasil. Nova sér., vol. 88)

Transcriptions of 65 songs primarily of black people of Minas Gerias, Brazil. The melodies appear with the accompanying words. Commentary and textual analyses appear on other pages. Included is a "crioulo" vocabulary, since language is also a concern of the author. In Portuguese.

1005. **Madani, Yousif Hassan.** BOAT BUILDING IN THE SUDAN: MATERIAL CULTURE AND ITS CONTRIBUTION TO THE UNDERSTANDING OF SUDANESE CULTURAL MORPHOLOGY. Dissertation. University of Leeds (United Kingdom), 1986. 258pp.

Chapter 6 has three song texts associated with boats. The first, a praise song composed by the wife of a sailor, describes the special qualities that distinguish him from men with other occupations. The second song is sung when a boat hits shallow water. The third, also a work song, is sung when the sails are hoisted. The author notices that certain words he doesn't understand are repeated frequently, but believes that the purpose is to keep the songs and work in rhythm. Madani is interested in the syncretism of diverse cultural influences. Apparently tapes accompanied the dissertation.

1006. **El-Mahdi, Salah** [Al-Mahdī, Ṣalāḥ]. "The problems of traditional music in Tunisia." In **Creating a wider interest in traditional music: proceedings of a conference held in Berlin in cooperation with the International Music Council, 12th to the 17th June, 1967**. [Edited by Alain Daniélou and others], 154-156. Berlin: International Institute for Comparative Music Studies and Documentation, [1967?].

Maina wa Kinyatti
See: **Thunder from the mountains, 1558.**

1007. **Makarius, Laura**. "Observations sur la legende des griots Malinke." **CAHIERS D'ÉTUDES AFRICAINES** 9, no. 4 (1969): 626-640.

1008. **Makeba, Miriam**, comp. *The world of African song*. Edited by Jonas Gwangwa and E. John Miller, Jr. Introduction by Solomon

Mbabi-Katana. Illustrated by Dean Alexander. Chicago: Quadrangle Books, 1971. 119pp.
Consists of unaccompanied song melodies with chord symbols. Words are in the original languages. Prefacing each song are notes concerning its origin, an English translation of the words, and one measure of suggested accompaniment for piano and guitar. The art work is quite spectacular.

1009. **Makeba, Miriam, and James Hall.** *Makeba: my story.* New York, N.Y.: New American Library, c1987. 249pp.
Written in present tense in a direct manner. We get to know this charismatic South African singer - a true survivor - not only as the glamorous performer she has always been, but also as a brave and vulnerable human being. There are nineteen absorbing chapters on the Makeba few know, with a number of black and white photos dating from her childhood to more recent times, pictures taken alone and with a variety of musicians and political figures of international fame.

1010. **Makiwane, Tennyson.** "African work songs." In *An African treasury: articles, essays, stories, poems, by black Africans.* Edited by Langston Hughes, 95-97. New York: Crown Publishers, 1969].
A very brief but pithy article on South African work songs, seen from an economic and sociological viewpoint. There are a few short texts. Makiwane makes the point that the most inspiring work songs are those composed as a direct reaction to "oppression, the color bar, and so on." He fears that these songs may disappear when mechanization causes the displacement of unskilled laborers, and urges that something be done to preserve "this wonderful heritage of the people."

1011. **Makuta-Nyim, and Minga Shanga.** "Les chansons traditionelles Lele et leur signification socioculturelle." In *Symbolique verbale et rituelle chez les Sakata, Lele, Wongo, Kuba, Lulua, Mbole et Vira (Rép. du Zaïre,* edited by Ize-Senze, Kabulampuka Kanyinda, *et. al.* Bandundu, République du Zaïre: Ceeba, 1984.

Malan, Jacques P.
See: **South African music encyclopedia, 1485.**

1012. **Malm, Krister.** *Fyra musikkulturer: tradition och förändring i Tanzania, Tunisien, Sverige och Trinidad.* Stockholm: AWE/Gebers, c1981. 223pp.
An interesting constellation of music cultures, studied with regard to change, and studied with regard to tradition. Tanzania, Tunisia, Sweden, and Trinidad and Tobago are under scrutiny. Written in Swedish. Bibliography and index. A number of interesting though darkish photos augment the essays.

1013. **Malm, Krister.** "Neue Musik und Veränderungen im Musikleben Tansanias nach Erlangung der Unabhängigkeit." In *Musikkulturen* *in Afrika*. Edited by Erich Stockmann, 282-291. Berlin: Verlag Neue Musik, 1987.

On new music and changes in the musical life of Tanzania since Independence: TANU songs (Tanganyika African National Union), national *ngoma*, *kwaya*, *muziki*, *Blasmusik*, jazz, and a more recent form called *taarab* music. No notes or bibliography.

1014. **MAMBO EXPRESS**.

Not seen, but **AFROPOP WORLDWIDE**, in its 1991 issue, indicates that this is a "Latin music newsletter," and that it contains information on "Afropop" music. It is not listed in the current **ULRICH'S**, but the address is given as 2272 Colorado Boulevard, Los Angeles, California 90041.

1015. **MAN**. New Series 1966- . London, England: Royal Anthropological Institute of Great Britain and Ireland.

Appears quarterly, and a likely source for occasional articles on African music. There were also quite a few in the earlier series. Incorporates **ROYAL ANTHROPOLOGICAL INSTITUTE OF GREAT BRITAIN AND IRELAND. JOURNAL**. Covers all areas of anthropology, physiology, sociology, and culture. Includes information on archaeology and linguistics. Indexed in **CURRENT CONTENTS AFRICA**, **BIOLOGICAL ABSTRACTS**, **CURRENT CONTENTS**, and others listed in **ULRICH'S**. Three, randomly selected articles follow. Currently, mention of music is rather rare.

- **Gibson, Gordon D.** "The Himba trumpet," vol. 62, no. 258 (1962): 161-163.
- **Vaughan, James**. "Rock paintings and rock gongs among the Marghi of Nigeria," vol. 62, no. 83 (1962): 49-52.
- **Wachsmann, Klaus**. "Some speculations concerning a drum chime in Buganda," vol. 65, no. 1 (1966): 1-8.

1016. **Manday Faborie, and other Mandingo stories and songs.** Collected by Heribert Hinzen, Abdullai Kallon, and S. A. Tejan Tamu. Freetown: People's Educational Association of Sierra Leone, 1988. 74pp. (Stories and songs from Sierra Leone, 30)

Illustrations.

1017. **Manford, Robert.** THE STATUS OF MUSIC TEACHER EDUCATION IN GHANA WITH RECOMMENDATIONS FOR IMPROVEMENT. Dissertation, Ohio State University, 1983. 160pp.

There is token mention of the importance of incorporating African music into the music curriculum, but sadly, Ghana in 1983 still seemed to be structuring its program basically on a British model - a great disservice to people for whom music is paramount, and who make such wondrous music of their own. Ghanaian musicologists and educators have been largely ignored in their recommendations that indigenous music resources be used, resulting in deplorable problems. Although Manford suggests a "Comprehensive Musicianship Strategy," in which the focus would be on music elements and "world musics," his long bibliography paradoxically lists primarily Western sources.

Manga, Charles
See: **Kissi stories and songs, 870.**

1017a. **Mann, Michael.** *A thesaurus of African languages: a classified and annotated inventory* of the spoken languages of Africa, with an appendix on their written representation by Michael Mann and David Dalby, with Philip Baker...*et al.* London; New York: Hans Zell, published for the International African Institute, 1987. 325pp.
The most complete inventory of African languages yet compiled, and a primary source for researching any languages mentioned in this bibliography. It traces its origins to a language map, published in initial form in 1977 by the International African Institute. Divided into: 1. Introduction, 2. Inventory of African Languages, 3. The Languages of African States, 4. Writing African Languages, 5. Documentation, and 6. Language Index. Somewhat off-putting for the non-specialist because of all the complex symbols and the complete absence of capital letters, but a masterpiece nonetheless. For the neophyte, the Language Index may be the best place to start.

1018. **Manniche, Lise.** *Ancient Egyptian musical instruments.* Münich; Berlin: Deutscher Kunstverlag, 1975. 111pp. (Münchner ägyptologische Studien; Heft 34) (Münchener Universitäts-Schriften: Philosophische Fakultät)
Includes bibliographical references and indexes.

1018a. **Manzanares, Rafael.** "Instrumentos musicales tradicionales de Honduras." In **Music in the Americas**. Edited by George List and Juan Orrego-Salas, 123-128. [Bloomington]: Indiana University Research Center in Anthropology, Folklore and Linguistics, 1967.
Photographs, illustrations.

Mapanje, Jack
See: **Oral poetry from Africa, 1294.**

1019. **Mapoma, Mwesa Isaiah.** THE DETERMINANTS OF STYLE IN THE MUSIC OF INGOMBA. Dissertation, University of California, Los Angeles, 1980. 433pp.
This has to do with the Bemba people of Zambia, also the subject of Mapoma's Master's Thesis, **1020.** He speaks of a "traditional musical copyright (shared) among the royal musicians, *ingomba*," living in Northern and Luapula Province. These are the only professional musicians among the Bemba. The copyright is expressed in the translated saying, "You never earn a living through the music of another musician." The study is concerned with Bemba criteria for important determinants of style in *ingoma* music. Maps, music, bibliography.

1020. **Mapoma, Mwesa Isaiah.** INGOMA: THE ROYAL MUSICIANS OF THE BEMBA PEOPLE OF LUAPULA PROVINCE IN ZAMBIA. Master's Thesis, University of California, Los Angeles, 1974.

M

1021. **Mapoma, Mwesa Isaiah**. *Survey of Zambian musical instruments. Case Study: Musical instruments of the Lala people of Serenje District*. Institute for African Studies, University of Zambia, Lusaka, 1982.

1022. **Mapoma. Mwesa Isaiah**. "The use of folk music among some Bemba church congregations in Zambia." **INTERNATIONAL FOLK MUSIC COUNCIL. Yearbook** 1 (1969): 72-88.

1023. **Marcus, Scott Lloyd.** ARAB MUSIC THEORY IN THE MODERN PERIOD [Egypt]. Dissertation: University of California, Los Angeles, 1989. 877pp.

1024. **Marcuse, Sibyl.** *Musical instruments: a comprehensive dictionary*. Corrected edition. New York: Norton, 1975. 608pp.
Approached from a global perspective by the former Curator of the Yale University Collection of Musical Instruments. Precise authoritative information is given on instruments the world over, including countless (if not all) African instruments with their varied names. The book is thoroughly cross-referenced. There are etymologies and foreign language equivalents of English terms. Written with clarity and an easy, delightful style that is learned but never stuffy. Bibliography of over 200 entries is identical to the 1964 edition, which was grander and contained remarkable photographs. This version, alas, has none, but was cheaper. ("Less is less.") Cheers for Marcuse's masterpiece!

1025. **Marcuse, Sibyl.** *A survey of musical instruments*. New York: Harper and Row, (1975). 863pp.
An intelligent and well-organized book showing great dedication. African instruments get their well- deserved attention, but not so many kinds or alternative names for them as in her dictionary. There is information about the diffusion and origin of instruments, separate subject and name indexes, and a glossary. Part One is classified by instrument types. Some not particularly inspired drawings and photographs appear. Few, if any, are of African instruments. Not as thorough as her remarkable dictionary, but not intended to be. "Survey" is the term she appropriately chose. Again, the writing style is delightful, and the "asides" refreshing.

1026. **Mariani, Myriam Evelyse.** A PORTRAYAL OF THE BRAZILIAN SAMBA DANCE WITH THE USE OF LABANALYSIS AS A TOOL FOR MOVEMENT ANALYSIS. Dissertation, University of Wisconsin - Madison, 1986. 528pp.
Laban Movement Analysis and Music Rhythmic Analysis were the methods used to describe patterns associated with the Samba, as expressed in dance movement and music rhythms. Video tapes from Samba School contests of 1983, 1985, and 1986 were data sources. The author compares African and contemporary Brazilian movement characteristics, pointing out their similarities and differences. Though dance is the core concern, Samba music and dance are so welded that examination of one art, of necessity involves the other.

1027. **Marre, Jeremy**. *Beats of the heart: popular music of the world*. New York: Pantheon Books, c1985. 254pp.
Selected chapter headings indicate why this book is included: Rhythm of Resistance (Black Music of South Africa), *Konkombé* (Nigerian Music), Roots Rock Reggae (Jamaican Music), Spirit of Samba (The Black Music of Brazil). Index, discography, illustrations.

1028. **Martin, György**. "Charakteristik und Typen der äthiopischen Tanze." In *Musikkulturen in Afrika*. Edited by Erich Stockmann, 252-281. Berlin: Verlag Neue Musik, 1987.
Even though the main concern is Ethiopian dance, there is enough scattered information about music and musical instruments to warrant inclusion. Excellent black and white photographs capture the vitality of the dances to such a degree that one can almost hear the accompanying singing, clapping, drumming.

Martin, Phyllis M.
See: •**Africa, 20.**
•**Africa**, 2d ed., **21.**

1029. **Martin, Stephen Harvey**. AFRICAN ACCULTURATED MUSIC: A PRELIMINARY STUDY OF THE MAJOR GENRES. Master's Thesis, University of Washington, 1974. 149pp.
Map, music.

1030. **Martin, Stephen Harvey**. MUSIC IN URBAN EAST AFRICA: A STUDY OF THE DEVELOPMENT OF URBAN JAZZ IN DAR ES SALAAM. Dissertation, University of Washington, 1980. 319pp.
Illustrations, maps, music, bibliography.

1031. **Martin, Stephen Harvey**. "Music in urban East Africa: five genres in Dar es Salaam." In **JOURNAL OF AFRICAN STUDIES** 9, no. 3 (1982): 155-163.
Maps, notes, glossary of Swahili terms, and a long transcribed excerpt - an example of Tanzanian urban jazz - by the NUTA Jazz Band.

1032. **Martins, Bayo**. *The message of African drumming*. Brazzaville, R.P. of the Congo; Heidelberg: P. Kivouvou Verlag, Éditions bantoues, 1983. 57pp.
A metaphysical book by a drummer known for his innovative style of "jazz-flavored drumming" of the 50s, and for introducing African rhythmic patterns into modern drumming. Learning music in his native Nigeria, and later studying music in Europe, Martins is well able to contrast modern drumming techniques with traditional African ones, and the fundamental differences in attitude of Westerners and Africans regarding music. The drummer's art is sacred in Africa, and the drummer must be socially, culturally, and politically involved - true of Martins. The drum is mystical and symbolizes Power. Thoughtful, thought-producing. Martin's *Drum Ballad* is included. Bibliography.

M

Mata Machado Filho, Aires da
See: **Machado Filho, Aires da Mata, 1004.**

Matondo ne Mansangaza Kanza
See: **Kanza Matondo ne Mansangaza, 813.**

1033. **Matshikiza, Todd.** *Chocolates for my wife.* Cape Town: David Philip, 1982, c1961. 127pp.
A moving narrative by the composer of South Africa's first jazz opera, *King Kong*, **1034**. The book initially was banned in South Africa. Matshikiza contrasts his experiences in London after his brutal treatment by South African police, even as rehearsals went on for his opera. Dramatic, sardonic, sad, witty, and written from an insider's view, the book is sometimes difficult to follow because of the idiomatic style, but always absorbing, full of poetic images, and emotionally powerful. The opera, about a notorious boxer, was popular in South Africa and London. Matshikiza is well respected in South Africa for his choral works.

1034. **Matshikiza, Todd.** *King Kong: an African jazz opera.* Book by Harry Bloom. Lyrics by Pat Williams. London: Collins, 1962. 96pp.
This is the libretto of the opera, *King Kong*, for which Matshikiza composed the music. "Kong" is an onomatopoetic word for the blow of a fist. The famed South African prizefighter gave himself the title, "King of the Kong," because of his boxing prowess. The name has nothing whatsoever to do with the old Hollywood movie about an outsized gorilla. (See also the preceding entry, **1033.**)

1035. **Maultsby, Portia K.** "Africanisms in African-American music." In **Africanisms in American culture.** Edited by Joseph E. Holloway, 185-210. Bloomington: Indiana University Press, c1990.
A wonderfully informative essay, particularly valuable in that it contains Maultsby's regularly revised, copyrighted chart showing the interrelationships of all major African-American music forms, and their derivations from West African musical roots. The essay is noteworthy in addition because it points out, in an original way, characteristics common to African-American and African musics as regards style of delivery, sound quality, and mechanics of delivery [time, text, and pitch]. Africanisms are also touched on in the section on music in the slave community. The two-paragraph summary is an important synthesis that deserves to be read and assimilated. Profuse notes.

1036. **Maultsby, Portia K.** "Africanisms retained in the spiritual tradition." In **INTERNATIONAL MUSICOLOGICAL SOCIETY. Congress. Report**, 75-82, 1977. Berkeley, California.

1037. **Maultsby, Portia K.** *Afro-American religious music: a study in musical diversity.* Springfield, Ohio: Hymn Society of America, [1981?]. 19pp. (The Papers of the Hymn Society of America, 35)
Portia Maultsby focuses on the unique character of the African-American religious experience and religious practices that derive from Africa. This monograph discusses spirituals, folk, and gospel music. Bibliography.

1037a. Maultsby, Portia K. AFRO-AMERICAN RELIGIOUS MUSIC: 1619-1861. Part I - HISTORICAL DEVELOPMENT. PART II. - COMPUTER ANALYSIS OF ONE HUNDRED SPIRITUALS. Dissertation, University of Wisconsin, 1974. 460pp.
Emphasis is given to the strong influence of West Africa.

1038. Maultsby, Portia K. "From backwoods to city streets: the Afro-American musical journey." In **Expressively Black: the cultural basis of ethnic identity**. Edited by Geneva Gay and Willie L. Baber, 109-136. New York: Praeger, 1987.
A knowledgeable overview. Maultsby affirms that the structural formula and performance style associated with folk spirituals and other black music derive from West African traditions. In both cases, there is a great emphasis on group participation, further reinforced by the common call-response structure of vocal music, not to mention numerous other shared features. Components common to black sacred and secular musical performances are also described. The conclusion is reached that even though outward manifestations of the music might change, underlying principles remain the same for each category. Bibliography.

1039. Maultsby, Portia K. "The use and performance of hymnody, spirituals, and gospels in the black church." **THE WESTERN JOURNAL OF BLACK STUDIES** 7 (1983): 161-171.
On the African aesthetic basis for the creation and performance of African-American religious music. Bibliography.

1040. Maultsby, Portia K. "West African influences and retentions in U.S. black music: a sociolcultural study." In **More than dancing: essays on Afro-American music and musicians.** Edited by Irene V. Jackson, 25-57. Westport, Connecticut: Greenwood Press, c1985.
Bibliography. Abstracted in **RILM**, 1985.

May, Elizabeth
See: **Musics of many cultures, 1133.**

1041. Mazauric, Catherine. "Salif Keita, un héritier singulier." In **Chansons d'Afrique et des Antilles**, 29-37. Paris: Harmattan, c1988.

1042. Mazouzi, Bezza. *Musique Algérienne et la question Räi.* Paris: Éditions Richard-Masse, c1990. (Revue musicale, no. 418-419-420)
Raï is a popular music of the Oran area of western Algeria that shows traditional influence but uses modern electric instruments. It is both danced to and sung, and has a compelling kind of perpetual motion.

M

1043. Mbabi-Katana, Solomon. *African class music course.* Vol. 2. [Kampala, Uganda]: Mbabi-Katana, c1987.

To date, no other volumes have been located for examination, though there are apparently three. The author states that it is designed for teacher use. Fifty songs from Uganda, Kenya, Tanzania and those of related peoples in neighboring states have been gathered and translated into English. Words under the notated music itself are not specified as to language. Tonic sol-fa indications are given. Teaching suggestions accompany each song, and are graded by difficulty into three categories that might include dance, drama, pageantry, or creative projects of the students. Specific school grades are not indicated, however. Brief annotations. Child-like illustrations enhance the songs.

1044. Mbabi-Katana, Solomon. *History of Amakondere: (Royal Trumpet Set) of the Interlacustrine States of East Africa.* [Bukavu, Zaïre]: s.n., [1982?]. 54pp.

Another beautiful example of Mbabi-Katana's thorough scholarship. This was originally a paper presented to the Regional Colloquium on the Cultural and Material Production of the Peoples of the Great Lakes and Neighboring Regions, Bukavu, 1982. It commences with a comprehensive geographical, historical and political orientation to the area, and ultimately zeroes in on the instruments themselves, even going so far as to show the step-by-step creation of the six trumpets that comprise the Royal Set. There are 11 maps, 15 photos, (2 representing rock drawings of long-horned cattle), footnotes, transcriptions, a chart, and bibliography.

1045. Mbabi-Katana, Solomon. AN INTRODUCTION TO EAST AFRICAN MUSIC FOR SCHOOLS. Master's Thesis, Washington State University, 1966. 57pp.

See next entry, **1046**, which represents the published version.

1046. Mbabi-Katana, Solomon. *An introduction to East African music for schools.* [Kampala, Milton Obote Foundation, 1966]. 57pp. (Publications of the Milton Obote Foundation)

The original Master's Thesis is directly above, **1045**.

1047. Mbabi-Katana, Solomon. PROPOSED MUSIC CURRICULUM FOR FIRST EIGHT YEARS OF SCHOOLING IN UGANDA. 3 vols. Dissertation, Northwestern University, 1972. 753pp.

1048. Mbabi-Katana, Solomon. "Similarities of musical phenomenon over a large part of the African continent as evidenced by the *irambo* and *empango* side-blown trumpet styles and drum rhythms." **AFRICAN URBAN STUDIES** vol. 5, no. 4 (1970): 25-41.

1049. Mbabi-Katana, Solomon. "A song for every season: music in African life from the cradle to the grave." **COURIER** 30, no. 5 (1977): 26-32.

1050. **Mbabi-Katana, Solomon**. *Songs of East Africa*. London: Macmillan, 1965. 62pp.
Fifty songs from Kenya, Uganda, and Tanzania are gathered. Melodies appear on the treble staff with tonic sol-fa indications. The table of contents gives brief statements about each song, either its subject or a short quotation. The book is designed "... for use by teachers and students in Africa. It will interest musicians and musicologists as well as ethnographers." Bravo to Mbabi-Katana for consistently working to acquaint peoples of East Africa with their heritage! This book was part of a research project funded by a Rockefeller Foundation Grant to the University of East Africa.

1051. **Mbabi-Katana, Solomon**. *The Uganda likembe: its history, tuning systems, notational and composition techniques*. [Kampala?: s.n.], c1986. [Kampala]: Makerere University Printery. 59pp.
Another name for *mbira*, *sansa*, "hand piano," etc. Bibliography.

1052. **Mbabi-Katana, Solomon**. "The use of measured rhythm to communicate messages among Banyoro and Baganda in Uganda." In **Studies in African music**. Co-editors, J. H. Kwabena Nketia, and Jacqueline Cogdell DjeDje, 339-353. [Los Angeles]: Program in Ethnomusicology, Department of Music, University of California, Los Angeles, 1984.
There is a brief review of sound elements that structurally constitute Runyoro and Luganda surrogate languages. Three types of measured rhythm messages in Runyoro and Buganda, identified as Bantu dialects, are presented and discussed: Royal Drum Beats, Clan Drum Beats of Buganda, and Communal Drum Beats. Many notated examples of these beats are given, using quarter and eighth notes, and three symbols for dynamic variations. Timbre and pitch, as aspects of speech, are also discussed, and there is a table to assist in correct pronunciation of vowel sounds. Notes and two references.

1053. **Mboniman, Gamaliel**. "Les chants traditionnels du Rwanda et la liturgie." In **Symposium musico-ethnologicum**. Edited by Johannes Overath, 184-203. MUSICES APTATIO 1980 (Roma: CIMS, 1980).
Text in English, French, and German. Bibliography. Abstracted in **RILM**, 1980.

1054. **McAllester, David P.** "In memoriam: Hewitt Pantaleoni (1929-1988)." ETHNOMUSICOLOGY 33, no. 2 (1989): 287-291.
The memorial essay is followed by a bibliography of Pantaleoni's written works and his compositions.

1055. **McAllester, David P.** "Music of the Americas." In **Music in world cultures**. Edited by Margaret Mead. MUSIC EDUCATORS JOURNAL 59, no. 2 (1972: 54-58.
continued

A survey with two paragraphs on African musical style persisting in the New World. Three photographs of interest from Haiti, Trinidad, and the United States.

1056. **McCoy, James A.** THE BOMBA AND AQUINALDO OF PUERTO RICO AS THEY HAVE EVOLVED FROM INDIGENOUS AFRICAN AND EUROPEAN CULTURES. Dissertation, Florida State University, 1968. 185pp.

1057. **McDaniel, Lorna Angela.** MEMORY SONGS: COMMUNITY, FLIGHT AND CONFLICT IN THE BIG DRUM CEREMONY OF CARRIACOU, GRENADA. Dissertation, University of Maryland, College Park, 1986. 311pp.
The Carriacou Big Drum had, and continues to have, an impact on people's memories of their national origins and kinship ties. The Nation Songs of the Big Drum are categorized as to national types - the historical West African origins of the people of Carriacou. Names such as Cromanti, Igbo, Manding, Temne, Congo, Chamba, Arada, Moko, and Banda do not only identify cultural traditions, but also indicate song and dance classifications. Cultural information of use to the researcher is stored in the ritual practice, song texts and song/dance classification of the Big Drum. **(UMI)**

1058. **McDougall, Russell John.** A CASEMENT, TRIPLE-ARCH'D CULTURAL KINETICS: THE FUSION OF MUSIC, THE DANCE AND THE WORD IN AFRICAN AND CARIBBEAN CULTURE. Dissertation, Queen's University at Kingston (Canada), 1986.
Music is mentioned in the title, but the abstract only uses the word "music" once: "In the West Indies, the African heritage of 'danced art' is transformed into a new aesthetic of the body absorbed into music." McDougall considers the dominant medium in African arts to be the dance, and says that his thesis examines the human body as a "cultural icon" in the work of two African writers: Chinua Achebe and Wọlé Ṣoyínká. Also examined are works of Caribbean writers, Derek Wolcott and Wilson Harris. The title speaks of the fusion of music, dance and the word, but actually, "the word" seems to get preferential treatment. **(UMI)**

1059. **McLeod, Norma.** "Musical instruments and history in Madagascar." In **Essays for a humanist: an offering to Klaus Wachsmann**, 189-215. Spring Valley, New York: Town Hall Press, 1971.
Footnotes, four maps of instrument distribution, bibliography.

1060. **McLeod, Norma.** SOME TECHNIQUES OF ANALYSIS FOR NON-WESTERN MUSIC. Dissertation, Northwestern University, 1966. 245pp.

Mead, Margaret
See: **Music in world cultures, 1130.**

1061. **Mecheri-Saada, Nadia.** "Audiographie Touarègue." In **Études touarègues: bilan des recherches en sciences sociales:**

institutions, chercheurs, bibliographie. Edited by Salem Chaker, 73-77. Aix-en-Provence: ÉDISUD, c1988.
Factual information on sound recordings and collections of Tuareg music.

1062. **Mecheri-Saada, Nadia.** "Ethnomusicologie." In **Études touarègues: bilan des recherches en sciences sociales: institutions, chercheurs, bibliographie.** Edited by Salem Chaker, 68-72. Aix-en-Provence: ÉDISUD, c1988.
Several pages on Tuareg music. Gives factual information on resources.

1063. **Melville J. Herskovits Library of African Studies.** *The Africana conference paper index.* 2 vols. Compiled and published by the Melville J. Herskovits Library of African Studies, Northwestern University. Boston: G. K. Hall, 1982.
The Index is based upon the collection of conference papers held in the Melville J. Herskovits Library of African Studies at Northwestern University. There are two volumes, the first entitled, Register of Conferences through Author Index; the second, Keyword Index. This is a valuable work encompassing 562 conferences, and 12,000 individual papers, all held by Northwestern University's Africana Library. Most date from the 1960s and 1970s, with a few from the 1980s; but some are significantly older. Organized in a most peculiar way by key words. (?) Music references are found on pages 1142-1143, but there may be others scattered elsewhere.

1064. **Mensah, Atta Annan.** "African civilization and the performing arts." In **The arts and civilizations of Black and African peoples.** Edited by Joseph Ohiomogben Okpaku, Alfred Esimatemi Opubor, and Benjamin Ọlátúnjí Ọlọ́runtìmẹhìn, Volume 1: 64-82. Lagos: Centre for Black and African Arts and Civilization, c1986.
Includes an informative section on the Arab presence in the performing arts, and marks left by Islam on African music. Mensah also discusses African courts that "have always been musical courts," and the contributions of institutions of worship, and secret societies to the performing arts. He includes the text of a royal song from Zambia, in *Nkoya* and English, and a transcribed excerpt from a *kadodi* band of Uganda as it accompanies a group of dancing novices for circumcision rites in Bagisu. Bibliography.

1065. **Mensah, Atta Annan.** "Le contact de l'Africain moderne avec la musique: l'expérience de la Zambie." In **La musique africaine, réunion de Yaoundé (Cameroun)** [sur les traditions musicales de l'Afrique subsaharienne], **23-27 février 1970, organisée par l'UNESCO**, 125-127. Paris: *La revue musicale*, Richard-Masse, 1972.
Listed below in English translation as, "The modern African's contact with music," **1071**.

1066. Mensah, Atta Annan. THE GUANS IN MUSIC. Master's Thesis, University of Ghana, Institute of African Studies, 1966. 176pp.

1067. Mensah, Atta Annan. "*Gyil*: the Dagara-Lobi xylophone." **JOURNAL OF AFRICAN STUDIES** 9, no. 3 (1982): 139-154.
Notes, tables.

1068. Mensah, Atta Annan. "The *Gyilgo* - a Gonja sansa." In **Papers in African studies,** 35-41. Legon: University of Ghana, Institute of African Studies, 1968.
Illustrations, transcription of a *Gyilgo* Prelude.

1069. Mensah, Atta Annan. "The impact of Western music on the musical traditions of Ghana." **JOURNAL OF THE COMPOSERS' GUILD OF GREAT BRITAIN** 19 (1966): 19-22.

1070. Mensah, Atta Annan. "Jazz - the round trip." **JAZZFORSCHUNG/JAZZ RESEARCH** 3, 4, 1971-72.

1071. Mensah, Atta Annan. "The modern African's contact with music: the Zambian experience." In **African music: meeting in Yaoundé (Cameroon) 23-27 February 1970, organized by UNESCO,** 127-129. Paris: *La revue musicale*, 1972.
This is a translation of "Le contact de l'Africaine moderne avec la musique: l'expérience de la Zambie," listed above, **1065**.

1072. Mensah, Atta Annan. *Music and dance in Zambia.* [Lusaka]: Zambia Information Services, [1971]. 22pp.
In addition to the written section, there are 18 pages of unusually clear and gleaming photographs. Following a brief introduction, the order of progression is: Elements, Instruments, Dances, Rituals of Good Health, Life Cycle, Order, Social Control, History, and Twentieth Century. There is explanatory information in each section, and a number of sections are subdivided. Mensah concludes with, "No music culture remains unchanged forever, but one speculation well worth the risk is that Zambia's rich heritage of music and dance will retain its distinctive quality through a long foreseeable future." (May his prediction prove true!)

1073. Mensah, Atta Annan. "Music south of the Sahara." In **Music of many cultures: an introduction.** Edited by Elizabeth May, 172-194. Berkeley: University of California Press, c1980.
Glossary, bibliography, map, photos of instruments and instrumentalists, notations. The discography is divided into: General: Traditional; and General: Twentieth Century New African Music. There are also sections on the traditional music of different areas. Films.

1074. **Mensah, Atta Annan**. "Musicality and musicianship in North-Western Ghana." **RESEARCH REVIEW** 2, no. 1 (1965): 42-45.

1075. **Mensah, Atta Annan**. "Performing arts in Zambia." **INTERNATIONAL COMMITTEE ON URGENT ANTHROPOLOGICAL AND ETHNOLOGICAL RESEARCH. BULLETIN** 13 (1971): 67-82.
This outstanding Ghanaian musicologist once more writes a thorough and informative essay. The elements of Zambian music, musical instruments, and dance are analyzed. In the following section, on the social significance of music and dance, Mensah classifies and discusses rituals that serve society in assorted ways. He speaks too of the integration of the arts, and includes paragraphs on a girl's puberty dance (*chimwangalala*), and the coming of age ceremony (*chinamwali*). Mensah is optimistic about the future, maintaining that through the ages, outside sources have only enriched Zambian music. He points to the many signs he sees in the music of "resilience and regeneration."

1076. **Mensah, Atta Annan**. *Sing, sing, sing: forty Ghanaian songs you enjoy* [including compositions in Twi, Fante, Ga, Ewe, Dagbani, and Nzema] Accra, Anowuo Educational Publications [1966?]. 31pp.

1077. **Mensah, Atta Annan**. "The source of the *kurubidwe* - a song type in Chokosi." In **Papers in African studies**, 45-52. Legon: University of Ghana, Institute of African Studies, 1968.
Includes a transcription, two maps of Ghana, one showing Chokosi territory, the other showing Chokosi villages visited by the author. There is one short song text, brief notes.

1078. **MERRIAM, ALAN P.**
See the volume entitled, **A Tribute to Alan P. Merriam (1586)**, for a complete bibliography and discography of his works, and his reviews of the works of others. Merriam was the first editor of **ETHNOMUSICOLOGY**, the Journal of the Society for Ethnomusicology, and produced the first major work in the field, *The anthropology of music*, 1964. (**1085**) In his dissertation, he first used the term "ethnomusicological" as an adjectival form of "ethnomusicology," replacing the earlier term, "comparative musicology," which denoted the study of non-Western and "folk musics."

1079. **Merriam, Alan P.** "The African idiom in music." **JOURNAL OF AMERICAN FOLKLORE** 75, no. 296 (1962): 120-130.

1080. **Merriam, Alan P.** "African Music." In *Continuity and change in African cultures*. Edited by William Bascom, and Melville J. Herskovits, 49-86. [Chicago]: University of Chicago Press [1962].
A significant and stellar essay that, to combine Merriam's own descriptive words, gives an "overview of underlying unities." The concern is primarily with subSaharan music. In a relatively small space, he gives an historical survey of the field, and interprets the research of numerous investigators, revealing always his

superior knowledge, and his cautious, analytical skills. The following subjects are examined: function; instruments; rhythm; melody and form; scales; harmony; vocal style, tone quality, and ornamentation; music areas; change; and problems. Important older references are listed in 96 footnotes. Includes a map of African music areas, and a few short transcriptions.

1081. **Merriam, Alan P.** *African music in perspective.* New York: Garland, 1982. 506pp. (Critical studies on Black life and culture, vol. 6)
Bibliography, index.

1082. **Merriam, Alan P.** *African music on LP: an annotated discography.* Evanston, Illinois: Northwestern University Press, 1970. 200pp.
Includes 390 discs. Information on the sleeve of each one has been classified. In addition, almost all recordings have been listened to by Merriam and assistants and briefly described. Main entries are under the name of the recording company or producing organization, arranged alphabetically. There are additionally eighteen indexes (!). A work that shows incredible dedication.

1083. **Merriam, Alan P.** *An African world: the Basongye village of Lupupa Ngye.* Bloomington: Indiana University Press, [1974]. 347pp.
Essentially an ethnographic study of the Songa people in the village of Lupupa Ngbe, Zaïre, but there are a number of musical references to be found under key words in the index. Try Gong, Xylophone, Musical instruments, Songs, etc. Bibliography.

1084. **Merriam, Alan P.** "An annotated bibliography of African and African-derived music since 1936." AFRICA 21, no. 4 (1951): 319-330.
(The cut-off date of 1960 has been waived in order to accommodate this early, important work.) Merriam's bibliography is divided alphabetically into two sections, one for references he saw personally, and one for those obtained from secondary sources. Merriam picked up where Varley's bibliography left off. Gaskin (1965), Thieme (1964), and Aning (1967) picked up where Merriam's bibliography left off, and so it goes...

1085. **Merriam, Alan P.** *The anthropology of music.* Evanston, Illinois: Northwestern University Press, 1971, c1964. 358pp.
An early work, still valuable. Merriam's intensive training in musicology and anthropology are well displayed. Because he presents music as the reflection of an entire culture, there are implications for scholars in related fields. Many references to the musics of African peoples occur (though North America and Oceania, are also included). He draws from a wealth of significant research of his own and of other distinguished figures. Comparison of the status of the "griot" (*jali*) to that of the American jazz musician is fascinating, as are some of

Merriam's other insightful juxtapositionings. Index and lengthy bibliography are models of excellence.

1086. **Merriam, Alan P.** "The bala musician." In *The traditional artist in African societies*. Edited by Warren L. d'Azevedo, 250-281. Bloomington: Indiana University Press, [1973].
Bala is the generic name of the xylophone in Mali and Guinea.

1087. **Merriam, Alan P.** "Melville Jean Herskovits: 1895-1963." **AMERICAN ANTHROPOLOGIST** 66, No. 1 (1964): 91-109.
This memorial essay in honor of Melville J. Herskovits is followed by a complete bibliography of his works, compiled by Anne Moneypenny and Barrie Thorne.

1088. **Merriam, Alan P.** "Music." **AFRICA REPORT** vol. 7, 1963 to vol. 14, 1969.
For the indicated years, a densely-packed, full page by Merriam on African music appeared in almost every issue. Current recordings received the most attention, though not exclusively.

1089. **Merriam, Alan P.** "Music and the dance." In *The African World: a survey of social research*. Edited by Robert A. Lystad for the African Studies Association, 452-468. New York: Praeger, [1965].
When he wrote this, Merriam said that music and dance were thought to be studied (by "people outside the field of ethnomusicology") in a highly technical way that treated these arts as products rather than as aspects of human behavior. He attempts to correct this image by discussing music and dance as symbolic behavior, functional behavior, and as historical phenomena. He raises questions of aesthetic preferences of Africans, and how a researcher's own cultural background might affect objectivity. There is much to contemplate here. Bibliography and cited literature at end of book.

1090. **Merriam, Alan P.** "Music change in a Basongye village." **ANTHROPOS** 72, no. 5/6 (1977): 806-846.
An excellent essay that incorporates a map, four transcriptions, photographs, a bibliography, and a chart of instruments used 1959-1960, and in 1973.

1091. **Merriam, Alan P.** *A prologue to the study of the African arts*. Yellow Springs, Ohio: Antioch Press [1961]. 37pp.
"Arts," of course, includes music.

1092. **Merriam, Alan P.** "Traditional music of black Africa." In *Africa*. Edited by Phyllis M. Martin, and Patrick O'Meara, 243-257. Bloomington: Indiana University Press, c1977.
An authoritative survey of subSaharan African music, including sections on music areas, the role of music in African societies, instruments, and structure and style. Merriam consistently and carefully examines, modifies, or invalidates earlier assumptions. He goes on to substantiate with appropriate data the theories more generally agreed upon at the time of writing, acknowledging always the vast areas

in which information was [is still] scanty and basic research must be done. Notes and a brief bibliography follow.

1093. **Michels-Gebler, Ruth**. *Schmied und Musik: über die traditionelle Verknüpfung von Schmiedehandwerk und Musik in Afrika, Asien und Europa.* Bonn: Verlag für systematische Musikwissenschaft, 1984. 201pp. (Orpheus-Schriftenreihe zu Grundfragen der Musik, vol. 37)
The African section, pages 73 to 136, includes Africa north and south of the Sahara. Many black and white photos of different peoples. The author is concerned with ethnomusicology in general, music and mythology, music and society, and blacksmithing. Bibliography. Index.

1094. **Milingo, Emmanuel**. "Presentation on African traditional music in liturgy." In **Symposium musico-ethnologicum**. Edited by Johannes Overath, 156-174. **MUSICES APTATIO** 1980 (Roma: CIMS, 1980).
Text in English, French, and German. Abstracted in **RILM**, 1980.

1095. **Mngoma, Khabi**. "The correlation of folk and art music among African composers." In **Symposium on Ethnomusicology**. (2nd: 1981: Rhodes University) *Papers presented at the Second Symposium on Ethnomusicology, Music Department, Rhodes University, 24th to 26th September, 1981.* Edited by Andrew Tracey, 61-69. Grahamstown: International Library of African Music, Institute of Social and Economic Research, Rhodes University, 1982.

1096. **Mngoma, Khabi**. "Music in African education." In **National Music Educator's Conference**. (1st: 1985: University of Natal) *Proceedings of the first National Music Educator's Conference.* Edited by Christine Lucia, 115-121. Durban [South Africa]: University of Natal, Department of Music, 1986.

1097. **Mngoma, Khabi**. "Music teaching at the University of Zululand." In **Symposium on Ethnomusicology**. [1st: 1980: Rhodes University] *Papers presented at the Symposium on Ethnomusicology, Music Department, Rhodes University, on 10th and 11th October, 1980*, 14-22. Grahamstown: International Library of African Music, Institute of Social and Economic Research, Rhodes University, 1981.

Modern Language Association
See: **MLA, 1003.**

1098. **Mokhali, A. G.** *Basotho music & dancing.* Roma, Lesotho: The Social Centre, St. Michael's Mission, [196-]. 11pp. (Anthropologica studies)

1099. **Moneypenny, Anne, and Barrie Thorne.** "Bibliography of Melville J. Herskovits." **AMERICAN ANTHROPOLOGIST** 66, no. 1 (1964): 91-109.
This complete bibliography of Herskovits' publications follows Alan P. Merriam's memorial essay, "Melville Jean Herskovits: 1895-1963." There are 479 entries, published between 1920 and the year of Herskovits' death, 1963.

1100. **Monts, Lester Parker.** "Conflict, accommodation and transformation: the effect of Islam on music of the Vai secret societies." **CAHIERS D'ÉTUDES AFRICAINES** 24, no. 3 (1984): 321-342.
Music, bibliography, map.

1101. **Monts, Lester Parker.** "Music clusteral relationships in a Liberian-Sierra Leonean region: a preliminary analysis." In **JOURNAL OF AFRICAN STUDIES** 9, no. 3 (1982): 101-115.
Map, photos, notated shorter examples, and longer transcriptions of music.

1102. **Monts, Lester Parker.** MUSIC IN VAI SOCIETY: AN ETHNOMUSICOLOGICAL STUDY OF A LIBERIAN ETHNIC GROUP. Dissertation, University of Minnesota, 1980. 359pp.
The study applies both ethnological and musicological dimensions in studying the role and significance of music in Liberian Vai society. The two dimensions are merged in a "holistic approach." Six major areas of socio-musical interest are examined in the study: (1) the concepts about music; (2) musical instruments as part of the overall material culture; (3) musicians and cultural specialists; (4) the uses and functions of music; (5) the structural characteristics of songs; and (6) music as an indicator of socio-cultural change. Illustrations, bibliography, music. **(UMI)**

1103. **Monts, Lester Parker.** "Vai women's roles in music, masking and ritual performance." In **African musicology: current trends: a festschrift presented to J. H. Kwabena Nketia**. Edited by Jacqueline Cogdell DjeDje, and William G. Carter, 219-235. [Atlanta, Georgia: Crossroads Press, 1988]- .
Music notations, bibliography, notes.

1104. **Moore, Bai T.** "Categories of traditional Liberian songs." **LIBERIAN STUDIES JOURNAL** 2, no. 2 (1970): 81-82.

M

1105. Moore, Carlos. *Fẹlá, Fẹlá: cette putain de vie.* Paris: Karthala, c1982. 305pp.

Discography. See following entry, **1106**, for the English translation.

1106. Moore, Carlos. *Fẹlá, Fẹlá: this bitch of a life.* Translated from French by Shawna Moore. London: Allison & Busby, 1982. 287pp.

(A translation of the preceding entry.) Carlos Moore, Cuban journalist and ethnologist, uses his professional skills to convey the complexities of Fẹlá Aníkúlápó-Kútì, musician, political activist, spiritual leader, thinker, mystic. The early section, "Presentation," gives a scholarly background of Yorùbá history. The biography itself is based upon interviews, mostly with Fẹlá, with his closest friend, his many wives. Fẹlá's dramatic life and sociopolitical convictions are emphasized more than his music, though there is a discography through 1981. Countless vivid photographs. Two poetic, spiritual *Afa Ojo* soliloquies by Carlos' wife, Shawna, appear at the beginning and end of the biography proper.

1107. Moore, Grace. *Cultural context of Lobi funeral xylophone music.* [s.l.: s.n., 1976]. 4pp.

Includes information on the construction of the xylophone, and a synopsis of Kakraba Lobi's professional career as an African musician and dancer. On xylophone tuning and musical texture.

1108. Moore, Joseph G. "Music and dance as expressions of religious worship in Jamaica." In **The performing arts: music and dance.** Edited by John Blacking, and Joann W. Kealiinohomoku, 219-318. New York: Mouton, c1979.

A significant study of music and dance of two religions of Jamaica: Cumina, a blend primarily of African, and New World innovations by people of African-descent (whose ceremonies are commonly known in Jamaica as "African Dances"), and Revival, also a syncretistic group, with characteristics of Western Christian and African beliefs and practices. Both religions incorporate spirit possession and have other similarities. Ceremonies are graphically described, and included are a number of small dynamic silhouettes of the Zombie Dances of Cumina. In the Appendices are transcriptions and texts of songs, and information on Possessing Spirits and their Dances.

1109. More than dancing: essays on Afro-American music and musicians. Edited by Irene V. Jackson. Westport, Connecticut: Greenwood Press, c1985. 281pp. (Contributions in Afro-American and African studies, no. 83)

These essays are also abstracted in **RILM**, 1985. (See also the next entry, **1110**.) The following three essays have been selected for listing here:

- **Maultsby, Portia K.** "West African influences and retentions in U.S. black music: a sociocultural study," 25-57.
- **Starks, George L.** "Salt and pepper in your shoe: Afro-American song tradition on the South Carolina sea islands," 59-80.
- **Wilson, Olly.** "The association of movement and music as a manifestation of a black conceptual approach to music-making," 9-23.

1110. **More than drumming: essays on African and Afro-Latin music and musicians.** Edited by Irene V. Jackson. Westport, Connecticut: Greenwood Press, c1985. 207pp. (Contributions in Afro-American and African studies, no. 80)

This book, together with the one directly preceding, **More than dancing,** comprise 22 articles growing out of a symposium on African and African-American music sponsored by the Center for Ethnic Music at Howard University in 1978. Articles in both books have been abstracted in **RILM**, 1985. The following have been selected for listing in this bibliography:

- **Amoaku, William Komla**. "Toward a definition of traditional African music: a look at the Ewe of Ghana," 31-40.
- **DjeDje, Jacqueline Cogdell**. "Women and music in Sudanic Africa," 67-89.
- **Fiagbedzi, Nissio**. "On signing and symbolism in music: the evidence from among an African people," 41-48.
- **Harrison, Daphne**. "Aesthetics and social aspects of music in African ritual settings," 49-65.
- **Jules-Rosette, Benetta**. "Ecstatic singing: music and social integration in an African church," 119-143.
- **Nicholls, Robert W.** "Music and dance guilds in Igèdè," 91-117.
- **Smith, Ronald R.** "They sing with the voice of drums: Afro-Panamanian musical tradition," 163-198.
- **Welch, David B.** "A Yorùbá/Nagô 'melotype' for religious songs in the African diaspora: continuity of West African praise song in the New World," 145-162.

Moreno Fraginals, Manuel
See: **•Africa en América Latin, 23.**
•Africa in Latin America, 24.

1111. **Moro, América, and Mercedes Ramírez.** *La macumba y otros cultos afro-brasileños en Montevideo.* Montevideo: Ediciones de la Banda Oriental, [1981]. 155pp. (Temas del siglo XX, 2)

Concerning Afro-Brazilian religions of Montevideo, Uruguay. Pages 56-58 describe a Candomblé ceremony, with mention of instruments, order of procedure, but little else pertaining to music.

1112. **Mounzeo-Bikohot**. *Musique, culture et société: la musique congolaise: essai de problématique sociologique.* Paris: Université de droit, d'économie et de sciences sociales de Paris, Paris 2, Institut français de presse et de science de l'information, [1982?]. 124pp.

On various aspects of Congo music (Brazzaville), including the social picture. This was originally a thesis for the Institut française de presse, Paris, 1982. Bibliography of six pages.

1113. **Mphahlele, Ezekiel**. "Africanist humanistic thought and belief: background to an understanding of African music." In **Symposium on Ethnomusicology**. (3rd: 1982: University of Natal) [4th: 1983:

Rhodes University] *Papers presented at the Third and Fourth Symposia on Ethnomusicology*, Music Department, University of Natal, Durban, 16th to 19th September 1982, 15-19; Music Department, Rhodes University, 7th to 8th October 1983.Grahamstown, South Africa: International Library of African Music, 1984.
Note that this paper is in the 3rd Symposium. (The 3rd and 4th Symposia are bound in one volume.)

1114. **Mthethwa, Bongani**. "Syncretism in church music: adaptation of Western hymns for African use." In **Symposium on Ethnomusicology**. (7th: 1988: Venda, South Africa). *Papers presented at the 7th Symposium on Ethnomusicology: Department of Anthropology and Ethnomusicology, University of Venda, 3rd to 5th September 1988*. Edited by Andrew Tracey, 32-34. Grahamstown, South Africa: Rhodes University, 1989.

1115. **Mthethwa, Bongani**. "Western elements in Shembe's religious dances." In **Symposium on Ethnomusicology**. (3rd: 1982: University of Natal) [4th: 1983: Rhodes University] *Papers presented at the Third and Fourth Symposia on Ethnomusicology*, Music Department, University of Natal, Durban, 16th to 19th September 1982, 34-37; Music Department, Rhodes University, 7th to 8th October 1983. Grahamstown, South Africa: International Library of African Music, 1984.
Isaiah Shembe published 219 songs, 5 percent of which were purely Zulu, and the rest, a fusion of African and European elements. In the latter category, the melodies are essentially European, but the rhythms are strongly African. The dances are generated by these two categories of songs. (Note that this paper is in the 3rd Symposium. The 3rd and 4th Symposia are bound in one volume.)

1116. **Mthethwa, Bongani**. "Zulu children's songs." In **Symposium on Ethnomusicology**. [1st: 1980: Rhodes University] *Papers presented at the Symposium on Ethnomusicology, Music Department, Rhodes University, on 10th and 11th October, 1980*, 23-28. Grahamstown: International Library of African Music, Institute of Social and Economic Research, Rhodes University, 1981.

1117. **Mukimbo, Mary**. *An appreciation of Amu women's poetry which was sung in the 1974/75 political campaign form parliamentary elections*. [Nairobi]: Institute of African Studies, University of Nairobi, [1978]. 11pp. (Paper. Institute of African

Studies, University of Nairobi, no. 105)
Political poetry sung by women.

Mukuna, Kazadi wa
See: **Kazadi wa Mukuna, 837-840.**

1118. **Müller, Alfons.** *La musique Zaïroise aux services liturgiques.* 2 vols. Introduction by Tamuzi Talekwene. [Bandundu]: Ceeba Publications, 1980. 545pp. (Publications Ceeba, Série 2, vols. 54-55)
Zaïrian music for liturgical use of three dioceses in the region of Bandundu. Primarily texts with many verses and one staff melodic notations. Introduction in French, music in Kongo. Index of composers. Each volume is a comfortable size for holding while singing.

1119. **Muller, Jean-Claude.** "Interlude pour charivari et tambour silencieux: l'intronisation des tambours chez les Rukuba (Plateau State, Nigeria)." **HOMME** 16, no. 4 (1976): 77-95.
This has to do with the fabrication and installation of drums of the Rukuba people of Nigeria. In French.

1119a. **Mulvaney, Rebekah Michele.** *Rastafari and reggae: a dictionary and sourcebook.* Bibliography by Carlos I. H. Nelson. Illustrations by Barbara Boyle. New York: Greenwood Press, 1990. 253pp.
Dictionary, videography, discography, and bibliography of reggae music.

1120. **Muñoz, María Luisa.** *La música en Puerto Rico: panorama historico-cultural.* Sharon, Connecticut: Troutman Press, 1966.

1120a. **Murdock, George Peter.** *Africa: its peoples and their culture history.* New York: McGraw-Hill, 1959. 456pp.
At the time it was written, this book was widely used and highly respected because of its abundant ethnological and historical information about African peoples. Discretion is required in its use today, however, since it reflects an older, rural Africa - frozen in time - and an older way of thinking about Africa. Terminology is obsolete, and the indicated areas where peoples once lived no longer applicable. There are 55 chapters [!], a 31 page index of "Tribal Names," and many valuable bibliographies at the ends of chapters. Thirteen maps include a large "Tribal Map of Africa" in the back pocket, that opens to the size of a table cloth and refolds (like travel maps) with difficulty.

1120b. **Murdock, George Peter.** *Atlas of world cultures.* Pittsburgh: University of Pittsburgh Press, c1981. 151pp.
This volume represents a selected sample of coded materials on culture that first appeared in **ETHNOLOGY**, from 1967 to 1971 in a running feature called "Ethnographic Atlas." Murdock chose 563 cultures from the 1,264 originally covered, and divided the world into six large geographical regions. He believed

that the book's primary value lay in its potential aid to cross-cultural research. Two ethnographic sources are given for each society. Information on Africa is limited, and emphasizes linguistic connections.

1121. **Murphy, Charles F.** STUDY AND COMPARISON OF THE MARIMBA AND XYLOPHONE IN CONTEMPORARY SYMPHONIC LITERATURE. Master's Thesis, Western Connecticut State University, 1970. 61pp.
Chapter 2 gives a comparative historical background of the marimba and xylophone. It is divided into: Places of Origin, Evolution of Mallet Instruments, Inclusion in Western Culture, and African and Guatemalan Marimba.

1122. **Murphy, Joseph M.** *Santería: an African religion in America.* Boston: Beacon Press, c1988.
The author studied Santería in the Bronx, New York over a period of several years. The early chapters cover the history of Santería and are written in a didactic style. Later, however, he writes subjectively as both a participant and observer of countless Santería ceremonies. The immediacy of his experiences, and his writing skill, make for fascinating reading. There is a useful chart of the *orisha* [Yorùbá = òrìṣa] including their associations with particular saints, their foods, colors, dances, postures, emblems, etc. A number of key words in the index relate to African music. Bibliography, glossary.

1124. **Musée d'ethnographie (Neuchâtel, Switzerland).** *Les sanza: collections d'instruments de musique.* Edited by François Borel. Neuchâtel, Suisse. Musée d'ethnographie, 1986. 181pp. (Collections du Musée d'ethnographie de Neuchâtel, no. 2)
The work is primarily a catalogue of *sanza* photos, two to a page. They are classified, described as to construction, tuning systems, playing techniques. The collections of which they are a part are listed at the back. There are *sanzas* with resonators, without resonators, with different shapes, sizes, materials comprising the tongues, different arrangements of the tongues on the board or resonator. There are anthropomorphic *sanzas.* Approximately one-third of the instruments are Angolan. (Borrel says that the *sanza* was first described in Ethiopia in 1586.) Bibliography. Discography. Index.

1125. **Musée du Louvre. Département des antiquités égyptiennes.** *Catalogue des instruments de musique égyptiens.* Musée du Louvre, Département des antiquités égyptiennes. [rédigé by Christiane Ziegler] Paris: Éditions de la Réunion des musée nationaux, 1979. 133pp.
Bibliography and index. Catalog of the Egyptian music collection of the Louvre.

1126. **Museo preistorico-etnografico Luigi Pigorini.** *Oggetti e ritmi: strumenti musicali dell'Africa: Museo Luigi Pigorini, Roma, Piazzale Marconi-EUR, maggio-ottobre 1980.* Rome: De Luca, c1980. 95pp.
Concerning an exhibition of subSaharan African musical instruments in Rome. Bibliographical references. Illustrations.

1127. **Museu do Estado de Pernambuco**. *Coleção culto afro-brasileiro: um testemunho do xangô pernambucano*. Museu do Estado de Pernambuco. Recife: Governo do Estado de Pernambuco, Secretaria de Turismo, Cultura e Esportes, 1983. 110pp.

Included are black and white photographs, with correlated descriptive information, on a number of drums, gongs, rattles, and other objects relating to beliefs, rituals and practices of Xangô, Pernambuco, Brazil.

MUSEUM OF MANKIND LIBRARY

See: **ANTHROPOLOGICAL INDEX TO CURRENT PERIODICALS IN THE LIBRARY OF THE MUSEUM OF MANKIND LIBRARY, 110.**

1128. **Music and ceremony of central and east Africa**. [Exhibit and catalogue organized by the Satellite Museum Program of the Museum and Laboratories of Ethnic Arts and Technology, UCLA]. [Los Angeles?: The Museum? 197-?]. [24pp].

All the museum objects in this exhibit came from central and eastern Africa, from savanna or rain forest areas. A wide variety of musical instruments are among items pictured, and these are succinctly described as to construction, use, and other significant facts. The following peoples are included, with a page of basic information about each group: Kuba, Tetela, Luba, Lega, Twa, Mangbetu, Yande, Tusi, Chiga, Nande and Soga. A good, simple map lists the groups, and outlines where they live with a corresponding number. Bibliography.

1129. **MUSIC EDUCATORS JOURNAL**. 1914- . Reston, Virginia: Music Educators National Conference.

Appears 9 times a year, and regularly contains articles on African-American music, and sometimes specifically on African music. There is an emphasis on study and teaching methods. The journal is indexed in **RILM, MUSIC INDEX**, and other sources mentioned in **ULRICH's**, and also available on microfilm from **UMI**. Some years ago there was a memorable special issue, with an introduction by Margaret Mead entitled, **Music in world cultures**. See entry **#1130** below.

MUSIC EDUCATORS JOURNAL

See also:
- **Arneson, Arne Jon**. ***The Music educators journal**: cumulative index 1914-1987*, **26**.
- **Music in world cultures** (Special issue of **MEJ** volume 59, no 2.), **1130**.

Music Educators National Conference

See: **Standifer, James A., and Barbara Reader**. *Source book for African and Afro-American materials for music educators*, **1494**.

1129a. **Music in the Americas**. Edited by George List and Juan Orrego-Salas. [Bloomington]: Indiana University Research Center in Anthropology, Folklore and Linguistics, 1967. 257pp. (Inter-

American music monograph series, vol. 1)

Besides the papers read at the First Inter-American Seminar of Composers, this book contains papers from the Second International Conference on Ethnomusicology. Both meetings were held at Indiana University, April 24-28, 1965. The introduction is in English and Spanish, written by George List and Juan Orrego-Salas, and the papers are in English, Spanish, or Portuguese. Those listed below have been selected from the Ethnomusicology Conference for their appropriateness:

•**Ayestarán, Lauro**. "El tamboril Afro-Uruguayo," 23-37.

•**Corrêa de Azevedo, Luiz H.** "*Vissungos* - Negro work songs of the diamond district in Minas Gerais, Brazil," 64-67.

•**Gillis, Frank**. "Hot rhythm in piano ragtime," 91-104.

•**List, George**. "The folk music of the Atlantic Littoral of Colombia, an introduction," 115-122.

•**Manzanares, Rafael**. "Instrumentos musicales tradicionales de Honduras," 123-128.

•**Ramón y Rivera, Luis Felipe**. "El mestizaje de la Música Afro-Venezolana," 176-182.

1130. **Music in world cultures**. Edited by Margaret Mead, *et al*. Special consultant and field editor, Barbara B. Smith. Washington: Music Educators National Conference, 1972. 214pp.

This is a splendid, special issue of the **MUSIC EDUCATORS JOURNAL** (volume 59, no. 2) devoted to world music. There are illustrations, photographs, notations, two disks, a bibliography, discography, filmography, map, and glossary of Music in World Cultures. The following articles are especially important, though other references to African and African-related musics can be found scattered throughout the issue. There is as essay by Mead, "Music is a human need," and one by Charles Seeger, "World Musics in American Schools."

•**Goines, Leonard**. "Music of Africa south of the Sahara," 46-51.

•**Klotman, Phyllis, and Robert H. Klotman**. "Impressions of music education in East Africa," 105-106.

•**McAllester, David P.** "Music of the Americas," 54-58

•**Slobin, Mark**. "Musics of West Asia-North Africa," 44-45.

1131. THE MUSIC INDEX. 1949- . Detroit: Information Service, Inc.

A primary reference tool for ferreting out periodical articles on African music. Appearing monthly, the index is entirely alphabetical, including authors, subjects, and geographical locations. "Book Reviews" is also inserted in proper alphabetical order, after which the index picks up with the next alphabetical word or phrase - an efficient organizational plan. The number of periodicals indexed regularly is impressive. These are listed in a separate section, with new journals added regularly. **AFRICAN MUSIC** is indexed, as is **ETHNOMUSICOLOGY,** not to mention other foreign and domestic journals that might contain articles on African music. The **INDEX** and **RILM ABSTRACTS** are excellent places to begin.

1132. **Music of Africa**. Washington, D.C.: The African-American Institute's African Performing Artist Program, [1978?]. 4pp.

This actually is a program of a few pages featuring small photos and brief biographies of a handful of African musicians, at that time on tour in the United States. They come from Zaïre, Zambia and Mali. One, Bourama Soumaoro, who plays the harp-lute, was taught by famed Mande hunter's *jali*, Seyidu Kamara. The names of their instrumental groups are also given.

Music of Africa (Book)
See also: **Nketia, J. H. Kwabena, 1205.**

1133. **Musics of many cultures: an introduction**. Edited by Elizabeth May. Foreword by Mantle Hood. Berkeley: University of California Press, c1980. 431pp.
Bibliographies, discographies, glossary, index, 3 discs. Of the 20 essays on a variety of musicological subjects, the following have been selected for listing:
•**Blacking, John**. "Trends in the black music of South Africa," 172-194.
•**Kimberlin, Cynthia Tse**. "The music of Ethiopia," 232-252.
•**Ladzekpo, Alfred Kwashie, and Kobla Ladzekpo**. "Anlo Ewe music in Anyako, Volta Region, Ghana," 216-231.
•**Mensah, Atta Annan**. "Music south of the Sahara," 172-194.
•**Olsen, Dale A.** "Folk music of South America - a musical mosaic," 386-425.

1134. **Musik der Götter, Geister und Menschen: die Musik in d. myth., fabulierenden u. histor. Überlieferung d. Völker Afrikas, Nordasiens, Amerikas u. Ozeaniens: eine Quellensammlung**. Edited by Wolfgang Laade. Baden-Baden: Koerner, 1975. 344pp. (Collection d'études musicologiques, vol. 58)
Bibliographical references and indexes. 28 illustrations.

1135. **Musik in Afrika: mit 20 Beiträgen zur Kenntnis traditioneller afrikanischer Musikkulturen**. By A. M. Dauer...*et al*. Compiled by Artur Simon. Berlin: Staatliche Museen Preussischer Kulturbesitz, Museum für Völkerkunde, c1983. 432pp. (Veröffentlichungen des Museums für Völkerkunde Berlin. New Series, 40. Abteilung Musikethnologie, 4)
Bibliography, filmography, discography, index, and two cassettes inside back cover.

1136. **Musikgeschichte in Bildern**. Leipzig, VEB Deutscher Verlag für Musik, 1974- .
An important series, and a source of significant works on African music. The following entries appear as separate entries in this bibliography:
•**Collaer, Paul**. *Nordafrika*, vol. 1, pt. 8, 1983.
•**Farmer, Henry George**. *Islam*, vol. 3, pt. 2, [1966].
•**Gansemans, Jos**. *Zentralafrika*, vol. 1, pt. 9, 1986.
•**Hickmann, Hans**. *Ägypten*, vol. 2, pt. 1, [1961].
•**Kubik, Gerhard**. *Ostafrika*, vol. 1, pt. 10, c1982.
•**Kubik, Gerhard**. *Westafrika*, vol. 1, pt. 11, c1989.

1137. **Musikkulturen Asiens, Afrikas und Ozeaniens im 19. Jahrhundert**. Edited by Robert Günther. Regensburg: G. Bosse, 1973. 360pp. (Studien zur Musikgeschichte des 19. Jahrhunderts, Volume 31)
A collection of articles emanating from a series of symposia at the Kölner Institut für Musikwissenschaft. English, French, or German. Includes bibliographies.

1138. **Musikkulturen in Afrika**. Edited by Erich Stockmann. Berlin: Verlag Neue Musik, 1987. 304pp.
A collection of brilliant essays on African music written in German by ethnomusicologists from a number of countries. The one by Rodriguez is concerned with African musical influence on Cuba. Includes bibliographies, illustrations (some in color), music, tables. The following list is alphabetical by last name:
- **Elscheková, Alica**. "Traditionelle afrikanische Mehrstimmigkeit: Za ihrer Typologie, Stratigraphie und historischen Erforschung," 62-81.
- **Garfias, Robert**. "Die Rolle der Träume und Geisterbesessenheit in der Mbira Dza Vadzimu - Musik der Shona in Zimbabwe," 221-245.
- **Kubik, Gerhard**. "Das Khoisan-Erbe im Süden von Angola," 82-196.
- **Malm, Krister**. "Neue Musik und Veränderungen im Musikleben Tansanias nach Erlangung der Unabhängigkeit," 282-291.
- **Martin, György**. "Charakteristik und Typen der äthiopischen Tänze," 252-281.
- **Nketia, J. H. Kwabena**. "Musik in afrikanischen Kulturen," 9-43.
- **Nketia, J. H. Kwabena**. "Zur Geschichtlichkeit der Musik in Afrika," 44-61.
- **Norborg, Åke**. "Musikinstrumente der Bini in Südwest-Nigeria," 197-220.
- **Rodriguez, Olavo Alén**. "Afrikanische Musikeinflüsse in Kuba," 292-304.
- **Wachsmann, Klaus P**. "Völkerwanderungen und afrikanische Harfen," 246-251.

1139. **Die Musikkulturen Lateinamerikas im 19. Jahrhundert**. Edited by Robert Günther. Regensburg: Gustav Bosse, 1982. 463pp. (Studien zur Musikgeschichte des 19. Jahrhunderts, volume 57)
Despite the title, there is only one essay in German - the first one, written by the editor. Other essays are primarily in Spanish, with some written in English. A cursory examination only yielded one "plum," though the book's general bibliography might, conceivably, lead one to Africa:
Lewin, Olive. "Musical Life of Jamaica in the 19th Century," 277-297.

1140. **La musique africaine, réunion de Yaoundé (Cameroun)** [sur les traditions musicales de l'Afrique subsaharienne], **23-27 février 1970, organisée par l'UNESCO**. Paris: "La Revue musicale," Richard-Masse, 1972. 152pp. (La Revue musicale, no. 288-289)
Includes an Introduction, a Report on the Yaoundé meeting by Charles Duvelle, Recommendations, and a List of Participants. This is also in English and in this bibliography under the title, **African music: meeting in Yaoundé (Cameroon), 39**. Essay titles are entered in both their French and English versions.
- **Almeida, Renato**. "L'influence de la musique africaine au Brésil," 135-140.
- **Collins, Elizabeth**. "Les traditions musicales au Liberia," 141-142.

continued

- **Daniélou, Alain**. "Les langages musicaux de l'Afrique noire," 49-55.
- **Duvelle, Charles**. "La musique orientale en Afrique noire," 95-116.
- **Eno Belinga, Samuel**. "La musique traditionelle de l'Afrique occidentale: genres, styles et influences," 69-74.
- **Euba, Akin**. "Évolution et diffusion de la musique africaine traditionelle," 117-124.
- **Ismail, Mahi**. "Les traditions musicales du Soudan," 87-93.
- **Kakoma, George W.** "Les traditions musicales de l'Afrique orientale," 75-86.
- **Kebede, Ashenafi**. "La musique africaine dans l'hémisphère occidental. La musique noire des Amériques," 129-134.
- **Mensah, Atta Annan**. "Le contact de l'Africain moderne avec la musique: l'expérience de la Zambie," 125-127.
- **Nketia, J. H. Kwabena**. "Les langages musicaux de l'Afrique subsaharienne: étude comparative," 7-42.
- **Nketia, J. H. Kwabena**. "Les sources de documentation historique sur les traditions musicales de l'Afrique," 43-48.
- **Ṣ̀ówándé, Fẹlá**. Le rôle de la musique dans la société africaine traditionelle," 57-68.

1141. **La musique dans la vie, étude realisée sous les auspices l'Ocora et sous la direction de Tolia Nikiprowetzky**. Paris, Office de coopération radiophonique, 1967- . Vol. 1, 241pp, Vol. 2, 297pp.

The work is written in French and consists of two volumes of essays. The first is entitled, *L'Afrique, ses prolongements, ses voisins*. The second volume, which bears the imprint, [Paris] Office de Radio Télévision Française, is entitled, *Rayonnement des cultures africaines. Regards sur les civilisations asiatiques. Quelques problemes du monde actuel*. Each volume contains musical examples, bibliographical references, an introduction by the editor, Tolia Nikiprowetzky, and sparse but quite wonderful photographs. Besides essays on Africa and African-related music, others appear on China, India, Vietnam, the Middle East, and more. Following is a select list:

Volume 1

- **Binon, Gisèle**. "Musique dans le Candomblé," 159-207.
- **Brandily, Monique**. "Un exorcisme musical chez les Kotoko," 30-75.
- **Eno Belinga, Samuel**. "*Oka'angana*: un genre musical et littéraire pratiqué par les femmes Bulu du Sud-Cameroun," 105-132.
- **Essyad, A.** "La musique berbère au Maroc," 241-260.
- **Zamiti, Khalil**. "Sources collectives du rythme musical en Tunisie," 225-240.
- **Zemp, Hugo**. "Comment on devient musicien: quatre exemples de l'Ouest-Africain," 77-103.

Volume 2

- **Rhodes, Willard**. "La musique noire dans le nouveau monde," 25-41.
- **Schaeffner, André**. "La musique noire d'un continent à un autre," 7-23.

1142. **Musique de l'Afrique noire: Metz, Musée d'art et d'histoires, 2 octobre-6 décembre 1982**. Metz: La Musée, [1982]. 23pp.

This French museum exhibition was organized on the occasion of the eleventh

"Recontres internationales de Musique contemporaine." General documentation was by Pierre Sallée. Music and musical instruments of subSaharan Africa were the subjects of the exhibition. Bibliography.

Musiques africaines
See: **Bridgman, Nanie.** *Musiques africaines*, **284.**

1143. **Mutere, Matilda E.** THE MUSIC OF KENYA: A SURVEY BASED ON BIBLIOGRAPHICAL SOURCES. Master's Thesis, University of California, Los Angeles, 1983. 151pp.

Mutloatse, Mothobi
See: **Umhlaba wethu, 1602.**

1144. **Un mvet...**[conte par] **Zwè Nguéma, chant épique fang.** Collected by Herbert Pepper. Reedited by Paul De Wolf and Paule De Wolf. Paris: A. Collin, 1972. 493pp.
The Mvet is a sung epic of the Fang of Gabon, the instrument, *mvet*, being the only accompanying instrument. The epic can comprise genealogies, homeric adventures, tales of combat, stories of the immortals, descriptions of places that have long since disappeared, and be concerned with other topics, as well. The text of this book is in Fan with French translations. Words to twelve songs are included. (Other peoples in this general area of Africa also perform Mvets.) Bibliography.

1145. **Mvet Moneblum = ou, L'Homme Bleu.** Edited by Samuel-Martin Eno Belinga. [Bilingual edition]. [s.l.: s.n.], c1978. 287pp. (Yaoundé: Centre d'édition et de production pour l'enseignement et la recherche)
The text to *Mvet Moneblum* is transcribed in Bulu, as declaimed by Daniel Osomo, a celebrated poet-singer, instrumentalist and dancer of this south Cameroonian epic. The French translation adjoins the Bulu. Eno Belinga defines "mvet," which originated in the countries of the Bulu, Fang and Beti (Cameroon, Gabon and Equatorial Guinea), in three ways: the instrument, *mvet*, the epic, Mvet, and the literary genre, Mvet, an ancient drama that incorporates the epic, and which is augmented by traditional dance and music. The instrument *mvet* is featured in performance. Bibliography, notes. See also related works by **Eno Belinga, Samuel-Martin, 523-531.**

Mvula Enoch S. Timpunza
See: **Timpunza Mvula, Enoch S., 1560.**

1146. **Mwaniki, Henry Stanley Kabeca.** *Categories and substance of Embu traditional folksongs.* [Nairobi]: University of Nairobi, Institute of African Studies, 1973. 21pp. (Discussion paper - University of Nairobi, Institute of African Studies, no. 44)
Music of the Embu of Kenya.

1147. **Myers, William Jackson, Jr.** THE SYNCRETISM OF EUROPEAN AND WEST AFRICAN INFLUENCES IN MUSIC OF THE UNITED STATES. Master's Thesis, Midwestern University, Wichita Falls, Texas, 1962. 113pp.

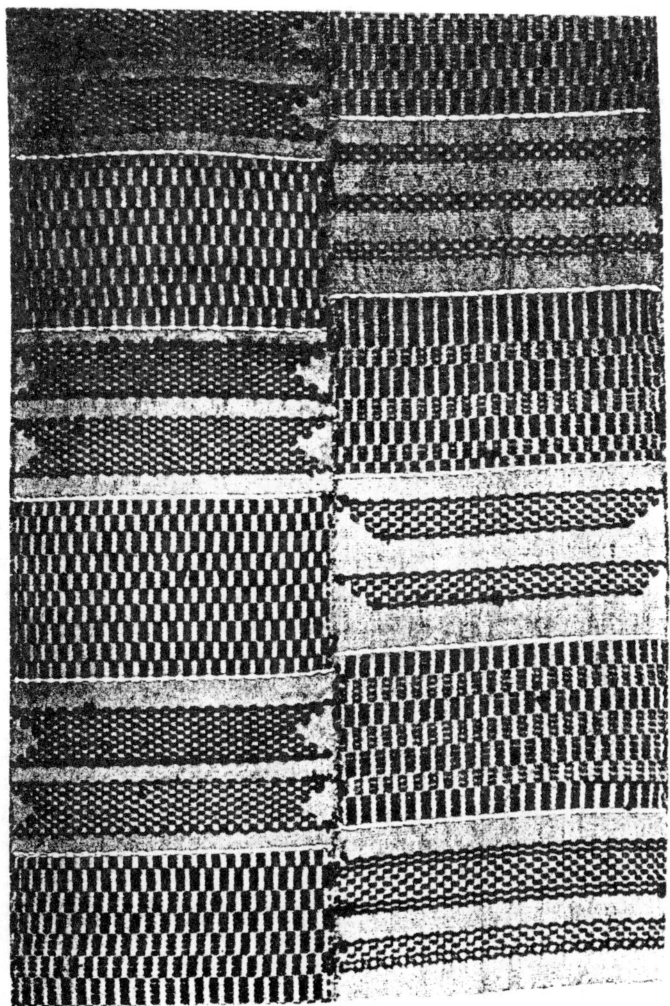

N

1148. **Nacib, Yomiussef.** "Oral tradition and the Algiers festival." In **African culture: Algiers Symposium July 21st - August 1st, 1969.** *The first Pan-African cultural festival*, 357-362. Alger: S.N.E.D. (Société Nationale d'Édition et de Diffusion), 1969.
Youssef Nacib, of the University of Algiers, goes from a consideration of "Ancestor worship" [a term that should be obsolete by now] to folk tales and legends, to African popular oral poetry and the permanent song. Consideration of music occupies several paragraphs appearing on pages 359 and 360.

1149. **Nagashima, Yolivshiko S.** *Rastafarian music in contemporary Jamaica: a study of socioreligious music of the Rastafarian movement in Jamaica.* Tokyo, Japan: Institute for the Study of Languages and Cultures of Asia and Africa, 1984. 227pp. (Performance in culture no. 3)
A scholarly, sociocultural study with an excellent bibliography, covering 15 pages, and a discography. Extremely comprehensive, with many chapters of informed analysis, plus photos, tables, song texts, diagrams. A primary reference tool for this African-influenced religion and music. Of particular value is the comparison of Rastafarian and reggae music in order to classify the differences between them. The author admittedly avoids discussion of the more popular forms of Jamaican music in this work.

Natanson, Rose Brandel
See: **Brandel, Rose, 275.**

1150. **National Library of Jamaica.** *Bob Marley: a bibliography.* Compiled by the National Library of Jamaica based on its collection. Kingston: National Library of Jamaica, 1985. 23pp. (Occasional bibliography series, no. 1)
A bibliography of Marley and other Jamaican singers.

1151. **National Music Educators' Conference** (1st: 1985: University of Natal) *Proceedings of the first National Music Educator's Conference.* Edited by Christine Lucia. Durban [South Africa]: University of Natal, Department of Music, 1986. 218pp. Cover title: "Music education in contemporary South Africa. These papers were presented at the first National Music Educators' Conference, held at the University of Natal, Durban, from September 16-18, 1985."
An important event, since it was the first conference of its kind to be held in South Africa. Aimed at music educators involved in teacher training at the tertiary level, nearly 100 delegates from Ledowa, KwaZulu, Venda, Ciskei, the Transvaal, Natal, Transkei and the Cape attended. Ten papers representing a variety of topics of special concern to South Africans are gathered together in this volume. Main speakers were: William Anderson, Sinclair Hoffman, Melveen Jackson, Christine Lucia, Khabi Mngoma, Elizabeth Oehrle, and Vevek Ram. The *continued*

entire collection is worth examining, but listed below are a few papers selected for particular relevancy:

- **Mngoma, Khabi**. "Music in African education," 115-121.
- **Oehrle, Elizabeth**. "The first South African National Music Educator's Conference in the context of world music education," 7-18. (The introductory address.)
- **Tracey, Andrew**. "Keywords in African music," 29-45.

1152. **Nayo, N. Z.** "Akpalu and his songs." In **Papers in African studies**, 24-34. Legon: University of Ghana, Institute of African Studies, 1968.
Nayo subdivides his essay according to categories of Akpalu's songs: Comments on Personal Experience, Songs of Self-Defence, Historical Songs, On Sorrows Caused by Death, and On Himself as a Composer. Includes song texts.

1153. **Ndlovu, Bernard**. "Indigenization of church music in Zimbabwe." In **Symposium musico-ethnologicum**. Edited by Johannes Overath, 341-349. **MUSICES APTATIO** 1980 (Roma CIMS, 1980).
Charts, tables. Abstracted in **RILM**, 1980.

1154. **Nelson, Karleen Emmrich**. *The African hand piano.* Lake Oswego, Oregon: Emmrich-Nelson Publishing Company, c1987. 20pp.
Instruction and study of the *mbira*. Map, illustrations, music, bibliography.

1155. **Nettl, Bruno**. *Folk and traditional music of the Western continents.* 3d ed. Revised by Valerie Woodring Goertzen. With chapter on Latin America by Gerard Béhague. Englewood Cliffs, New Jersey: Prentice Hall, c1990. 286pp. (Prentice-Hall history of music series)
Chapters of particular interest are, Music of Sub-Saharan Africa, Latin American Folk Music, (by Gerard Béhague), and one by Nettl and Béhague entitled, Afro-American Folk Music in North and Latin America. There are profuse bibliographical and discographical notes at ends of chapters, an index, bibliography, and many illustrations. An enormous amount of valuable information is contained in this book, but it is suggested that in the 4th edition - which surely will occur - obsolete terminology be given a thorough up-dating.

1156. **Nettl, Bruno**. *Reference materials in ethnomusicology: a bibliographic essay.* 2d ed., rev. Detroit: Information Coordinator, Inc., 1967.
This essay is directed to the librarian and student to help them find general information in the field. Nettl stresses that it is not a survey of research studies, but rather a summary of surveys and compendiums, and an attempt to provide substitutes where surveys and compendiums don't exist. Of use to the musicologist studying African music, if only for the listing and description of likely sources. There are a few specific references to African music, but no

elaboration. The book is dated but still has its value. The List of Publications Cited includes certain old classics.

1157. **Nettl, Bruno**. *Theory and method in ethnomusicology*. New York: The Free Press of Glencoe, Macmillan), 1964. 306pp.
Useful information is given in chapters on bibliographic resources, field work, transcription, description of musical compositions, style, instruments, music in culture (historical and geographical approaches), and music in culture (context and communication). An appendix gives "Some Preliminary and Preparatory Exercises and Problems." African references have to do with the music in general, with style, music areas, instruments, polyphony, tone languages. Bibliographies after each chapter, and an index.

1158. **Nettl, Bruno**. "The Western impact on world music: Africa and the American Indians." In *Contemporary music and music cultures*. Edited by Charles Hamm, Bruno Nettl, and Ronald Byrnside, 101-124. Englewood Cliffs, New Jersey: Prentice-Hall, [1975].
Subheadings of special interest are: Traditional Music in Africa, African Music in the New World, Highlife Music in Modern West Africa, and Music in East Africa and South Africa. Two notated African rhythm examples are given. Bibliography.

Nettl, Bruno
See also: **Eight urban musical cultures, 500.**

1159. **New, Leon**. "The traditional *Ebe* school for girls at Adazi, Igboland, Nigeria: the problem of traditional culture in the modern world." In **Symposium on Ethnomusicology**. (7th: 1988: Venda, South Africa). *Papers presented at the 7th Symposium on Ethnomusicology: Department of Anthropology and Ethnomusicology, University of Venda, 3rd to 5th September 1988*. Edited by Andrew Tracey, 35-42. Grahamstown, South Africa: Rhodes University, 1989.
Music-making during *Ebe* is described. The author says that origins of the *Ebe* schools are unclear, but that the schools probably were instituted in the 18th or early 19th centuries as a formalized instruction for the daughters of a few wealthy families, who would be much sought-after as wives. He mentions that they would "retain certain privileges for life."

1160. **New directions in African bibliography**. Edited by Patricia M. Larby. London: Standing Conference on Library Materials on Africa, 1988. 159pp.
See: **Barber, Karin**. "Popular theatre and music," 51-68.

1161. **The new Grove dictionary of music and musicians**. Edited by Stanley Sadie. 20 vols. Washington, D.C.: Grove's Dictionaries of
continued

Music, 1980.
This edition is a major source for information on African music and musicians. The roster of world-renowned contributors to the publication is dazzling: Wachsmann, Mensah, Seeger, Nketia, Merriam, Blacking, Euba, and many more. (Regrettably, few women's names are included.) A special feature is Appendix A: a lengthy "Index of Terms Used in Articles on Non-Western Music, Folk, and Kindred Topics." Every imaginable word is found that might relate to musical forms, genres, repertoires, instruments, ensembles, theory, musicians, musical events, performance practices, song texts, music drama, and dance. Diacritics abound! Photographs, charts, diagrams, bibliographies, etc.

1162. **The new Grove dictionary of musical instruments.** Edited by Stanley Sadie. 3 vols. London: Macmillan Press; New York, N.Y.: Grove's Dictionaries of Music, c1984.

1163. **The new Harvard dictionary of music.** Edited by Don Michael Randel. Cambridge, Massachusetts: Belknap Press of Harvard University Press, 1986.
This a revised edition of **Harvard dictionary of music**, edited by Willi Apel, 2d ed., 1969.

Ngandu Nkashama Pius
See: **Pius Ngandu Nkashama, 1331.**

1164. **Ngirabanyiginya, Dominique.** "Interaction entre les paroles et la musique avec accent particulier sur le langage tonal african et en l'occurrence le Kinyarwanda." In **Symposium musico-ethnologicum**. Edited by Johannes Overath, 237-298. **MUSICES APTATIO** 1980 (Roma CIMS, 1980).
Illustrations, bibliography. Text in French, English, and German. Abstracted in **RILM**, 1980.

1165. **Ngumu, Pie-Claude.** *Maîtrise des chanteurs à la croix d'ébène de Yaoundé.* [Yaoundé?: s.n.], 1971. 88pp.
In French and Oyenga. The Maîtrise, directed by Father Pie-Claude Ngumu, consists of a chorus, an orchestra of nine African instruments (including a *mvet* when available), and incorporates dancing. As part of its program, the *Maî trise* adapts the Christian liturgy to the "African soul." Instruments are pictured, as well as photographs and texts for: the *Passion du Christ*, *Psalms*, the Catholic Mass, and Ngumu's own, *Oratorio de Noël*, and *Mystère de Noël en dix tableaux*. Includes words of commendation by various dignitaries. The *Maî trise* scored a great success at the Festival des Arts Nègres de Dakar in 1966.

1166. **Ngumu, Pie-Claude.** *Les Mendzan: des chanteurs de Yaoundé: histoire, organologie, fabrication, système de transcription.* Vienna: Maria Enzersdorf: Elisabeth Stiglmayr, 1976. 81pp. (Acta ethnologica et linguistica, no. 34; Series

musicologica, 2)
Bibliography, discography, illustrations. Music of Cameroon.

1167. **Ngumu, Pie-Claude**. "Les recherches ethnomusicologiques en Afrique Centrale: le cas du Cameroun." **RECHERCHE, PÉDAGOGIE ET CULTURE** no. 65-66 (1984): 64-69.

1168. **Niane, Djibril Tamsir**. *Sundiata: an epic of old Mali*. Translated by G. D. Pickett. London: Longman; Atlantic Highlands, New Jersey: distributed by Humanities Press, 1979. 96pp.
The work gives *Jali* Mamadou Kouyaté's version of this famous epic. The preface contains brief information on the *jali*'s role and status. Notes at the end of the book about *Sundiata* itself are illuminating. There is almost nothing mentioned in the book about a music component. (Several versions of *Sundiata* may be found in this bibliography.)

1169. **Niangoran-Bouah, G.** *Introduction à la drummologie*. [Ivory Coast]: Université nationale de Côte d'Ivoire, Institut d'ethno-sociologie, 1981. 199pp. (Collection Sankofa)
Entirely in French. The term "drummologie" was coined by the author to mean the science of studying the oral expression of African societies of the precolonial period by means of talking drums texts. He studies the Abron-Gyaman people in particular. Following presentation of his theoretical framework, there are translations of over 150 drum texts. Niangoran-Bouah's explanation of what he calls, "the Law of Silence," operating in drum texts (i.e., unfortunate incidents in the life of a celebrity are omitted), and his way around this obstacle is fascinating. 26 black and white plates, bibliography.

1170. **Niangoran-Bouah, G.** *The role of the drum in traditional African communications*. Boston, Massachusetts: African-American Issues Center, [1984?]. 15pp. (Discussion paper. African-American Issues Center, no. 8)
This paper, written in English, is a translation of a lecture given in French by Niangoran-Bouah. There is not too much here of a concrete nature on the subject of the talking drum. However, a comprehensive listing of the myriad functions of the drum - any drum - in African society is impressive and useful. The author considers the future of the talking drum, especially vis-à-vis radio. No index or bibliography.

1171. **Nicholls, Robert W.** "Music and dance guilds in Ìgèdè." In **More than drumming: essays on African and Afro-Latin music and musicians**. Edited by Irene V. Jackson, 91-117. Westport, Connecticut: Greenwood Press, c1985.
Map, notes, bibliography, photographs. Abstracted in **RILM**, 1985.

1172. **Nicklin, Keith**. "*Agiloh*: the giant Mbube xylophone." **NIGERIAN FIELD** vol. 40, no. 4 (1975): 148-158.

Nidzgorska Olenka Darkowska
See: **Darkowska-Nidzgorska, Olenka, 425.**

1173. **Nidzgorski, Denis.** *Arts du spectacle africain: contributions du Gabon*. Bandundu, République du Zaïre: Ceeba, c1980. 373pp. (Publications Ceeba, Série 2, vol. 48)
Touches on every kind of Gabon performance art imaginable. The section on *Mvet, Ngombi et Mandâtô*, three forms of lyric expression, is important. "Musique + joueur + message = mvet" is the definition given by Tsira Ndong Ndoutoure for what has been called the most "original" lyric genre. Found particularly among the Fang people of Cameroon, Gabon, and Equatorial Guinea, more recent studies show the *mvet* to be in Chad and the Central African Republic, as well. Parallel to the art of the *mvet* is that of the *ngombi*, an 8-stringed harp, and the *mandâtô*, the latter associated with weddings. Photographs. Bibliography.

Nidzgorski Olenka Darkowska
See: **Darkowska-Nidzgorska, Olenka, 53, 425.**

1174. NIGERIA MAGAZINE. 1927-1988. Ministry of Culture and Social Welfare (Federal Department of Culture P.M.B. 12524, Lagos, Nigeria).
This journal, which was called **NIGERIA** until 1970, is a particularly rich source for articles on African music, dance, and other aspects of Nigerian culture. The 1989-1990 **ULRICH'S** indicates that back issues are available, even though the journal ceased in 1988. A few articles that appeared are:

- **Euba, Akin**. "European influences in Nigerian musical life," no. 101 (1969): 477-478. [Full title of the essay, of which this is a section, is "Music in traditional society," 475-480.]
- **Lo-Bámijoko, Joy Ifeoma Nwosu**. "Music education in Nigeria," no. 150 (1984): 40-47.
- **Nwajel, George U.** "Methods of musical composition and production among Nigerian urban professional musicians," no. 151 (1984): 63-68.
- **Ṣówándé, Fẹlá**". Nigerian music and musicians: then and now," no. 94 (1967): 253-261.
- **Uzoigwe, Leroy, and Landeg White**. "Forms of resistance songs and perceptions of power in colonial Mozambique," vol. 54, no. 3 (1986): 53-60.

1175. **Nigeria tourist guide. Guide du tourisme nigerien.** 1969- Lagos: Nigerian Tourist Association.
The guide for 1973/74 was examined. Pages 95-104 briefly describe eleven Nigerian festivals and which ones include drumming, dancing or singing. Most space is given to *Sallah*, a festival presided over by all the Muslim traditional rulers in northern Nigeria. A photo is incorporated, and mention of music and drums. In French and English. For another tour guide edited by the same dignitary and published by the same association, see also **Atigbi, I. A., 151.**

1176. NIGERIAN FIELD: THE JOURNAL OF THE NIGERIAN FIELD SOCIETY. 1931- . Nigerian Field Society, Department of Botany,

University of Ìbàdàn, Ìbàdàn, Nigeria.
Issued quarterly. Indexed in **BIOLOGICAL ABSTRACTS** (not listed in this bibliography as a separate entry), and **MLA**. Following are a few articles that have appeared during its long tenure:
- **Nicklin, Keith**. "*Agiloh*: the giant Mbube xylophone," vol. 40, no. 4 (1975): 148-158.
- **Omibìyí, Mosúnmọ́lá Àyínkẹ́**. "The gourd in Nigerian folk music," vol. 48, no. 1-4 (1983): 30-53.
- **Omibìyí, Mosúnmọ́lá Àyínkẹ́**. "Musical instruments as art objects," vol. 51 (1986): 63-78.

1177. **NIGERIAN MUSIC REVIEW**. 1977- . [Ilé-Ifẹ̀, Nigeria]. Department of Music, University of Ifẹ̀.
Volume 1, Number 1 (the only issue located for examination) may represent the grand beginning of yet another excellent African musicology journal that subsequently faded away. This number is fine enough to stand on its own, however. Editor is Akin Euba, who indicates that the journal includes all categories of music practiced in Nigeria, and who paves the way for "informants" to contribute, as well as professional musicians and scholars. Three substantive articles (listed below alphabetically) are included, along with reviews, general news and information, and notes on the contributors. An obituary for composer, Ayọ̀ Bánkọ́lé, appears at the end.
- **Ekwueme, Lazarus Edward Nnanyelu**. "Blackie na Joseph: the sociological implications of a contemporary Igbo popular song," 39-65.
- **Euba, Akin**. "An introduction to music in Nigeria ," 1-38.
- **Vidal, Túnjí**. "Traditions and history in Yorùbá music," 66-92.

1178. **Nigerian universities dissertation abstracts (NUDA): a comprehensive listing of dissertations and theses undertaken in the universities of Nigeria**. Edited by Stephen A. Osiobe...*et. al*. Port Harcourt: University of Port Harcourt Press, c1989- .
Covers all disciplines taught in Nigerian universities. Arranged by broad subject categories, then alphabetically by author. For each entry, there is title, author, degree awarded, institution, date, pages, and an abstract. Subject and author indexes. Most useful.

1179. **Nikiprowetzky, Tolia**. *Les instruments de musique au Niger, communication présentée à la conférence: East and West in Music; Jérusalem, août 1963*. Paris: Office de cooperation radiophonique [1963?]. One unpaginated volume.
In French. Musical instruments of Niger. Illustrations.

1180. **Nikiprowetzky, Tolia**. "Means of preservation and diffusion of traditional music in French-speaking Africa." In **Creating a wider interest in traditional music: proceedings of a conference held in Berlin in cooperation with the International Music Council, 12th to the 17th June, 1967**. [Edited by Alain Daniélou and others], 132-134. Berlin: International Institute for Comparative Music Studies and Documentation, [1967?].

1181. Nikiprowetzky, Tolia. *Trois aspects de la musique africaine, Mauritaine, Sénégal, Niger.* Paris: Office de Coopération radiophonique [1966?]. 93pp.
In French and English. On music of Mauritania, Senegal, Niger. Illustrations.

Nikiprowetzky, Tolia
See also: •**African music: meeting in Yaoundé, 39.**
•**La musique dans la vie, 1141.**

1182. Njoku, Akuma-Kalu Johnston. OKECHUKWU NDUBUISI'S CONTRIBUTION TO THE DEVELOPMENT OF ART MUSIC TRADITION IN NIGERIA. Master's Thesis, Michigan State University, 1987. 202pp.
The writer laments the lack of adequate information in Nigeria on art music. He is particularly concerned with the works of composer, Okechukwu Ndubuisi, whom he has interviewed, corresponded with, and whose music he has collected, classified and analyzed. Njoku speaks of searching through journals and reference books almost in vain for related information on art music in Nigeria. He stresses the need for "a comprehensive collection, classification, edition, and assessment of the growing number of musical compositions in Nigeria." **(UMI)**

1183. Nkamba, Simon C. H. *Development of music curriculum and instructional materials for primary schools in Zambia.* Nairobi: ACO Project, 1980. 29pp. (African studies in curriculum development and evaluation, no. 9)
Illustrations.

Nkashama
See: **Pius Ngandu Nkashama, 1331.**

1184. NKETIA, J. H. KWABENA
This world renowned musicologist from Ghana has published untold numbers of scholarly books, articles, monographs, essays, music compositions, and more. Following are but a few items selected from his vast output. For a comprehensive list of his major works representing the period 1949-1987, however, see **African musicology: current trends: a festschrift presented to J. H. Kwabena Nketia, 41.** In this work, his biography and bibliography are combined on pages 3-29, entitled **J. H. Kwabena: A Biobibliographic Portrait.**

1185. Nketia, J. H. Kwabena. *African gods and music.* Legon: Institute of African Studies, University of Ghana, 1970. 12pp.
An abundantly footnoted compendium of 10 pages backs up the initial statement that the gods in Africa are "music-loving." West African traditional religions receive particular, though not exclusive attention, as do specific associated musical instruments. (The range goes from pottery whistles to bull-roarers!) Dances, too, are noted. Nketia points out that music effective with one god or pantheon of

gods might not be so for another, even in the same locality. There is much more information about differentiation in musical forms, differentiation in the use of musical instruments, and about religion and worship in general in Africa.

1186. **Nketia, J. H. Kwabena**. "African music and Western praxis: a review of Western perspectives on African musicology." **CANADIAN JOURNAL OF AFRICAN STUDIES** 20, no. 1 (1986): 36-56.

1187. **Nketia, J. H. Kwabena**. *African music in Ghana*. [Evanston, Ill.] Northwestern University Press, 1963. 148pp. (Northwestern University, Evanston, Ill. African studies, no. 11)
Bibliography, illustrations, maps, music, tables. Songs for 1-2 voices, pages 115-146.

1188. **Nketia, J. H. Kwabena**. *African music in Ghana: a survey of traditional forms*. Accra: Longmans [1962a]. 148pp.
Maps, music, bibliography.

1189. **Nketia, J. H. Kwabena**. "African roots of music in the Americas: an African view." In **INTERNATIONAL MUSICOLOGICAL SOCIETY. Congress. Report**, 82-88, 1977. Berkeley, California.
Source is **RILM**, 1981.

1190. **Nketia, J. H. Kwabena**. "Akan poetry." In *An African treasury: articles, essays, stories, poems, by black Americans*. Edited by Langston Hughes, 102-109. New York: Crown Publishers [1969].
A most instructive article that divides Akan poetry into four categories: The Oral Poetry Tradition (poetry that is recited and not sung); Recitative (verse that is half-spoken/half-sung, used in dirges and the poetry of hunter's celebrations); Lyric Types; and The Poetry of Horns and Drums. There are several sub-groups in the last two categories.

1191. **Nketia, J. H. Kwabena**, comp. *Ayan: the poetry of the Atumpan drums of the Asantehene*. [Legon]: Institute of African Studies, University of Ghana, 1966.
All the texts were played and interpreted verbally by Okyerema Kwaku Pon (alias Kyirifufuo)

1192. **Nketia, J. H. Kwabena**. *Drumming in Akan communities of Ghana*. [Accra]: Published on behalf of the University of Ghana by Thomas Neldon [1963]. 212pp.
Bibliography, illustrations, diagrams, music, tables.

1193. **Nketia, J. H. Kwabena**. *Ethnomusicology in Ghana*. Accra: Ghana Universities Press, 1970. 23pp.
This was an inaugural lecture delivered on the 20th of November, 1969 at the

University of Ghana, Legon. An overview of the field is given - especially valuable because it represents an African perspective. It is delightful to hear *Nketia* evaluate *Western* evaluations of African music! He quotes early short-sighted visitors to Africa: Thomas E. Bowdich, Richard A. Freeman, H. O. Northcott, and William Bosman. At least, W. E. F. Ward managed to say in 1927, "African rhythm is so complicated that it is exceedingly difficult for a European to analyse it." No truer words were ever said.

1194. **Nketia, J. H. Kwabena**, ed. *Folk songs of Ghana.* Legon: University of Ghana, 1963. 205pp.
In this collection, Akan folk songs are analyzed, with discussion of their socio-cultural backgrounds. The text is in Akan.

1195. **Nketia, J. H. Kwabena**. *Funeral dirges of the Akan people.* New York: Negro Universities Press, [1969]. 296pp.
This was originally published in 1955. The texts of the dirges are in English, Twi and Fante. Bibliography.

1196. **Nketia, J. H. Kwabena**. *Ghana: music, dance and drama: a review of the performing arts of Ghana.* Script by J. H. Kwabena Nketia, Institute of African Studies, University of Ghana. [Accra-Tema: Ghana Information Services]. 1965. 50pp.
Illustrations.

1197. **Nketia, J. H. Kwabena**. "History and organization of music in West Africa." In *Essays on music and history in Africa.* Edited by Klaus P. Wachsmann, 3-25. Evanston: Northwestern University Press, 1971.
Divided into headings: Musical Change, The Effects of Political and Social Institutions (the latter subdivided into The Bambara, The Fon of Dahomey, Ashanti, The Ewe), The Effects of Trade, The Effects of Religion, and Conclusion. Two maps, many footnotes.

1198. **Nketia, J. H. Kwabena**. *History and the organization of music in West Africa.* Legon: Institute of African Studies, University of Ghana, [196?]. 28pp.
A carefully considered essay that disputes old die-hard ideas that African music is static or somehow represents the music of early humankind. Nketia further argues against the false idea that historical information on Africa is unobtainable (an assumption resulting from the fact that the usual Western historical methods don't work). He demonstrates enlightened and productive approaches to gathering historical music data in Africa. When it comes to instruments, their uses, dissemination, and incorporation into a given culture, Nketia is particularly brilliant, though the entire work is significant. Unfortunately, notes and references at the end are incomplete and poorly organized.

N

1199. **Nketia, J. H. Kwabena**. "The hocket technique in African music." **INTERNATIONAL FOLK MUSIC COUNCIL. Journal** 14 (1962a): 44-52.

1200. **Nketia, J. H. Kwabena**. "The instrumental resources of African music." In **Papers in African studies**, 1-23. Legon: University of Ghana, Institute of African Studies, 1968.
Includes a one-page chart that lists rattles, bells, gourd drums, hourglass drums, closed (double-headed) cylindrical drums, and bottle-shaped talking drums in pairs, followed by their names in several West African languages. Notes, photographs.

1201. **Nketia, J. H. Kwabena**. "Les langages musicaux de l'Afrique subsaharienne: étude comparative." In **La musique africaine, réunion de Yaoundé (Cameroun)** [sur les traditions musicales de l'Afrique subsaharienne], **23-27 février 1970, organisée par l'UNESCO**, 7-42. Paris: *La revue musicale*, Richard-Masse, 1972.
The English translation of this essay can be found under: **Nketia, J. H. Kwabena**, "The musical languages of Subsaharan Africa," **1206**.

1202. **Nketia, J. H. Kwabena**. "Music in African Culture." In **Festac '77**. 4pp. London: Africa Journal Ltd., c1977.
A brief essay in a souvenir book.

1203. **Nketia, J. H. Kwabena**. "Music in African Culture." In **Colloquium on Negro Art, Dakar, 1966**, 143-186. Organized by the Society of African Culture (S.A.C.) [Paris, Présence africaine, 1968]
Though this essay has the same title as the immediately preceding one (**1202**) it is an entirely different work - a translation of "La musique dans la culture africaine" that first appeared in **Colloque sur l'art nègre**.

1204. **Nketia, J. H. Kwabena**. *Music in African cultures: a review of the meaning and significance of traditional African music*. [Legon]: Institute of African Studies, University of Ghana, 1966. 75pp.
The subjects presented are: The African Heritage of Music; Music in Communal Life; Contextual Organization; The Social Organization of Traditional Music; and, Artistic Values in Traditional Music. A Summary/Conclusion follows. The bibliography has tried and true older references.

1205. **Nketia, J. H. Kwabena**. *The music of Africa*. New York: Norton, 1974. 278pp.
A *magnum opus*. The first two sections treat musical traditions in Africa, the place of music in the community, the role in society of performing groups, how they are recruited and trained, and musical instruments. The third section, on forms and the elements of music, departs from the gradually unfolding style of

earlier chapters and becomes quite technical, with complex music notations and musicological terminology apt to be beyond the comprehension of "the general reader and college student" for whom the book is designed. The last section concerns music and related arts. Transcriptions, photographs, maps, charts, song texts, glossary, more.

1206. **Nketia, J. H. Kwabena**. "The musical languages of Subsaharan Africa." In **African music: meeting in Yaoundé (Cameroon) 23-27 February 1970, organized by UNESCO**, 7-42. Paris: *La revue musicale*, 1972.
Notes. See Nketia's, "Les langages musicaux de l'Afrique subsaharienne" (**1201**) for the French version of this essay.

1207. **Nketia, J. H. Kwabena**. "The musician in Akan society." In *The traditional artist in African societies*. Edited by Warren L. d'Azevedo, 79-100. Bloomington: Indiana University Press, [1973].

1208. **Nketia, J. H. Kwabena**. "Musik in afrikanischen Kulturen." In *Musikkulturen in Afrika*, 9-43. Edited by Erich Stockmann. Berlin: Verlag Neue Musik, 1987.
A broad undertaking by a preeminent scholar. Subjects covered in this chapter, to name only a few, are: Music in Communal Life, Music and Ritual, The Social Structure of Traditional Music. Emphasis is given to the meaning of music to those who perform it. Many informative notes in margins.

1209. **Nketia, J. H. Kwabena**. "La musique dans la culture africaine." In **Colloque sur l'art nègre**. Rapports. Vol. 1 (1967): 147-191. [Paris: Présence africaine]

1210. **Nketia, J. H. Kwabena**. *Musique, danse, théâtre: un examen des arts ludiques du Ghana*. Legon: Institut des études africaines, Université du Ghana, 1965. 52pp.
Illustrations.

1211. **Nketia, J. H. Kwabena**. "On the historicity of music in African cultures." In INTERNATIONAL MUSICOLOGICAL SOCIETY. **Congress. Report**, 48-57, 1981. Bayreut.
Source is **RILM**, 1984. This same paper also appears as the next entry.

1212. **Nketia, J. H. Kwabena**. "On the historicity of music in African cultures." In JOURNAL OF AFRICAN STUDIES 9, No. 3 (1982): 91-99.
Copious notes.

N

1213. **Nketia, J. H. Kwabena**. *Our drums and drummers*. Accra: Ghana Publishing House, 1968. 48pp.
Profusely illustrated. Includes drum poetry.

1214. **Nketia, J. H. Kwabena**. *The performing musician in a changing society*. Legon: Institute of African Studies, University of Ghana, 1977. 13pp.
Nketia describes the traditional musician's primary dedication to service. Often exploited by commercial houses, the contemporary musician, on the other hand, though often lacking in the traditional musician's intensity, breadth of knowledge, and full acceptance of the cultural heritage, enjoys a special sort of freedom and far more opportunities. Nketia comforts those who would fear for the future of music in Africa, and suggests a realistic view about change, stressing the need to explore and reinforce "the present trend towards tradition," thereby helping to bridge the gap between traditional and contemporary African societies.

1215. **Nketia, J. H. Kwabena**. "Les sources de documentation historique sur les traditions musicales de l'Afrique." In **La musique africaine, réunion de Yaoundé (Cameroun)** [sur les traditions musicales de l'Afrique subsaharienne], **23-27 février 1970, organisée par l'UNESCO**, 43-48. Paris: *La revue musicale*, Richard-Masse, 1972.
Notes. See next entry (**1216**) for an English translation of this essay.

1216. **Nketia, J. H. Kwabena**. "Sources of historical data on the musical cultures of Africa." In **African music: meeting in Yaoundé (Cameroon) 23-27 February 1970, organized by UNESCO**, 43-49. Paris: *La Revue musicale*, 1972.
Notes. Preceding entry is the original French version.

1217. **Nketia, J. H. Kwabena**. "Traditional music in Ghana." In **Creating a wider interest in traditional music: proceedings of a conference held in Berlin in cooperation with the International Music Council, 12th to the 17th June, 1967**. [Edited by Alain Daniélou and others], 120-127. Berlin: International Institute for Comparative Music Studies and Documentation, [1967?].

1218. **Nketia, J. H. Kwabena**. "Unity and diversity in African music: a problem of synthesis." In *International Congress of Africanists, 1st, Accra, 11th-18th, December 1962*. Edited by Lalage Brown and Michael Crowder, 256-264. Evanston, Illinois: Northwestern University Press, 1964.
After overwhelming us with the enormous number of variables operating in the music of continental Africa, and stressing furthermore how vast are the present unknowns, Nketia nevertheless points the way to future research that will

emphasize "the synthesis of divergent forms and the recognition of the aggregate as a basis of generalization." He stresses once more the importance and vitality of African music, and quotes William Hicken who said, [The African] "...is born, named, initiated into manhood, warriored, armed, housed, betrothed, wedded and buried to music." Footnotes.

1219. **Nketia, J. H. Kwabena**. "Zur Geschichtlichkeit der Musik in Afrika." In *Musikkulturen in Afrika*. Edited by Erich Stockmann, 44-61. Berlin: Verlag Neue Musik, 1987.
An historical view of African music with an indication of possible directions for future study.

1220. **Nketia, J. H. Kwabena, and Jacqueline Cogdell DjeDje**. "Trends in African musicology." In **Studies in African music**. Co-editors, J. H. Kwabena Nketia, and Jacqueline Cogdell DjeDje, ix-xx. [Los Angeles]: Program in Ethnomusicology, Department of Music, University of California, Los Angeles, 1984. 387pp.
This, the introductory essay that launches the book, is at once an overview of approaches used in the past by pioneers in the field, and a preparation for new trends, exemplified by the essays that follow. African musicology was once characterized by Wachsmann as a "search after wholeness of vision." The authors believe that the papers selected exemplify this quest.

Nketia, J. H. Kwabena
See also: •**African musicology: current trends: a festschrift presented to J. H. Kwabena Nketia, 41.**
•**Studies in African music, 1514.**

1221. **Nkinda, Masengo**. "The adaptation of traditional musical instruments to sacred music: the example of Zaïre." In **Symposium musico-ethnologicum**. Edited by Johannes Overath, 129-153. MUSICES APTATIO 1980 (Roma CIMS, 1980).
Bibliography. Text in French, English, and German. Abstracted in **RILM**, 1980.

1222. ***"Nkosi Sikelel' iAfrika."*** SING OUT: THE FOLK SONG MAGAZINE 31, no. 3 (1985): 22-23.
Melody and words are given for this significant freedom song, the unofficial national anthem of South Africa, sung with reverence when black South Africans gather. Enoch Sontonga is the composer. There are other references to this song in the Index.

Non-Western music: a selected bibliography
See: **Johnson, Sheila J.**, 2d ed., **769.**
Smith, Donna Ridley, 3d ed., **1470.**

1223. **Norborg, Åke**. *A handbook of musical and other sound-producing instruments from equatorial Guinea and Gabon.* Stockholm: [s.n.], 1989 (Lund [Sweden]: Wallin and Dalholk

Boktryckeri). 469pp. (Musikmuseets skrifter, 16)
This is a twin in format of the book that immediately follows, except that the featured countries and their individual instruments differ. Even *one* of these handbooks could represent the life's work of a lesser (or slower!) scholar. An incredible achievement, resulting in a most welcome research tool.

1224. **Norborg, Åke.** *A handbook of musical and other sound-producing instruments from Namibia and Botswana.* Stockholm: Norborg, 1987. 454pp. (Musikmuseets skrifter, 13)
Remarkably complete. The handbook begins with notes on the orthography, followed by background information on geography, history, ethnic groups and "main sources." Instruments are classified with fastidious care as to their types, uses, construction, distribution and history, playing techniques, and vernacular names. Sketches but no photos. A section on ensembles is followed by a general outline of instrumental resources of the people of Namibia and Botswana. Besides a 24 page bibliography, discography, and index of vernacular names of instruments, there are explanatory, notes and personalized remarks throughout that keep this from being a stuffy reference tool. Instrument distribution maps.

1225. **Norborg, Åke.** *Musical instruments from Africa south of the Sahara.* Musikhistorisk museum og Carl Claudius' samling, 1982. 91pp.
Discography, indexes, bibliographical references.

1226. **Norborg, Åke.** "Musikinstrumente der Bini in Südwest-Nigeria." In *Musikkulturen in Afrika.* Edited by Erich Stockmann, 197-220. Berlin: Verlag Neue Musik, 1987.
A wide variety of Bini musical instruments and instrumental ensembles are treated, including drums, harps, horns, as well as clappers, bells, rattles and plucked idiophones. Instruments are carefully sketched. The bibliography has a broad subject range, approximately one-third of the listings dealing specifically with music. Some of the historical entries go far back in time. Black and white photographs of a dancer and two of instrumental groups are overly dark and too static to add much to the article.

1227. **Norris, H. T.** *S̲hinqīṭī folk literature and song.* Oxford: Clarendon Press, 1968. 200pp.
S̲hinquīṭ has become the name for the homeland of the Moors, inhabitants of a vast region of the Western Sahara adjoining the Atlantic Ocean. Originally, S̲hinquīṭ, in northern Mauritania, was a prosperous caravan town. Three chapters in this book pertain to music: 6. Musicians and poetry, 7. Mauritanian musical instruments, recitals and dances, 8. The background of Mauritanian music. The text is partly in Arabic. Includes illustrations, a map, and a genealogy table.

1228. **NOTES ON EDUCATION AND RESEARCH IN AFRICAN MUSIC.** 1967-1975. Legon, Institute of African Studies, University of Ghana.
Too late for listing as separate entries, the following items are noted:
•**Cooke, Peter R.** "A music course in Uganda," vol. 1 (1967): 32-37.
•**Edet, Edna M.** "Music education in Nigeria," 1 (1967): 38-42.

1229. **Nourrit, Chantal, and William Pruitt.** *Musique traditionnelle de l'Afrique Noire: discographie.* Paris: Radio-France Internationale, Centre de documentation africaine, 1978-[1985]. 17 volumes (Radio-théques)

A spectacular series of comprehensive discographies of traditional black African music. In French. Each volume treats a separate country. Volume numbers and associated countries are [translated] as follows: 1. Mali, 2. Upper Volta, 3. Mauritania, 4. Senegal and Gambia, 5. Niger, 6. Côte d'Ivoire, 7. Benin, 8. Togo, 9. Cameroon, 10, Chad, 11. Central Africa, 12. Gabon, 13. Congo, 14. Zaïre, 15. Burundi, 16. Rwanda, 17. Djibouti. Each volume contains a number of subject indexes, an introductory essay on the music of the area, and an annotated discography by manufacturer. See also the next entry, **1230**.

1230. **Nourrit, Chantal, and William Pruitt.** *Musique traditionelle de l'ocean Indien: discographie.* Paris: Radio-France Internationale, Centre de documentation africaine, 1981-[1988]. 4 vols. (Radio-théques)

Another series of discographies, related to the immediately preceding entry, also in French, and with the same features. African islands of the Indian Ocean are treated. Volumes by island are [translated from the French] as follows: 1. Mauritius, 2. Seychelles, 3. Madagascar, 4. Comores.

1231. **Nsibu, Kalokora J.** *Traditional musical instruments of Tanzania.* [Dar es Salaam?]: Music Conservatoire of Tanzania, [197-?]. 6pp.

The text is in English and Swahili.

1232. **Nundlall, Iswarduth.** *Dialogues on music.* Vacoas, Mauritius: Sargam Publications, 1984. 116pp.

A useful non-technical book designed to teach the basics of Indian music to the people of Mauritius. There are twelve informative lessons in a teacher-pupil, question and answer, format, and a number of notated songs in several Indian languages. One is a hymn to Mauritius. There are a few photos of the author with various visiting dignitaries, and one blurry photo picturing four Indian instruments. Brief index, no bibliography.

1233. **Nundlall, Iswarduth.** *Music in Mauritius.* Vacoas, Mauritius: Sargam Publications, 1984- . [178pp].

Dated. Issued as a Master's Thesis in 1957 at Bhatkande University of Music, Lucknow. Since little is available on the music of this Indian Ocean island, however, the book is included here. Western "classical," "light," and Indian music, are included. The chapter on "Creole" music and dance has song texts in Creole and English. Song pitches are expressed as syllables later in the book. The *Sega*, a rhythmic, style of Creole syncopated song in quick waltz tempo associated with dance is described ethnoocentrically. Perhaps researchers can separate chaff from wheat and pinpoint possible Africanisms. Bibliography of 7 flimsy, undated entries.

N

1234. **Nuñez, Benjamin**. *Dictionary of Afro-Latin American civilization*. Benjamin Nuñez with the assistance of the African Bibliographic Center. Westport, Connecticut: Greenwood Press, 1980. 525pp.

Most useful. The author says that the dictionary comprises a systematic and documented survey of Afro-Latin American civilization, and that to the best of his knowledge, it is the first of its kind in English. The Subject Index lists many entries under music, musical instruments, folklore, religious practices, and other related aspects of culture. Caribbean references are admittedly more abundant than continental Latin America. Though perhaps not everyone would agree with each definition, this work still represents a major achievement and a giant step forward. Excellent bibliography.

1235. **Nwabuoku, Chukwuemeka 'Tony**. A FIELD STUDY OF MUSIC AS A CULTURAL AND EDUCATIONAL SYSTEM: THE CASE OF THE ANIOCHA IBOS OF BENDEL STATE OF NIGERIA. Dissertation, Rutgers University, 1979. 226pp.

1236. **Nwabuoku, Chukwuemeka 'Tony**. BENIN COURT MUSIC: PROPOSALS FOR FUTURE RESEARCH. Master's Thesis, Columbia University, 1974. 105pp.

1237. **Nwajel, George U.** "Methods of musical composition and production among Nigerian urban professional musicians." **NIGERIA MAGAZINE** 151 (1984): 63-68.

Music and illustrations.

1238. **Nyabongo, Ada Naomi**. TRADITIONAL MUSICAL INSTRUMENTS OF THE BAGANDA AND AKAN IN THEIR SOCIAL CONTEXTS. Dissertation, New York University, 1986. 157pp.

The purpose of this study was to investigate and to compare selected traditional musical instruments of the Baganda in Uganda and the Akan in Ghana. This project focuses only on the physical properties of traditional musical instruments. Illustrations, maps, bibliography.

Nyberg, Anders
See: **Freedom is coming, 599.**

1239. **Nzewi, Meki**. MASTER MUSICIANS AND THE MUSIC OF ESA UKOM AND MGBA ENSEMBLES IN NGWA IGBO SOCIETY. 2 vols. Dissertation, Queen's University of Belfast (Northern Ireland). 1977. 927pp.

Listed as **M. E. Nzewi** in **THE BRITS index**, and in the bibliography of Meki's Nzewi's own paper. Nzewi also lists the title of this dissertation slightly differently from that in **BRITS**, i.e., "The Master Musician and the Music of Ese, Ukom and Mgba in Ngwa, Igbo Society." Since the dissertation itself was not seen, the precise title is not certain.

1240. **Nzewi, Meki.** "Philological derivations of melo-rhythmic improvisation." **AFRICAN MUSICOLOGY** 1, no.1 (1983): 1-13.
Illustrations, music, bibliography.

1241. **Nzewi, Meki.** "The rhythm of dance in Igbo music." **THE CONCH** 3, No.2 (1971): 104-108.

1242. **Nzewi, Meki.** "Some reflections on research methodology in ethnomusicology." **IKENGA** 4, no.2 (1980): 66-70.
Good to read an African scholar's perspective, for a change, on the subject of ethnomusicology. Theories of many prominent ethnomusicologists are explored, compared, evaluated. Nzewi feels that a comparative approach "implicates ethnocentric bias, even if not intended." He believes that Western and non-Western literary musical traditions and non-Western non-literary traditions have a great deal to offer if those "involved in musical promotion, usage and discussion would lay aside ethnocentric prejudices and vain cultural airs, and approach their studies with a genuine spirit of reciprocity and respect." He does not minimize problems of ethics and morality.

1243. **Nzewi, Meki.** "Traditional strategies for mass communication: the centrality of Igbo music." **In Studies in African music.** Co-editors, J. H. Kwabena Nketia, and Jacqueline Cogdell DjeDje, 319-338. [Los Angeles]: Program in Ethnomusicology, Department of Music, University of California, Los Angeles, 1984.
Nzewi describes his paper as an attempt to investigate the "structural-formal configurations underlying the process of communicating information to a wide audience through non-verbal, non-literary sound media." Musical sound is the focus. There are a number of figures included, the most important being a grid schema for the "efficiency/efficacy of mass communication, with an "axis of emotivity" and an "effectiveness axis." These axes, Nzewi says, furnish the surface and deep structures of mass communication. Many examples of music notations in the Appendix are meant to accompany the several sections of the essay. Notes, bibliography, photographs, map.

O

1244. **Obama, Jean-Baptiste.** "La musique africaine traditionelle, ses fonctions sociales et sa signification philosophique." In **Colloque sur l'art nègre**. Rapports. Vol. 1 (1967): 193-230. [Paris: Présence africaine]
The original French version. The English translation is the next entry, **1245**.

1245. **Obama, Jean-Baptiste.** "Traditional African music." In **Colloquium on Negro Art, Dakar, 1966**, 187-222. Organized by the Society of African Culture (SAC) [Paris: Présence africaine]
A translation of the immediately preceding entry, **1244**.

1246. **Obenga, Théophile.** "La chanson Mbochi." In **Chansons d'Afrique et des Antilles**, 55-62. Paris: Harmattan, c1988.

1247. **OBJETS ET MONDES**. 1961- . Paris: Musée de l'Homme.
Appeared quarterly, but was discontinued in the winter of 1982. Covered ethnology, anthropology, and prehistory. There were a few fine articles on African music. Examples follow:
- **Gessain, Monique**. "Les Malinke des chants de chasseurs Bassari," vol. 12, no. 4 (1972): 355-360.
- **Johnston, Thomas F.** "Musical instruments and dance uniforms in Southern Africa," vol. 13, no. 2 (1973): 81-90.

1248. **O'Brien, James Patrick.** *Non-western music and the western listener*. Dubuque, Iowa: Kendall/Hunt Publishing Company, c1977. 107pp.
There is indication that this book was intended to be part of a university survey course following the exposure of students to Western music. Some caution is required, however. Good reference materials are interpreted unevenly. China, India, Japan, and Indonesia get full chapter elaboration. Chapter 6, entitled "Primitive Music," dumps Africa and Australia together, and gives the music slight - and collective - treatment. At the beginning we read: "Primitive society! Primitive art and music! This is an inadequate classification that reflects an inappropriate Western viewpoint." So why perpetuate it? Bibliography includes Nettl, Nketia, Wachsmann, Tracey, and Ekwueme. Short discography.

1249. **ODÙ: A JOURNAL OF WEST AFRICAN STUDIES**. New Series, 1969- [Older series]: 1964-1968. [Initial series]: 1955-1963. Obáfẹ́mi Awólọ́wọ̀ University, Ilé-Ifẹ̀, Nigeria.
This journal, initially called, **ODÙ: A JOURNAL OF YORÙBÁ, EDO AND RELATED STUDIES**, ran from 1955 to 1963, numbers 1 to 9. Only one article from this period (by Akin Euba) appears below, since other music articles predated 1960. In 1964, the journal acquired its present title, and by 1968 four volumes had appeared. In 1969, a New Series was inaugurated, and numbers (no longer called volumes) were issued semiannually. (To further complicate the journal's history, the former University of Ifẹ̀ at Ìbàdàn is now called Obáfẹ́mi Awólọ́wọ̀ University.) Indexed in **HISTORICAL ABSTRACTS, MLA, AICP**. Examples follow:

- **•Àjùwọ̀n, Bádé**. "The metaphorical language of *ìrèmòjé* chants," New Series no. 18 (1978): 106-116.
- **•Babábọ̀lá, S. A.** "The characteristic features of outer form of Yorùbá *ìjálá* chants," vol 1, no. 1 (1964): 33-34; Part 2, vol. 1, no. 2 (1965): 47-77.
- **•Darah, G. G.** "Aesthetic socialization of youth through dance and music in Urhobo society," New Series no. 28 (1985): 46-56.
- **•Euba, Akin**. "Six Yorùbá songs," [Initial Series] no. 9 (1963): 5-12.
- **•Euba, Akin**. "Musicology in the context of African culture," New Series no. 2 (1969): 3-18.
- **•Harper, Peggy**. "The role of dance in the Gẹ̀lẹ̀dẹ́ ceremonies of the village of Ìjìó," New Series no. 4 (1970): 67-94.
- **•Iṣọ̀lá, Akínwùmí**. "The artistic aspects of Ṣàngó-pípè," New Series no. 13 (1976): 80-103.
- **•Uzoigwe, Joshua**. "A cultural analysis of Akin Euba's musical works," New Series no. 24 (1983): 44-60.

1250. **Oehrle, Elizabeth**. "The first South African National Music Educator's Conference in the context of world music education." In **National Music Educator's Conference**. (1st: 1985: University of Natal) *Proceedings of the first National Music Educator's Conference*. Edited by Christine Lucia, 7-18. Durban [South Africa]: University of Natal, Department of Music, 1986.

1251. **Oehrle, Elizabeth**. *A new direction for South African music education: a creative introduction to African, Indian and Western music*. 2d ed. Pietermaritzburg, South Africa: Shuter & Shooter, 1988. 82pp.
On instruction and study of music and musical instruments of South Africa. Indian and Western musics are also included. Bibliographical references, illustrations.

1252. **Ofei, Patrick Sakyi**. A BASIS FOR THE DEVELOPMENT OF A MUSIC CURRICULUM FOR GHANAIAN ELEMENTARY SCHOOLS. Dissertation. University of Colorado, 1973. 205pp.

1253. **Offei, W. E.** *Adonten music album*. [Accra?: s.n., 1978?-] (Accra: Multipress)
Twi or English words. Volume 1, part 1 is a revised version of the 1966 publication entitled, "Twi and English songs," **1254**. Volume 1, part 2 is a revised version of the 1969 publication "20 melodies." Written in both staff and tonic sol-fa notation.

1254. **Offei, W. E.** *Twi and English songs*. [Accra: Catholic Press, 1966]. 31pp.
Songs in English and Twi (a Ghanaian language). Includes music.

O

Ogbalu, F. Chidozie
See: **Igbo poems and songs, 718.**

1255. **Ògúnbà, Oyinadé**. "The poetic content and form of Yorùbá occasional festival songs." **AFRICAN NOTES** 6, no. 2 (1971): 10-30.

1256. **Ògúnbà, Oyinadé**. RITUAL DRAMA OF THE ÌJẸ̀BÚ PEOPLE [NIGERIA]: A STUDY OF INDIGENOUS FESTIVALS. Dissertation, University of Ìbàdàn, 1967. 535pp.
The festival, referred to as the "idiom of the people," is a dynamic and vital cultural institution that makes use of many fine arts. Above all, however, it is the art of poetic musical chant that provides the excitement and atmosphere of a festival.

1257. **Ògúnmọ̀lá, Kọ́lá**. *The palmwine drinkard: opera, after the novel by Amos Tutùọlá.* Transcribed and translated by R. G. Armstrong, Robert L. Awujoola and Val Ọláyẹmí. [Ìbàdàn]: University of Ìbàdàn, Institute of African Studies, [1968]. 118pp. (University of Ìbàdàn. Institute of African Studies. Occasional Publication no. 12)
Ògúnmọ̀lá is an actor, accomplished composer and director. This is the text of his opera in Yorùbá and English (based on Tutùọlá's famous novel) derived from a tape recording made of a performance in 1963. Sung and spoken parts are indicated, and there are interpolations of what kinds of music and dances occur at given points. No transcriptions or finer details about the music itself are given.

1258. **Ògúnnáìkè, Anna**. CONTEMPORARY NIGERIAN ART MUSIC: THE WORKS OF BANKỌLE, EUBA AND EKWUEME. Master's Thesis, University of Lagos, 1986.

1259. **Ojaide, Tanure**. "The poetry of the *udje* songs." **BĀ SHIRU** no. 1 (1981): 31-38.
Several clans of the Urhobo people of the Niger Delta of Nigeria perform a unique dance known as *udje*. Accompanying dance-songs (also called *udje* and sung for Uhwagha the dance god) are studied with particular attention to their poetic aspects, and their relationship to the dance. There are notes, and texts to three songs.

Ojehomon, Agnes A.
See: **University of Ìbàdàn. Institute of African Studies**. *Catalogue of recorded sound*, **1605.**

1260. **Òjó, Jerome O.** "Ògbóni drums." **AFRICAN ARTS** vol. 6, no. 3 (1973): 50-52, 84.

1261. **Òjó, Jerome O.** *Yorùbá customs from Ondó.* Vienna: Elisabeth Stiglmayr, 1976. 112pp. (Acta ethnologica et linguistica, no. 37: Series africana, 10)
Two-page bibliography, 4 pages of plates.

1262. **Òjó-Adé, Fẹ́mi.** *Analytical index of Présence africaine, 1947-1972.* [Washington]: Three Continents Press, c1977. 181pp.
A useful index for researching **PRÉSENCE AFRICAINE** for likely old articles on African music.

1263. **Okafor, Richard Chijioke.** IGBO MINSTRELS. Dissertation, Queen's University of Belfast (Northern Ireland), 1980. 313pp.
Another brilliant dissertation supervised by John Blacking. Okafor uses "minstrel" to signify a genre of solo-musicians who are either professional or semi-professional music specialists. Chapters examine literature on minstrelsy, the role and status of master-musicians, perceptions of minstrels by themselves and others in society, pertinent terminology, minstrel training and transmission of the tradition, song texts and themes, social contexts, and minstrelsy as music, its influence on the Igbo modern orchestra. Photos, figures, maps, bibliography, discography. Appendix of recorded musical illustrations.

1264. **Okelo, Anthony.** "Intonation of words in the Acholi language in relation to church music." In **Symposium musico-ethnologicum.** Edited by Johannes Overath, 204-236. **MUSICES APTATIO** 1980 (Roma CIMS, 1980).
Illustrations. Text in French, English, and German. Abstracted in **RILM**, 1980.

1265. **Okoreaffia, C. O.** "*Igeri Ututu*: an Igbo folk requiem music dance ritual." In **The performing arts: music and dance.** Edited by John Blacking, and Joann W. Kealiinohomoku, 265-276. New York: Mouton, c1979.

Okpaku, Joseph Ohiomogben
See: **The arts and civilization of Black and African people, 137.**

1266. **Okpewho, Isidore.** *The epic in Africa: toward a poetics of the oral performance.* New York: Columbia University Press, 1979. 288pp.
Songs, epic poetry, oral tradition. Bibliography and index.

Okpewho, Isidore
See also: •**The heritage of African poetry, 674.**
•**The oral performance in Africa, 1293.**

1267. **Ọláníyan, O. C.** THE COMPOSITIONS AND PERFORMANCE TECHNIQUES OF DÙNDÚN-ṢẸ̀KẸ̀RẸ̀ MUSIC OF SOUTH-WESTERN

NIGERIA. Dissertation, Queen's University of Belfast (Northern Ireland), 1984. 450pp.

1268. **Ọlátúnjí, Olátúndé O.** "Issues in the study of oral poetry in Africa." **JOURNAL OF AFRICAN STUDIES** 6, No. 1 (1979): 112-119.
Song is mentioned throughout this essay. Notes and a bibliography of 55 entries.

1269. **Ọláyẹmí, Val.** "Forms of the song in Yorùbá folktales." **AFRICAN NOTES** 5, no. 1 (1968): 179-207.

1270. **Ọláyẹmí, Val**, ed. and trans. *Orin ìbejì (Songs in praise of twins).* Ìbàdàn, Nigeria]: University of Ìbàdàn, Institute of African Studies, [c1971].
In English and Yorùbá.

1271. **Oldham, June Page.** SOME ASPECTS OF AFRICAN MUSIC SOUTH OF THE SAHARA. Master's Thesis, Austin Peay State University, Clarksville, Tennessee, 1973. 93pp.

1272. **Olema, Debhonvapi.** "Société Zaïroise dans le miroir de la chanson populaire." **CANADIAN JOURNAL OF AFRICAN STUDIES** 18, no. 1 (1984): 122-130.

1273. **Oliveira, Alda de Jesus.** A FREQUENCY COUNT OF MUSIC ELEMENTS IN BAHIAN FOLK SONGS USING COMPUTER AND HAND ANALYSIS. Dissertation, University of Texas at Austin, 1985. 321pp.
The frequency of selected elements in Bahaian songs was analyzed, using computer and hand analysis. Fifty-six songs of various types were used, and ten musical elements chosen. After presenting his findings, the author concludes that the study "demonstrates the efficacy of computer analysis as a tool for the ethnological, theoretical, and educational study of music, and provides an important analytical perspective concerning representative folk-songs from Bahia-Brazil." **(UMI)**

1274. **Oliver, Paul.** "Africa influence and the blues." **LIVING BLUES** no. 8 (1972): 13-17.

1275. **Oliver, Paul.** *Savannah syncopators: African retentions in the blues.* London: Studio Vista, 1970. 112pp. (Blues paperbacks)
Interesting, somewhat random compilation of information on the music of West Africa, with little information on the blues. Though no serious scholar doubts the African retentions in almost all African-American music, this attempt to connect the blues so directly to the Savannah area of West Africa (even as to noses, cheek bones and skin tones of blues singers) is a bit far-fetched. Maps, Glossary of Instruments, "Index of Tribes and People," many photographs, chapter notes, a record list, and mention of an accompanying record (not seen).

Oliver, Paul
See also: **Black music in Britain, 240.**

1276. **Olivera Pinto, Tiago de.** "'Making ritual drama:' dance, music, and representation in Brazilian Candomblé and Umbanda." **THE WORLD OF MUSIC** 33, no. 1, 1991.

1277. **Oliverson, Cathy Anine.** DANCE MUSIC OF THE GIRIAMA OF KENYA. Master's Thesis, University of California, Los Angeles, 1984. 86pp.

1278. **Olsen, Dale A.** "Folk music of South America - a musical mosaic." In **Musics of many cultures: an introduction.** Edited by Elizabeth May, 386-425. Berkeley: University of California Press, c1980.
Contains a large map showing where slaves were situated during the colonial period, places where, with the exception of Chile, there is a sizeable black population today. The essay presents a knowledgeable overview of the contributions of various cultures. The African component is not slighted. Many long notations, glossary, bibliography, discography, films, transcription of a guitar solo, photographs of instruments.

1279. **Olson, Howard S.**, comp. *Lead us on, Lord: a collection of African hymns.* Minneapolis: Augsburg, c1977. 22pp.
Hymns are in English. Music.

1280. **Omibìyí, Mosúnmọ́lá Àyìnkẹ́.** "Folk music and dance in African education." **INTERNATIONAL FOLK MUSIC COUNCIL. Yearbook** 4 (1972): 87-94.

1281. **Omibìyí, Mosúnmọ́lá Àyìnkẹ́.** "The gourd in Nigerian folk music." **NIGERIAN FIELD** vol. 48, no. 1-4 (1983): 30-53.
Bibliography, photographs.

1282. **Omibìyí, Mosúnmọ́lá Àyìnkẹ́.** "Human migration and diffusion of musical instruments in Nigeria. **INTERNATIONAL COMMITTEE ON URGENT ANTHROPOLOGICAL AND ETHNOLOGICAL RESEARCH. BULLETIN** 25 (1983): 77-93.
Map, bibliography, illustrations.

1283. **Omibìyí, Mosúnmọ́lá Àyìnkẹ́.** A MODEL OF AFRICAN MUSIC CURRICULUM FOR ELEMENTARY SCHOOLS IN NIGERIA. Dissertation, University of California, Los Angeles, 1972. 175pp.
Illustrations, music, bibliography.

O

1284. **Omibìyí, Mosúnmọ̀lá Àyìnkẹ́**. "Musical instruments as art objects." NIGERIAN FIELD vol. 51 (1986): 63-78.
References, photographs.

1285. **Omídèyí, Ọláolú**. "The place of traditional music in African society (with particular reference to Nigeria." In **African culture: Algiers Symposium July 21st - August 1st, 1969**. *The first Pan-African cultural festival*, 243-245. Alger: SNED (Société Nationale d'Édition et de Diffusion), 1969.
The author uses that unfortunate borrowed old term, "primitive," to refer to African music. He also refers to "higher cultural development," "upper classes," lower classes," and the like. Listed in the publication as "Musician," Omídèyí has an interesting theory involving conjunct and disjunct melody motion. He believes that conjunct melodies - meaning that the intervals are close together - are "dynamic and strongly emotional, full of excitement and tension, whereas disjunct melodies are more "'static' or restrained." He also considers these latter melodies with large skips to represent a "more advanced stratum than the former." (Has this man ever heard *Wozzeck*?)

1286. **Omondi, Washington A.** *An introduction to the music of the Luo I*. [Nairobi]: University of Nairobi, Institute of African Studies, 1971. 23pp. (Discussion paper - University of Nairobi, Institute of African Studies, no. 16)
After this first paper of Omondi's, on music of the Luo of Kenya, no more were published.

1287. **Omondi, Washington A.** "The lyre in Luo society: an observation." AFRICAN MUSICOLOGY 1, no.1 (1983): 41-44.
Bibliography.

1288. **Omondi, Washington A.** THUM: TRADITIONAL LYRE MUSIC OF THE LUO PEOPLE OF KENYA. Dissertation, London University, 1981. 650pp.

1289. **Omondi, Washington A**. "Tuning of the *thum*, the Luo lyre: a systematic analysis." In **Studies in African music**. Co-editors, J. H. Kwabena Nketia, and Jacqueline Cogdell DjeDje, 263-281. [Los Angeles]: Program in Ethnomusicology, Department of Music, University of California, Los Angeles, 1984. 387pp.
Illustrations, examples of pitch notations corresponding to *thum* strings, tables, notes, bibliography, map.

1290. **Opoku, A. A.** *Festivals of Ghana*. Accra: Ghana Publishing Corporation, 1970. 80pp.
This attractively executed book gives a realistic idea of how music operates within culture, a refreshing change from studies that abstract music from context. Ghana

is a country of many festivals, and twelve (from a total list of thirty-eight!) are explicated here. The African perspective is valuable. Music is mentioned in passing but is not given the attention some musicologists might have wanted. Included are excellent black and white photographs showing people participating in ceremonies in various ways. A few of the pictures show musicians. There are several talking drum translations into English. No index or bibliography.

1291. **Opoku-Boahen, Kwame.** SYMBOLIC AND REPRESENTATIONAL VALUES OF THE AKAN MUSIC IN GHANA. Master's Thesis, Washington University, 1985. 81pp.

1292. **Oppong, Christine.** "A note on a Dagomba chief's drummer." **RESEARCH REVIEW** 4, no. 2 (1968): 63-65.

1293. **The oral performance in Africa.** Edited by Isidore Okpewho. Ìbàdàn, Nigeria: Spectrum Books in association with Safari Books (Export), St. Helier, Jersey, Channel Islands, United Kingdom, 1990. 277pp.
This consists of a selection of papers presented at the Sixth Annual African Literature Conference held at Ìbàdàn University, July 27-August 1, 1988. Includes bibliographical references and index. Oral tradition, folk literature, and traditional African music were the subjects of the papers.

1294. **Oral poetry from Africa: an anthology.** Compiled by Jack Mapanje and Landeg White. Isidore Okpewho, Adviser. New York: Longman, 1983. (1984 printing). 216pp.
Bibliography.

1295. **Orin Yorùbá = Yorùbá songs,** by J. O. Ajíbọ̀lá. Preface by Akin Euba. 2d ed. Ilé-Ifẹ̀, Nigeria: University of Ifẹ̀ Press, c1974. 126pp.
A compilation of traditional and contemporary popular songs that also includes some of Chief Ajíbọ̀lá's original compositions. The first part comprises 38 sacred songs intended for Christian religious service. The second part contains 34 secular songs for assorted ceremonies and other social occasions. The songs, in from one to four parts with piano accompaniment, are all written in staff notation. The texts are in both Yorùbá and English.

1296. **Orpheus-Schriftenreihe zu Grundfagen der Musik.**
For entries in this series, see:
- **Engel, Hans.** *Die Stellung des Musikers im arabisch-islamischen Raum*, 1987.
- **Michels-Gebler, Ruth.** *Schmied und Musik: über die traditionelle Verknüpfung von Schmiedehandwerk und Musik in Afrika, Asien und Europa*, 1984.
- **Pilipczuk, Alexander.** *Elfenbeinhörner im sakralen Königtum Schwarzafrikas*, 1985.

O

1297. **Osei, W. A.** MUSICAL INSTRUMENTS AT TAFO PALACE [Ghana]. Master's Thesis. Kumasi, Ghana: University of Science and Technology, 1966. 91pp.
The main chapter headings are: Musical Instruments and their Description, Musical Examples and their Occasions, Conclusion - Summary.

Osiobe, Stephen A.
See: **Nigerian universities dissertation abstracts, 1178.**

1298. **Osorio, Oswaldo.** *Cantigas de trabalho: tradiçöes orais de Cabo Verde: recolha, transcrição, tradução, introdução, comentários, notas.* Comissão nacional para as Comemorações do 5 Aniversário da Independência de Cabo Verde. Praia: Platano Editora, [1980].

1299. **Osterland, David Conrad.** THE ANUAK TRIBE OF SOUTH WESTERN ETHIOPIA: A STUDY OF ITS MUSIC WITHIN THE CONTEXT OF ITS SOCIOCULTURAL SETTING. Dissertation, University of Illinois at Urbana-Champaign, 1978. 532pp.

1300. **Otieno, Samuel A.** *Africa's voices: Luo spirituals.* Nairobi, Kenya, African Centre for Technology Studies: Acts Press, 1990. 70pp.
A collection of five notated sacred choral arrangements and compositions by Samuel A. Otieno. In Dholuo and English, this represent a newer kind of dynamic music that draws, nonetheless, from traditional Luo musical idioms. The publisher claims that this is the first publication of choral works by a Kenyan composer.

1301. **Oven, Cootje van.** *An introduction to the music of Sierra Leone.* [Sponsored by the Minister for Development Co-Operation of the Netherlands.] [Wassenaar?]: C. van Oven, c1981. 85pp.
This is a vibrant, vital book containing texts to 49 songs and instrumental pieces, 76 handsome black and white plates, illustrations, and music notations. The book is intended for secondary schools and teachers' colleges in Sierra Leone. Seven chapters cover: Types of songs and instrumental pieces; Musical instruments; Singing style, phrasing and form; Rhythms; Scales on which the music is built; Part-singing; and How to do your own research. Accompanied by sound cassette. See also the following supplement, **1302.**

1302. **Oven, Cootje van.** *Supplement to An introduction to the music of Sierra Leone.* [Sponsored by the Minister for Development Co-operation of the Netherlands.] [Wassenaar?]: C. van Oven, c1982. 47pp.
The supplement has the same chapters as the preceding original book, with the exception of the last chapter. It also includes a sound cassette containing pieces not included on the cassette accompanying the original book. This handsomely

executed work is augmented by 16 fine black and white photographs showing instrumentalists at work. Six chapters cover all but the last chapter listed in the preceding original book. Written in a pleasing, communicative style. Brief music notations throughout.

1303. **Oyèṣakin, Adéfióyè.** *Yorùbá oral poetry for children as an aid to moral education.* [s.l.: s.n., 1984?]. 20pp.
In English. The first section discusses the importance of children in the life of Yorùbá people, and the concern there is for their moral, physical and spiritual development. The subject is oral poetry and songs used for teaching and socializing children - many used by children themselves against the deviating child. Some of the songs are intended to be performed by moonlight. This is part of a program existing at that time called, WAI (War against Indiscipline). Texts, no music. Bibliography.

P

1304. **PAIS BULLETIN**. 1915- . New York, N.Y.: Public Affairs Information Service, Inc.
Appears monthly. Indexes several journals entered in this bibliography. Formerly knows as **PUBLIC AFFAIRS INFORMATION SERVICE. BULLETIN**. Available online and on **CD-ROM**.

PEA (People's Educational Association of Sierra Leone)
See: **Stories and songs from Sierra Leone, 1513.**

1305. **Pacere Titinga**. *La poésie des griots*. 2d ed. Paris: Silex, c1982-1983. 113pp.
Song texts from Burkina Faso.

1306. **Paden, John N.** *Ahmadu Bello Sardauna of Sokoto: values and leadership in Nigeria*. Zaria: Hudahuda Publishing Company, 1986. 799pp.
The book concerns the impact of Ahmadu Bello, Premier of the Northern Region of Nigeria, during the years 1956 to 1966. Hausa praise poems written for him during his lifetime and upon his death are incorporated into the book (listed in an appendix). Primarily, they celebrate and glorify Ahmadu Bello's leadership qualities. Fifteen of the prominent poet-musicians who honored him appear in a table. Pages 31-34 contain information specifically on music, including the use of Hausa poetry and song as part of the political process, and the categories and roles of Hausa musician-poets. Traditional poetry sources are also given.

1307. **Paden, John N.** *Religion and political culture in Kano*. Berkeley: University of California Press. [1973]. 461pp.
Contains scattered references to the use of drums (*bandiri*) for Islamic worship services of the *Qādiriyyah* Brotherhood in Kano. Several references are to be found under Drumming in the index. Under Praise Poetry, there are also references to a few included poetry texts that are sung by poet/musicians (though there is no actual mention of music). No musical instruments are listed in the index.

Paden, John N.
See also: **The African experience, 35.**

1308. **Palmer, Robert**. "Introduction." [On African popular music] **AFROPOP WORLDWIDE: LISTENER'S GUIDE**. (1990): 4-7. Washington D.C., National Public Radio.

1309. **Panofsky, Hans E.** *A bibliography of Africana*. Westport, Connecticut: Greenwood Press, 1975. 350pp. (Contributions in Librarianship and Information Science, no. 11)
Hans E. Panofsky, Curator of Africana Emeritus, Northwestern University Library, is the author of this informative book. It is divided into six parts: The Study of Africa; Bibliographies and Serials; Guide to Resources by Subject and Discipline; Guide to Resources on Non-African Areas; Guide to Resources in

African Nations; and On Collecting and Disseminating Africana. The two pages of informative comments on music bibliographies, to which Hans Panofsky initially introduced me, helped to launch the present bibliography. Map, index.

1310. **PANTALEONI, HEWITT**
Upon Pantaleoni's death in 1988 a memorial essay was published, followed by a bibliography of Pantaleoni's written works and musical compositions. The essay, by David McAllester (**ETHNOMUSICOLOGY** 33, no. 2, 1989: 287-291) besides being a biography, also selects a few of Pantaleoni's memorable, and what McAllester calls "refreshing and sometimes startling" definitions and opinions. A smiling photo of the musicologist/composer prefaces the essay.

1311. **Pantaleoni, Hewitt**. "The possibility of objective rhythmic evidence for African influence in Afro-American music." In **The performing arts: music and dance**. Edited by John Blacking, and Joann W. Kealiinohomoku, 287-291. New York: Mouton, c1979.

1312. **Pantaleoni, Hewitt**. THE RHYTHM OF ATSIA DRUMMING AMONG THE ANLO (EVE) OF ANYAKO. Dissertation, Wesleyan University, 1972. 524pp.

Pantaleoni, Hewitt
See also: **Serwadda, W. Moses**. *Songs and stories from Uganda*, **1441**.

1313. **Panzacchi, Cornelia**. *Griot: seine Darstellung in der frankophonen westafrikanischen Literatur*. Rheinfelden, [Switzerland]: Schauble Verlag, 1990. 185pp. (Dritte Welt, 5)
Entirely in German. The focus is on the *griot* as depicted in West-African literature. There is little mention of music. The work is scholarly, with many footnotes. Table, map, bibliography, chronological list of relevant ethnological literature on the *griot* and the oral tradition.

1314. **Papers in African studies**. Legon: University of Ghana, Institute of African Studies, 1968. 80pp.
This is a valuable collection of essays on African music by highly esteemed musicologists, perhaps not so widely known as it should be because of the non-informative title. Listed in alphabetical order below:
•**Aning, Ben A.** "Melodic analysis of Adenkum," 64-80.
•**Aning, Ben A.** "Wangara xylophone and its music," 57-63.
•**Laing, E.** "Regulative beat and phrase duration in Ghanaian songs," 53-56.
•**Mensah, A. A.** "The *gyilgo* - a Gonja sansa," 35-41.
•**Mensah, A. A.** "The source of the Kurubidwe - a song type in Chokosi," 42-52.
•**Nayo, N. Z.** "Akpalu and his songs," 24-34.
•**Nketia, J. H. Kwabena**. "The instrumental resources of African music," 1-23.

1315. **Pareles, Jon**. "Introduction." [On African popular music] **AFROPOP WORLDWIDE: LISTENER'S GUIDE**. (1989): 2-5. Washington D.C., National Public Radio.

P

1316. **Parker, Judith Wirthlin.** EGYPTIAN MUSIC: AN HISTORICAL STUDY WITH CURRICULUM MODEL FOR AMERICAN ELEMENTARY GRADES. Dissertation, University of Utah, 1979. 283pp.

Patel, Essop
See: **Umhlaba wethu, 1602.**

Paudrat, Jean-Louis
See: •**Huet, Michel**. *The dance, art, and ritual of Africa*, **697.**
•**Huet, Michel**. *Danses d'Afrique*, **698.**

1317. **p'Bitek, Okot.** *Song of Lawino: a lament.* [Translation of *Wer pa Lawino* by the author]. Nairobi, East African Publishing House, 1966. 216pp.
This is a long prose poem drawing from traditional proverbs, songs, and oral narratives of the Acholi. Interwoven song fragments and dance descriptions convey the major role of song and dance. Using the inspired technique of word-for-word translation, an oral song has been artfully conveyed to print, and the satiric song, a traditional medium of expression among the Acholi, has been transformed to make unambiguous statements about neo-colonial forces holding Africa back, and the need to reinstate traditional African values. The theme, "Let no one uproot the pumpkin," from a traditional Acholi song, appears again and again.

1317a. **p'Bitek, Okot.**
Following are a few related works by this author based on Acholi oral tradition, and written in Acholi or other languages. (They are not entries in this bibliography)
•**The horn of my love.**
•**Song of a prisoner.**
•**Song of Malaya.**
•**Song of Ocol**, and others.

Pearson, J. D.
See: **International African bibliography, 1973-1978. (729)**

1318. **Peek, Philip M., R. Dogbu, and N. E. Owheibor**, trans. "*Isoko* and *ijaw* songs." **BLACK ORPHEUS** no. 22 (1976): 4-5.

Peek, Philip M.
See also: **Indiana University, Bloomington. Archives of Traditional Music, 723, 724.**

People's Educational Association of Sierra Leone
See: **Stories and songs from Sierra Leone, 1513.**

1319. Pepper, Herbert. "La notion d'unité, notion clé de l'expression nègre-africaine." In **Colloque sur l'art nègre**. Rapports. Vol. 1 (1967): 231-241. [Paris: Présence africaine]

1320. Pepper, Herbert. "The notion of unity: the key to Negro-African expression." In **Colloquium on Negro Art, Dakar, 1966**, 223-232. Organized by the Society of African Culture (S.A.C.) [Paris: Présence africaine, 1968]

Pepper, Herbert
See also: **Un Mvet, 1144.**

1321. PERCUSSIONIST. 1961- . Urbana, Illinois: Percussive Arts Society, Incorporated.
There are six issues a year, and a cumulative index. Available as microform, or as reprints from **UMI**. There are occasional articles on African percussion. Three have been selected, below. Indexed by **RILM, MUSIC INDEX**. This journal was formerly called **PERCUSSIVE NOTES**.
•**Avorgbedor, Daniel**. "Double bell techniques among the Anlo-Ewe of Ghana," vol. 20, no. 2 (1981): 77-80.
•**Bakan, M.** "West African drum languages," vol. 24, no. 2 (1986): 29-30.
•**Locke, David**. "The rhythm of Takai," 23, no. 4 (1985): 51-54.

PERCUSSIVE NOTES
See: **PERCUSSIONIST, 1321.**

1322. Pérez, Fernández, Rolando Antonio. *La binarizacion de los ritmos ternarios Africanos en América Latina.* Ciudad de la Habana, Cuba: Casa de las Américas, 1986. 139pp.
In Spanish. Pérez gives an historical background of studies of African influence on Latin American music, finding African rhythms throughout Latin America, not just near original sites where slaves toiled. The main concentration is on rhythm and documenting what Pérez calls "binarization," a process that modifies what he identifies as basically "ternary" African rhythms. Use of the term "ternary," however, which is a Western concept growing out of a monometric rhythmic system with regularly recurring accents, seems an unwarranted generalization when applied wholesale to African music, especially when so much African music is polymetric and without regularly recurring accents. Bibliography, notations, maps.

1323. Performance in contemporary African arts. Edited by Ruth M. Stone. [Bloomington, Indiana]: African Studies Program, Indiana University, 1988. 139pp.
Includes bibliographies, illustrations, and information on African music.

1324. Performance practice: ethnomusicological perspectives. Edited by Gerard Béhague. Westport, Connecticut: Greenwood Press,

c1984. 262pp. (Contributions in intercultural and comparative studies, no. 12)
Béhague's introduction is a general essay on ethnomusicology. Five exceptionally fine and long essays are included, an index, and brief notes on contributors. There are many music transcriptions, song texts, charts, but no photographs. Each essay has a solid bibliography. The three items of especial interest are:
- **Béhague, Gerard**. "Patterns of Candomblé music performance: an Afro-Brazilian religious setting," 222-254.
- **Knight, Roderic**. "Music in Africa: the Manding contexts," 53-90.
- **Schuyler, Philip D**. "Berber professional musicians in performance," 91-148.

1325. **The performing arts: music and dance**. Edited by John Blacking, and Joann W. Kealiinohomoku. New York: Mouton, c1979. (World anthropology)
This represents a collection of papers submitted to the performing-arts sessions of the 9th International Congress of Anthropological and Ethnological Sciences, Chicago, 1973. There is a Preface by Sol Tax, and an Introduction by Blacking in which he briefly discusses the papers that follow. The book itself has a subject and name index, and biographical notes on the authors. Most papers have their own bibliographical notes, and assorted charts, line drawings, graphs, but no photographs. A wide range of subjects are covered, and cultures from all over the world are treated. Following are essays relating to African music:
- **Kauffman, Robert**. "Tactility as an aesthetic consideration in African music," 251-253.
- **Kubik, Gerhard**. "Pattern perception and recognition in African music," 221-249.
- **Moore, Joseph G**. "Music and dance as expressions of religious worship in Jamaica," 293-318.
- **Okoreaffia, C. O**. "*Igeri Ututu*: an Igbo folk requiem music dance ritual," 265-276.
- **Pantaleoni, Hewitt**. "The possibility of objective rhythmic evidence for African influence in Afro-American music," 287-291.
- **Seaton, S. Lee, and Karen Ann Watson**. "Continuity and discontinuity in song styles: an ordinal cross-cultural classification," 93-107.
- **Sithole, Elkin M. T**. "*Ngoma* music among the Zulu," 277-285.

1326. **Perspectives on African music**. Edited by Wolfgang Bender. Bayreuth, Germany: Bayreuth University, c1989. 139pp. (Bayreuth African studies series, 9)
In English and German. Bibliographies, discographies, photographs. Includes nearly all of the papers presented at a colloquium on African music organized by Bender in 1984. Following are the essays, arranged alphabetically by last name:
- **Bender, Wolfgang**. "Ebenezer Calender: an appraisal," 43-68. (Note: In some publications, this name appears as "Ebenezar Calendar.")
- **Harrev, Fleming**. "Jambo records and the promotion of popular music in East Africa: the story of Otto Larsen East African Records Ltd. 1952-1963," 103-137.
- **Johnson, Alex**. "Transcription and translation of Ebenezer Calender's repertoire list," 70-90.

continued

•**Johnson, Rótìmí**. "The language and content of Nigerian popular music," 91-102.
•**Kubik, Gerhard**. "Afrikanische Musik, ideologischer Kolonialismus und Identitätskrise der Zöglingsgeneration 1945-1970," 7-24.
•**Simon, Artur**. "Musical traditions, Islam and cultural identity in the Sudan," 25-42.

1327. **Petersen, Alvin Benito**. AFRICAN MUSIC AND ITS USE IN THE SCHOOL: AN INVESTIGATION. Master's Thesis, University of Cape Town (South Africa), 1981.

1328. **Pevar, Susan Gunn**. "Teach-in: the Gambian *kora*." **SING OUT: THE FOLK SONG MAGAZINE** 25 (1977): 15-17.

1329. **Pike, Charles A.** THE LUYIA *OLUKANO*. Dissertation, University of Wisconsin, Madison, 1981. 325pp.
The Luyia *olukano* is a formal medium of communication among the Luyia-speaking peoples of western Kenya. Its fundamental nature is a narrative movement from conflict to resolution, but it also includes songs or chants, the creation and interrelationship of images, audience participation and rhythm. It includes wide varieties of themes that relate to important aspects of peoples' lives. Bibliography. **(UMI)**

1330. **Pilipczuk, Alexander**. *Elfenbeinhörner im sakralen Königtum Schwarzafrikas*. Bonn: Verlag für Systematische Musikwissenschaft, 1985. 136pp. (Band 42 of Orpheus-Schriftenreihe zu Grundfragen der Musik)
On subSaharan musical instruments. Wind instruments. Bibliography. Index.

1331. **Pius Ngandu Nkashama**. "La chanson de la rupture dans la musique du Zaïre." In **Chansons d'Afrique et des Antilles**, 63-75. Paris: Harmattan, c1988.
In French. A critical evaluation of social conditions in Zaïre as manifested by contemporary song. The author examines the themes of song texts, as well as the people who sing them. He uses the term "rupture" to signify the breaking away from traditional values and cultural history, and regards the music as a representation of the "social crisis" in Zaïre. The music does not evoke, he says, but diverts, and, at its limits, "perverts." He speaks of "the languages of the new Churches surging in the country" as better indicating the path of the rupture.

1332. **Plumley, Gwendolen Alice**. *El tanbur: the Sudanese lyre or the Nubian kissar*. Cambridge: Town and Gown Press, c1976. 70pp.
Concerns Nubian and Sudanese lyres. Illustrations, map, music.

P

1333. **Polfliet, Leo.** *Bodies of resonance: musical instruments of Zaïre = Resonanz-Korper: Musikinstrumente aus Zaïre.* Münich: F. and J. Jahn, c1985. 71pp.
Musical instruments of Zaïre. In German and English. Illustrations, map.

Pommerol, Patrice Julien de
See: **Contes et chants du Tchad, 377.**

1334. **Pongweni, Alec J. C.** *Songs that won the liberation war.* Foreword by C. S. Banana. [Harare, Zimbabwe]: College Press, [1982]. 167pp.
Revolutionary songs and ballads of Zimbabwe. Text in English, Ndebele, and Shona. Bibliography.

1335. POPULAR MUSIC. 1982 - . New York: Cambridge University Press.
Since 1987, published three times a year. This is a scholarly journal that provides, multi-disciplinary coverage of all aspects of popular music; musicology, literary studies, sociology, economics, and social history. Contains music, illustrations, and articles pertinent to this bibliography. Two issues a year cover *all* aspects of popular music. The third issue is thematic, as, for example, Volume 8, no. 3 (1989) on African music, and Volume 10, no. 1 (1991), the "John Blacking Issue." The African issue contains a selected discography, bibliography, and essays by prominent names in the field of African urban music. Indexed in **MUSIC INDEX**.

1336. **Porter, Dorothy Burnett.** *Afro-Braziliana: a working bibliography.* Boston: G. K. Hall, c1978. 294pp.
This is the most impressive bibliographic source for African influence on Brazilian culture seen to date. Entries tend to be of older materials, and consist of books, pamphlets, and periodical articles not apt to be easily obtainable outside Brazil. Part 1 is organized into subject headings, such as social conditions and race relations, history, folklore, African influence on Brazilian Portuguese, to name but a few. Part 2 lists writings by selected authors, with critical and bibliographical references. There are twelve vital pages under the sensible, combined heading: Music, Dance and Carnival. Comprehensive and careful. Occasional annotations, maps, index.

1337. **Póvoas, Ruy do Carmo.** *A linguagem do candomblé: níveis sociolingüisticos de integração afro-portuguesa.* Rio de Janeiro, RJ-Republica Federativa do Brasil: J. Olympio Editora, c1989
This was originally the author's dissertation at the Universidade Federal do Rio de Janeiro, in 1983. The terminology of Candomblé is the subject. There are occasionally references to the musical aspects of Candomblé, particularly in the section entitled, Reflexos Culturais no Português do Brasil, which includes some poetic texts having close affinities to music, and references to instruments. In general, however, the book only grazes the subject of music. The lengthy glossary of Candomblé terms is impressive, and does include some music-related terms, primarily in Yorùbá (with diacritical faithfulness). Discography, bibliography.

1338. **Powe, Edward L.** HAUSA COMBAT LITERATURE: AN EXPOSITION, ANALYSIS AND INTERPRETATION OF ITS FORM, CONTENT, AND EFFECT. Dissertation, University of Wisconsin-Madison, 1984. 626pp.

Powe defines Hausa combat literature as, "the aggregate of highly stylized linguistic behavior associated with the performance of such Hausa competition as *dambe* (local boxing), *shanci* (wristlet fighting), and *farauta* (hunting)." The study ends with the suggestion that "perhaps the hitherto mysterious and unexplained effects of poetry and song upon modern man may possibly be viewed as the subliminal survival of a former belief that reality could be shaped and influenced through the practice of sympathetic magic." Maps, bibliography. **(UMI)**

1339. **Powe, Edward L.**, comp. *Hausa studies: a select bibliography of B.A., M.A., and Ph.D. papers available in Northern Nigerian universities.* Revised edition. [Madison, Wisconsin: African Studies Program, University of Wisconsin], 1983. 29pp.

On pages 15 to 17, under Oral Literature, subheading, Songs, there are 40 entries. Almost all of the theses listed were completed for the Bachelor of Arts degree, and are in Hausa. A useful reference tool. Indexed.

1340. **Powne, J. Michael F.** SOME ASPECTS OF INDIGENOUS COPTIC AND ETHIOPIAN MUSIC. Master's Thesis, University of Durham, 1964.

1341. **The praises of Dingana (Izibongo zikaDingana).** Edited by D. K. Rycroft, and A. B. Nycobo. Durban [South Africa]: Killie Campbell Africana Library; Pietermaritzburg South Africa: University of Natal Press, 1988. 258pp. (Killie Campbell Africana Library publications, no. 3)

This is a collection of praise poetry for the Zulu king, Dingana, who reigned from 1828 to 1840. Even though Zulus do not themselves categorize *izibongo* as music, there are a number of reasons (see pages 54 to 69), involving phenomena of pitch, tempo, pause and style, that warrant inclusion in this bibliography. Pitches are notated on a treble staff, and analyzed in other ways. Comparisons are made of various realizations of the *izibongo* based upon recordings listed at the end of the book, and covering 1927-1976. These recordings are transcribed and translated, with commentary in English. Index. Bibliography.

1342. **PRÉSENCE AFRICAINE: REVUE CULTURELLE DU MONDE NOIR**. New Series 1947- . Paris, France: Société Nouvelle Présence Africaine.

Issued quarterly, text in English and French. A likely source through the years for articles on African music. Indexed in **MLA, CURRENT CONTENTS AFRICA, CERDIC** (now ceased), and others listed in **ULRICH'S**. See also the entry for the book that indexes 1947-1972 of this publication, under the author's name, **Òjó-Adé, Fẹ́mi (1262)**. It appears as though articles on African music were more apt to appear in the earlier issues. Several randomly selected articles follow:

•**Jones, A. M.** "Instruments de musique africains," vols 6-7. nos. 34-35 (1961): 132-150.

•**Kotchy, B. Nguessan**. "Fonction sociale de la musique traditionelle," no. 93 (1975): 80-91.

•**Shelton, Austin S.** "The problem of *griot* interpretation and the actual cause of war in Sondjata," no. 66 (1968): 145-152.

1343. Price, Christine. *Talking drums of Africa.* New York: Scribner [1973].
Juvenile literature. A rhythmic interpretation of how African drums are made, and how they serve the Yorùbá and Ashanti cultures.

1344. Price, Sally, and Richard Price. *Afro-American arts of the Suriname Rain Forest.* Los Angeles: Museum of Cultural History, University of California; Berkeley: University of California, c1980. 237pp.
Really a sensitive, informed, probing ethnological study, though also a pictorially beautiful book about the arts of the Maroons of Suriname, descendants of African slaves who escaped from coastal plantations in the seventeenth and eighteenth centuries and set up new societies and cultures in the rain forest. The Prices ensconced themselves in a Saramaka village for two years, returned five times. Though visual arts fill the book, music and dance receive notice in Chapter 6, entitled, Performance. Pages 35, 36, 38, 40, 41 also have information on music. There are breath-taking old and new photographs, extensive notes, bibliography.

1345. Prince, Rob. "Baaba Maal talks to Rob Prince about the importance of traditional music." In **FOLK ROOTS** no. 95 (1991): 34-37.
Baaba Maal is a popular Senegalese musician.

1346. Proceedings of a sesquicentennial conference on human development: held at the Institute of International Relations, University of the West Indies, St. Augustine, 30th July to 1st August 1984. Edited by Max B. Ifill. Port of Spain, Trinidad: Economic and Business Research, 1989. 193pp.
A rather unexpected twosome. The bipartite conference had as its themes, slavery, and calypso music of Trinidad and Tobago.

PUBLIC AFFAIRS INFORMATION SERVICE. BULLETIN
See: **PAIS BULLETIN, 1304.**

1347. Publications Ceeba. Série 2. Zaïre. (Publications du Centre d'études ethnologiques)
The following volumes of this series have been selected for listing because of their references to African music. (There may be others.)

•**Chants mongo,** vol. 76.

continued

•**Darkowska-Nidzgorska, Olenka**. *Théâtre populaire de marionnettes en Afrique sub-saharienne*, vol. 60.
•**Hulstaert, G.** *Berceuses mongo*, vol. 36..
•**Hulstaert, G.** *Chansons de danse mongo*, vol. 78.
•**Instrumente de musique de Gandajika**, vol. 35/2.
•**Ize-Senze**. *Symbolique verbale et rituelle chez les Sakata, Lele, Wong, Kuba, Lulua, Mbole et Vira*, vol. 93.
•**Je désire danser!**, vol. 49.
•**Müller, Alfons**. *La musique Zaïroise*, vol. 54-55.
•**Nidzgorski, Denis**. *Arts du spectacle africain*, vol. 48.
•**Voilà la nouvelle lune!**, vol. 44.

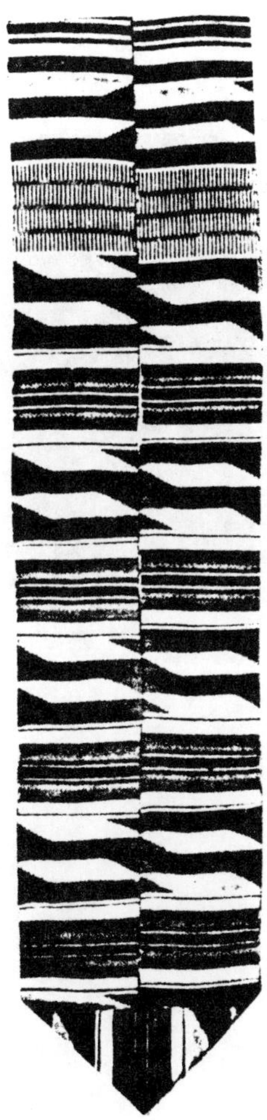

Q

1348. **Quarcoo, A. K.** "African civilization and the performing arts." In **The arts and civilization of Black and African peoples**. Edited by Joseph Ohiomogben Okpaku, Alfred Esimatemi Opubor, and Benjamin Ọlátúnjí Ọlọ́runtìmẹ̀hìn, Volume 1: 35-53. Lagos: Centre for Black and African Arts and Civilization, c1986.

The section entitled, The Arts, Dance and Theatre and African Culture, contains a kernel of information on Ghanaian *Klama* (a musical type), and a significant quotation by Mawere Opuku, artist director of the Ghana Dance Ensemble, who speaks of the primacy of Dance in African society, and the vital role of drum and choral ensembles in what he calls the "Drama of Life." "Life to us with its rhythms and cycles," he says, "is Dance." Bibliography, but nothing on music.

1349. RE. 1968- . Vienna, Austria: Institut für Völkerkunde.
This journal, originally called **RESEARCH REVIEW,** appears semi-monthly, and contains book reviews, charts, indexes. It is indexed in **AICP**. Articles by Mensah, Kubik, Blacking, Rycroft, and other luminaries have appeared in past issues. More recent issues were not examined.

1350. **Raab, Claus**. "Afrikanische Musik." In **Institut für neue Musik und Musikerziehung Darmstadt.** *Musik fremder Kulturen: 5 einfuhrende Studien.* Edited by Rudolf Stephan, 66-108. Mainz: Schott, 1977.
In German. The essay is accompanied by footnotes, music notations, a chart, and bibliography in two sections.

1351. **Raab, Claus**. *Trommelmusik der Hausa in Nord-West-Nigeria.* Münich, Kommissionsverlag Klaus Renner, 1970. 249pp.
Drum music of the Hausa of Northwest Nigeria. Bibliography, music.

1352. **Racy, Ali Jihad** ['Alī Jihād]. "The impact of commercial recording on the musical life of Egypt, 1904-1932." **ESSAYS IN ARTS AND SCIENCES** 6, No. 1, March 1977. (Special issue)

1353. **Racy, Ali Jihad** ['Alī Jihād]."Music in nineteenth-century Egypt: an historical sketch." **SELECTED REPORTS IN ETHNOMUSICOLOGY** 4 (1983b): 157-179.
Detailed notes and a bibliography with many entries, a good portion of which are in Arabic. The illustrations are fascinating: photographs of instruments from a source book published in 1823, portraits of musicians of the past, a photograph of the Cairo Opera House, 1969.

1354. **Racy, Ali Jihad** ['Alī Jihād]. MUSICAL CHANGE AND COMMERCIAL RECORDING IN EGYPT, 1904-1932. Dissertation, University of Illinois at Urbana-Champaign, 1977. 373pp.
Between 1904 and 1932 commercial sound recordings played a complex musical role in Egypt, according to Racy. He outlines this role as a "network of interaction among 3 entities: the live music, the record industry, and the recorded music." After the Introduction, the chapters are entitled: Changes in the Musical Life of Modern Egypt, The Origins and Development of Commercial Recording in Egypt, The Impact of Recording on Musical Life, Musical Change in the Recorded Qaṣtdah, and Conclusion. Included are a bibliography, disk catalog, transcriptions, tables, and photographs.

1355. **Racy, Ali Jihad** ['Alī Jihād]. "Sound and society: the *Takht* music of early-twentieth century Cairo." **SELECTED REPORTS IN ETHNOMUSICOLOGY** 4 (1983a): 157-179.
This article is an attempt to understand the connections between professional music-makers as a social group and the music they perform. *Tahmila Rast Suznak*, transcribed in this paper, is included in the cassette that accompanies the

entire volume. It was recorded in Egypt and released as a 78 rpm disk by Columbia around 1927. Photographs of musicians, brief notations, the transcription (cited above), notes, and bibliography.

1356. **Racy, Ali Jihad** ['Alī Jihād]. "The Waṣlah: a compound-form principle in Egyptian music." **ARAB STUDIES QUARTERLY** 5, No. 4 (1983B): 396-403.

1357. **Rácz, István, and P. Hugo Huber.** *Die Antilopenfrau: Lieder und Märchen zu den Lebenszeiten, Bildwerke und Gesänge aus Westafrika.* Olten, Urs Graf-Verlag [c1965]. 60pp. (Dreiklang Test, Bild, Ton, Volume 8)
Illustrations, and phonodisc in pocket.

1358. **Rakotomala, Mireille.** *Bibliographie critique d'intérêt ethnomusicologique sur la musique malagasy.* Isoraka, Antananarivo: Musée d'art et d'archéologie de l'Université de Madagascar, 1986. 107pp. (Travaux et documents/Musée d'art et d'archéologie de l'Université de Madagascar, 23)
A critical bibliography of the music of Madagascar. Includes indexes, a map.

1359. **Rakotoson, Michéle.** "Dix ans de chanson à Madagascar." In **Chansons d'Afrique et des Antilles**, 99-106. Paris: Harmattan, c1988.

1359a. **Ramón y Rivera, Luis Felipe.** "El mestizaje de la Música Afro-Venezolano." In **Music in the Americas**. Edited by George List and Juan Orrego-Salas, 176-182. [Bloomington]: Indiana University Research Center in Anthropology, Folklore and Linguistics, 1967.
Contains many notations.

Randel, Don Michael
See: **The new Harvard dictionary of music, 1163.**

1360. **Raphael, Allison.** "From popular culture to microenterprise: the history of Brazilian Samba Schools." **REVISTA DE MÚSICA LATINAMERICANO: LATIN AMERICAN MUSIC REVIEW** 11, no. 1 (1990): 73-83.

1361. **Rashīd, Bahijah Ṣidqī.** *Egyptian folk songs in Arabic and English.* New York: Oak, 1964.
The author does not consider his work to be a scientific study. He expresses its purpose as an effort to preserve a folklore that is fast-disappearing.

1362. **Rattray, R. S.** *Some folk-lore stories and songs in Chinyanja, with English translation and notes.* Preface by Alexander Hetherwick. New York: Negro Universities Press [1969]. 224pp.
This is a reprint of the 1907 edition.

1363. **Readings in Black American music.** Compiled and edited by Eileen Southern. 2d ed. New York: W. W. Norton, c1983.
The book starts with accounts by Richard Jobson, Mungo Park and Thomas Edward Bowdich, early British travelers to Africa, of their on-the-site observations of African music and music practices. (Bowdich went so far as to notate some of the music he heard.) Distorted though these accounts may be, they are nevertheless valuable - even spellbinding. Furthermore, it is a great convenience to find them all in one place. Early chapters are particularly informative about African continuities manifested on the plantation, in music, dance, and celebration. The index leads directly to many significant references to African music. An important book.

1364. **RECHERCHE, PÉDAGOGIE ET CULTURE**. Paris: AUDECAM.
This journal continued **DOSSIERS PÉDAGOGIQUES**. Date of first issue was not determinable at time of writing, but final issue was December, 1984.
It was issued bimonthly. Examples follow:
•**Augier, Pierre**. "La musicologie africaine à l'Institut National des Arts d'Abidjan," no. 65-66 (1984): 55-63.
•**Ngumu, Pie-Claude**. "Les recherches ethnomusicologiques en Afrique Centrale: le cas du Cameroun," no. 65-66 (1984): 64-69.

1365. **Redina, José.** *Instrumentos musicais de Angola: sua construção: notas históricas e etno-sociológicas da música angolana.* Coimbra: Instituto de Antropologia, 1984. 230pp. (Publicações do Centro de Estudos Africanos, no. 3)
Musical instruments of Angola. Includes bibliographies. Entirely in Portuguese.

THE REGGAE AND AFRICAN BEAT
See: **THE BEAT, 190.**

1366. **Repercussions: a celebration of African-American music.** Edited by Geoffrey Haydon and Dennis Marks. London: Century Publications, 1985. 192pp.
A splendid collection of essays (abstracted in **RILM** 1985, and reviewed in **KESKIDEE** 1, 1986). The book is based on the British RM Arts and Channel Four television series, *Repercussions.* Haydon's introduction describes formative stages in the development of the film project. Mark's "Afterword" makes the point that any African links to music beyond the continent may be so distant and modified that these musics should be regarded as indigenous, and "resonant" culture"[s] in their own right. There is an index, abundant black and white photographs, notes on the authors. (Available as a videorecording also.) Essays have bibliographies, discographies. Four concerned specifically with Africa follow:

R

- **Bilby, Kenneth**. "Caribbean crucible," 128-151.
- **Chernoff, John Miller**. "Africa come back: the popular music of West Africa," 152-178.
- **Chernoff, John Miller**. "The drums of Dagbon," 101-127.
- **Jatta, Sidia**. "Traditional music from the Gambia," 14-29.

1367. RESEARCH REVIEW. 1965, new series, vol. 1, 1985- . Legon,. Ghana: University of Ghana, Institute of African Studies.

Originally, until 1985, there were three issues a year. Now there are only two. Publication was suspended 1982-1984, and volume 10, no. 2-3, and volume 11 were never published. This is a rich resource for essays on African music. Examples:

- **Fiagbedzi, Nission**. "Notes on membranophones of the Anlo-Ewe," vol. 8, no. 1 (1971): 90-97.
- **Mensah, Atta Annan**. "Musicality and musicianship in North-Western Ghana," vol. 2, no. 1 (1965): 42-45.
- **Oppong, Christine**. "A note on a Dagomba chief's drummer," vol. 4, no. 2 (1968): 63-65.
- **Turkson, Adolphus Acquah Robertson**. "Evolution of the Fante sacred lyric," vol. 9, no. 3 (1973): 1-12.

REVIEW OF ETHNOLOGY
See: **RE, 1349.**

1368. REVISTA DE MÚSICA LATINAMERICANO: LATIN AMERICAN MUSIC REVIEW. 1980 - . Austin, Texas: University of Texas Press.

Issued semiannually. Articles are in English, Portuguese, or Spanish. Available on microform from **UMI**, which also provides reprint services. Indexed in **CURRENT CONTENTS, MLA, RILM, MUSIC INDEX, ARTS AND HUMANITIES CITATION INDEX**. Not yet examined in depth, but there are certain to be key materials here. One example follows:

- **Raphael, Alison**. "From popular culture to microenterprise: the history of Brazilian Samba Schools," vol. 11, no. 1 (1990): 73-83.

1369. REVUE DE MUSICOLOGIE. 1917- . Paris, France: Société Française de Musicologie.

Issued semi-annually. Even though a superficial examination of more recent issues might seem to indicate that the focus is primarily on Western art music, the journal's track record actually reveals that quite a good number of important and fine articles on African music have appeared throughout the years. Available on microform through **UMI**, which also provides reprint services. It is indexed in **CURRENT CONTENTS, RILM, MUSIC INDEX**, and **ARTS AND HUMANITIES CITATION INDEX**. Examples follow:

- **Arom, Simha**. "La 'mémoire collective' dans les musiques traditionnelles d'Afrique Centrale," vol. 76, no. 2 (1990): 149-162.
- **Rouget, Gilbert**. "Sur les xylophones équiheptaphoniques des Malinke," vol. 55, no. 1 (1969): 47-77.
- **Rouget, Gilbert**. "Tons de la langue en Gun (Dahomey) et tons du tambour," vol. 50, no. 128 (1964): 3-29.

1370. **Rhodes, Willard.** "La musique noire dans le nouveau monde." In **La musique dans la vie, étude realisée sous les auspices l'Ocora et sous la direction de Tolia Nikiprowetzky**, 25-41. Vol. 2. Paris, Office de coopération radiophoniques, 1967.
Overviews New World black music, looking always to Africa as the source for characteristic features. Footnotes, song texts, music transcriptions.

1371. **Ribeiro, José.** *Tambores d'África.* Rio de Janeiro, RJ: Editora-Ezpiritualista, [197-?]. 231pp.
In Portuguese. Despite the title, not about drums or even much about music, though a great deal about African-related religions in Brazil is included. The individual characteristics of the *orisha* [Yorùbá = Òrìṣà] are given, along with their chants. There is brief mention of instruments used in ceremonies and the characteristics of associated rhythms.

1372. **RILM ABSTRACTS OF MUSIC LITERATURE.** 1967- . New York: Association of Music Libraries. (International Repertory of Music Literature)
One of the most useful sources available for researching music in general, and African and New World music in particular - not only articles that appear regularly in standard periodicals, such as **ETHNOMUSICOLOGY**, and **AFRICAN MUSIC**, but also abstracts of conferences, *Festschriften*, collected works, and obscure papers from far corners of the earth, always translated into English. Appears quarterly, available online. Volumes lag markedly behind actual dates - 1986 was issued in 1991 - but plans are afoot to produce two volumes a year in the future. No matter how long the delay, **RILM** is always well worth the wait. May they find an angel!

1373. **Rinzler, Paul E.** "LAYERS," AN ORIGINAL COMPOSITION FOR WIND ENSEMBLE BASED ON AFRICAN RHYTHM. Dissertation, University of Northern Colorado, 1988. 198pp.
The composition, *Layers*, is constructed according to principles of African rhythm, i.e., polyrhythm, additive rhythm, a fixed time-background, and repetition. The African Dance Ensembles, analyzed in A. M. Jones book, *Studies in African music*, was used as a role-model to illustrate the essentials of African polyrhythm. **(UMI)**

1374. **Risério, Antônio.** *Carnaval Ijexá: notas sobre afoxés e blocos do novo carnaval afro-baiano.* Salvador [Brazil]: Corrupio, 1981. 156pp. (Baianada, 2)
In Portuguese. Not an abundance of information on the music itself, but the book conveys a good deal of the *affect* of the Bahian carnival, in which African-influenced music and dance are essential. Includes Afro-Bahian poetry. No bibliography or index.

1375. **Roberts, Doris.** *Music and dance periodicals: an international directory and guidebook.* Voorheesville, New
continued

York: Peri Press, 1989. 382pp.
A most useful reference book intended to provide comprehensive coverage of periodicals in the fields of music and dance. Brief annotations. Only those issued at least once yearly are included. Material is subdivided into close to 20 subject headings. Musicology and Ethnomusicology lists periodicals pertinent to this bibliography, but related entries can be found elsewhere. Indexes are by Title, Publisher and Organization, Subject, Country of Publication, and ISSN number. Subject index had only 2 entries under Africa Music, and these did not include that major periodical, *African Music*, listed in another section. Careful scouring for likely entries, therefore, is recommended.

1376. **Roberts, John Storm**. *Black music of two worlds*. New York: Original Music, 1982. 286pp. (First published in 1974 by William Morrow)
A remarkable - even monumental! - book. The good news is that it once more is available, and now includes photographs from the original hardback. Recognized as a classic, this book asserts its worth by appearing in the bibliographies of countless prestigious publications. It still may be the only book on black music of *all* the Americas. Covers the Caribbean, South, Central and North America, from neo-African music to soul, salsa and "Sparrow," as well as the early days of "Afropop." Contains an almost overwhelming amount of information, casually tossed off by an extremely well-informed musicologist who thinks globally.

1377. **Roberts, John Storm**. *The Latin tinge: the impact of Latin American Music on the United States*. New York: Original Music, 1985. 246pp.
A much-needed book on a neglected subject, with countless examples of the prefix "Afro" followed by a hyphen, and frequently, the word "Cuban." Two important parts of the book for Africanists are: **1**, the much-welcome Glossary, which explains with authority major terms relating to Latin dances, instruments, and other music-related terms (a number of listed items pertain directly to Africa), and **2**, the first chapter, Roots, which contains basic information on the African tinge superimposed on the Latin one. Roberts discusses how resistant Latin American forms are to being "pinned down." Discography, bibliography, index. Fascinating photos.

Roberts, John Storm
See also: **WORLD MUSIC CATALOG, 1687.**

1378. **Robinson, Adjai**. *Singing tales of Africa*. Retold by Adjai Robinson. Illustrated by Christine Price. New York: C. Scribner's Sons [c1974]. 80pp.
Includes seven singing tales primarily from West Africa. A few measures of some melodies are notated. There are five pages of notes about the tales, passed along by the author's mother and grandmother. The bold illustrations all but dance across the page or leap from it. The author mentions the importance of song and dance in African storytelling, that some action stories tell *themselves* in song and body.

1379. **Robinson, Gertrude Roberts.** "Moods for Flute and Piano." In **African musicology: current trends: a festschrift presented to J. H. Kwabena Nketia.** Edited by Jacqueline Cogdell DjeDje, and William G. Carter, 321-331. [Atlanta, Georgia: Crossroads Press, 1988]- .

This composition, dedicated to J. H. Kwabena Nketia, is printed in entirety in his *festschrift*. Ethnomusicologist Robinson says that new dimensions and insights were added to her musical understanding as a result of hearing Nketia's lectures, reading his publications, and hearing some of his early piano compositions. She is grateful for his assistance in securing Ghanaian master drummers to teach at UCLA. In her work, *Mood II*, there is a place for a guitarist to improvise in the "manner of a West African drummer."

1380. **Robinson, J.** "African aesthetics and its implication for institutionalized music education in Black South African schools. 56-58. In **Symposium on Ethnomusicology.** (3rd: 1982: University of Natal) [4th: 1983: Rhodes University] *Papers presented at the Third and Fourth Symposia on Ethnomusicology*, Music Department, University of Natal, Durban, 16th to 19th September 1982; Music Department, Rhodes University, 7th to 8th October 1983, 56-58. Grahamstown, South Africa: International Library of African Music, 1984.

Note that this paper is in the 4th Symposium. (The 3rd and 4th Symposia are in one volume.)

1381. **Rodrigues, Ana Maria.** *Samba negro, espoliação branca.* São Paulo: Editora Hucitec, 1984. 143pp. (Ciências sociais)

In Portuguese. Very little on the music itself, but still warrants inclusion. References to Afro-Brazilian rhythm. Carnival photos, two of drummers. One rather congested photograph shows Brazilian instruments of African derivation. Carnival and Samba Schools get ample coverage. Bibliography.

1382. **Rodriguez, Olavo Alén.** "Afrikanische Musikeinflüsse in Kuba." In *Musikkulturen in Afrika.* Edited by Erich Stockmann, 292-304. Berlin: Verlag Neue Musik, 1987.

A short overview of African influence on Cuban music is followed by transcriptions of two versions of the same song perpetuated by one family. The song, along with other African carry-overs in the music of Cuba, shows a strong connection to Creole-speaking Haitians who came to Cuba in 1800 as a consequence of the revolution there. There are frequency and interval studies, and linguistic comparisons of a few terms related to music-making. No notes or bibliography.

1383. **Rosfeld, John Ezra.** CHEWA MUSIC: TRANSCRIPTION AND ANALYSIS OF MUSIC RECORDED IN "THE SOUND OF AFRICA." Master's Thesis, University of Illinois, Urbana-Champaign, 1970.

1384. **Rouget, Gilbert.** "Une convergence remarquable entre langages tambourinés, codes nerveux et langages machines." **HOMME** 17, no. 1 (1977): 117-121.
This is a technical study of what the author calls "a remarkable convergence" between drum language, nervous codes, and language machines. Footnotes, detailed figures. In French.

1385. **Rouget, Gilbert.** "Court songs and traditional history in the ancient kingdoms of Porto-Novo and Abomey." [Benin] In *Essays on music and history in Africa.* Edited by Klaus P. Wachsmann, 27-64. Evanston: Northwestern University Press, 1971.
Rouget said in 1971 that though were no longer any reigning kings in Dahomey, royal courts still existed there "in more or less decaying form." Of the different kingdoms still surviving at that time, in the southern part of the country, Abomey, which ruled the Fon people, is best known to anthropologists; Porto-Novo, which is less well known, ruled the Gun people. Both are branches of the of the ancient kingdom of Alada, from which they originated at the beginning of the seventeenth century. Footnotes, song texts, historical accounts.

1386. **Rouget, Gilbert.** *Music and trance: a theory of the relations between music and possession.* Translation from the French revised by Brünhilde Biebuyck in collaboration with the author. Chicago: University of Chicago Press, 1985. 395pp.
This is a translation of *La musique et la transe* (**1387**). It includes a bibliography, discography and filmography. A University of Chicago flier quotes Gerard Béhague as follows: "This is undoubtedly the most comprehensive and in-depth study to date of the relationships of music and spirit possession...Written in an engaging, vivid style, this book belongs on the shelf of all ethnomusicologists."

1387. **Rouget, Gilbert.** *La musique et la transe: esquisse d'une théorie générale des relations de la musique et de la possession.* Preface by Michel Leiris. [Paris}: Gallimard, c1980. 494pp.
This is the original version in French. See preceding entry (**1386**) for English translation.

1388. **Rouget, Gilbert.** "Sur les xylophones équiheptaphoniques des Malinke." **REVUE DE MUSICOLOGIE** 55, no. 1 (1969): 47-77.

1389. **Rouget, Gilbert.** "Tons de la langue en Gun (Dahomey) et tons du tambour." **REVUE DE MUSICOLOGIE** 50, no. 128 (1964): 3-29.
In French. Footnotes, a fold-out table.

ROYAL ANTHROPOLOGICAL INSTITUTE OF GREAT BRITAIN AND IRELAND. JOURNAL.
See: **MAN, 1015.**

ROYAL ANTHROPOLOGICAL INSTITUTE OF GREAT BRITAIN AND IRELAND. LIBRARY. ANTHROPOLOGICAL INDEX
See: •**ANTHROPOLOGICAL INDEX TO CURRENT PERIODICALS IN THE LIBRARY OF THE MUSEUM OF MANKIND LIBRARY, 110.**
(Acronym = **AICP**)

1390. Rubin, Libby Antarsh. GOTTSCHALK IN CUBA. Dissertation, Columbia University, 1974. 223pp.
Louis Moreau Gottschalk, early American composer, is best remembered for his singular pieces, many showing strong influence of music and dance of people of African ancestry. His famous *Bamboula, Danse de Nègres* is one example. Later, when he lived in various Caribbean islands, Gottschalk continued to write in a style that was markedly African in rhythm, style, and associated dance-forms, ultimately latching on to the Havana *contradanza*, whose rhythm he incorporated into myriad compositions. Rubin gives the background of this *contradanza* (pages 141-154), and its transformation from an English country dance into a spirited, rhythmic, Africanized form.

1391. Rugamba, Sipiriyani. *Chansons rwandaises.* Butare: I.N.R.S., 1979. 298pp.
The text is in French. Rugamba composed the melodies and texts in this collection, and explains that inspiration came from his ancestral heritage. Melodies are notated. Words are in Kinyarwanda. The 25 songs are also translated into French. Rugamba wishes to promote song, dance, and sung-texts that draw from the traditional culture of Rwanda.

1392. Rugamba, Sipiriyani. *Melodies du ballet Amasimbi n'Amakombe.* Butare: INRS, 1981. 277pp.
The initials stand for "L'Institut National de Recherches Scientific," the goal of this organization being to preserve the Rwandan cultural heritage and demonstrate the work of Rwandans. The ballet troupe of the title was launched in 1976 as an agent for this desired cultural conservation. The choral component was created in 1978. The songs for the ballet are revived old melodies or newly created ones. Some, though new, are written in a traditional style. Eight songs associated with eight ballets are notated (though difficult to read) with matching Kinyarwanda text. The introduction and later translation of the song texts are in French.

1393. Rycroft, David K. "Evidence of stylistic continuity in Zulu 'town' music." In **Essays for a humanist: an offering to Klaus Wachsmann**, 216-260. Spring Valley, New York: Town House Press, 1977.
Illustrations, transcriptions, bibliography.

1394. Rycroft, David K. "The musical bow in southern Africa." In **Symposium on Ethnomusicology**. (2nd: 1981: Rhodes University) *Papers presented at the Second Symposium on Ethnomusicology, Music Department, Rhodes University,*

24th to 26th September, 1981. Edited by Andrew Tracey, 70-76. Grahamstown: International Library of African Music, Institute of Social and Economic Research, Rhodes University, 1982.

1395. Rycroft, David K. "Nguni vocal polyphony." **INTERNATIONAL FOLK MUSIC COUNCIL. Journal** 19 (1967): 88-103.

1396. Rycroft, David K. "The relationships between speechtone and melody in South African music." In *South African music encyclopedia.* Vol. 2. Edited by Jacques P. Malan, 301-314. Cape Town: Oxford University Press, 1979-1986.

1397. Rycroft, David K. "Stylistic evidence in Nguni song." In *Essays on music and history in Africa.* Edited by Klaus P. Wachsmann, 213-241. Evanston: Northwestern University Press, 1971.
A survey of the musical style of Zulu, Swazi, and Xhosa songs. Many notations, song texts, two charts of "Bow Notes and Vocal Tones," one chart entitled, "The Evolution of Scale in Nguni Music by Accretion of Analogous Whole Tones." Footnotes.

1398. Rycroft, David K. "Zulu and Swazi music." In *South African music encyclopedia.* Vol. 2. Edited by Jacques P. Malan, 314-344. Cape Town: Oxford University Press, 1979-1986.

1399. Rycroft, David K. "Zulu melodic and non-melodic vocal studies." In **Symposium on Ethnomusicology**. (5th: 1984: University of Cape Town). *Papers presented at the fifth Symposium on Ethnomusicology: Faculty of Music, University of Cape Town, August 30th-September 1st, 1984,* 50-53. Grahamstown: International Library of African Music, 1985.

1400. Rycroft, David K. *Zulu, Swazi en Xhosa instrumentale en vocale muziek.* Tervuren, Koninklijk Museum voor Midden-Afrika; [Brussel], Belgische Radio en Televisie, [Flageyplein, 18], 1969. 54pp.
On South African music. English and Flemish, with summary in French and German. Illustration, map, music.

Rycroft, David K.
See also: **The praises of Dingana, 1341.**

SAS
See: **Stories and songs from Sierra Leone, 1513.**

SEM
See: **Society for Ethnomusicology, 1475.**

SSCI
See: **SOCIAL SCIENCES CITATION INDEX, 1474.**

Saane, Kelefa
See: **Kelefa Saane, 851.**

1401. **Sabry, Hoda Nicola.** THE ADAPTION OF CLASS PIANO METHODS AS USED IN THE UNITED STATES OF AMERICA FOR USE IN THE EGYPTIAN EDUCATIONAL SYSTEM. Dissertation, Indiana University, 1965. 192pp.
The author states that her focus on class piano stems from her belief as an educator that this approach "offers a means of worthwhile and beneficial instruction in support of a successful music education program." Her study covers all aspects of the subject, including the problems inherent in trying to teach Egyptian music that uses quarter tones, on a fixed-pitched instrument that uses half tones. She brings a sensitive, informed approach to problems inherent in working simultaneously within two music systems. There are 13 technical exercises and 26 songs of both cultures.

1401a. SACHS, CURT.
Most of the writings of this renowned musicologist were written well before 1960, hence are not included here. A bibliography of his works, compiled by **Kurt Hahn**, is in **ACTA MUSICOLOGICA** 29 (1957): 94-106. See also **Bruno Nettl's**, *Theory and method in musicology* (**1157**) for an overview and evaluation of Sach's major works.

1402. **Sachs, Curt.** *The history of musical instruments.* New York: Norton, 1968.
Norton first published this in 1940, and renewed the copyright in 1968. The book is regarded as the first comprehensive history of musical instruments, covering prehistoric times to the twentieth century, and scanning five continents. Instruments can be as basic as the bullroarer or as complicated as the electric organ.

1403. **Sachs, Curt.** *Real-Lexicon der Musikinstrumente, zugleich ein Polyglossar für das gesammte Instrumentengebiet.* [Revised and enlarged edition]. New York, Dover Publications [1964]. 451pp. (American Musicological Society - Music Library Association. Reprint Series)
In German. A dictionary of musical instruments that includes African instruments, many illustrations, notations of instrumental ranges, and a bibliography. The first edition of this work was published by Julius Bard in Berlin, 1913. The present edition contains a note to the effect that it is the only version that contains

"emendations and additions" introduced by Sachs after the first publication of his work.

1404. **Sachs, Curt.** *Vergleichende Musikwissenschaft: Musik der Fremdkulturen.* 3d ed. Wilhelmshaven: Heinrichshofen, 1974. 76pp. (Musikpädagogische Bibliothek, 2)
This reprint fortunately falls within our elected time frame. Contains many of Sach's theories and observations, substantiated by universal examples. Only two references to Africa are found. On page 44 is mention of the music of islands off East Africa, in which singers change from octaves to fourths and fifths in the same song, with an example of a Wanyamezi dance song (transcribed by Hornbostel). On page 46, there is reference to African antiphonal singing (likened to European canon). A Bateke dance song is transcribed.

1405. **Sachs, Curt.** *The wellsprings of music.* Edited by Jaap Kunst. New York: Da Capo Press, 1977. 256pp.
A "classic" in the field of musicology, also Sach's final and perhaps greatest work. (Originally copyrighted by Nijhoff in 1961.) Kunst says in the preface, "The sum and substance of the book is a truly monumental discussion of the development of the melodic element is all its aspects (including rhythm)." Other elements are also treated, and so are instruments. Music is approached on a world-wide basis, with many references to Africa, though one wishes for a subject index to locate these places more easily. There are bibliographic footnotes, and musical illustrations.

Sacramento Library
See: **Johnson, Sheila.** *Non-Western music*, **769.**

Sadie, Stanley
See: **•The new Grove dictionary of music and musicians, 1161.**
•The new Grove dictionary of musical instruments, 1162.

1406. **Saighoe, Francis A. Kobina.** THE MUSIC BEHAVIOR OF DAGABA IMMIGRANTS IN TARKWA, GHANA: A STUDY OF SITUATIONAL CHANGE. Dissertation, Columbia University, 1988. 304pp.
This study, which "examines the utility of 'situational change' as a tool for explaining the extent to which rural music may be transformed when its performers migrate and adjust to an urban environment," ultimately concludes that there is no correlation between the many changes in the social situation and changes in the music behavior of the Tarkwa Dagaba. The focus is the music of Dagaba immigrants, as performed in Tarkwa, a gold-mining Ghanaian town. Bibliography. **(UMI)**

1407. **Sallée, Pierre.** *Un aspect de la musique des Batéké du Gabon: le grand pluriarc Ngwomi et sa place sans la danse Onkila: essai d'analyse formelle d'un document de musique africaine.* 2d ed. Libreville, République gabonaise: ORSTOM, 1971. 53pp.
Includes music.

1408. **Sallée, Pierre.** *Deux études sur la musique du Gabon.* Paris: ORSTOM, 1978. 87pp. (Travaux et documents de l'ORSTOM, no. 85)
The two studies are: "Un aspect de la musique des Batéké: le grand pluriarc *Ngwomi* et sa place dans la danse *onkila*," and "Un musicien chez les Nkomi: le harpiste Rampano Mathurin." A 45rpm accompanying disc demonstrates the *pluriarc*, a harp/lute, and Mathurin singing to an eight-stringed harp, called *ngombi*. Meticulous musicological investigation is demonstrated, including transcriptions and the two-page bibliography. Some black and white photographs accompany the first essay - even an engraving from 1662 showing a *pluriarc* being played. Rampano's personality and his qualities as musician and theoretician are described. A photo would have been nice.

1409. **Sancho, Ignatius (1729-1780), an early African composer in England: the collected edition of his music in facsimile.** Edited by Josephine R. B. Wright. New York: Garland Publishing Company, 1981. 90pp. (Critical studies on Black life and culture, vol. 3)
A toss-up whether to include this, but Sancho *was* African (born on a slave ship en route from the coast of Guinea to northern Colombia) and he became a composer (though no signs of any Africanisms in his minuets, gavottes, or similar genteel works with figured basses, ornaments, etc.). Brought to England when 2 years old, having already shown signs of genius, he received a Western education, rubbed shoulders with the aristocracy, and produced 62 compositions. A fascinating and informative historical study. (In 1770, there were approximately 15,000 to 20,000 black men and women living in England.)

1410. **Santoro, Claudio.** "Means of preservation and diffusion of traditional music in Latin America." In **Creating a wider interest in traditional music: proceedings of a conference held in Berlin in cooperation with the International Music Council, 12th to the 17th June, 1967.** [Edited by Alain Daniélou and others], 128-131. Berlin: International Institute for Comparative Music Studies and Documentation, [1967?].

1410a. **Santos Barbosa, Guilherme dos.** "*Capueira* de Angola: a personal view of a *capueira* master." THE WORLD OF MUSIC 30, no. 2 (1988): 69-85.
The *capueira* (commonly called *capoeira regional*) and the accompanying sound of the *berimbau*, are considered by the author to be a vital reflection of the history and culture of blacks in Brazil. Notes, bibliography, illustrations, photographs.

1411. **Savador-Daniel, Francisco.** *Musique et instruments de musique du Maghreb* [al-Maghrib]. Paris: La Boîte à Documents, 1986. 175pp.
The music history and musical instruments of northern Africa. Bibliography.

S

1412. **Scaramuzzo, Gene.** "*Zouk*: magic music of the French Antilles." **THE BEAT** 5, no. 4 (1986): 27-33.
This was the beginning of a series. Photographs.

1413. **Schaeffner, Hugo.** "La musique noire d'un continent à un autre." In **La musique dans la vie, étude realisée sous les auspices l'Ocora et sous la direction de Tolia Nikiprowetzky**, 7-23. Vol. 2. Paris, Office de coopération radiophoniques, 1967.
An evaluative survey, heavily footnoted, written in French.

1414. **Schapera, Isaac.** *Rainmaking rites of Tswana tribes.* Leiden: Afrika-Studiecentrum, 1971. 144pp. (African social research documents, vol. 3)
The monograph concerns the beliefs and practices associated with rain-making among the Kgatla of south-eastern Botswana. Includes the words of approximately eight rain-making songs. No transcriptions.

1415. **Scheub, Harold.** *African oral narratives, proverbs, riddles, poetry, and song.* [2d ed.]. Boston: G. K. Hall, c1977. 393pp. (Bibliographies and guides in African studies)
The first edition was published in 1971 under the title, *Bibliography of African oral narratives.* Includes indexes.

1416. **Scheub, Harold.** THE NTSOMI: A XHOSA PERFORMING ART. Dissertation, University of Wisconsin-Madison, 1969. 1020pp.

1417. **Scheven, Yvette.** *Bibliographies for African studies, 1970-1986.* London; New York: Hans Zell, 1988. 615pp.
An important and extremely useful reference book edited by the Bibliographer for African Studies at the University of Illinois (Urbana-Champaign). The focus is subSaharan Africa. Thorough and impeccably organized, this on-going and cumulative bibliography includes entries written in major European languages as well as in Afrikaans. Along with the many subjects covered, there are a number of music references in this volume, as well as in earlier ones in the series. Includes an index.

1418. **Schmidt, Cynthia Elizabeth.** "Interlocking techniques in Kpelle music." In **Studies in African music**. Co-editors, J. H. Kwabena Nketia, and Jacqueline Cogdell DjeDje, 195-216. [Los Angeles]: Program in Ethnomusicology, Department of Music, University of California, Los Angeles, 1984.
There are 10 notated examples, some corresponding to music recorded on the cassette that accompanies the book. Extensive notes, bibliography, and a map augment the study. The author indicates the musical and social goals achieved by Kpelle music-makers by their use of interlocking and hocket techniques. The creation of cohesion in structures that allow performers to express themselves in separate parts, Schmidt says, "is the single Kpelle musical ideal."

1419. **Schmidt, Cynthia Elizabeth.** MULTI-PART VOCAL MUSIC OF THE KPELLE OF LIBERIA. Dissertation, University of California, Los Angeles, 1985. 336pp.

A stunning example of high-level scholarship matched only by the author's exemplary ethical standards. Schmidt's detailed study combines the "descriptive and the interpretive," as proposed by J. H. Kwabena Nketia. She follows his lead by focusing on musical culture rather than general culture, using the "musical event" as the unit for analysis. She chooses recreational music and work songs for her research, the issue of relationships in multi-part music being an important concern. This in-depth examination of choral techniques and their contextual use in West Africa may well be a "first." Transcriptions, texts, bibliography, Kpelle glossary.

1420. **Schmidt, Cynthia Elizabeth.** ṢHÀNGÓ CULT MUSIC OF TRINIDAD: THE ANNUAL CEREMONY. Master's Thesis, University of California, Los Angeles, 1974.

1421. **Schmidt, Cynthia Elizabeth.** "Womanhood, work and song among the Kpelle of Liberia." In **African musicology: current trends: a festschrift presented to J. H. Kwabena Nketia**. Edited by Jacqueline Cogdell DjeDje, and William G. Carter, 237-263. [Atlanta, Georgia: Crossroads Press, 1988]- .

A number of song texts in Kpelle, translated into English. Music notations, photographs, notes, bibliography.

1422. **Schmidt, Nelly.** "Chanson des 'nouveaux libres' de Guadeloupe et de Martinique 1848-1851." In **Chansons d'Afrique et des Antilles**, 107-135. Paris: Harmattan, c1988.

1423. **Schmidt-Wrenger, Barbara.** *Rituelle Frauengesänge der Tshokwe: Untersuchungen zu einem Säkularisierungsprozess in Angola und Zaïre.* [Tervuren: Musée royal de l'Afrique centrale], 1979. 3 vols. (Annalen. Series in-8°, Menselijke wetenschappen. Koninklijk Museum voor Midden-Afrika, Tervuren, Belgium, no. 98-100 = Annales. Série in-8°, Sciences humaines. Musée royal de l'Afrique centrale, Tervuren, Belgium, no. 98-100)

Music of Angola, Zaïre, Chokwe people. Some texts in Chokwe with German translation. Volume 3 consists of music. Bibliography.

1424. **Schneider, Harold K.** *Concordance of words in the titles of* **AFRICAN ABSTRACTS**. [Bloomington, Indiana, 1971]. 515pp.

This covers volumes 1-17 of **AFRICAN ABSTRACTS**, omitting the linguistic abstracts. Choosing only the prefix "mus" one is already led to "music," "musica," "musical," "musicale," "musicaux," "musician," and still more music-related words. Other key words in titles, not necessarily the *word* "music," also will produce similar salutary results. See also: **AFRICAN ABSTRACTS, 29**.

S

1425. **Schneider, Marius**. "Le langage tambouriné des Doula." In *Musiques africaines*. Edited by Nanie Bridgman. [Paris]: Musique de tous les temps, [1967]. 1 vol. (unpaginated, but approximately pages 6-20, including plates). (Musique de tous les temps, 44/45)

1426. **Schüller, Dietrich**. BEZIEHUNGEN ZWISCHEN WEST- UND WESTZENTRALAFRIKANISCHEN STAATEN VON 1482 BIS 1700. EINE ETHNOHISTORISCHE UNTERSUCHUNG AN HAND DER SCHALLINSTRUMENTE IN HÄUPTLINGSKULT UND KRIEGSWESEN AUF GRUND SCHRIFTLICHER QUELLEN. Dissertation, Universität Wien, 1970. 169pp.

This dissertation resulted in the following book, published two years later.

1427. **Schüller, Dietrich**. *Beziehungen zwischen west- und westzentralafrikanischen Staaten von 1482 bis 1700. Eine ethnohistorische Untersuchung an Hand der Schallinstrumente in Häuptlingskult und Kriegswesen auf Grund schriftlicher Quellen*. Vienna, Verlag Notring, 1972. 169pp.

This was originally presented as the author's thesis at the University of Vienna. (See preceding entry, **1426**.) On percussion instruments and African ethnology. Illustrations, bibliography.

1428. **Schuller, Gunther**. *The history of jazz*. Vol. 1. *Early jazz: its roots and musical development*. New York: Oxford University Press, 1986 -. 401pp.

There is more on African rhythm in the first chapter of Schuller's book on jazz than in many a monograph purporting to deal with this subject. Insights are brilliant and expressed with rare directness: "But until now we have lacked musically documented proof of the fact that the syncopation of jazz is no more than an idiomatic corruption, a flattened-out mutation of what was once the true polyrhythmic character of African music." Additional inspired ideas vitalize the book. Abundant notes, glossary, index. Other references to African music, some to Arabic music.

1429. **Schuyler, Philip Daniel**. AL-MILḤŪN: THE FUSION OF FOLK ART TRADITIONS IN MOROCCAN SONG FORM. Master's Thesis, University of Washington, 1974. 249pp.

Illustrations, music, tape recording.

1430. **Schuyler, Philip Daniel**. "Berber professional musicians in performance." In **Performance practice: ethnomusicological perspectives**. Edited by Gerard Béhague, 91-148. Westport, Connecticut: Greenwood Press, c1984.

The study is of professional musicians (*rwais*) from the tashlḥit-speaking region of southwestern Morocco. (Tashlḥit is a Berber language dialect.) Thorough notes, excellent bibliography, glossary, with linguistic origins of terms indicated.

1431. **Schuyler, Philip Daniel.** A REPERTORY OF IDEAS: THE MUSIC OF THE "RWAIS," BERBER PROFESSIONAL MUSICIANS FROM SOUTHWESTERN MOROCCO. Dissertation, University of Washington, 1979. 355pp.
Illustrations, maps, music, bibliography.

1432. **Sealey, John, and Krister Malm.** *Music in the Caribbean.* Introduction by the Mighty Chalkdust (Hollis Liverpool). London: Hodder and Stoughton, 1983, c1982. 44pp.
The is a textbook for older children. West Indians are reminded of the worth of their *own* music. The book is informative, and comprehensive: shanties, Shango [Ṣàngó], parang, and fête music, reggae, calypso, steelpan, the Jonkanoo masquerade, kalinda, and much more. African, European, and East Indian components of Caribbean music are discussed, other cultures mentioned, but one reads later, "We could say that the many Afro-European musical types in the Caribbean are the creation of black musicians, and are chiefly based on the African musical tradition." African references throughout. Glossary, bibliography, attractive photographs.

1433. **Seaton, S. Lee, and Karen Ann Watson.** "Continuity and discontinuity in song styles: an ordinal cross-cultural classification." In **The performing arts: music and dance.** Edited by John Blacking, and Joann W. Kealiinohomoku, 93-107. New York: Mouton, c1979.
Represents further research into Cantometrics. In this paper a taxonomic world song style map is given for ninety sample cultures, and interpreted in accordance with the underlying "circumplex structure." (Africa, of course, represents a major component.) According to the authors, the overall display of this map corresponds essentially to the culture regions of Murdock's *Ethnographic atlas* (1967). Seaton says that the musicological "split was between Lomax's 'individualized' Model A and 'group-oriented' Model B." Directions for future research are suggested. Highly technical language. Bibliography.

1434. **Seavoy, Mary Hermaine.** THE SISAALA XYLOPHONE TRADITION [Ghana]. Dissertation, University of California, Los Angeles, 1982. 575pp.
The study presents a comprehensive examination of one instrument, the Sisaala *jengsi*, the musical tradition of which it is part (*gokung*), and the musical culture surrounding its use, covering in detail repertoire, tonal system, performers, contextual use, and *jengsi* morphology (shown to be related to the broader Western Sudanic xylophone complex). It focuses on the modes of integration between the musical culture and Sisaala religious, social, economic and ceremonial life. The two parts are: The Social Context, and Sounds, Structures, and Modes of Expression. She employs Nketia's "cultural factor" approach. Keen scholarship, nothing left undone. Illustrations, maps, music, bibliography. **(UMI)**

S

1435. **Seck, Nago, and Sylvie Clerfeuille.** *Musiciens africains des années 80: guide.* Paris: L'Harmattan, 1986. 168pp.
In French. Discographies, photos, bibliographical references, biographies of African musicians of the 80s. There is factual information for forty-six separate musicians or groups, with occasional photos - often less-familiar ones. The six categories of music considered are: *Le makossa, Le umbaganga, Le mbalax, Le matacumbi ou socope, La jùjú, La soukous*, and the areas with which these music styles are associated.

1436. **Seeger, Pete.** *The incompleat folksinger.* Edited by Jo Metcalf Schwartz. New York: Simon and Schuster [1972]. 596pp.
Bibliographies and discographies. Illustrations. Many references to African music. Includes words and music to older South African freedom songs.

1437. **SELECTED REPORTS IN ETHNOMUSICOLOGY.** 1966- . [Los Angeles] Department of Music, University of California, Los Angeles. Continues: California. University. University at Los Angeles. Institute of Ethnomusicology. Selected Reports. Vol. 2, no. 1 issued by the Institute of Ethnomusicology, UCLA; Vol. 2, no. 2- by the Department of Music. Following are essays concerned with African or African-related music. They are listed alphabetically by author rather than chronologically:

- **Cornelius, Steven.** "Encapsulating power: meaning and taxonomy of the musical instruments of Santería in New York City," vol. 8 (1990): 125-141.
- **Koetting, James.** "Analysis and notation of West African drum ensemble music," vol. 1, no. 3 (1970): 115-147.
- **Nketia, J. H. Kwabena, and Jacqueline Cogdell DjeDje**, co-editors. vol. 5, in entirety, 1984. (See **Studies in African music, 1514.**)
- **Racy, 'Ali Jihad.** "Music in nineteenth-century Egypt: an historical sketch," vol. 4 (1983): 157-179.
- **Racy, 'Ali Jihad.** "Sound and society: the Takht music of early-twentieth century Cairo," vol. 7 (1988): 139-170.
- **Wachsmann, Klaus P.** "The trend of musicology in Africa," vol. 1, no. 1 (1966): 61-65.
- **Woodsen, Craig.** "The effect of a snare on the tone of a single-headed frame drum, the Moroccan Bender," vol. 2, no. 1 (1974): 102-117.

1438. **Seminar on Yorùbá Oral Tradition: Poetry in Music, Dance and Drama (1974: University of Ifẹ̀).** *Yorùbá oral tradition: selections from the papers presented at the Seminar on Yorùbá Oral Tradition: Poetry in Music, Dance and Drama.* Edited by Wándé Abímbọ́lá. [Ilé-Ifẹ̀, Nigeria: Department of African languages and literatures, University of Ifẹ̀], 1975. 33pp. (Ifẹ̀ African languages and literatures series, no. 1)
This is essentially a program of events of the seminar, with information and notes on oral tradition, various art forms, rituals, music, and dance.

1439. Senoga-Zake, George W. *Folk music of Kenya.* Nairobi, Kenya: Uzima Press, 1986.
Musical instruments of Kenya also receive attention. Illustrations, music.

1440. Sephula, Moshe. *Sing again, Africa!: twelve more South African urban folk songs.* Great Yarmouth, Norfolk: Galliard Ltd.; New York: Galaxy Music Corporation, c1970. 17pp.
Texts in both original language and English translation. Piano accompaniment.

1441. Serwadda, W. Moses. *Songs and stories from Uganda.* Transcribed and edited by Hewitt Pantaleoni. Illustrated by Leo Dillon and Diane Dillon. New York: Crowell [1974]. 80pp.
Thirteen songs with accompanying stories retold from Ugandan folklore.

1442. Shapiro, J. H. "Learning to play [the ṣẹ̀kẹ̀rẹ̀, a West African instrument]." HERESIES 7, no. 1: (1990): 80-92.

1443. El-Shawan, Salwa Aziz. AL-MUSIKA AL-'ARABIYYAH [AL-MŪSĪQA AL- 'ARABIYYAH]: A CATEGORY OF URBAN MUSIC IN CAIRO, EGYPT, 1927-1977. Music Dissertation, Columbia University, 1981. 349pp.
"*Al-musika al- ('c) arabiyyah*, a category of Egyptian urban secular music, is examined as it was practiced in Cairo from 1927 to 1977. The focus of this work is on the documentation and explanation of the changes which have occurred in *al-musika al- ('c) arabiyyah*'s performance groups and music products, and the relationship of these changes to their larger political, social and musical contexts." **(UMI)**

1444. Shelemay, Kay Kaufman. THE LITURGICAL MUSIC OF THE FALASHA OF ETHIOPIA. Dissertation, University of Michigan, 1977. 226pp.

1445. Shelemay, Kay Kaufman. "The music of the Lalibeloč: music mendicants of Ethiopia." In JOURNAL OF AFRICAN STUDIES 9, no. 3 (1982): 128-138.
"Lalibeloč" is the name given to lepers or descendants of lepers in Ethiopia. They perform dawn serenades outside the homes of wealthy Ethiopians, and their music has been termed "the most original element in Ethiopian music."

1446. Shelemay, Kay Kaufman. *Music, ritual, and Falasha history.* East Lansing, Michigan: African Studies Center, Michigan State University, c1986. 415pp. (Ethiopian series no. 17)
Music of the Falashas of Ethiopia is examined in this detailed historical study. Similarities and differences of music traditions of the Falashas and the Ethiopian Christians are studied, as is the liturgy of Judaism. Glossary, many transcriptions, bibliography.

S

1447. **Shelemay, Kay Kaufman**. "Recording technology, the record industry, and ethnomusicological scholarship." In **Comparative musicology and anthropology of music: essays on the history of ethnomusicolog**. Edited by Bruno Nettl and Philip V. Bohlman, 277-292. Chicago: University of Chicago Press, 1991.
A brilliant assessment, with important implications regarding the ongoing proliferation of recorded African and African-influenced urban music today. Notes, bibliography.

1448. **Shelton, Austin S.** "The problem of *griot* interpretation and the actual cause of war in Sondjata." PRÉSENCE AFRICAINE no. 66 (1988): 145-152.
Footnotes.

1449. **Sherman, Jessica**. "Songs of the Chimurenga (Zimbabwean revolution): from protest to praise." In **Symposium on Ethnomusicology**. (2nd: 1981: Rhodes University) *Papers presented at the Second Symposium on Ethnomusicology, Music Department, Rhodes University, 24th to 26th September, 1981.* Edited by Andrew Tracey, 77-79. Grahamstown: International Library of African Music, Institute of Social and Economic Research, Rhodes University, 1982.

1450. **Shona praise poetry**. Compiled by A. C. Hodza. Edited with introduction, translations and notes by G. Fortune. New York: Oxford University Press, 1979. 401pp. (Oxford library of African literature)
Although this is a collection of praise poetry, texts of two poems honor musicians: Tribute to a Mbira Player, pages 358-361, and Tribute to a Good Singer, 362-364.

Sidibe, B. K.
See: **Sunjata, 1516.**

1451. **Sidran, Ben**. *Black talk*. New York: Holt, Rinehart and Winston [1970]. 201pp.
Based on Sidran's dissertation, completed at the University of Sussex. (See the following entry, **1452.**) Bibliography.

1452. **Sidran, Ben**. A CULTURAL HISTORY OF BLACK MUSIC IN AMERICA: THE FOUNDATIONS AND FUNCTIONS OF AN ORAL CULTURE. Dissertation, University of Sussex, 1970. 189pp.
Ideas, later expressed in Sidran's book, *Black talk*, are still powerful. At the time of his research, no book treated black culture in America as an oral culture, nor regarded black music as a perpetrator of this orality. In Sidran's words: "This study attempts to tell the *why* of black music using socio-historical events and cultural terminology under a conceptual umbrella which is the examination of an

oral culture in the context of literate America." Sidran's keen insights into perceptual, philosophical and musical differences deriving from African oral culture are nothing less than brilliant. Notes. Bibliography.

1453. **Silver, David**. "Reggae epiphanies: Freetown, Sierra Leone." In **Reggae international**. Edited by Stephen Davis, and Peter Simon, 184. New York: R & B [Roger and Bernhard], c1982.
On a single page there are two columns of information on reggae in Sierra Leone at the time of writing. An interesting contrast is made between African reggae versus Jamaican reggae. (By now it has become a familiar pattern for African-influenced music created in far distant lands to be greeted with open arms in Africa, emulated and reinterpreted there, tossed back in modified form, only to be reinterpreted once more. The process has been going on for years.)

1454. **Simmons, Donald C.** *Extralinguistic usages of tonality in Efik folklore*. University of Alabama: University of Alabama Press, c1980. 150pp.
Information in this book was obtained in Calabar Province, Nigeria, from 1952-1953. The Introduction treats technicalities of the Efik language. Chapter headings reveal the music tie-in: Signal Communication [the drum and gong used for this purpose], Tone Riddles, Tone Poems, Song Lyrics. The appendix contains free translations of Efik texts, notes, bibliography, and index. The author stresses the importance of tonality in Efik folklore, and establishes the Tone Riddle as a definite form of African folklore. He draws a number of other conclusions, raises some interesting questions - one being the possible prior use of tonality by the Chinese in ways not yet documented.

1455. **Simmons, Sandra Kay**. INDIGENOUS FORMS OF MUSIC IN FOREIGN MISSION STATIONS OF THE SOUTHERN BAPTIST CONVENTION. Dissertation, Baylor University, 1981. 108pp.
The study is based on questionnaires sent to 110 Southern Baptist music missionaries, then serving in 45 countries, nine African. Sixty-eight missionaries responded. Twenty-eight resultant tables of various aspects of performance practice are included, plus other information. Vocal and instrumental music are apparently widely used for evangelistic purposes, and selections performed "reflected national culture, customs, habits, and beliefs" of the peoples involved. The author recommends that music missionaries have one or more courses in ethnomusicology, and that "nationals" be allowed to structure their own Christian worship services independent of American missionary influence.

1456. **Simon, Artur**. "Musical traditions, Islam and cultural identity in the Sudan." In *Perspectives on African music*. Edited by Wolfgang Bender, 25-42. Bayreuth, Germany: Bayreuth University, c1989.

1457. **Simon, Artur**. STUDIEN ZUR ÄGYPTISCHEN VOLKSMUSIK. Dissertation, University of Hamburg, 1971.
This is the original. The following entry, **148**, represents the published book.

S

1458. **Simon, Artur**. *Studien zur ägyptischen Volksmusik*. 2 vols. Hamburg: Verlag der Musikalienhandlung, 1972. (Beiträge zur Ethnomusikologie, vol. 1)

Simon gives Egyptian vocal and instrumental music exacting treatment. Volume 1 presents an historic overview with source materials. There are analyses of melodies, elaborate computations of frequencies and intervals, and charts that open out. Volume 2 is divided into three appendices with descriptions of select recordings, transcriptions of them, and sandwiched in-between, some highly technical tables of a mathematical nature. These appendices do not relate in an easily discernible way. An extensive bibliography that includes many significant books and articles in assorted languages follows. Fortunately, many entries deal directly with Egyptian music. An index is present.

1459. **Simon, Artur**. "Trumpet and flute ensembles of the Berta people in the Sudan." In **African musicology: current trends: a festschrift presented to J. H. Kwabena Nketia**. Edited by Jacqueline Cogdell DjeDje, and William G. Carter, 183-217. [Atlanta, Georgia: Crossroads Press, 1988]- .

Notes, bibliography, photographs, one illustration. There are tables that analyze fine points such as pitches, intervals, patterns, etc. Photographs. One illustration.

1460. **Sims, Michael, and Alfred Kagan**. *American and Canadian doctoral dissertations and master's theses on Africa, 1986-1974*. Waltham, Massachusetts: African Studies Association, Brandeis University, c1976.

This volume is an updating and expansion of *American doctoral dissertations on Africa, 1886-1972*, by Anne Schneller and Michael Bratton. It was a useful source for dissertations included in this bibliography. Includes indexes. See also the work bearing the same title but covering 1974-1987, by **Lauer, Joseph J., *et al.*, 951**.

1461. **SING OUT: THE FOLK SONG MAGAZINE**. 1950- . Bethlehem, Pennsylvania: Sing Out Corporation.

Issued quarterly. Contains a selection of songs reflecting a diversity of folk music styles: blues, blue grass, country, gospel, country folk, Celtic traditional, women's, topical, and seasonal. Besides the songs themselves, there are regular features, such as a column by Pete Seeger that has continued for years. Not too many recent articles relate to Africa, though a thorough search through back issues might produce a few. The publication has a cumulative index, and is also indexed by **MUSIC INDEX** and **CURRENT CONTENTS**. Available in microform and as reprints, from **UMI**. A recent scanning produced the following rewards:

- **Kivnick, Helen**. "Singing in South Africa: a conversation with Victoria Mxenge," vol. 31, no. 3 (1985): 12-19.
- ***"Nkosi Sikelel' iAfrika."*** (words and melody), vol. 31, no. 3 (1985): 22-23.
- **Pevar, Susan Gunn**, "Teach-in: the Gambian *kora*," vol. 25 (1977): 15-17.
- ***"Tshotsholosa."*** (lyrics and melody), vol. 31, no. 3 (1985): 20-21.

1462. Sithole, Elkin M. T. "Black folk music." In **Rappin' and stylin' out: communication in urban black America**. Compiled by Thomas Kochman, 65-82. Urbana: University of Illinois Press [1972].

A unique essay on aspects of black culture and performance practices that have not been presented exactly this way before. Sithole, a Zulu musicologist and anthropologist, has an almost philosophically resigned way of invading the Western psyche, zeroing in on arrogance, with its associated misconceptions, and persisting with his necessary logical, patient - but firm - corrective work. Irony and wit are his tools, not the bitterness to which he is entitled. This essay ought to be required reading for any teacher or person specializing in African music. Zulu song texts, notations, charts.

1463. Sithole, Elkin M. T. "*Ngoma* music among the Zulus." In **The performing arts: music and dance**. Edited by John Blacking, and Joann W. Kealiinohomoku, 277-285. New York: Mouton, c1979.

Ngoma, not discussed from 1957 until this essay, is still alive and well after more than fifty years of nonacceptance in Christian missions. It "dominates the international scene as no other music from southern Africa does." Fascinating are Zulu ethnomusicologist, Sithole's, technical and human-interest descriptions of varieties of *ngoma*. One learns of *umbholoho* ("bombing" songs), *sikwela Jo*, (music that demands a sharp forceful attack on each choral yell), a dance form known as *sikhunzi* (or "grumbling," since the cherished deep voices seem to grumble), school-influenced songs, known as *mnyuziki*, and many others. Informative, while entertaining. Bibliography.

1464. Sithole, Elkin M. T. THE ROLE OF GOSPEL MUSIC IN THE BLACK CHURCHES OF CHICAGO. Dissertation, Queen's University of Belfast (Northern Ireland), 1975. 622pp.

This is an exhaustive study of the gospel music scene in Chicago, explored from every possible angle - historical, musical, religious, socioeconomic, cultural, *ad infinitum*, by a Zulu ethnomusicologist/composer who brings his special knowledge and vision to the study. Gospel personalities, their groups, and their churches are treated in depth. Sithole, who was a student of John Blacking, finds surprising similarities in gospel music practices to those of his South African homeland, (although we are now finding out much more about contact between the two areas in the past). No finer work exists on gospel music. Many photos, bibliography.

1465. Sithole, Elkin M. T. ZULU MUSIC AS A REFLECTION OF SOCIAL CHANGE. Master's Thesis, Wesleyan University, 1968. 125pp.

Regrettably, this remarkable work has not to date been published. Written by South Africa's outstanding musicologist, himself a Zulu, this thesis demonstrates that the author not only has a deep understanding of his entire culture, and the ability to convey this to others, but that he is bicultural in his musical understanding. Music is always interpreted *within* culture, but the music itself gets scholarly treatment - transcriptions, analyses, skilled English translations. Notable is Sithole's wry humor, his admirable objectivity. Does any other scholar have such insight, such inside knowledge, of so many aspects of Zulu life and culture? Excellent bibliography.

1466. **Siwela, Elias W. M.** *Ngoma dze kunyumwa kwe mashona, "songs of social consciousness of the Shona of Zimbabwe".* [Nairobi]: Institute of African Studies, University of Nairobi, [1979]. 31pp. (Paper. Institute of African Studies, University of Nairobi, no. 109)
Shona songs.

1467. **Slawson, Wayne**. "Features, musical operations, and compositions: a derivation from Ewe drum music." In **African musicology: current trends: a festschrift presented to J. H. Kwabena Nketia**. Edited by Jacqueline Cogdell DjeDje, and William G. Carter, 307-319. [Atlanta, Georgia: Crossroads Press, 1988]- .
Notations, tables, notes, bibliography.

1468. **Slobin, Mark**. "Musics of West Asia-North Africa." In **Music in world cultures**. Edited by Margaret Mead. MUSIC EDUCATORS JOURNAL 59, no. 2 (1972): 44-45.
General information is packed into two columns bordered by photographs of an Egyptian woman playing a *tar*, a Tunisian man playing a *zurna*, a North African bowed lute, and two photos, one showing a drum, the other, two reed instruments. Origin of the instruments is not indicated.

1469. **Smith, C. C., and Gerard Tacite Lamothe**. "Legends of Haitian music." THE BEAT 6, no. 2 (1987): 14-18.
This was the beginning of a series. Illustrations, photographs.

1470. **Smith, Donna Ridley**, comp. *Non-Western music: a selected bibliography of materials in the California State University, Sacramento Library*. 3d edition. The Library. California State University, Sacramento, 1982. 45pp. 45pp.
(The second edition of this work - only five pages shorter - is listed under **Johnson, Sheila J., 769.)** In the present updated edition there are: general reference tools, ones for specific geographic areas, bibliographies, music and musical instrument sources, indexes to periodicals and collections. General works on "non-Western" musics are followed by a section that treats specific geographical areas. Africa is covered from page 25 to 30. No annotations appear here, but they appear later in the book, where various useful items relating to Africa in different formats may be found: monographs, songbooks, filmstrips, audiotapes, videotapes.

1471. **Smith, Edna Marilyn**. MUSIC IN WEST AFRICA. Dissertation, Columbia University, 1961. 221pp.

Smith, Edna Marilyn
See also: **Griot sings, 642.**

1472. **Smith, Ronald Richard.** THE SOCIETY OF LOS CONGOS OF PANAMA: AN ETHNOMUSICOLOGICAL STUDY OF THE MUSIC AND DANCE-THEATER OF AN AFRO-PANAMANIAN GROUP. Dissertation, Indiana University, 1975. 342pp.

1473. **Smith, Ronald Richard.** "They sing with the voice of drums: Afro-Panamanian musical tradition." In **More than drumming: essays on African and Afro-Latin music and musicians.** Edited by Irene V. Jackson, 163-198. Westport, Connecticut: Greenwood Press, c1985.
Tables, music notations, bibliography, map, notes, photographs. Abstracted in **RILM**, 1985.

1474. **SOCIAL SCIENCES CITATION INDEX.** 1969- . Philadelphia, Pennsylvania: Institute for Scientific Information.
Multidisciplinary indexing of research in all fields of social science. Appears three times a year. A likely source for references in African music. There are Cumulative indexes appear every five years. Available online and on magnetic tape. Issued in parts: Citation Index; Source Index and Corporate Index; Permuterm Subject Index; and Journal Citation Reports. Abbreviated as **SSCI.**

SOCIÉTÉ DES AFRICANISTES
See: **JOURNAL DES AFRICANISTES, 788.**

1475. **Society for Ethnomusicology.** *S.E.M. Newsletter.* 1967- . Bloomington, Indiana.
The newsletter, which is a vehicle for the exchange of ideas, news, and information among the Society's members, has been issued quarterly since 1985. It contains reports about people, conferences, prizes, committee meetings, and the like, all items of general concern to the ethnomusicologist. A few advertisements for new publications usually appear.

Society for Ethnomusicology
See also: **ETHNOMUSICOLOGY: JOURNAL OF THE SOCIETY FOR ETHNOMUSICOLOGY, 551.**

1476. **Söderberg, Bertil.** "Afrikanische Musikinstrumente und bildende Kunst." In **Festschrift to Ernst Emsheimer on the occasion of his 70th birthday, January 15th 1974.** Edited by Gustaf Hilleström, 214-223. Stockholm: Nordiska Musikförlaget, 1974.
Bibliography.

1477. **Söderberg, Bertil.** "Les instruments de musique africains et leurs décoration." **ARTS D'AFRIQUE NOIRE** 24 (1977): 18-33.

Many excellent photographs of musical instruments, some of wood, some of metal, all handsomely decorated. Included is an example of the human-sized Bembe wooden trumpets. Interesting are whistles made of antelope horns, and a three-headed sanza. The majority of decorations photographed appear in one way or another to be anthropomorphic.

1478. **Söderberg, Bertil.** Les sifflets sculpté du Bas-Congo." **ARTS D'AFRIQUE NOIRE** 9 (1975): 25-44.
Photographs and sketches of many beautiful sculptured whistles, most often anthropomorphic. The majority of miniature masterpieces pictured are carved from antelope horns.

1479. **Soko, Boston-Jaston.** STYLISTIQUE ET MESSAGES DANS LE VIMBUZA: ESSAI D'ÉTUDE ETHNIOLINGUISTIQUE DES CHANTS DE POSSESSION CHEZ LES NGONI-TUMBUKA DU MALAŴI - 1900-1963. Dissertation (3e cycle): Université de Paris III, 1984. 622pp.
In French. An ethnolinguistic study of the songs of the Vimbuza possession dance. One hundred thirty-one texts are first presented in their original versions, with notes as to the languages in which they appear. This is accompanied by a literal translation and a literary French translation. The author maintains that the songs of possession represent an oral genre that is part of African oral literature. Chapter 5 is concerned with "stylistique" in the songs of Vimbuza. Three maps, bibliography.

1480. **Somalia. Wasaaradda Warfaafinta iyo Hanuuninta Dadweynaha.** *Somali culture and folklore.* Mogadishu: Ministry of Information and National Guidance, c1974. 64pp.
The songs and dances of Somalia, along with other ethnological information. (In October, 1972 the Ministry of Information and National Guidance was changed to the Somali form of name listed above.)

1481. **Songs of Kenya: Embu, Gĩkũyũ na Meru.** Edited by John Kamenyi Wahome. Corrected edition, with new illustrations. Nairobi, Kenya: East African Publishing House, c1981. 1 score (46pp).
The foreword states that the songs are drawn mainly from the "folk music" of the three peoples listed in the title. There are melody lines, sol-fa indications, and Swahili texts. There is one song per page, usually with several verses written at the bottom, and animated, shaded illustrations that add considerable interest. Pages 43-47, written in English, are entitled, "What the songs are about." (Note: Other works of Kamenyi's in this bibliography can be found in the Author Index.

1482. **Songs of the Ethiopian revolution = Chansons de la révolution ethiopienne.** Compiled by Aleme Eshete. Addis Ababa: Published under the auspices of the Ministry of Culture, 1979. 118pp.
Texts drawn from some 1,000 revolutionary ballads and songs of Ethiopia in

English, French or Amharic. The songs relate primarily to the socialist movement.

1483. **Songs of Zambia**. Compiled and edited by Jackie Ehlers and Joan Child. Lusaka: Longman, 1975. 107pp.
Songs are in 20 African languages with English translations.

1484. **Sounding forms: African musical instruments**. Edited by Marie-Thérèse Brincard. Text by Arthur P. Bourgeois, *et al*. New York: American Federation of Arts, c1989. 205pp.
This pertains to an touring exhibition on African musical instruments, and African musical instruments in art. Bibliography, index.

SOUTH AFRICAN JOURNAL OF AFRICAN AFFAIRS
See: **AFRICA INSIGHT, 25**.

1485. **South African music encyclopedia**. Jacques P. Malan, General Editor. 4 vols. Cape Town: Oxford University Press, 1979-1986. ("A publication of the Human Sciences Research Council, Pretoria")
A "mixed bag" of four volumes issued different years. Racism by omission or condescension, especially in Volume I, A-D, under "Bantu [*sic*] Composers of South Africa." Only 4 of 318 black South African composers listed in Huskisson's books bearing a similar title (**704**, **705**) are included in the entire Encyclopedia. "Indigenous Musics of South Africa," however, is an excellent, 243 page compendium of scholarly essays. (See: Blacking (**250**), Huskisson (**707, 708**), Johnston, (**776**), Kirby (**868**), and Rycroft (**1398**.) One needs a curry-comb to find anything else on black South African music or musicians. "South African Music Collections," biographies of the Traceys, and other ethnomusicologists are worthwhile.

1486. **Southern, Eileen**. "African retentions in Afro-American music in the nineteenth century." In **INTERNATIONAL MUSICOLOGICAL SOCIETY. Congress. Report**, 88-98, 1977. Berkeley, California.
Source is **RILM**, 1981.

1487. **Southern, Eileen**. *Biographical dictionary of Afro-American and African musicians*. Westport, Connecticut: Greenwood Press, 1982. 478pp.
Southern hopes by this work to "throw into focus the 'oneness' of black music." Musicians of African descent from distant places are united by the welcoming arms of the alphabet. Biographical information is concise, comprehensive, well-researched, often filling an entire column of a large thick book with bold, legible type. For the most part, Southern excludes musicians born after 1945. Particular gratitude is due for providing hard-to-find information on prominent African musicians. Appendices list Period of Birth, Place of Birth, Musical Occupation. The latter category incorporates every imaginable activity having a musical core. Significant achievement! Select bibliography.

S

1488. **Southern, Eileen.** *The music of black Americans: a history.* 2d ed. New York: Norton, c1983. 602pp.

A work of the highest quality by an esteemed musicologist. The first chapter, The African Heritage (pages 1-24) gives a succinct and informative overview of African culture, the music component, and its carry-over into the New World. There are fascinating old illustrations of African musicians, music notations, accounts from long ago of travelers to Africa. The book has a bibliography, discography, index, and includes a useful 2-page map entitled, Tribes of the West African Coast in the period of the slave trade.

1489. **Southern, Eileen, and Josephine Wright.** *African-American traditions in song, sermon, tale, and dance, 1600s-1920: an annotated bibliography of literature, collections, and artworks.* New York: Greenwood Press, 1990. 365pp.

One could browse for hours in this superior compendium of priceless historical references. With a little time and patience, and working with the subject index, one can find African music references galore. Under "African tradition," the subheading "Antebellum Period" alone incorporates 114 entries. Often references are to performance practices of slaves that involve songs, dances or instruments related directly or indirectly to Africa. A few of many key subject words are: Dahomey, Festivals, Field Hollers, Juba Dance Song, Instruments Used for Signaling, Place Congo, Ring-Game Dances, Voodoo, Worksongs, and countless more. All entries are carefully annotated.

Southern, Eileen
See also: **Readings in Black American music, 1363.**

1490. **Ṣówándé, Fẹlá.** "Nigerian music and musicians: then and now." NIGERIA MAGAZINE no. 94 (1967): 253-261.

1491. **Ṣówándé, Fẹlá.** "Le rôle de la musique dans la société africaine traditionelle." In **La musique africaine, réunion de Yaoundé (Cameroun)** [sur les traditions musicales de l'Afrique subsaharienne], **23-27 février 1970, organisée par l'UNESCO**, 57-68. Paris: *La revue musicale*, Richard-Masse, 1972.

This is the original French version of the essay that follows.

1492. **Ṣówándé, Fẹlá.** "The role of music in traditional African society."In **African music: meeting in Yaoundé (Cameroon) 23-27 February 1970, organized by UNESCO**, 59-69. Paris: *La revue musicale*, 1972.

A translation of the preceding essay.

1493. **Städtisches Museum Braunschweig.** *Katalog der afrikanischen Sammlung im Städtischen Museum Braunschweig.* Braunschweig, Waisen-Buchdruckerci und Verlag, 1968. 394pp.(Braunschweiger Werkstüke, vol. 37) *continued*

A catalogue of African art objects found in the Museum. Pages 285-313 encompass the collection of musical instruments of all kinds, gathered from all over Africa, with detailed information concerning them. Technical, with very few photographs. Bibliography.

1494. **Standifer, James A., and Barbara Reeder [Lundquist].** *Source book of African and Afro-American materials for music educators.* [Washington]: Contemporary Music Project, [1972]. 147pp.
The dramatic black cover features the serene sculpture of a Bakuba ruler. Even though this book might need slight updating at some point, it cannot be surpassed as a valuable teaching resource for educators. Divided into African Music, and Afro-American Music, neither section is of the book is slighted. The African Music section has a bibliography subdivided into books on Africa, Music, Musical Instruments, Dance, Art, and Books for Elementary Grades. Tapes, films, film strips, and a discography are included. There are innovative classroom exercises in each section. Illustrations, notations, charts, scores, and a general bibliography.

1495. **Stapleton, Chris.** "African connections: London's hidden music scene." In *Black music in Britain: essays on the Afro-Asian contribution to popular music.* Edited by Paul Oliver, 87-101. Milton Keynes [England]; Philadelphia: Open University Press, 1990.

1496. **Stapleton, Chris.** "Golden Guinea." **FOLK ROOTS** no. 61 (1988): 27, 29.

1497. **Stapleton, Chris, and Chris May.** *African all stars: the pop music of a continent.* Illustrations by Andy Isham. Photographs by Jak Kilby. London; New York: Quartet Books, 1987. 373pp.
This is known as *African rock* in the British edition. History of popular African music, with a bibliography, discography, index, plates, illustrations. **AFROPOP WORLDWIDE** says, "best overall background book available on contemporary African music; highly recommended."

1498. **Starks, George Leroy.** BLACK MUSIC IN THE SEA ISLANDS OF SOUTH CAROLINA: ITS CULTURAL CONTEXT - CONTINUITY AND CHANGE. Dissertation, Wesleyan University, 1973. 239pp.
This dissertation was an outgrowth of field research conducted in the sea islands off the coast of South Carolina in 1972-1973. Music, and the role of music for black sea island residents, is examined in cultural context. It is doubtful that the word, "Africa," is mentioned at all. On the other hand, there are many Africanisms manifested in the presence of call-response, ring games, use of body percussion, and other resourceful percussive devices. Interesting is a brief passage concerning aesthetics, and what is desirable in voice quality. Bibliography, illustrations, song transcriptions.

S

1499. **Starks, George L.** "Salt and pepper in your shoe: Afro-American song tradition on the South Carolina sea islands." In **More than dancing: essays on Afro-American music and musicians.** Edited by Irene V. Jackson, 59-80. Westport, Connecticut: Greenwood Press, c1985.

A few historical references to Africanisms in the songs of the sea islands. Notes, excellent bibliography for those interested in this area. Selected discography, music notations. Abstracted in **RILM**, 1985.

1500. **Stefaniszyn, Bronislaw.** *African lyric poetry in reference to the Ambo traditional poem-songs.* Edited by Alice Diane Coughlan. [Portland, Oregon, HaPi Press, 1974], 208pp.

The Ambo are people of Zambia. Bibliography.

1501. **Stephenson, Mark H.** AFRICAN MUSIC IN THE METHODIST CHURCH OF SOUTHERN AFRICA: A CASE STUDY IN THE WESTERN CAPE. Master's Thesis, University of Cape Town (South Africa), 1985.

Sternberg, Ilse
See: **African studies: papers presented at a colloquium at the British Library, 44.**

1502. **STERNS WORLD MUSIC REVIEW: TRADEWIND.**

Listed in **AFROPOP WORLDWIDE** as having current information on new releases, record reviews, and world music news, and published monthly. (Available from Stern's African Music Centre, 116 Whitfield Street, London W1P 5RW, England.) The only number seen - but a recent one - consisted of two-pages slightly longer and narrower than typewriter paper. Three sides of these two pages had four columns, each densely packed with information such as is described above, but also including chitchat about personalities, clubs, events, gigs, and even obituaries. Paper bright pink. Not found in the 1990-1991 issue of **ULRICH'S**.

Stockmann, Erich
See: **Musikkulturen in Afrika, 1138.**

1503. **Stoller, Paul.** *Fusion of the worlds: an ethnography of possession among the Songhay of Niger.* Chicago, Illinois: University of Chicago Press, 1989. 243pp.

Stoller has studied possession among the Songhay for almost twenty years, both as a keen observer and also as an initiate into the private world of sorcerers. A long-time student of Adamu Jenitongo, the priest (or *zima*) of the possession troupe of Tillaberi, Niger, Stoller has interviewed Jenitongo at length, as well as the mediums, violinists, and drummers who comprise the troupe. Stoller discusses the relationship between what he calls the Social World and the Spirit World, and how possession occurs when these two worlds fuse. An authoritative and thoroughly-researched work that is also fascinating to read. Bibliography and index.

1504. **Stone, Ruth M.** "African music performed." In *Africa*. 2d ed. Edited by Phyllis M. Martin, and Patrick O'Meara, 233-248. Bloomington Indiana Press, c1986.
Written in an almost rhapsodic style, contrasting with Merriam's didactic essay of the 1977 edition. The writer uses an assortment of sources, including folklore, written accounts by scholars, and comments of Africans selected from different cultures, more often from West Africa, on the meaning of music, its effects on the individual and the community, stories about the origin of music and musical instruments, and more. There are interesting comments on timbre and its primacy to Africans. A number of fine photographs. Several statements, and the drawing of a 12 beat time-line, could be more precise.

1505. **Stone, Ruth M.** COMMUNICATION AND INTERACTION PROCESSES IN MUSIC EVENTS AMONG THE KPELLE OF LIBERIA. Dissertation, Indiana University, 1979. 323pp.

1506. **Stone, Ruth M.** *Dried millet breaking: time, words, and song in the Woi epic of the Kpelle*. Bloomington: Indiana University Press, c1988. 150pp.
This work has been called by Lester P. Monts, "a major contribution to the field of ethnomusicology. The *American Anthropologist* says, "a commendable piece of work that should be of interest to a range of scholars in anthropology and other disciplines. Index, bibliography, plates, illustrations. Stone has done intensive research among the Kpelle of Liberia.

1507. **Stone, Ruth M.** *Let the inside be sweet: the interpretation of music event among the Kpelle of Liberia*. Bloomington: Indiana University Press, c1982. 180pp.
Bibliography, discography, index, illustrations.

1508. **Stone, Ruth M.** "Meni-Pelee: a musical-dramatic folktale of the *Kpelle*." **LIBERIAN STUDIES JOURNAL** 4 (1972): 31-46.

1509. **Stone, Ruth M.** "Motion film as an aid in transcription and analysis of music." In *Discourse in ethnomusicology: essays in honor of George List*. Edited by Caroline Card, *et al*., 65-68. Bloomington: Ethnomusicology Publications Group, Indiana University, c1978.
For her study, she focuses on the work of Kubik, Rouget and List.

1510. **Stone, Ruth M.** MUSIC OF THE KPELLE PEOPLE OF LIBERIA. Master's Thesis, Hunter College, 1972. 211pp.

1511. **Stone, Ruth M.** "Unity of the arts in the aesthetics of *Kpelle* performance." In **Explorations in ethnomusicology: essays in honor of David P. McAllester**. Edited by Charlotte J. Frisbie,

179-185. Detroit: Information Coordinators, 1986.
The *Kpelle* are a Liberian people. Notes, bibliography, summary of Kpelle orthography.

1512. **Stone, Ruth M., and Frank J. Gillis**. *African music and oral data: a catalog of field recordings, 1902-1975*. Bloomington: Indiana University Press, c1976. 412pp.
Discography of African music and oral tradition.

Stone, Ruth M.
See also: **Performance in contemporary African arts, 1323.**

1513. **Stories and songs from Sierra Leone**
This excellent series is published by the People's Educational Association (PEA) of Sierra Leone, Freetown. Editors are Heribert Hinzen and Sheikh Tejan Tamu. Following is an alphabetical list of individual PEA entries in this bibliography that are known to involve music:
- **Benjei**. *The origin of the white race*, 1987.
- **Fishing in rivers of Sierra Leone**, 1987.
- **Fyle, C. Magbaily**. *Tradition, song and chant of the Yalunka*, 1986.
- **Gbomba, Lele**. *The bossy wife*, 1987.
- **Kissi stories and songs**, 1987.
- **Koroma, Salia**. *Salia Koroma: my life story*, 1985.
- **Koroma, Salia**. *The spider's web*, 1986.
- **Launching and reporting**, 1986.
- **Limba stories and songs**, 1986.
- **Manday Faboric, and other Mandingo stories and song**, 1988.
- **Temne stories and songs**, 1986.
- **A trap for men and other Susu stories and songs from Rokel, Mambolo, Rotain and Kamboa**, [1987?].

1514. **Studies in African music**. Co-editors, J. H. Kwabena Nketia, and Jacqueline Cogdell DjeDje. [Los Angeles]: Program in Ethnomusicology, Department of Music, University of California, Los Angeles, 1984. 387pp. (Selected reports in ethnomusicology, vol. 5)
Published in honor and memory of Klaus P. Wachsmann, this monumental book belongs in every academic library, should be the guarded possession of every ethnomusicologist. Beyond the merits of its essays, a brilliant collection by luminaries in the field, the book has an Introduction by Nketia and DjeDje, a 19 page Glossary of African terms from the text, a cassette, for which recording information and transcriptions appear, photographs, maps, sketches, charts, pull-out melograms, notes on contributors. The subject sections are: Style and Performance, Multipart Relationships, Organology, Notation and Transcription, and Communication: Speech Surrogates and Music. Essays have individual bibliographies.
- **Anderson, Lois Ann**. "Multipart relationships in xylophone and tuned drum traditions in Buganda," 121-144.

continued

- **Arom, Simha**. "The music of the Banda-Linda horn ensembles: form and structure," 173-193.
- **DeVale, Sue Carole**. "Prolegomena to a study of harp and voice sounds in Uganda: a graphic system for the notation of texture," 285-315.
- **DjeDje, Jacqueline Cogdell**. "The interplay of melodic phrases: an analysis of Dagomba and Hausa one string fiddle music," 81-118.
- **Godsey, Larry**. "The use of variation in Birifor funeral music," 67-80.
- **Kauffman, Robert**. "Multipart relationships in Shona vocal music," 145-159.
- **Knight, Roderick**. "The style of Mandinka music: a study in extracting theory from practice," 3-66.
- **Koetting, James**. "Hocket concept and structure in Kasena flute ensemble music," 161-172.
- **Mbabi-Katana, Solomon**. "The use of measured rhythm to communicate messages among Banyoro and Baganda in Uganda," 339-353.
- **Nketia, J. H. Kwabena, and Jacqueline C. DjeDje**. "Trends in African musicology," ix-xx.
- **Nzewi, Meki**. "Traditional strategies for mass communication: the centrality of Igbo music," 319-338.
- **Omondi, W. A.** "Tuning of the *thum*, the Luo lyre: a systematic analysis," 263-281.
- **Schmidt, Cynthia E.** "Interlocking techniques in Kpelle music," 195-216.
- **Tse, Cynthia, and Jerome Kimberlin**. "The morphology of the *mansinqo*: Ethiopia's bowed spike fiddle," 249-262.
- **Woodson, Craig**. "Appropriate technology in the construction of traditional African musical instruments in Ghana," 217-248.

1515. **Summers, Lynn S.** "African influence and the blues: an interview with Richard A. Waterman." **LIVING BLUES** no. 6 (1971): 30-36.

1516. **Sunjata**. Compiled and edited by B. K. Sidibe. Introduction by Winifred Galloway. Banjul: The Gambia: Oral History and Antiquities Division, Vice-President's Office, [1980]. 47pp.
Illustrations.

1517. **Sunjata: three Mandinka versions**. Edited by Gordon Innes. London: School of Oriental and African Studies, University of London, 1974. 326pp.
The epic of Sunjata, the man regarded by historians as the founder of the Mali empire, is presented here in three versions by different *jali*. The interest is less on history, more on Sunjata as literature. The introduction is valuable because of the information it gives on the *jali*'s role and status, and description of the three possible styles of vocalization (and how these relate to the accompanying music). Five essential notations are given that are common to either of the two possible accompanying instrument, the *kora*, or the *balo* (a xylophone referred to as *bala* in other sources). Three other notations are only used in the song mode. Gambian Mandinka text and English translation. Bibliography.

S

1518. **Sutner, Karl**. "Musik und Tanz im Reich des Löwen von Juda." In *Äthiopien: Musik der koptischen Kirche*, by Ashenafi Kebede. [Berlin: E. Blaschker], 1969.

Music and dance in the Kingdom of the Lion of Juda [Ethiopia]. This is the original version, in German.

1519. **Sutner, Karl**. "Musique au royaume du lion de Juda." In *Éthiopie: musique de l'Église copte*, by Ashenafi Kebede. Berlin: Institut International d'Études Comparatives la Musique, 1969.

French version of the preceding entry, **1518**, though this translation says nothing about dance.

1520. **Świderski, Stanislaw, and Marie-Laure Girou-Swiderski**. *Laoésie populaire et les chants religieux du Gabon*. Ottawa, Canada: Editions de l'Université d'Ottawa, 1981. 290pp.

Summary in English, French, German, Italian, Polish and Spanish. Includes bibliographical references.

1521. **Symposium musico-ethnologicum**. Edited by Johannes Overath. MUSICES APTATIO 1980 (Roma: CIMS, 1980) 382pp.

This is a collection of papers presented at the second symposium held in June 1980 in Bonn, on the subject of church music in east and central Africa. There are illustrations, music, bibliographies, charts and tables. Individual papers listed below are abstracted iu **RILM**, 1985.

- **Bispo, Antonio**. "Zur Kirchenmusik in Zaïre nach den Darstellungen in der missions- und musikwissenschaftlichen Literatur," 364-382.
- **Chima, Alex B**. "The suitability of instruments in the liturgy," 84-114.
- **Gilombe, Mudiji-Malamba**. "Community life and the Church: selected perspectives and points of contact as exemplified in the Phende society of Zaïre," 56-69.
- **Mboniman, Gamaliel**. "Les chants traditionnels du Rwanda et la liturgie," 184-203.
- **Milingo, Emmanuel**. "Presentation on African traditional music in liturgy," 156-174.
- **Ndlovu, Bernard**. "Indigenization of church music in Zimbabwe: a report," 341-349.
- **Ngirabanyiginya, Dominique**. "Interaction entre les paroles et la musique avec accent particulier sur le langage tonal africain et en l'occurence le Kinyarwanda," 237-298.
- **Nkinda, Masengo**. "The adaptation of traditional musical instruments to sacred music: the example of Zaïre," 129-153.
- **Okelo, Anthony**. "Intonation of words in the Acholi language in relation to church music," 204-236.
- **Tangang, Yakime**. "La musique au service du message," 299-320.
- **Thiel, Paul van**. "An historical outline of the growth of African church music in some Bantu countries," 350-363.

1522. **Symposium on African Art, Music and Literature (1977).** [Papers from the Symposium on African Art, Music and Literature: sponsored by the African Studies Association of the United Kingdom, September 20, 1977]. [England?: s.n., 1977?].
The papers are photocopied. Bibliographical references are included.

1523. **Symposium on Ethnomusicology.** [1st: 1980: Rhodes University] *Papers presented at the Symposium on Ethnomusicology, Music Department, Rhodes University, on 10th and 11th October, 1980.* Grahamstown: International Library of African Music, Institute of Social and Economic Research, Rhodes University, 1981. 35pp.
- •**Clegg, Johnny**. "The music of Zulu immigrant workers in Johannesburg - a focus on concertina and guitar," 2-9.
- •**Dargie, David**. "Group composition and church music workshops," 10-13.
- •**Mngoma, Khabi**. "Music teaching at the University of Zululand," 14-22.
- •**Mthethwa, Bongani**. "Zulu children's songs," 23-28.
- •**Tracey, Andrew**. "White response to African music," 29-35.

1524. **Symposium on Ethnomusicology.** (2nd: 1981: Rhodes University) *Papers presented at the Second Symposium on Ethnomusicology, Music Department, Rhodes University, 24th to 26th September, 1981.* Edited by Andrew Tracey. Grahamstown: International Library of African Music, Institute of Social and Economic Research, Rhodes University, 1982. 91pp.
- •**Axelsson, Olof**. "The development of African church music in Zimbabwe," 2-7.
- •**Clegg, Johnny**. "Towards an understanding of African dance: the Zulu *Isishameni* style," 8-14.
- •**Dargie, David**. "A theoretical approach to composition in Xhosa style," 15-22.
- •**Erlmann, Veit**. "Music and body control in the Hausa *bori* spirit possession cult," 23-27.
- •**Gildenhuys, Cecilia**. "Musical instruments of South West Africa/Namibia," 28-33.
- •**Hansen, Deirdre**. "The categories of Xhosa music," 34-52.
- •**Kierman, Sean**. "Audiometric characteristics of the ethnic ear," 53-60.
- •**Mngoma, Khabi**. "The correlation of folk and art music among African composers," 61-69.
- •**Rycroft, David**. "The musical bow in southern Africa," 70-76.
- •**Sherman, Jessica**. "Songs of the *Chimurenga* (Zimbabwean revolution): from protest to praise," 77-79.
- •**Strydom, Frikkie**. "The music of the Rehoboth basters," 80-83.
- •**Weinberg, Pessa**. "Some aspects of my research into Zulu children's songs," 84-90.

1525. **Symposium on Ethnomusicology.** (3rd: 1982: University of Natal) [4th: 1983: Rhodes University] *Papers presented at the Third and Fourth Symposia on Ethnomusicology,* Music Department, University of Natal, Durban, 16th to 19th September

1982; Music Department, Rhodes University, 7th to 8th October 1983. Grahamstown, South Africa: International Library of African Music, 1984. 70pp.

These two Symposia are bound in one volume, and all papers are abstracted in **RILM**, 1985. Contents of each Symposium are listed below.

3rd Symposium

•**Dargie, David**. "Music and liberation," 9-14.
•**Gourlay, Kenneth A.** ""The necessity of theory," 2-8.
•**Gourlay, Kenneth A.** "Songs of the *Karimojong*: a talk with slides," 20-24.
•**Mphahlele, Ezekiel**. "Africanist humanistic thought and belief: background to an understanding of African music," 15-19.
•**Mthethwa, Bongani**. "Western elements in Shembe's religious dances," 34-37.
•**Weinberg, Pessa**. "An analysis of semi-rural and peri-urban Zulu children's songs," 34-37.

4th Symposium

•**Axelsson, Olof**. "African music and its relation to education," 61-63.
•**Ballantine, Chris**. "Taking sides - or music, music departments and the deepening crisis in South Africa," 52-55.
•**Bigalke, Erich**. "An historic overview of southern *Nguni* musical behaviour," 38-47.
•**Clegg, Johnny**. "An examination of the *Umzansi* dance style," 64-70.
(Note: though this paper is listed at the bottom of the contents page of this 4th Symposium, it is preceded by the statement: "3rd Symposium - Durban.")
•**James, Debba**. "Some inter-disciplinary problems in the teaching of African music," 59-60.
•**Kubik, Gerhard**. "How my research developed from 1959 to now," 48-51.
•**Robinson, J.** "African aesthetics and its implication for institutionalized music education in Black South African Schools," 56-58.

1526. **Symposium on Ethnomusicology**. (5th: 1984: University of Cape Town). *Papers presented at the fifth Symposium on Ethnomusicology: Faculty of Music, University of Cape Town, August 30th-September 1st, 1984*. Grahamstown: International Library of African Music, 1985. 67pp.

All of the following papers are abstracted in **RILM**, 1985.
•**Dargie, David**. "Some recent discoveries and recordings in Xhosa music," 29-35.
•**Davids, Achmat**. "Music and Islam," 36-38.
•**Desai, Desmond**. "'Cape Malay' music," 39-44.
•**Hai, Tran Quang**. "Vietnamese music," 57-61.
•**Henning, C. G.** "Indian musical instruments," 62-66.
•**Kruger, Jaco**. "The state of Venda chordophones," 8-12.
•**Kubik, Gerhard**. "Meaning and cultural context of masks and masked dancing in Central Africa," 45-49.
•**Ralushai, Victor**. "The origin and social significance of *Malombo*," 2-7.
•**Rycroft, David**. "Zulu melodic and non-melodic vocal styles," 13-28.
•**Sharvit, Uri**. "Jewish Yemenite wedding ceremonies," 54-56.
•**Sharvit, Uri**. "Old and new in the musical cultures in Israel," 50-53.

1527. **Symposium on Ethnomusicology**. (6th: 1987: Rhodes University). *Papers presented at the Sixth Symposium on Ethnomusicology: Music Department, Rhodes University, 1st-3rd October, 1987*. [Grahamstown]: International Library of African Music, 1988.

Note: This symposium was not available in sufficient time to include each paper as a separate entry.

- **Ballantine, Christopher**. "From *marabi* to exile: a brief history of black jazz in South Africa," 2-5.
- **Blacking, John**. "Percy Grainger's contribution to ethnomusicology and music education," 6-8.
- **Dontsa, Luvuyo**. "Performing arts and politics in South Africa," 9-15.
- **Honore, Jasmine**. "Some observations on Xhosa dance in the 1980's," 16-18.
- **Jackson, Melveen**. "Aspects of music amongst Indian South Africans in Natal 1920-1948: towards a politico-cultural understanding," 19-23.
- **Kruger, Jaco**. "The construction of the Venda xylophone," 24-27.
- **Lucia, Christina**. "The ethnomusicologist and the educator," 36-39.
- **Merwe, Peter van der**. "Shifting tonal levels in Africa, Europe and America," 53-56.
- **Mthethwa, Bongani**. "The songs of Alfred A. Kumalo: a study in Nguni and Western musical syncretism," 28-32.
- **Oehrle, Elizabeth**. "Role of the ethnomusicologist in altering the course of South African music education," 40-42.
- **Petersen, Alvin**. "Making African music relevant in the school: some implications," 33.
- **Rose-Joubert, Margaret**. "Practical discussion points concerning music education in South Africa," 33.
- **Tonder, Tossie Van**. "I am a performer," 42.
- **Tracey, Andrew**. "Workshop in transcription of African music," 43-52.

1528. **Symposium on Ethnomusicology**. (7th: 1988: Venda, South Africa). *Papers presented at the 7th Symposium on Ethnomusicology: Department of Anthropology and Ethnomusicology, University of Venda, 3rd to 5th September 1988*. Edited by Andrew Tracey. Grahamstown, South Africa: Rhodes University, 1989. 55pp.

The majority of the following papers have bibliographies and various explanatory devices:

- **Ballantine, Christopher**. "'Africans in America.' "'Harlem in Johannesburg:'" the ideology of Afro-America in the formation of black jazz and vaudeville in South Africa before the mid-1940s," 5-10.
- **Espi-Sanchis, Pedro**. "African stories in education," 11-13.
- **Honore, Jasmine**. "A transcription system for Xhosa dance-songs," 14-21.
- **Jackson, Melveen**. "The advent of the 'Indian' orchestra and a local Indian record company: music into the Indian South African economy." 22-27.
- **Kruger, Jaco**. "Introduction to the social context of two Venda dances: *Tshikona* and *Tshigombela*, 28-31.
- **Mthethwa, Bongani**. "Syncretism in church music: adaptation of Western hymns for African use," 32-34.

continued

- **New, Leon**. "The traditional *Ebe* school for girls at Adazi, Igboland, Nigeria: the problem of traditional culture in the modern world," 35-42.
- **Tracey, Andrew**. "The system of the Mbira," 43-55.

1529. Szwed, John F. "Afro-American musical adaptations." In *Afro-American anthropology: contemporary perspectives*. Edited by Norman E. Whitten, Jr., and John F. Szwed, 219-228. Foreword by Sidney W. Mintz. New York: Free Press, [1970].

Szwed's maintains "that song forms and performances are themselves models of social behavior that reflect strategies of adaptation to human and natural environments." Much of the paper is spent on discussing the dichotomy between church song and the blues. He finds church songs and spirituals to be closer to West African song style, in contrast to the blues, which, according to the Lomax study he cites, are stylistically mid-way between African and Western European song forms. He also examines calypso, gospel, soul, and Colombian and Ecuadorian forms, searching for the same dichotomy, sometimes finding it, sometimes not. Notes.

1530. Szwed, John F. and Roger D. Abrahams, with Robert Baron *et al. Afro-American folk culture: an annotated bibliography of materials from North, Central, and South America, and the West Indies*. Philadelphia: Institute for the Study of Human Issues, c1978. 2 vols. (Publications of the American Folklore Society, Bibliographical and special series, vol 31-32)

A comprehensive, meticulous work showing incredible dedication. Volume 1 is on North America; Volume 2 is on Central America, South America, and the West Indies. The index has countless entries under Music, and related headings. The theme of the bibliography, presented in italics in the book, is "...*Afro-American cultures exist, cultures which are neither entirely African nor Euro-American in origin, but which contain elements of both, plus the inevitable developments attendant upon enslavement, the plantation experience, Native American contact, poverty, and racism, as well as the vigor and creativity of human beings*."

1531. **Tahmen, George W. W.** *Tarditional [i.e., traditional] music and dances of Liberia.* [s.l.: s.n., 19--?] 17pp.
Liberian songs are discussed from pages 3 to 6, starting with a brief essay followed by a list of 25 examples of traditional songs. Some are briefly described or explained. Others have texts in various Liberian languages. Descriptions of 20 selected dances are followed by 9 examples of the Liberian National Troupe's dance dramas. No transcriptions.

1532. TAKE COVER. 1990- . London: Southern Rag Ltd.
This is a relative of what the editor Chris Stapleton calls their "senior sibling publication **FOLK ROOTS**," but differs from the latter in that it does not include world music. The same is true for reggae, felt to be well covered elsewhere. The stated aim is to provide news, views and information on African pop music and the Latin and Caribbean sounds related through history to the mother continent. Issued quarterly.

1533. **Tamene, Asmare.** *Instruments musicaux = Musical instruments: Ethiopia.* Illustrated by Jill Poole. [Addis Ababa: Ethiopian Tourist Office, 1976?]. 25pp.
In English and French.

1534. **Tangang, Yakime.** "La musique au service du message." In **Symposium musico-ethnologicum**. Edited by Johannes Overath, 299-320. MUSICES APTATIO 1980 (Roma CIMS, 1980).
Illustrations, music. In French, English, and German. Abstracted in **RILM**, 1960.

1535. TANZANIA NOTES AND RECORDS. 1966- . Dar es Salaam, Tanzania Society.
In earlier years, i.e., 1936-1965, when this journal was called **TANGANYIKA NOTES AND RECORDS**, there were occasional articles on African music, (Hans Cory, 1937, 1962, Z. Hall, 1936, Pamela Gulliver, 1955). Perhaps there were others. Though its present policy is unknown, mention of music articles in connection with this journal has not been noted recently in standard sources. Indexed in **CURRENT CONTENTS AFRICA**, and **HISTORICAL ABSTRACTS**.

1536. **Tatar, Elizabeth.** THE DEFINING CRITERIA OF ANLO EVE VOCAL STYLE. Master's Thesis, University of California, Los Angeles, 1973.

Tax, Sol
See: **International Congress of Americanists, 733.**

1537. **Taylor, Frederick Jerome.** THE DEVELOPMENT AND EVALUATION OF A BLACK MUSIC COURSE OF STUDY DESIGNED FOR JUNIOR HIGH STUDENTS. Dissertation, Temple University, 1981. 77pp.
The course that the writer describes and evaluates starts off with information on west African music and Yorùbá drumming before continuing with black American idioms, composers, conductors, performers. He makes a good case for including

both black and white music in music courses, and found in his study that black students did better than whites when black music was included.

1538. **Temne stories and songs.** Collected by Ibrahim Bangura, Heribert Hinzen, and Lansana Kamara. Illustrated by Maliki Koroma. Freetown: People's Educational Association of Sierra Leone, 1986. 96pp. (Stories and songs from Sierra Leone, 21)
Members of the Stories and Songs Project of PEA gathered materials from the Port Loko District area [Sierra Leone]. Contributions were by story-tellers, singers and instrumentalists - men, women, and children - from Magborognoh and Fanya. Neighboring people also contributed. Besides 13 stories, there are 20 songs, primarily in call-response form, falling into four categories: Circumcision Songs, Traditional Chieftain Songs, Women's Moonlight Activity Songs, and General Songs. Texts in English, but no notations.

1539. **Tenaille, Frank.** *Toure Kunda.* [Paris]: Seghers, c1987. 159pp. (Le Club des stars) (Livre compact)
Toure Kunda is a ten-piece fusion band from Senegal and one of the most popular and well-known of commercial African groups. Biographies of Senegalese musicians are included. Discography, bibliography, illustrations.

1540. **Tersis-Surugue, Nicole, and Bernard Surugue.** *La mare de la vérité: contes et musique zarma, Niger.* Paris: SELAF, 1976. 129pp. (Langues et civilisations à tradition orale, 19)
Includes five Nigerien tales, a narrative in the form of riddles, and a girl's song. Two 33 1/3 rpm discs in back pocket give a complete record of the tales, of the song, and musical examples of a monochord lute, and an"idioglottal clarinet," with musicological remarks by Bernard Surugue. Summary in English, French, German and Russian. Bibliography, indexes.

1541. **Thiel, Paul van.** "Divine worship and African church music." **AFRICAN ECCLESIASTICAL REVIEW** 3, no. 1 (1961): 73-76; vol. 3, no. 2 (1961): 144-147.

1542. **Thiel, Paul van.** "An historical outline of the growth of African church music in some Bantu countries." In **Symposium musico-ethnologicum**. Edited by Johannes Overath, 350-363. **MUSICES APTATIO** 1980 (Roma CIMS, 1980).
Abstracted in **RILM**, 1960.

1543. **Thiel, Paul van.** *Multi-tribal music of Ankole: an ethnomusicological study including a glossary of musical terms.* Tervuren, (Steenweg op Leuven 13): Musée royal de l'Afrique centrale, 1977. 234pp. (Annalen - Koninklijk Museum voor Midden-Afrika: Series in-8°, Menselijke wetenschappen, no. 91)
Includes bibliographies and indexes.

1544. **Thiel, Paul van**. "Spontaneous creativity and African sacred music." **MUSICES APTATIO** 1982: 15-20.
Abstracted in **RILM**, 1985.

1545. **Thiel, Paul van**. "Text, tone and tune in African sacred music." **AFRICAN ECCLESIASTICAL REVIEW** 6, no. 3 (1964): 250-257; vol. 8, no. 1 (1966): 53-62.

1546. **Thieme, Darius L.** A DESCRIPTIVE CATALOGUE OF YORÙBÁ MUSICAL INSTRUMENTS. Dissertation, Catholic University of America, 1969. 429pp.

1547. **Thieme, Darius L.** "Music history in Africa." In *Development of materials for a one year course in African music for the general undergraduate student (project in African music).* Edited by Vada E. Butcher, *et al.*, 101-104. [Washington]: Office of Education, 1970.

1548. **Thieme, Darius L.** "Music in Yorùbá society." In *Development of materials for a one year course in African music for the general undergraduate student (project in African music).* Edited by Vada E. Butcher, *et al.*, 107-111. [Washington]: Office of Education, 1970.

1549. **Thieme, Darius L.** A SELECTED BIBLIOGRAPHY OF PERIODICAL ARTICLES ON THE MUSIC OF THE NATIVE PEOPLES OF SUB-SAHARAN AFRICA. Master's Thesis, Catholic University of America, Washington D.C., 1963.
This work surveys "the complete runs of 12 selected periodicals and serials in various fields of study." Thieme says that it lists all articles that discuss African music appearing in print up to November 1, 1962. Gaskin (**614**) lists this same title as appearing in **AFRICAN MUSIC** 3, no. 1 (1962): 103-110. See also **Library of Congress. Music Division**, for Thieme's, *African music: a briefly annotated bibliography*, **975**.

1550. **Thieme, Darius L.** "Social organization of Yorùbá musicians." In *Development of materials for a one year course in African music for the general undergraduate student (project in African music).* Edited by Vada E. Butcher, *et al.*, 115-117. [Washington]: Office of Education, 1970.

1551. **Thieme, Darius L.** "Style in Yorùbá music." **ÌBÀDÀN** 24 (1967): 33-39.

T

1552. **Thieme, Darius L.** "Training and musicianship among the Yorùbá." In *Development of materials for a one year course in African music for the general undergraduate student (project in African music)*. Edited by Vada E. Butcher, *et al.*, 121-122. [Washington]: Office of Education, 1970.

Thieme, Darius L.
See also: **Library of Congress. Music Division.** *African music: a briefly annotated bibliography*, **975.**

1553. **Thomas, Jacqueline M. C.** *Contes, proverbes, devinettes ou énigmes, chants et prières ngbaka-ma'bo (République centrafricaines.* With the collaboration of Simha Arom, and Marcel Mavode. Paris: Klincksieck, 1970. 908pp. (Langues et littératures de l'Afrique noire, 6)
Bibliography.

1555. **Thompson, Robert Farris.** "Afro-Atlantic music in the nineties: making space for African futures." AFROPOP WORLDWIDE. LISTENER'S GUIDE. (1991): 2-6. Washington D.C., National Public Radio.
Africanist Thompson points out African continuities in *all* "Afropop" - the African song of allusion become "social critique voiced to a swinging beat." He points out the similarities of instruments and their uses, and the deeper connections to Yorùbá religion. Thompson coins the term "Afro-Atlantic" for this music, though how appropriate it will be as the music reaches points far beyond the Atlantic - and perhaps ultimately the entire globe - remains to be seen.

1556. **Thompson, Robert Farris.** *Flash of the spirit: African and Afro-American art and philosophy.* New York: Random House, c1983. 317pp.
Only inadvertently about music, but Thompson works in a few brilliant insights about African music and other African arts. His comprehension is so unified and profound that he can point out the same general symbolic, aesthetic, and philosophical principles operating in many forms of African artistic expression. Narrow-strip fabrics, he calls "rhythmized," saying that the designs are meant to be "scanned metrically, in visual resonance with the famed off-beat phrasing of melodic accents in African and Afro-American music." He treats *nsibide* (an indigenous African form of script) similarly. Other musical references may be found via the index.

1557. **Thompson, Robert L.** MUSIC AND HEALING IN WEST AFRICA: THE HAUSA BORI CULT. Master's Thesis, Western Washington University, 1986.

1558. **Thunder from the mountains: Mau Mau patriotic songs.** Edited by Maina wa Kinyatti. London: Zed Press, 1980. 116pp. (Africa series)
Revolutionary songs and ballads from Kenya with texts.

1559. **Timpunza Mvula, Enoch S.** "Mngeniso ritual and Ngomi ethnic identify." **Cross rhythms** 3 (1989): 109-128.
Mngeniso is a communal dance, song and beer drinking ceremony, observed in this case by the Ngoni people of Mchinje district, central Malaŵi. It marks a son-in-law's incorporation into his parents-in-law's house and affinity group.

1560. **Timpunza Mvula, Enoch S.** *Tumbuka pounding songs: a device for resolving familial conflict.* Bloomington, Indiana: African Studies Program, Indiana University, c1984. 19pp.
This paper was co-winner in the seventh annual graduate student term paper competition, 1984. Timpunza believes that work songs and their functions in a sociocultural context deserve far more study than they have received to date. He starts his essay with a sociocultural background of the Tumbuka people of northern Malaŵi, and proceeds to the women's pounding songs, which he regards as most effective in resolving family conflicts arising between the woman, her husband, mother-in-law, and co-wives. Bibliography.

1561. **Timpunza Mvula, Enoch S.** "Tumbuka pounding songs in the management of familial conflicts." **Cross Rhythms** 2 (1985): 93-113.
See the directly preceding (**1560**) and following (**1562**) entries.

1562. **Timpunza Mvula, Enoch S.** WOMEN'S ORAL POETRY AS A SOCIAL STRATEGY IN MALAWI. Dissertation, Indiana University, 1987. 361pp.
Women's sung poetry is examined to show the position of women and sex roles in a Maseko Ngoni community of Malaŵi. The author claims that this medium is used by women as a "social and communicative strategy to define, redefine, evaluate and interpret their positions." Illustrations, bibliography. **(UMI)**

1563. **Tinhorão, José Ramos.** *Os negros em Portugal: uma presença silenciosa.* Lisbon: Caminho, c1988. 460pp. (Colecção Universitária, 31)
A thorough record - with an emphasis on history - of people of African descent in Portugal. Though music and dance are not treated in any depth, there are still enough cues as to their possible African derivations to warrant the dedicated researcher's at least scanning the work. As might be expected, some of the dance and music forms are also common to Brazil. The notes and comprehensive bibliography might also lead in the right direction. Entire work in Portuguese. Notes.

T

1564. Tinhorão, José Ramos. *Os sons dos negros no Brasil: cantos, danças, folguedos: origens.* São Paulo: Art Editora, 1988. 138pp.

Written in Portuguese. This author has a number of other books to his credit on the popular music of Brazil, listed at the beginning of his book. There are four parts, starting with the 15th Century, leading through the 20th, in which the music, dance, and song of people of African descent in Brazil are presented, particularly the origins of their arts. Music *per se* seems to receive the least notice. There is a fairly extensive bibliography of books, articles, and dictionaries at the end, through few entries specify *música*. Each part is also followed by notes.

1565. Titouh, Tassadit Yacine. *Aït Menguellet chante...: chansons berbères contemporaines: textes berbères et français.* Tassadit Yacine-Titouh. Paris: La Découverte/AWAL, 1989. 343pp.

Some of the songs are political, some are about love, nostalgia, and various other subjects. They are in Berber and French on facing pages. Includes bibliographical references.

1566. Toffolon, Elsa, comp. *Songs of Nigeria.* Ìbàdàn: New Culture Studios, 1982. 58pp. (Music production series, no. 1)

This collection of traditional Nigerian songs is meant to be used in primary and secondary schools, and corrects what had been an unfortunate lack in Nigeria of suitable textbooks. Songs are of the Igbo, Yorùbá, and Bini peoples; words are in associated languages, and in English. Music students, under the direction of W. Wilberforce C. Echezona, contributed to this book, transcribed the songs. Suggestions are given for ways in which the teacher can improvise percussion instruments as an accompaniment to the songs. It is also suggested that the songs be dramatized. (Elsa Toffolon also arranged the piano accompaniments.)

1567. Tompkins, William David. THE MUSICAL TRADITIONS OF THE BLACKS OF COASTAL PERU. 2 vols. Dissertation, University of California, Los Angeles, 1981. 594pp.

Examines Afro-Peruvian music history chronologically, describes and analyzes the major musical instruments and music and dance genres. There are plates and numerous transcriptions. The goal of the author is to be carefully objective in an extremely complex field. Though African influence figures in the study, Tomkins is concerned with other cultures as well, including the Spanish and Indian strands. He speaks of origins of Afro-Peruvian music, rather than one "origin."

1568. Tons et accents dans les langues africaines. Edited by Gladys Guarisma. Paris: SELAF, 1981. 143pp.

In French. On tones and accents in African languages. Summaries in English, German, and Spanish. Includes bibliographical references.

1569. Topan, Farouk. ORAL LITERATURE IN A RITUAL SETTING: THE ROLE OF SPIRIT SONGS IN A SPIRIT-MEDIUMSHIP CULT OF MOMBASA, KENYA. Dissertation, University of London, 1972.

1570. **Torrend, Julius**, comp. and trans. *Specimens of Bantu folklore from Northern Rhodesia: texts (collected with the help of the phonograph)*. London: K. Paul, Trench & Company; New York: E. P. Dutton & Company, 1921; New York: Negro Universities Press, [1969]. 187pp.
Map, music, illustrations.

1571. **Touma, Habib**. *Der Maqām Bayati im arabischen Taqsīm*. 2. unveränderte Aufl. Hamburg: K. D. Wagner, 1976. 104pp. (Beiträge zur Ethnomusikologie, vol. 3)
Originally the author's thesis, Berlin, 1968.

1572. **Tracey, Andrew T. N.** *How to play the mbira (dza vadzimu)*. [Roodepoort, Transvaal]: International Library of African Music, c1970. 25pp.
Bibliography.

1573. **Tracey, Andrew T. N.** "Keywords in African music." In **National Music Educator's Conference.** (1st: 1985: University of Natal) *Proceedings of the first National Music Educator's Conference.* Edited by Christine Lucia, 29-45. Durban [South Africa]: University of Natal, Department of Music, 1986.

1574. **Tracey, Andrew T. N.** "The system of the mbira." In **Symposium on Ethnomusicology**. (7th: 1988: Venda, South Africa). *Papers presented at the 7th Symposium on Ethnomusicology: Department of Anthropology and Ethnomusicology, University of Venda, 3rd to 5th September 1988.* Edited by Andrew Tracey, 43-55. Grahamstown, South Africa: Rhodes University, 1989.

1575. **Tracey, Andrew T. N.** "White response to African music." In **Symposium on Ethnomusicology**. [1st: 1980: Rhodes University] *Papers presented at the Symposium on Ethnomusicology, Music Department, Rhodes University, on 10th and 11th October, 1980*, 29-35. Grahamstown: International Library of African Music, Institute of Social and Economic Research, Rhodes University, 1981.

1576. **Tracey, Andrew T. N., and Gei Zantzinger.** *A companion to the films "Mgodo wa mbanguzi" and "Mgodo wa mkandeni."* Johannesburg: International Library of African Music, 1976. 47pp.
Although this book is intended to accompany two films, it contains enough enlightening information about African music to stand on its own. The films are real time documentations of performances of the *mgodo* dance in the villages of

Mbanguzi and Mkandewni [southern Mozambique] in 1973 - the term *mgodo* referring to the whole performance or work. There are details about the music, its structure, order of presentation. The xylophones, *timbili*, get special attention, as do the accompanying dances. Included are choreographic comments and notations by Nadia Nahumck. One experiences the *mgodo* event even without viewing the films.

1577. **Tracey, Hugh**. *Catalogue: the Sound of Africa series: 210 long play records of music and songs from Central, Eastern, and Southern Africa.* 2 vols. in 1. Roodepoort, South Africa: International Library of African Music, 1973.
A detailed and comprehensive catalogue that furnishes far more information about African music than the title alone might indicate. Recordings cover a broad geographic range, and were made between 1943-1940, and 1948-1970. In all, there are 210 long play records covered. Eighteen subject sections include a map of the home territories of the people who were recorded; a map of African language zones; records classified by types of performances (in itself instructive); a section explaining how musical instruments are classified; information on scales, with diagrams; photographs; glossaries of vernacular terminology for languages and instruments. This is a veritable treasure-trove.

1578. **Tracey, Hugh**. *Chopi musicians: their music, poetry, and instruments: [1st ed. reprinted] with a new introduction.* New York: Oxford University Press, 1970. 193pp.
"First published 1948."

1579. **Tracey, Hugh**. *The evolution of African music and its function in the present day.* Johannesburg: International Library of African Music, 1963. 24pp. (Institute for the Study of Man in Africa. Publications)

1580. **Tracey, Hugh**. *The lion on the path, and other African stories.* Illustrations by Eric Byrd. Music transcribed by Andrew Tracey. London: Routeledge & K. Paul, c1967. 129pp.
Tracey reiterates frequently that a printed oral text is only a half-way stage in its reproduction, and that it is not meant to be read as a written story or to produce the same effect. Since most of us may never get to hear original, memorized and spontaneously sung African tales, however, the author's careful transcriptions are a welcome substitute. Melodies are transcribed at the ends of the stories. A brief guide to pronunciation of vernacular words is included. Imaginative, African-style illustrations enhance. (Many tales, à la Grimm, not noteworthy for happy endings or eliciting pleasant dreams.)

1581. **Tracey, Hugh, Gerhard Kubik, and Andrew T. N. Tracey**. *Codification of African music and textbook project. A primer of practical suggestions for field research.* [Roodepoort, South Africa: International Library of African Music,
continued

1969]. 54pp.
An enlightening handbook with everything an ethnomusicologist working in Africa ought to know. Although attention is given to the operation and coordination of the Codification Project itself, there are specific instructions for almost every aspect of researching the music of a given culture. Tracey is concerned that investigation be carried on without cultural bias, and recommends ways for maintaining scrupulous objectivity. African music is always a primary concern, along with an admirable commitment to make the results of research available to African people for their own needs.

1582. **Tracey, Peggy**. *The lost valley*. Cape Town: Human & Rousseau, 1975. 139pp.
A sensitive, poetic narrative by Peggy Tracey, who accompanied Hugh Tracey in an expedition to record the music of the Tonga people in Zimbabwe. This documents their daily lives, including the recording sessions that took place in a stretch of the Zambezi valley, now the bed of the great man-made Lake Kariba. Between chapters, there are texts of songs that include some Tsonga words, preceded by brief summaries as to who sang what, and with which instrument. One can almost hear the music that is described in context as the journey unfolds. The book is beautifully written, deeply human.

TRADEWIND
See: **STERNS WORLD MUSIC REVIEW, 1502.**

1583. **Tradition and renewal: essays on twentieth-century Latin American literature and culture**. Edited by Merlin H. Forster. Urbana: University of Illinois Press, [1975]. 240pp.
•**Béhague, Gerard**. "Notes on regional and national trends in Afro-Brazilian cult music," 68-80.

1584. **The traditional artist in African societies**. Edited by Warren L. d'Azevedo. Bloomington: Indiana University Press, [1973]. 454pp.
A major collection of important essays. The book includes a comprehensive bibliography of its own, though many essays have individual notes. At the end are commentaries on the essays by Peter Etzkorn, George Mills, John Ladd, and Ray Sieber. Though all of the essays are of high quality, those listed alphabetically below focus in particular on African music:
•**Ames, David W.** "A sociocultural view of Hausa musical activity," 128-161.
•**D'Azevedo, Warren L.** "Sources of Gola artistry," 282-340.
•**Merriam, Alan P.** "The bala musician," 250-281.
•**Nketia, J. H. Kwabena**. "The musician in Akan society," 79-100.

1585. **A trap for men and other Susu stories and songs from Rokel, Mambolo, Rotain and Kambia**. Collected 19th-21st February, 1987, by Heribert Hinzen, Jim Sorie and E. D. A. Turay. Translated by Shebora S. Suma and Jim Sorie. Freetown: People's

Educational Association of Sierra Leone, [1987?]. 67pp. (Stories and songs from Sierra Leone, 33)
Includes Sierra Leone songs, illustrations.

1586. **A tribute to Alan P. Merriam**. Edited by Caroline Card, *et al*. Bloomington, Indiana: Indiana University. (Archives of Traditional Music), c1981. 266pp.
This is a volume of essays on ethnomusicological subjects, plus a complete bibliography and discography of works of the renowned ethnomusicologist, Alan P. Merriam. The latter has been compiled by Caroline Card and Carl Rahkonen (pages 237-266) and lists 317 books, articles, reviews, and records by Merriam, as well as works of others he has reviewed. The following essays from this volume have been selected for listing:
- **Boyd, James T.** "Music in Islam: Lamu, Kenya, a case study," 83-98.
- **Coplan, David, and David Rycroft**. "*Marabi*: the emergence of African working-class music in Johannesburg," 43-65.
- **Johnson, Joyce Marie**. "The black American folk preacher and the chanted sermon: parallels with a West African tradition," 205-222.

1587. **TRINIDAD CARNIVAL: THE WORLD'S MOST COLOURFUL FESTIVAL**. 1973- . Port-of-Spain, Trinidad: Key Caribbean Publications Ltd.
ULRICH'S says this is issued annually. The 1973 copy, and the only one seen, has as its subtitle, "The Greatest Spectacle on Earth." It is a sumptuous picture book commemorating the Trinidad carnival of that year. Advertising, pictures of competition winners, and popularly written articles appear. Carnival terms are explained, texts given of the most acclaimed calypsos from 1961 on. Steel pan is featured, contest winners of past years listed. One page refers to variations on African themes as being "endless." Contents of subsequent issues cannot be vouched for at this time, but it is likely that they are similar.

1588. **Trowbridge, Antony V**. "Hugh Travers Tracey." **AFRICA INSIGHT** 15, no. 1 (1985): 4-9.

1589. **Tse, Cynthia**. ETHIOPIAN CONTEMPORARY POPULAR SONG. Master's Thesis, University of California, Los Angeles, 1968.

1590. **Tse, Cynthia, and Jerome Kimberlin**. "The morphology of the mansinqo: Ethiopia's bowed spike fiddle." In **Studies in African music**. Co-editors, J. H. Kwabena Nketia, and Jacqueline Cogdell DjeDje, 249-262. [Los Angeles]: Program in Ethnomusicology, Department of Music, University of California, Los Angeles, 1984.
Includes sketches of the *mansinqo*, notes, bibliography, map. Tables show variations in *mansinqo* dimensions, and their sound box volumes. Comparisons are made of instruments designed by four *masinqo* craftsmen.

1591. ***"Tshotsholosa."*** **SING OUT: THE FOLK SONG MAGAZINE** 31, no. 3 (1985): 20-21.
Melody and words are given for this song that was included in the very successful African musical, *King Kong*, by Todd Matshikiza, in which Miriam Makeba appeared. (Pete Seeger is credited with introducing it to the Western world.)

1592. **Tsukada, Kenichi.** LUVALE PERCEPTIONS OF "MUKANDA" IN DISCOURSE AND MUSIC. Dissertation, Queen's University of Belfast (Northern Ireland), 1988. 370pp.
Mukanda is a traditional African educational institution of the Luvale of Zambia, involving circumcision and seclusion in the bush. Music considerations start particularly with Chapter 8, on Mukanda Songs, and continue through other chapters that examine these songs as they are sung by different groups, and performed in ritual. In the 12th Chapter, Tsukada, expresses his concern with the "epistemotological issue of how the Luvale perceive music in their own terms in contrast to 'ours.'" Tsukada, who is well-trained in music and social anthropology, analyzes the Luvale tonal system in detail. Many notations. Illustrations, maps, bibliography.

1593. **Die tunesische Nuba ed Dhil = La nouba tunisienne ed Dhil.** Edited by K. Khatchi, *et al.* Regensbury: Gustav Bosse, 1971. 15pp. (Studien zur Mittelmeermusik = Études de musique méditeranéenne, 1)
The *nouba*, a kind of Tunisian suite composed of 5 to 8 movements, evolved in the *maqām ed Dhil*. The fundamental meters executed by the drums in the *nouba* vary considerably from movement to movement. This work has German on the left side of the page, French on the right. There are three main sections: The Material, Analysis [of the movements, includes notations of the underlying rhythmic pattern, metronome indications, and other descriptive data] and Interchangeable Movements. In a large pocket at the end of the book is the score, consisting of 27 pages.

1594. **Turkson, Adolphus Acquah Robertson.** EFFUTU ASAFO MUSIC: A STUDY OF A TRADITIONAL MUSIC STYLE OF GHANA WITH SPECIAL REFERENCE TO THE ROLE OF TONAL LANGUAGE IN CHORAL MUSIC INVOLVING STRUCTURAL AND HARMONIC ANALYSIS. Dissertation, Northwestern University, 1972. 365pp.
Asafo is an ancient warrior organization common to all Akan societies of Ghana. In the past, the main objective of all *asafo* was to defend society, children, women, the aged, and the infirm. The defense of property was an additional responsibility. Turkson was inspired to research *asafo*, he says, because of the musical aspect of the institution. Map, figures, song texts, and bibliography.

1595. **Turkson, Adolphus Acquah Robertson.** "Evolution of the Fante sacred lyric." **RESEARCH REVIEW** 9, no. 3 (1973): 1-12.

T

1596. Turnbull, Colin M. *The forest people: a study of the pygmies of the Congo.* [New York]: Simon and Schuster, [1961]. 295pp.

This distinguished study has long been a classic in the field of anthropology. Beautiful and sensitively written, it is about the BaMbuti of the Ituri Forest of Zaïre. In prophetic words, Turnbull says that it "tries to convey something of the lives and feelings of a people who live in a forest world, something of their intense love for that world and their trust in it. It is a world that will soon be gone forever, and with it the people." Music references, memorable photographs, maps, glossary, pronunciation guide, index.

1597. Twenty-four songs of Uganda [music]. Compiled for use in primary schools by Peter Cooke. Kampala, Uganda: National Institute of Education, c1966. 40pp.

Unaccompanied songs of 9 Ugandan peoples. Believed to be the first book of its kind relating to Uganda alone. Transcriptions of unaccompanied melodies on the standard staff have been modified to allow for differences between African and European songs, one manifestation being that there are no bar lines or key signatures, Two special symbols have been added for glides and indefinite pitches. Titles and words in English, but African words inserted under staff pitches. Background information and performance instructions given for each song.

1597a. Twining, Mary Arnold. *Caribbean folklore.* Atlanta: Atlanta University, [1972]. 13pp. (Center for African and African-American Studies. CAAS bibliography, no. 6)

Twining, at the time of writing, hoped to expand this brief bibliography in the future, time and resources permitting. Entries, many of them older, are listed only alphabetically by author, but since there are but 13 pages, contents can be easily scanned. There is some mention of Cuba and Puerto Rico, but in general the author has limited herself to other areas of the Caribbean. Includes a number of references to music and dance, some of which connect directly or indirectly to Africa. No annotations.

1598. **UMI**. (University Microfilms International, 300 North Zeeb Road, Ann Arbor, Michigan 48106).
UMI is the micro publisher of a CD-ROM ("Compact Disc Read Only Memory") used as a major reference in this bibliography for information on doctoral dissertations. The acronym, **UMI**, has been used throughout to indicate when information has been provided via this source.

1598a. **UNESCO** (United Nations Educational, Scientific and Cultural Organization)
See: •**AFRICAN ABSTRACTS, 29.**
- •**African music: meeting in Yaoundé, 39.**
- •**América Latina en su música, 83, 121.**
- •**Bertonoff, Debora**. *Dance towards the earth: on a UNESCO grant*, **224.**
- •**Colloque sur l'art nègre, 368.**
- •**COURIER, 393.**
- •**INTERNATIONAL BIBLIOGRAPHY OF SOCIAL AND CULTURAL ANTHROPOLOGY, 730.**
- •**INTERNATIONAL COMMITTEE ON URGENT ANTHROPOLOGICAL AND ETHNOLOGICAL RESEARCH. BULLETIN, 731.**
- •**Kanza Matondon ne Mansangaza**. *Musique zaïroise*, **814.**
- •**La musique africaine, réunion de Yaoundé, 1140.**
- •**Ládipọ [Ládiípọ], Dúró**. *Morèmi*, **940.**
- •**Locatelli de Pérgamo, Ana Maria**. "Raices musicales," **983.**
- •**Lopes, Helena Theodoro** [*et all*]. *Negro e cultura no Brasil*, **997.**
- •**Universe of music: a history, 1603a.**
- •**YEARBOOK FOR TRADITIONAL MUSIC, 1695.**
- •**Zemp, Hugo**. *Die Musique der Dan*, **1700.**

1599. **Ude, Walter C.** THE RISE AND GROWTH OF INDIGENOUS ART MUSIC IN THE ANGLICAN DIOCESE OF OWERRI. Master's Thesis, University of Lagos, 1986.

1600. **Uka, N.** "The *ikoro* and its cultural significance." **IKOROK** 3, no.1 (1976): 21-27. Nsukka, Nigeria.
The Journal is named for the subject of this article, a large wooden drum that looks like a dug-out canoe. It is made from a large tree trunk, and distributed widely over much of southeastern Nigeria, particularly among the Ibibio, Ekoi, and Cross River groups, and also among the Igbo (where it is called *Ikoro* or *Ikolo*). It has traditionally been used for conveying information, as well as for signalling.

1601. **ULRICH'S INTERNATIONAL PERIODICALS DIRECTORY**. 1932- . New York: R. R. Bowker, Database Publishing Group, Division of Reed Publishing USA, New York.
With this amazing directory, vital information can be found on almost any periodical in print. **ULRICH'S** appears annually, is augmented during the year by quarterly updates. Arranged by subject, it includes periodicals, newsletters,

and annuals and irregular serials published worldwide. Separate indexes exist for title, online availability, cessations, publications of international organizations, and International Standard Serial Number. Individual entries include title, complete publisher address, description, and subscription price. Though **ULRICH'S** is a bit intimidating at first, if only because of its comprehensiveness and overwhelming amount of data, with a little patience, it can become an extremely useful reference tool.

1602. Umhlaba wethu. Edited by Mothobi Mutloatse. Foreword by Essop Patel. Johannesburg: Skotaville Publishers: Thorold's Africana Books [distributor], c1987. 164pp.

Of seven parts to this book, which seeks to correct historical misrepresentation of the history of South Africa, two pertain to music: "Music is a Healing Force" comprises brief essays by Ibrahim, Masekela, Matshikiza, Makeba, Leshoai, Nakasa, and Moeketsi. Part Seven is "A Brief History of the Anthem *Nkosi Sikelel' iAfrika*" ["God Bless Africa," by Enoch Sontonga]. The book is dedicated to "the oppressed majority in Namibia, to the Father of Black choral music, Reuben Tholakele Caluza, and the Future of Humanity - the children of Africa." In English. A bibliography.

1603. Underwood, Lois S. A FIELD STUDY OF THE USE OF INDIGENOUS AFRICAN MUSIC IN THE CHRISTIAN CHURCHES OF CONGO. Master's Thesis, University of Kansas, 1967.

UNITED NATIONS EDUCATIONAL, SCIENTIFIC AND CULTURAL ORGANIZATION
See: **UNESCO, 598a.**

1603a. Universe of music: a history. Barry Brook, General Editor. New York; Paris: UNESCO/International Music Council.

This is a projected, multi-volume series on world music. Though in process for several years, no volume had appeared at the time of writing. Eminent musicologists, specialists in musics of various areas of the world, are involved in its preparation. (There are unconfirmed indications that volume 5 will be on Africa.)

UNIVERSITY MICROFILMS INTERNATIONAL
See: **UMI, 1598.**

1604. University of Ghana. Institute of African Studies. *Descriptive notes on a selection of African dances*. [s.l.: s.n., 198-?]. 8pp.

At head of title: University of Ghana, School of Music and Drama, Institute of African Studies. This is a short pamphlet, popularly written. About a dozen dances, largely Ghanaian, are briefly described, along with their significance and backgrounds. The instrumentation for about one-third of the selected dances is mentioned, but not in any detail. Although this certainly is not a primary reference tool, it might be useful for quickly verifying dance titles, the character of certain dances, and sometimes an idea of the instruments involved and the pace they use for a particular dance.

1605. University of Ìbàdàn. Institute of African Studies. *Catalogue of recorded sound* [compiled by Agnes A. Ojehomon, Ìbàdàn], 1969. 39pp. (University of Ìbàdàn. Institute of African Studies. Occasional Publication no. 20)
In the introduction by R. G. Armstrong, this catalog and discography of sound recordings is described as containing the "major part of the recordings of Nigerian music and oral literature." A fine index is at the beginning. An appendix lists films, some of which are music-related. In 1969, at least, one could write to the Librarian at the University for further details and/or copies. A detailed Catalogue of the Odù of Ifá was/is? available. Recordings for some Nigerian performance texts contained in this bibliography are likely to be found in the catalog.

1606. Urfé, Odilio. "Music and dance in Cuba." In *Africa in Latin America: essays on history, culture, and socialization.* Edited by Manuel Moreno Fraginals, 170-188. New York: Holmes and Meier, 1984.
Much research has gone into this remarkable compendium of essentials about the African influence on Cuban music and dance. The musicologist, Urfé, has done his homework about the *cabildos*, their identifying characteristics, associated rites, instruments (with their descriptions and African names), the origin, evolution and names of countless dance styles, popular music and theater in Cuba of the day, *ad infinitum*. Commendable, too, is the lucid writing style and exceptional organizational skills Urfé brings to this difficult and complex subject. (One misses footnotes and/or precise information on resource materials at the end of the book.)

1607. Uzoigwe, Joshua. AKIN EUBA: AN INTRODUCTION TO THE LIFE AND MUSIC OF A NIGERIAN COMPOSER. Master's Thesis, Queen's University of Belfast (Northern Ireland), 1978.

1608. Uzoigwe, Joshua. THE COMPOSITIONAL TECHNIQUES OF UKOM MUSIC OF SOUTH-EASTERN NIGERIA. Dissertation, Queen's University of Belfast (Northern Ireland), 1981.

1609. Uzoigwe, Joshua. "A cultural analysis of Akin Euba's musical works." ODÙ New Series no. 24 (1983): 44-60.
"References" (i.e., notes), and music notations.

1610. Uzoigwe, Leroy, and Landeg White. "Forms of resistance songs and perceptions of power in colonial Mozambique." NIGERIA MAGAZINE 54, no. 3 (12986): 53-60.
Chart, music, photographs.

V

1611. **Vail, Leroy**. *Forms of resistance: songs and perceptions of power in colonial Mozambique*. [Cape Town]: Centre for African Studies, University of Cape Town, [1983]. 49pp. (Africa seminar)

1612. **Valbert, Christian**. "L'avenir des danses traditionnelles en Côte d'Ivoire." **ARTS D'AFRIQUE NOIRE** 29 (1979): 7-23.
Only occasional brief mention of music, but there are photographs of instrumentalists accompanying the dancers - a kora, played by a man in splendid regalia, a flutist, and perhaps another picture or two.

1613. **Vamos cantar, crianças: cancioneiro**. Illustrated by Ivone Luis. [Mozambique]: Instituto Nacional do Livro do Disco, [1981?]-. 95pp.
In Portuguese. Songs for children. The melodies are on one staff on the left page, and the words are on the right. Songs are indexed as: National, International, and by first lines, themes, and even musical difficulty. Distinctive, fanciful illustrations are a joy.

1614. **Vangroenweghe, Daniel**. *Bobongó: la grande fête des Ekonda (Zaïre)*. Berlin: D. Reimer, c1988. 332pp. (Mainzer Afrika-Studien, vol. 9)
On funeral customs/rites of the Ekonda people. *Bobongó* is a spectacular form of the final rite of passage, divided into many parts. These consist of songs, that are often polyphonic and accompanied by dancing. The *iyaya* consists primarily of dances and acrobatics with declaimed or sung texts. This book contains edited texts, in lekonda, of two *bebongó* [plural] and two *bayaya*. There is only a page and a half that describes the musical instruments involved, but the author directs the reader to musical examples in the Musée Royal de l'Afrique Central (Tervuren, Belgium). Bibliography. See also the next entry, **1615**.

1615. **Vangroenweghe, Daniel**. *La grande fête bobongó chez les Ekonda* 1978. Documents iconographiques (introduction de 37 pages + 300 photos), in Archives and Documents. Micro-édition (I 78 867 178) Institut d'ethnologie. Musée'de l'Homme, Paris. 300pp.
This was seen as a microfiche that did not contain all of the specific information listed above (in Vangroenweghe's own bibliography). There are abundant photographs of the *bobongó* and an ethnographic introduction of 37 pages. The Ekonda are described as being of the equatorial forest of Zaïre, and divided in each village into two distinct population groups, les *Baotó* and les *Batwá*. There are 239 photographs and 1 map.

1616. **Vann, Kimberly R**. *Black music in Ebony: an annotated guide to the articles on music in Ebony magazine, 1945-1985*. Chicago: Center for Black Music Research, Columbia College. c1989. 119pp.
Only moderately useful when it comes to African or African-related music. See

the book's index for: African Music and Musicians, Brazil, Calypso Singers, Jamaica, Lemmy Mabaso (his experiences as a South African musician), Mambo, Trinidad, and one or two other references. A popular approach that skims the surface.

1617. **Varley, Douglas Harold**, comp. *African native music: an annotated bibliography*. 1st edition reprinted; with additional note. "First published in 1936." Folkestone: Dawsons, 1970. 116pp.
The "additional note" merely refers people to Merriam's, Thieme's and Gaskin's bibliographies, and two journals, **ETHNOMUSICOLOGY** and **AFRICAN MUSIC**. No change otherwise since 1936. Nevertheless, this remains an important bibliography, a pioneer study, and an historical landmark in the field. It is a smallish book containing brief annotations and 11 subject headings, all pertaining to subSaharan music, with the exception of one, African Survivals in the New World. Lists museums with African music collections. Certain terms now sound dated. Bibliographies, author index.

1618. **Vaughan, James**. "Rock paintings and rock gongs among the Marghi of Nigeria." **MAN** 62, no. 83 (1962): 49-52.

1619. **Vega-Drouet, Hector**. HISTORICAL AND ETHNOLOGICAL SURVEY ON PROBABLE AFRICAN ORIGINS OF THE PUERTO RICAN BOMBA: INCLUDING A DESCRIPTION OF SANTIAGO APOSTOL FESTIVITIES AT LOIZA ALDEA. Dissertation, Wesleyan University, 1979. 162pp.
At the time of his research, the author was aware that there was no written material on the *bomba* that might assist his investigation into possible connections between this Puerto Rican song/dance form and Ashanti traditions. After living in Ghana, however, and studying Ashanti music and dance in depth, Vega-Drouet not only found general African features in the *bomba*, but a particular, constant, and indispensable rhythmic element, known as the *mpintin* pattern in Ghana, that he believes indicates the *bomba*'s Ashanti origin. Music, bibliography.

1620. **Vega-Drouet, Hector**. SOME MUSICAL FORMS OF AFRICAN DESCENDANTS IN PUERTO RICO: BOMBA, PLENA, AND ROSARIO FRANCÉS. Master's Thesis, Hunter College, The City University of New York, 1969. 110pp.
The author says that Spanish and African influences have strongly affected the music of Puerto Rico - "molded it," is the way he puts it. After an intriguing introduction that treats the early history of Puerto Rico, and the so-called *Ladinos* (people of African descent brought from Castille or Portugal), and *Bozales* (those who knew Portuguese or Spanish traditions, or the languages, or who had lived in either country for 2 years, or been born there). A sizeable section is devoted to each dance and song form, and at the end, Vega summarizes the elements all three have in common [some notably African, some not].

1621. **Vickers, Jonathan**. "British Library African resources: (2) archival; The National Sound Archive: spoken recordings." In *African studies: papers presented at a colloquium at the*

British Library, 7-9 January 1985. Edited by Ilse Sternberg and Patricia M. Larby, 231-237. London, British Library in association with SCOLMA, 1986.

Vickers states that "...when considering African performance arts it is inappropriate to separate music and speech because orature (or oral literature) exists in spoken or chanted forms as well as in sung or musically accompanied forms." And so, even though we learn in this report of recordings by great African personages during great moments of history, we cannot overlook the Archive's additional holdings of African plays in live performance. Just because they might be classified technically as "spoken" does not mean that the researcher might not also find a wealth of associated music information here.

1622. **Vidal, Túnjí**. "African oríkì in traditional Yorùbá music." **AFRICAN ARTS** vol. 3, no. 1 (1969): 56-59.

1623. **Vidal, [Túnjí] Augustus Olátúnjí**. ORÍKÌ: PRAISE SONGS OF THE YORÙBÁ. Master's Thesis, University of California, Los Angeles, 1971.

1624. **Vidal, Túnjí**. "The role and function of music at Yorùbá festivals." In **African musicology: current trends: a festschrift presented to J. H. Kwabena Nketia**. Edited by Jacqueline Cogdell DjeDje, and William G. Carter, 111-127. [Atlanta, Georgia: Crossroads Press, 1988]- .

Yorùbá song texts with English translation, music transcriptions, notes, bibliography.

1625. **Vidal, Túnjí**. "Traditions and history in Yorùbá music." **NIGERIAN MUSIC REVIEW** 1, no.1 (1977): 66-92.

1626. **Vidal, Túnjí**. "The Westernization of African music: a study of Yorúbà liturgical church music." In **Ifẹ̀: annals of the Institute of Cultural Studies**, 70-82 (Vol. 1). Ilé-Ifẹ̀, Nigeria: Institute of Cultural Studies, University of Ifẹ̀, 1986- .

1627. **Vogels, Raimund**. *Tanzlieder und liturgische Gesänge bei den Dagaaba in Nordwestghana: zur Verwendung einheimischer Musik im katholischen Gottesdienste.* 2 vols. Hamburg: Verlag der Musikalienhandlung K. D. Wagner, 1988. (Beiträge zur Ethnomusikologie, vol. 18)

Maps, music, bibliography.

1628. **Vohs, Leonard**. MARAVI-MUSIK: BEITRÄGE ZUR MUSIKETHNOLOGIE MALAŴIS UND SAMBIAS: TRANSCRIPTIONEN, ETHNOLOGISCHE ÜBERSICHT. Dissertation, Musikwissenschaftliches Institut der Universität Köln, 1967.

1629. **Voilà la nouvelle lune! Dansons!: chansons populaires de la Zone de Gandajika (Rép du Zaïre).** Katende Cyovo. Bandundu, République du Zaïre: Ceeba, 1977. 184pp. (Publications Ceeba, Série 2, vol. 44)
In French and Luba. Has bibliography and index. Sequel is **Je désire danser!** (758)

1630. **Volavka, Zdenka.** "Le *Ndunga*: un masque, une danse, une institution social au *Ngoyo*." **ARTS d'AFRIQUE NOIRE**. 17 (1976): 28-43.
In French. *Ndunga* is known to the Bakongo people as "the sacred dance," a term that incorporates a mask, a dance, and the organizers and performers of that dance. Performed by men, women are merely viewers. The *ndunga* is a long, decorated drum that opens the ceremony; a shorter, female drum, *Missaku*, joins in later. The drums are pictured but not discussed in any detail. (The region known as Ndunga embraces the western part of Zaïre and the Cabinda territory.)

1631. **Von Gnielinski, Anneliese.** *Traditional music instruments of Tanzania in the National Museum.* [Dar es Salaam?]: National Museum of Tanzania, [between 1985 and 1988]. 46pp. (Occasional paper, National Museums of Tanzania, no. 6)
Bibliography.

1632. **Vorbichler, Anton.** *Die Oralliteratur der Balese-Efe im Ituri-Wald (Nordost-Zaïre)*; mit einem musikwissenschaftlichen Anhang von Rudolph Maria Brandl. St. Augustin bei Bonn: Verlag des Anthropos-Instituts, 1979. 349pp. (Studia Instituti Anthropos, vol. 34)
Includes music and oral literature of the Balese-Efe, with texts in Balese and German. The music section is written by Rudolph M. Brandl.

1633. **Vzoigwe, Joshua.** "Operational and hierarchial forms of creativity in Igbo music: the *Ukom* music system as a case study." **In Ifẹ̀: annals of the Institute of Cultural Studies**, 65-83 (Vol. 2). Ilé-Ifẹ̀, Nigeria: Institute of Cultural Studies, University of Ifẹ̀, 1986- .

W

1634. **WACHSMANN, KLAUS P.**

For a complete bibliography of the works of this renowned musicologist, see **Essays for a humanist: an offering to Klaus Wachsmann**, pages 390-393 **(549)**.

1635. **Wachsmann, Klaus P.**, ed. *Essays on music and history in Africa.* Evanston: Northwestern University Press, 1971. 268pp.

The essays derive from the Symposium on Music and History in Africa and Asia, sponsored by the Royal Anthropological Institute in 1962. Added are two essays prepared for the African Studies Association meeting at Montreal in 1969, but not actually presented. The latter are by Lois Anderson and Akin Euba. The book contains a Preface by Wachsmann, maps, figures, music notations, and notes on contributors. Divided into sections on West Africa, East Africa, Islam and African Music, Southern Africa, and Music and History. (A critical review of the essays, written by David Ames, can be found in **ETHNOMUSICOLOGY** 17, no.2 (1973): 351-353.)

- **Anderson, Lois Ann**. "The interrelation of African and Arab musics: some preliminary considerations," 143-169.
- **Blacking, John**. "Music and the historical process in Vendaland," 185-212.
- **Dark, Philip J. C., and Matthew Hill**. "Musical instruments on Benin plaques," 65-78.
- **Dixon, David M.** "A note on Kushite contact with the South," 135-139.
- **Euba, Akin**. "Islamic musical culture among the Yorùbá: a preliminary survey," 171-181.
- **Fage, John D.** "Music and history: a historian's view of the African picture," 257-266.
- **Jones, A. M.** "Africa and Indonesia: an ancient colonial era?" 81-92.
- **Kirby, Percival R.** "The changing face of African music south of the Zambezi," 243-254.
- **Nketia, J. H. Kwabena**. "History and organization of music in West Africa," 3-25.
- **Rouget, Gilbert**. "Court songs and traditional history in the ancient kingdoms of Porto-Novo and Abomey," 27-64.
- **Rycroft, David K.** "Stylistic evidence in Nguni song," 213-241.
- **Wachsmann, Klaus P.** "Musical instruments in Kiganda tradition and their place in the East African scene," 93-134.

1636. **Wachsmann, Klaus P.** "Ethnomusicology in Africa." In **The African experience**. Edited by John N. Paden, and Edward W. Soja, 128-151. 4 vols. Evanston: Northwestern University Press, 1970.

1637. **Wachsmann, Klaus P.** "Ethnomusicology in African studies: the next twenty years." In *Expanding horizons in African studies. Program of African Studies, Northwestern University; proceedings of the twentieth anniversary conference, 1968.* Edited by Gwendolen M. Carter and Ann Paden, 131-142. Evanston: Northwestern University Press, 1969.

Many years have passed, and it is interesting to read Wachsmann's thoughts about the future, back in 1969. Once more, he is particularly concerned with aesthetics, sociology, and language. He speaks of the dichotomy in ethnomusicological research between sound and human behavior and argues that the two be integrated in the future. He makes predictions of those "pressures" and "responses" he anticipates in years to come, and concludes with suggestions for (1) An interdisciplinary program at the university level and (2) Regular meetings of African and non-African scholars. A brief response follows by J. H. Kwabena Nketia.

1638. **Wachsmann, Klaus P.** "Musical instruments in Kiganda tradition and their place in the East African scene." In *Essays on music and history in Africa.* Edited by Klaus P. Wachsmann, 93-134. Evanston: Northwestern University Press, 1971.

With dazzling scholarship, Wachsmann synthesizes vast amounts of data, some factual, some flimsy, as he attempts to trace the history of Kigandan instruments, trying to understand what might have gone on musically in prehistoric East Africa. Drawing from whatever materials he could find, Wachsmann uses, as required, hard logic, conjecture, or even wild guesses trying to unravel the past. From such fragmentary resources, dependable conclusions are not likely to be reached. "The music historian...may feel that there is not much fun working on a jigsaw puzzle in which so many pieces are missing," says Wachsmann. Charts, map. 136 footnotes!

1639. **Wachsmann, Klaus P.** "Some speculations concerning a drum chime in Buganda." **MAN** 65, no. 1 (1965): 1-8.

1639a. **Wachsmann, Klaus P.** "Traditional music in Uganda." In **Creating a wider interest in traditional music: proceedings of a conference held in Berlin in cooperation with the International Music Council, 12th to the 17th June, 1967.** [Edited by Alain Daniélou and others], 128-131. Berlin: International Institute for Comparative Music Studies and Documentation, [1967?].

1640. **Wachsmann, Klaus P.** "The trend of musicology in Africa." **SELECTED REPORTS IN ETHNOMUSICOLOGY** 1, No. 1 (1966): 61-65.

Well-footnoted.

1641. **Wachsmann, Klaus P.** "Völkerwanderungen und afrikanische Harfen." In *Musikkulturen in Afrika.* Edited by Erich Stockmann, 246-251. Berlin: Verlag Neue Musik, 1987.

Several informative pages about African harps. Wachsmann describes three types of existing harp, including a map showing migration patterns and distribution. Several notes in margins.

W

Wachsmann, Klaus P.
See also: **•Essays for a humanist: an offering to Klaus Wachsmann, 549.**
•Gaskin, L. J. P. ***A select bibliography of music of Africa*****, 614.**
•Studies in African music, 1514.

Wahome, John Kamenyi
See: **Kamenyi, John W., 812.**

1642. **Walker, Judith Ann.** RHYTHMIC NONALIGNMENT IN ABORIGINAL AUSTRALIAN, WEST AFRICAN, AND TWENTIETH-CENTURY ART MUSICS. Dissertation, University of Wisconsin-Madison, 1983. 599pp.
"Among repertoires not permeated by functional tonality, one means of achieving musical interest and momentum is the use of regular rhythmic nonalignment among two or more simultaneous layers." The author analyzes three such "repertoires, representing geographical and chronological diversity," including West African, aboriginal Australian, and twentieth-century art musics. "Non-alignment in West African music, generally occurring between a number of rhythmic layers...is evaluated and re-notated based on the rhythmic predominance of a frequently additive bell pattern..." **(UMI)**

1643. **Wallis, Roger, and Krister Malm.** *Big sounds from small people: the music industry in small countries.* New York, N.Y.: Pendragon Press, c1984. 419pp. (Sociology of Music, no. 2)
Summarizes the results of a three-year study of the Music Industry in Small Countries (MISC). Twelve sample countries on four continents include for our particular interest: Tanzania, Kenya, Tunisia, and Zaïre; Jamaica and Trinidad. Resulting data is summarized for each country regarding: government policy; work opportunities for musicians; radio, TV, film, video; trends in music, and more. One encounters the following thought-provoking statement: "The Seventies have taught us that music industry technology penetrates faster than any other technological development in the history of mankind." Many questions are raised about the future.

1644. **Wallis, Shona Sibson.** PUBLIC AND PRIVATE MUSIC COLLECTIONS IN SOUTH AFRICA. Master's Thesis, University of the Witwatersrand, Johannesburg (South Africa), 1977.
University Microfilms indicates that this is not available. On the assumption that it certainly ought, at least, to have some information about the Kirby collection - and hopefully others pertinent to the scope of this book - it is being included.

1645. **Walton, Ortiz M.** "A comparative analysis of the African and the Western aesthetic." In *The Black aesthetic*. Edited by Addison Gayle, 154-164. Garden City, New York: Doubleday, 1971.
This takes all prizes for "most amusing entry." Contains a tongue-in-cheek analysis of the Western symphony orchestra, seen through African-American eyes as an assembly line operation "...set into motion by a foreman, the conductor." The ludicrous metaphors continue, along with pointing out the dangers of coughing during a performance, or the "utter madness to dance or pop the

fingers." One learns more about the African aesthetic through this cool view of the Western one than if Africa itself were the subject. Good reading for the culturally smug.

1646. **Wanjala, Chris**. *East Africa's traditional cultural expressions*. [Nairobi]: Institute of African Studies, University of Nairobi, [1985?]. 21pp. (Seminar paper -Institute of African Studies, University of Nairobi, no. 167)
When discussing oral traditions, or performing arts in Africa, there is almost always an implied music component. Music weaves in and out of this somewhat loosely-constructed essay, without particular emphasis, more attention being given to oral literature, especially works of Ngugi wa Thiong'o. The word "folk" is rejected by Wanjala because of its "allusion to primitivism." He expresses other strong convictions. Important is a several paragraph quotation by *Djeli* Mamondon Konyate on his many societal roles. This paper emphasizes the need for redefining the terms of Africa's cultural traditions, and expanding techniques for its collection and preservation. Bibliography.

1647. **Ware, Naomi**. "Popular music and African identity in Freetown, Sierra Leone." In **Eight music cultures: tradition and change**. Edited by Bruno Nettl, 296-320. Urbana: University of Illinois Press, 1978.
Bibliography. Abstracted in **RILM**, 1985.

1648. **Warner, Keith Q.** *Kaiso! the Trinidad calypso: a study of the calypso as oral literature*. Washington, D.C.: Three Continents Press, c1982. 155pp.
Bibliography, discography, illustrations.

1649. **Warnock, Paul Willard**. TRENDS IN AFRICAN CHURCH MUSIC: A HISTORICAL REVIEW. Master's Thesis, University of California, Los Angeles, 1983. 354pp.

1650. **Warren, Fred, and Lee Warren**. *The music of Africa; an introduction*. Illustrations and photographs by Penelope Naylor. Englewood Cliffs, New Jersey, Prentice-Hall [1970]. 87pp.
Described inside the cover as an introduction to African music discussing melody, rhythm and form, musical instruments, and music in traditional and contemporary African life. A gem. Could be used for the education of younger people because of its simple language. On the other hand, it is so well done, and represents such a brief but good basic summation, that adults without prior knowledge concerning African music could well profit from reading it. Good line drawings. Brief bibliography and discography.

1651. **Waterman, Christopher Alan**. *Jùjú: a social history and ethnography of an African popular music*. Chicago: University of Chicago Press, 1990. 277pp. (Chicago studies in ethnomusicology)

A definitive work on jùjú - also handsomely executed. Gives a detailed account of the evolution and social significance of an important popular music form originating in Nigeria more than fifty years ago. The development of jùjú is traced from early origins in Lagos, through the days of Nigerian independence, the rise of Yorùbá nationalism, and the oil boom of the 1980s. But there is too much in this comprehensive book to do justice to it here. There are maps, photographs, notations, song texts, notes, a glossary of Yorùbá terms, cassette tape, index, and bibliography.

1652. **Waterman, Christopher Alan**. JÙJÚ: THE HISTORICAL DEVELOPMENT, SOCIOECONOMIC ORGANIZATION, AND COMMUNICATIVE FUNCTIONS OF A WEST AFRICAN POPULAR MUSIC. Dissertation, University of Illinois at Urbana-Champaign, 1986. 447pp.

A probing investigation confirming Waterman's hypotheses that: "1)...African syncretic popular musics may be usefully viewed as systems of social and aesthetic communication; 2) that they have played vital roles in the emergence of coherent patterns of urban African identity under conditions of pervasive and profound economic and political change; 3) that the communicative role of musical style in urban African contexts may strongly condition the developmental trajectories of popular musics; and 4) that musical style may come to play a constitutive and not merely reflexive role in the formulation of ideologies and the emergence of socioeconomic classes." A 23 page bibliography!

1653. **Waterman, Christopher Alan**. *Jùjú performance practice and African social identity in colonial Lagos*. [s.l.: s.n., 1986?]. 30pp.

Waterman says that there are two broad purposes to his essay: to present ethnomusicological and ethnographic data concerning a syncretic stylistic system developed by African musicians in a "West African colonial power nexus trade and entrepot;" and to respond through the data he presents on early jùjú to theoretical concerns of Fabian, Coplan, Barber and other contemporary scholars of African pop culture. His approach to the study is in terms of styles, practice, identity, and what he terms, "power." (Since his dissertation is listed in the bibliography, it must have predated this paper.)

1654. **Waterman, Christopher Alan**. "The uneven development of Africanist ethnomusicology: three issues and a critique." In **Comparative musicology and anthropology of music: essays on the history of ethnomusicology**. Edited by Bruno Nettl and Philip V. Bohlman, 169-186. Chicago: University of Chicago Press, 1991.

He answers the two important questions he himself poses: "1. African and modern European music are constructed on entirely different principles, and therefore, 2. there cannot be fusion into one, but only the one or the other can be used without compromise." Notes, bibliography.

1655. **WATERMAN, RICHARD ALAN**
Inspired insights of Richard Alan Waterman, eminent anthropologist/musicologist - also father to Christopher Alan Waterman - still reverberate. Unfortunately, most of his publications on African music retentions in the New World were published before 1960, and are therefore not within the time-scope of this bibliography. A complete list of his published - and unpublished - works follows the excellent and informative memorial biography, written two years after his death, by Alan P. Merriam. Compiled by Frank J. Gillis and Merriam, the bibliography contains entries from 1941 to 1971, and is found in **ETHNOMUSICOLOGY** 17, no. 1 (1972): 72-94.

1656. **Waterman, Richard Alan**. "African influence on the music of the Americas." In **International Congress of Americanists, 29th, New York, 1949.** *Acculturation in the Americas: proceedings and selected papers.* Edited by Sol Tax, 207-218. New York, Cooper Square Publishers, 1967 [c1952].
In this reprint we encounter first-hand some of Waterman's brilliant and original ideas that are still being discussed decades later. Presented here is his famous theory of the "metronome sense," along with his familiar and frequently-quoted expressions, "off-beat phrasing of melodic accents," "overlapping call-and-response," and "hot rhythm." Seldom is it mentioned, however, that in this paper Waterman also makes the point that harmony not only *exists* in African music, but is a *common* element. He explains what might have contributed to this misconception. The same essay is included in **Alan Dundes'**, *Mother wit...*, **486.**

1657. **Waterman, Richard A.** "On flogging a dead horse: lessons learned from the Africanisms controversy." **ETHNOMUSICOLOGY** 7, no. 2 (1963): 83-87.
For skeptics who still deny that Africanisms exist in New World music, this lucid, brilliant, ever-timely historical overview should be mandatory reading. Waterman distills what he believes has been learned from the Africanisms controversy: 1. "Get the Relevant Facts," 2. "Observe the Context," 3. "Beware Unexamined Assumptions." He believes that the major lesson learned by ethnomusicologists from the Africanisms controversy is that any attempt to deal with the dynamics of musical culture without reference to all the anthropological tools available for dealing with the dynamics of culture in general, can only be "unsatisfying, frustrating, and...a complete waste of time."

1658. **Waters, Anita M.** *Race, class, and political symbols: Rastafari and reggae in Jamaican politics.* New Brunswick, U.S.A.: Transaction Books, c1985. 343pp.
Includes reggae music, but emphasis on politics and the Ras Tafari Movement. Bibliography, index.

1659. **Wegner, Ulrich**. *Afrikanische Saiteninstrumente.* Berlin: Staatliche Museen Preussischer Kulturbesitz, Museum für Völkerkunde, c1984. 305pp. (Veröffentlichungen des Museums für

Völkerkunde Berlin, 41. Abteilung Musikethnologie, 5)
On African stringed instruments. Cassette in container at end. Bibliography and index.

1660. **Weinberg, Pessa**. "An analysis of semi-rural and peri-urban Zulu children's songs." In **Symposium on Ethnomusicology**. (3rd: 1982: University of Natal) [4th: 1983: Rhodes University] *Papers presented at the Third and Fourth Symposia on Ethnomusicology*, Music Department, University of Natal, Durban, 16th to 19th September 1982, 34-37; Music Department, Rhodes University, 7th to 8th October 1983. Grahamstown, South Africa: International Library of African Music, 1984.
Note that this paper is in the 3rd Symposium. (The 3rd and 4th Symposia are bound in one volume.)

1661. **Weinberg, Pessa**. "Some aspects of my research into Zulu children's songs." In **Symposium on Ethnomusicology**. (2nd: 1981: Rhodes University) *Papers presented at the Second Symposium on Ethnomusicology, Music Department, Rhodes University, 24th to 26th September, 1981.* Edited by Andrew Tracey, 84-90. Grahamstown: International Library of African Music, Institute of Social and Economic Research, Rhodes University, 1982.

1662. **Weinberg, Pessa**. ZULU CHILDREN'S SONGS. Master's Thesis, University of South Africa, 1980.

Weinberg, Pessa
See also: **Hlabelela mntwanami, 685.**

1663. **Welch, David.** ASPECTS OF VOCAL PERFORMANCE IN ṢÀNGÓ PRAISE-POETRY AND SONG. Dissertation, Northwestern University, 1972. 294pp.
Welch says that his work is devoted to a sadly neglected area common to all African peoples - the verbal arts. This term comprises praise names, poems, prose narratives, riddles, and "thousands of proverbs." Welch believes that there are two primary reasons for preserving oral literature - to "act as a revitalizing force in shaping contemporary artistic expression," and as a way of "providing a cultural identity to the modern (educated) African." Welch's stunning dissertation, in light of increasing emphasis today on the oral traditions of Africa, was way ahead of its time. Contains a comprehensive Glossary of Yorùbá terms, and is enhanced by additional special features.

1664. **Welch, David**. "West African cult music retentions in Haitian urban *vaudou*: a preliminary report." **In Essays for a humanist: an offering to Klaus Wachsmann**, 337-349. Spring Valley, New

York: Town House Press, 1977.
Footnotes, notations, song texts, bibliography.

1665. **Welch, David.** "A Yorùbá/Nagô 'melotype' for religious songs in the African diaspora: continuity of West African praise song in the New World." In **More than drumming: essays on African and Afro-Latin music and musicians.** Edited by Irene V. Jackson, 145-162. Westport, Connecticut: Greenwood Press, c1985.
Abstracted in **RILM**, 1985.

1666. **Welch, Evie Adams.** LIFE AND LITERATURE OF THE SUKUMA IN TANZANIA, EAST AFRICA. Dissertation, Howard University, 1974. 542pp.
The purpose of Welch's study is to discuss the major religious, social and socio-economic aspects of Sukuma life. For literature, Welch examines folktales; for the music component, wedding songs. Since marriage represents the major social process of Sukuma society, and songs represent the traditional poetry, analysis of wedding songs was felt to offer a balanced view of both the prose and poetry of the society. Chapter 4, entitled Sexual Imagery in Wedding Songs, treats the *Ngoma* (dance); the Song as Poetry; Content of the Wedding Songs; and The Function of Wedding Songs. Texts, no music notations. Bibliography, glossary, no index.

1667. **Weman, Henry.** *African music and the church in Africa.* [Translated by Eric J. Sharpe]. Uppsala, Svenska Institutet för Missionsforskning [1960]. 296pp. (Studia missionalia Upsaliensia, 3)
"Also published as Uppsala universitets arsskrift 1960: 3. Acta universitatis Upsalienses."
Illustrations (chiefly music), bibliography.

1668. **WEST AFRICA.** 1917- . Camberwell, London: West Africa Publishing Company.
A durable journal, issued weekly. Has frequent articles on African music - with emphasis on urban music and its leading exponents. Indexed in **MLA**, **CURRENT CONTENTS AFRICA**, and others.

1668a. **Western, Dominique Coulet.** *A bibliography of the arts of Africa.* Waltham, Massachusetts: African Studies Association, Brandeis University, c1975. 123pp.
The "arts" are classified as: Art, Architecture, Oral Literature, Music, and Dance. The bibliography of music is extensive, covering pages 79-102 and divided into general geographic areas (i.e., Central, West, South, and East Africa). Under each heading, entries are classified according to peoples of the area. The dance section covers pages 103-110. There are no annotations. Indexed.

W

1669. **Whipple, Emory Clark.** MUSIC OF THE BLACK CARIBS OF BRITISH HONDURAS. Master's Thesis, University of Texas, Austin, 1971. 151pp.

1670. **White, Garth**. "Voices crying in the wilderness." In **Reggae International**. Edited by Stephen Davis, and Peter Simon, 25-32. New York: R & B [Rogner and Bernhard], c1982.
White continues after his first chapter, which was an early history of Jamaica starting with the Arawak Indians and the advent of Christopher Columbus. This chapter continues by documenting the development of Jamaican music from 1494-1957. The diffusion to Jamaica of musical forms from Cuba and Trinidad is also discussed. Many uniquely Jamaican dance and music forms are explained, as are African-derived religions. Chapter sub-headings are: African Foundation; European Incursion; The African Spirit in Jamaica; and Cuba, Calypso and Carnival. A well-researched essay. Notes, many fine photographs.

1671. **White, Timothy**. "Rebel music: a history of Bob Marley and the Wailers." In **Reggae International**. Edited by Stephen Davis, and Peter Simon, 75-86. New York: R & B [Rogner and Bernhard], c1982.
Concerns Marley, that most famous and revered - now mourned - reggae musician of Jamaica, and the equally renowned group he headed. Interesting factual information on the Wailers, and an intimate insight into Marley, the man. Stunning photographs.

1672. **Whitney, Malika Lee, and Dermott Hussey**. *Bob Marley: reggae king of the world.* With a foreword by Rita Marley. Kingston, Jamaica: Kingston Publishers, 1984. 197pp.
Includes illustrations and a bibliography.

1673. **Whitten, Norman E., Jr.** "Personal networks and musical contexts in the Pacific low-lands of Colombia and Ecuador." In *Afro-American anthropology: contemporary perspectives.* Edited by Norman E. Whitten, Jr., and John F. Szwed, 203-215. Foreword by Sidney W. Mintz. New York: Free Press, [1970].
Under the subheading, Music and Social Relationships, five cultural events that incorporate music are considered: the *currulao*, or marimba dance; the *chigualo*, or *arrullo* (wake for a dead child); the *alabado* and *novenario* (which includes the wake and post-interment rites for a dead adult); the *arrullo* for a special saint; and the musical expression of the saloon or dance hall. Three diagrams with circles and triangles demonstrate links in human relationships that exist within the *currulao*, *chigualo*, and *alabado*.

1674. **Whitten, Norman E. Jr., and John F. Szwed**, eds. *Afro-American anthropology: contemporary perspectives.* Foreword by Sidney W. Mintz. New York: Free Press, [1970]. 468pp. *continued*

Still a stunning compendium. Includes 22 papers from a 1967 American Anthropological Association Symposium entitled, *Negroes in the New World*. Even before the main body begins, one can hardly get past the Foreword, the impressive Contributors List, the Preface (by the editors), a magnificent Pictorial Essay, and the lengthy Introduction, so absorbing and informative are these preliminaries in themselves. Papers are concerned with the United States, the Caribbean and South America, many including notes. A grand bibliography is at the end of the book. Of particular interest (though the entire book should be read) are:

- **Lomax, Alan**. "The homogeneity of African-African-American musical style," 181-201.
- **Szwed, John F.** "Afro-American musical adaptations," 219-228.
- **Whitten, Norman E., Jr.** "Personal networks and musical contexts in the Pacific low-lands of Colombia and Ecuador," 203-215.

1675. **Widman, Ragnar**. "Le culte du *Niombo* des *Bwendé*." **ARTS D'AFRIQUE NOIRE** 2 (1972): 13-41.

In French. Dramatic photographs and description of the *Niombo*, a term used by the Bwende [of the lower reaches of the Congo River and adjacent North and South coasts] for: a deceased person, the associated internment ritual, and the gigantic, presiding black "puppet-mummy" (so named in Darkowska-Nidzgorska's book on African puppet theater, **53**). He also describes the *Niombo* as the "portrait of a dead chieftain...composed of dried human remains, raphia, cotton, grasses and flexible wood." One arm is stiffly outstretched, the other, raised. Mostly, the paper describes the ritual, and the formidable *Niombo* figure, but instruments are mentioned, as well as the role of music. Photo shows musicians preceding the *Niombo* to burial.

1676. **Widstrand, Carl Gösta**. "A Masai musical instrument." In **Festschrift to Ernst Emsheimer on the occasion of his 70th birthday, January 15th 1974**. Edited by Gustaf Hilleström, 252. Stockholm: Nordiska Musikförlaget, 1974.

Bibliography.

1677. **Willet, Frank**. "A contribution to the history of musical instruments among the Yorùbá." In **Essays for a humanist: an offering to Klaus Wachsmann**, 350-386. Spring Valley, New York: Town House Press, 1977.

1678. **Williams, H. C. N., and J. N. Maselwa**, eds. *Choral folksongs of the Bantu, for mixed voices*. Introductory notes and English lyrics by Peter Seeger. New York: G. Shirmer, 1960. 58pp.

Fifteen songs, all notated in four parts with piano, the latter indicated as "only for rehearsal." Contains lullabies, work songs, songs for specific ceremonies, wedding songs, children's songs. Chord changes are provided, occasional key changes, and English lyrics, which Seeger says are different from the original African ones. This is music typical of Capetown Province at a particular time. "Bantu," used in this way, is not acceptable, and characteristic of an unfortunate period in South African history. For a number of reasons, nevertheless, this is a pioneer work.

W

1679. **Williams, Raymond**. *The African drum*. Highland Park, Michigan: Highland Park College Press, 1973. 55pp.

1680. **Wilson, Olly**. "The association of movement and music as a manifestation of a black conceptual approach to music-making." In INTERNATIONAL MUSICOLOGICAL SOCIETY. **Congress. Report**, 98-105, 1977. Berkeley, California.
Source is **RILM**, 1981. This bears the same title as the following item.

1681. **Wilson, Olly**. "The association of movement and music as a manifestation of a black conceptual approach to music-making." In **More than dancing: essays on Afro-American music and musicians**. Edited by Irene V. Jackson, 9-23. Westport, Connecticut: Greenwood Press, c1985.
The more obvious characteristics shared by African and African-American musics have been stressed, Wilson observes, at the expense of the importance of body movement in religious music, work songs, and marching bands. Bibliography. Abstracted in **RILM**, 1985.

1682. **Witmer, Robert**. "African roots: the case of recent Jamaican popular music." In INTERNATIONAL MUSICOLOGICAL SOCIETY. **Congress. Report**, 105-113, 1977. Berkeley, California.
Source is **RILM**, 1981.

Wonji, Christopher
See: **La chanson populaire en Côte d'Ivoire, 332.**

1683. **Woodson, Craig DeVere**. "Appropriate technology in the construction of traditional African musical instruments in Ghana." In **Studies in African music**. Co-editors, J. H. Kwabena Nketia, and Jacqueline Cogdell DjeDje, 217-248. [Los Angeles]: Program in Ethnomusicology, Department of Music, University of California, Los Angeles, 1984.
Woodson is concerned that musical artifacts be preserved, and that there be continuity in the art and technology surrounding them. The paper uses the *atumpan* (paired talking drums) of the Akan people of Ghana as its focus, but implications far exceed concern for this instrument alone. "Musical instrument technology," he says, "must now be considered in many cases the 'life support system' of music." Illustrations, notes, bibliography, map, photographs.

1684. **Woodson, Craig DeVere.** THE ATUMPAN DRUM IN ASANTE: A STUDY OF THEIR ART AND TECHNOLOGY. 2 vols. Dissertation, University of California, Los Angeles, 1983. 765pp.
The atumpan, a pair of single-headed, goblet-shaped membranophones with a sound modifier, are the major talking drums of the Asante in Ghana. The instrument is studied in terms of its details of construction, parts and variations,

social context and distribution, historical development, and finally selected examples of the speech mode of its music, each with the emphasis on art and technology... The approach is simultaneously "etic" and "emic." Woodson points to the lack of available literature on the atumpan, and is concerned that continuity of traditional drum and drum carving in Asante is threatened. Illustrations, maps, bibliography. **(UMI)**

1685. **Woodson, Craig DeVere.** "The effect of a snare on the tone of a single-headed frame drum, the Moroccan Bender." **SELECTED REPORTS IN ETHNOMUSICOLOGY** 2, NO. 1 (1974): 102-117.
Bibliography.

1686. **Woodson, Dorothy C.** *Drum: an index to "Africa's leading magazine," 1951-1965.* [Madison]: African Studies Program, University of Wisconsin-Madison, c1988. 207pp.
Useful to this bibliography because of a number of music references in an historically important South African publication. Subjects are arranged chronologically under such likely headings as: Music, Jazz, Musical Instruments, author's and musician's names. Elsewhere related words also lead to music. Contains a bibliography that does not pertain to African music. This index is a valuable contribution, however, since the contents of *Drum* had not been indexed -and therefore accessible - in this way before. Todd Matshikiza's name (composer of choral music and the opera, *King Kong*), appears often, among names of other renowned musicians.

1687. **WORLD MUSIC CATALOG**. 1989- . Tivoli, New York: Original Music.
Issued seasonally. Though it may be irregular to include a catalog in a bibliography, when the publisher is John Storm Roberts, who writes breezy, intriguing and informed annotations about countless world musics, there is no hesitation. We learn of books, recordings, videocasettes, and materials, sometimes in sets, for "Teaching/Learning/Doing." There is an emphasis on popular styles of the world, but not exclusively. For the Africanist, there is always something worthwhile going on under "Africa," "Caribbean," and "Latin Continuum." The "Middle East" section includes Egypt. An informative little booklet.

1688. **THE WORLD OF MUSIC/LE MONDE DE LA MUSIQUE/DIE WELT DER MUSIK: JOURNAL OF THE INTERNATIONAL INSTITUTE FOR COMPARATIVE STUDIES AND DOCUMENTATION**. 1958 - . Basel, Switzerland. 1958 - .
The title alone indicates how likely a source this is. Since 1978, it has been issued three times a year. The text is in English, with French and German summaries. Indexed in **CURRENT CONTENTS, RILM, ARTS AND HUMANITIES CITATION INDEX**. Particularly recommended is the issue on South Africa, Volume 31, no. 1, 1989; and the issue on Brazil, Volume 30, no. 2, 1988. Several essays have been selected for listing below. *continued*

W

- **Erlmann, Veit.** "A conversation with Joseph Shabala of Ladysmith Black Mambazo: aspects of African performers' life stories," vol. 31, no. 1 (1989): 31-58.
- **Gottheim, Vivian I.** "*Bumba-meu-boi*, a musical play from Maranhão," volume 30, no. 2 (1988): 40-66.
- **Knight, Roderic C.** "Music out of Africa: Mande *jaliya* in Paris," vol. 33, no. 1, 1991.
- **Kubik, Gerhard.** "The Southern Africa periphery: banjo traditions in Zambia and Malaŵi," vol. 31, no. 1 (1989): 3-29.
- **Olivera Pinto, Tiago de.** "'Making ritual drama:' dance, music, and representation in Brazilian Candomblé and Umbanda," vol 33, no. 1, 1991.
- **Santos Barbosa, Guilherme dos.** "*Capueira* de Angola: a personal view of a *capueira* master," vol. 30, no. 2 (1988): 69-85.

1689. WORLDBEAT.

This has not been seen but is listed as an "Afropop" periodical in **AFROPOP WORLDWIDE**, where it is described in the 1991 issue as a colorful new London journal featuring "gossip, news, gigs, reviews from the very active world music scene there." The journal is served by a "worldwide network of correspondents." Available by subscription from: Lazahold Lts., Pallion Industrial Estate, Roper Street, Sunderland, England SR4 68N. It was not found in the current **ULRICH'S**.

Wright, Josephine R. B.
See: **Sancho, Ignatius (1729-1780), an early African composer in England, 1409.**

1690. Wymeersch, Patrick. *Ritualisme et fonction des tambours en Afrique interlacustre.* Rome: Pioda, 1979. 104pp. (Collana di studi africani, 4)

An informative and probing work concerned with drums of the interlacustrine region of Central and East Africa, including: Burundi, Rwanda, Buganda, Bunyoro, and Ankole. The author first gives an historical survey of the territory, with his own hypotheses about the origin of the drums. He describes them and their fabrication, and how they are stored or conserved. He explains the rituals with which they are associated in each territory, and classifies the rituals when appropriate. A few dark [or poorly printed?] photos, are sprinkled about. There is a 3-page bibliography.

Yacine, Tassadit
See: **Amrouche, Jean**. *Chants berbère de Kabyile*, **91.**

1691. Yamoah, Mills Afful. MUSIC EDUCATION IN THE ELEMENTARY SCHOOLS OF GHANA. Master's Thesis, Northeast Missouri State University, 1977. 93pp.

1692. Yanco, Jennifer. "Lingala: 'La Langue la plus chantée d'Afrique.'" In **Curriculum materials for teachers.** 2d ed, 233-234. Urbana, Illinois: University of Illinois at Urbana-Champaign, [1985].
The author points out that Lingala is the most important language in Central Africa, and gives brief background information on its history. She speaks of Lingala's association with Zaïrian or Congolese music, saying that the exceedingly popular music is "as eclectic as the language in which most of it is sung." Lists two recordings under Producers/Distributors of African Records - one resource with three addresses.

1693. Yankah, Kwesi. "Beyond the spoken word: *aural* literature in Africa." **Cross rhythms** 2 (1985): 114-146.
The author proposes the term *aural literature*, and divides literature into *written*, and *aural*. The latter category is further divided into *oral* and *drums*. He explains that he uses the term aural literature to sensitize scholars to the wide-range of non-oral phenomena that are interwoven with the expressive realization of non-written literature. He goes on to describe the important structural differences between drum praise and oral praise, and spends considerable time on drum language and drum poetry. This is a thoughtful and informative essay that includes a number of poetry texts, and an impressive list of notes and references.

1694. Yartey, Francis. OTUFO: A STUDY OF MUSIC AND DANCE OF THE GA-MASCHIE (ACCRA) PUBERTY RITE. Master's Thesis, University of Ghana, 1971.

1695. **YEARBOOK FOR TRADITIONAL MUSIC.** Vol. 13, 1981- . New York: Columbia University. International Council for Traditional Music.
This publication grew out of the **INTERNATIONAL FOLK MUSIC COUNCIL. JOURNAL (734)**, which became the **INTERNATIONAL FOLK MUSIC COUNCIL. YEARBOOK (735)**, which became the **YEARBOOK FOR TRADITIONAL MUSIC**. It is published annually by the "International Council for Traditional Music, a founding member organization of the International Music Council under the auspices of the United Nations Educational, Scientific and Cultural Organization (UNESCO). Indexed in **MUSIC INDEX**, fully abstracted in **RILM**.

Z

1696. Zamiti, Khalil. "Sources collectives du rythme musical en Tunisie." In **La musique dans la vie, étude realisée sous les auspices l'Ocora et sous la direction de Tolia Nikiprowetzky**, 225-240. Vol. 1. Paris, Office de coopération radiophoniques, 1967.
In French. Solidly written information about Tunisian society, particularly the family, with brief mention of music. The word "rythme" in the title is used more in a poetic sense; no specific treatment of "rhythm" as an element of Tunisian music is to be found in the essay.

1697. Zell, Hans M. *The African studies companion: a resource guide and directory.* London; New York: Hans Zell, 1989. 165pp.
This excellent general African reference book can aid the researcher in finding likely music resources. Chapter headings augur well for ferreting out desired information: Major General Reference Resources; Current Bibliographies and Continuing Sources; Journals and Magazines; Major Libraries and Documentation Centres; Publishers with African Studies Lists; Dealers and Distributors of African Studies Materials; Organizations; African Studies Associations and Societies; Foundations, Donor Agencies, Network Organizations in African Studies; Awards and Prizes; Abbreviations and Acronyms in African Studies. It's all there, in one convenient package.

1698. Zemp, Hugo. "Comment on devient musicien: quatre exemples de l'Ouest-Africain." In **La musique dans la vie, étude realisée sous les auspices l'Ocora et sous la direction de Tolia Nikiprowetzky**, 77-103. Vol. 1. Paris, Office de coopération radiophoniques, 1967.
An interesting exploration, in French, of the status of professional musicians and their instruments among the Baole, Dan, Senufo and Malinke. There are magnificent, representative photographs of single musicians from each society. Heavily footnoted, bibliography, discography.

1699. Zemp, Hugo. "La legende des griots Malinke." **CAHIERS D'ÉTUDES AFRICAINES** 6, no. 24 (1966): 611-642.

1700. Zemp, Hugo. *Die Musik der Dan.* Kassel-Wilhelmshöhe, Bärenreiter-Verlag, 1966. (UNESCO Collection: An Anthroplogy of African Music.)
Dan music. Music from Liberia and Côte d'Ivoire.

1701. Zemp, Hugo. *Musique Dan. La musique dans la pensée et la vie sociale d'une société africaine.* Paris: La Haye, Mouton, [1971]. 318pp. (Cahiers de l'homme. Nouvelle série, 11) (École pratique des hautes études, Sorbonne. 6 section: Sciences economiques et sociales. Cahiers de l'homme: ethnologie, géographie, linguistique, nouvelle série, 11)
Music of the Dan people of Liberia. Bibliography, illustrations, maps, plates.

1702. Zemp, Hugo. MUSIQUE ET MUSICIENS CHEZ LES DAN (CÔTE D'IVOIRE). Dissertation, Université de Paris, 1968. 446pp.

1703. Zindi, Fred. *Roots rocking in Zimbabwe.* Gweru, Zimbabwe: Mambo Press, 1985. 98pp.

Concerned with the development of contemporary music in Zimbabwe, starting from the early fifties. Includes effects successive Rhodesian governments had on music. African, American, European and Caribbean influences are discussed. Contains biographies and interviews with popular musicians, especially Thomas Mapfumo. (The author is also a recording artist.) Includes a reference section on clubs, promoters, music shops, the musicians' union, assorted media, along with other important commercial information. Music and words of Zimbabwe's national anthem, *Nkosi Sikelel' iAfrika* (shared by other African countries) are given in Shona, English, Ndebele and Zulu. Many handsome photos of musicians. Informative and useful.

AUTHOR INDEX

The following list includes all authors of entries in this bibliography, the term author implying either a person, institution, or corporate body. Dissertations and theses are listed by both the individual author's name, and the degree-granting university. In the absence of a designated author, the names of editors, or other key individuals are given to make the search for a particular work less difficult. Although names of all important people who have contributed to a publication are not listed here, every effort has been made to include their names in entries themselves, whether they wrote prefaces, or served as photographers, compilers, translators, artists, transcribers, designers, advisers, illustrators, etc.

Some individuals listed in the Author Index are also associated with publications they either did not author, or in which they played a subsidiary role. This information is indicated in entries, but their numbers are not included here. There are also examples in which prominent persons - not only authors - are treated as subjects, indicated either within the title of a work, or included in the annotation for it. Many of these names will be found in the Subject Index. Material of the bibliography is too dense, however, to have allowed for every name mentioned in an annotation to be included. The reader is encouraged to survey entries and their annotations carefully, and to go to original publications whenever possible.

AUTHOR INDEX

AUTHOR INDEX

AUTHOR INDEX

AUTHOR INDEX

AUTHOR INDEX

AUTHOR INDEX

AUTHOR INDEX

AUTHOR INDEX

AUTHOR INDEX

AUTHOR INDEX

SUBJECT INDEX

This index contains the names of people who are either the main subjects of entries, or who are mentioned in annotations. Many names are duplicated in the Author Index. A sincere attempt was made to include as many names as possible, but due to the enormous volume of data, absolute comprehensiveness cannot be claimed. The index covers: African musicology, bibliographies, countries, dance, discographies, ethnomusicology, instruments, languages, music styles and types, oral tradition, peoples, periodicals, poetry, popular music, regions, religions, songs, and more. In some ways the index serves also as a kind of glossary. Due to space limitations, a certain amount of compressing was necessary.

SUBJECT INDEX

SUBJECT INDEX

SUBJECT INDEX

SUBJECT INDEX

SUBJECT INDEX

SUBJECT INDEX

SUBJECT INDEX

SUBJECT INDEX

SUBJECT INDEX

SUBJECT INDEX

SUBJECT INDEX

SUBJECT INDEX